VIRGILIO MARTÍNEZ | PÍA LEÓN | MALENA MARTÍNEZ

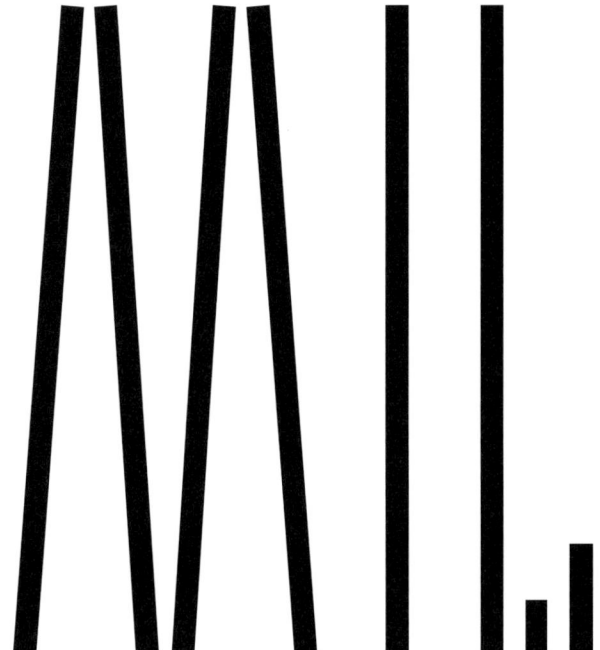

Catapulta

p. 10 — COMING FULL CIRCLE
p. 28 — SHARING SPACES, WORKING TOGETHER

p. 52 — FRANCISCO QUICO MAMANI AND TRINIDAD MAMANI CASCAMAYTA
p. 58 — DESTILERÍA ANDINA
p. 64 — DWIGHT AGUILAR MASÍAS
p. 70 — MANUEL CHOQQUE BRAVO
p. 76 — ANDEA
p. 82 — ORQUIMIEL

PRESERVATION[1]
ANDEAN FOREST[3]
EXTREME ALTITUDE[5]
FROZEN CORDILLERA[7]

p. 88 — TRACING ORIGINS

p. 110 — VIRGILIO MARTÍNEZ
p. 116 — VERÓNICA TABJA
p. 118 — MANUEL CONTRERAS
p. 120 — PÍA LEÓN

ANDEAN PLACE — p. 126

p.204 — TRIBUTE TO HERITAGE

MALENA MARTÍNEZ — p. 216
MANUEL ACURIO — p. 220
NILVER MELGAREJO — p. 222
LUIS VALDERRAMA — p. 224

²ANDES PLATEAU
⁴DIVERSITY OF CORN
⁶CENTRAL ANDES
⁸HUATIA OF CACAO

MIRRORING THE ANDEAN COLOR PALETTE — p. 226
DOWN-TO-EARTH CREATIONS — p. 244

ORGÁNICA LAMAY — p. 258
CERVECERÍA DEL VALLE SAGRADO — p. 264
MERCEDES CHAMPI AND FAMILY — p. 270
RÓMULO CÁMARA MONCADA — p. 276
ROSA FERRO GIRALDO — p. 282

THE SACRED VALLEY — p. 288

COMING FULL CIRCLE

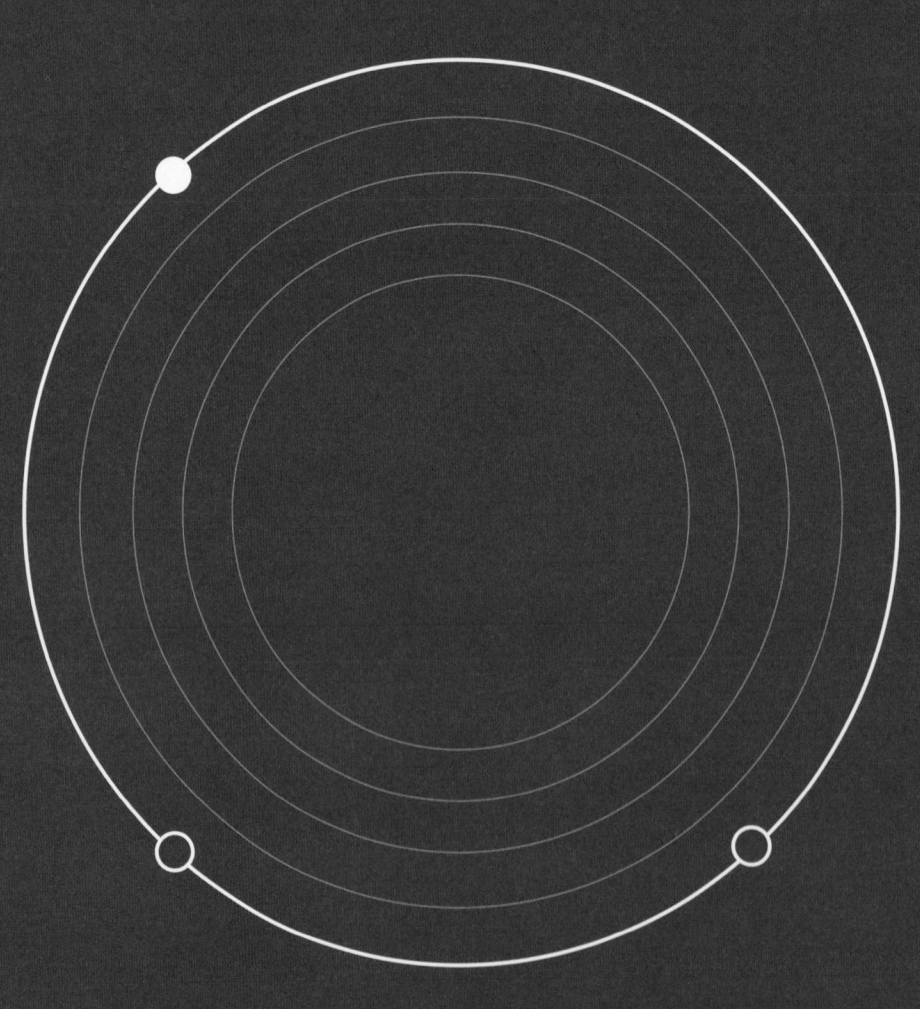

Meteorites leave their mark when they fall to earth. In the case of Moray, a series of depressions at 11,515 feet above sea level from thousands, perhaps millions, of years ago. Given the concentrations of feldspar [rock-forming tectosilicate minerals] found in the ground, this is one of the theories about how Moray's high-altitude topography came to exist, and from which the agricultural terraces were fashioned at the Quechua agricultural experimental station located just a few steps away from Mil; a group of concentric formations with an otherworldly appearance that inspire the menus through which we share the story behind Peru's elevations and ecosystems.

While archeological evidence hints these cavities were used by pre-Columbian Andean civilizations prior to our Quechua ancestors, there's little extant record of that, or even to what ends.[1] The Wari (700-1200AD) cultivated crops on terraces[2] but the Quechuas' exceptional civil engineering skills took this farming technique several steps further, fully using the geography and climate to their advantage.

Mitimaes [people from ethnic groups conquered by the Quechua and forced to relocate] were brought to work across the Cusco region including at Moray, a few miles from Maras, and it was here that they built a trio of concentric, irrigated *muyus* or circular terraces (the largest is called H'atun, followed by Chaupi, and Huch'uy, which is located closest to the Andes) and a single rectangular one. You can appreciate H'atun standing at the boundary of Mil's land and looking down into this ringed bowl.

Intricate and solid examples of Quechua architecture designed to withstand earthquakes, they have done their job well, resisting the movements of one mighty convulsion in 1650 and, exactly 300 years later, a second in 1950. Curiously, both measured 6.5 on the Richter scale yet despite the intensity, little to no damage was caused here. (In the Quechua language, Moray translates as 'territory taken from times of earthquakes'.)

---

1. Moray's archaeological complex, Marc Cárdenas, 2019
2. Ibid

The multi-function aspect is open to speculation but this outdoor laboratory likely also operated as a seed bank and nursery for plant species, also acting as a thermometer that gauged regional microclimates or extreme weather periods such as prolonged drought through the behavior of crops on the terraces.

This would trigger appropriate decision making at higher [administrative] levels before the entire Cusco harvest could be damaged.[3] Aside from the concave appearance of an amphitheater, it's notable for the thermal amplitude range between the lowest and highest platforms (the largest and deepest, H'atun, has 13 platforms). Depending on the time of day and the time of year, the mean temperature difference can vary as much as 59°F (15°C) between the highest and lowest terraces, which means one extra growing day is required for each successive 33 feet of altitude. That makes for a month's delay in the maturation cycles of plants that have been sown at 985 feet higher in altitude.[4]

While other agricultural terraces such as Pisaq, Ollantaytambo and Chinchero were also constructed around and near the Sacred Valley, these were intense crop producers designed to feed the empire's significant 4.5 million to six-million-strong population; it was estimated in a 2002-published paper in *American Anthropologist* written by B.S. Bauer and R.A. Covey, that the Quechua built 193,050 miles^2 of terraces around the empire.

Moray, however, was a one-of-a-kind, experimental research center because of the advanced technological approaches incorporated: it was "a socio-technological system for risk reduction, to enhance agricultural productivity at local scales and to facilitate effective agricultural coordination at large scales".[5] That is, its objective was to create a selection of microclimates represented at different levels[6] where crops from different regions would thrive under controlled cultivation, whose seeds could then be distributed across the empire, while also adhering to the astronomical calendar to celebrate significant rituals such as the equinoxes and solstices.

---

3. Inka Cosmology in Moray, John C. Earls and Gabriela Cervantes
4. Ibid
5. Ibid
6. Ibid

Living Andean heritage, Moray is a series of concentric formations by which the Quechua, using the geography and climate to their advantage, created a multi-function, agricultural research center from where Mil draws inspiration to share the stories behind the Cusco region's elevations and ecosystems. Today, Moray is a bustling sightseeing destination for tourists, but communities have long made the accompanying rolling landscape and its *apu* mountain gods their home.

Our Quechua ancestors understood thermal amplitude and its effect on agriculture, and studied it: warmer air, greater exposure to UV light and soil temperatures found at the top of a *muyu* would allow cacao, coffee and coca leaf to flourish, while cooler temperatures lower down, which would barely allow the aforementioned plants to start photosynthesizing, generated an ideal environment for cereals, maize, quinua and *kiwicha* (Amaranthus caudatus). Also understanding weather conditions, from humidity to frost or managing heat through stone reflection, was key. The eight terraces shaped in rectangular form were dedicated solely to tubers, and it's estimated up to 250 varieties were cultivated at Moray.

They were also irrigation masters, as seen at Tambomachay water palace near Cusco city, routing water from rivers through underground canals, as is the case with Moray and also Maras. Moray's water sources came from the south of the site, six from Misminay and three from Moray itself,[7] and flowed down through man-made waterfalls, vertical channels constructed within the terraces' stone walls.

Did the Quechua create a microcosm of the Sacred Valley's diverse ecosystems gathered in a single location? Was Moray a vertical farm and storage facility whose produce fed select armies and communities across the Cusco region, or were seeds cultivated then dispatched around the empire, redistributed with the ultimate aim of feeding millions of subjects? There are so many questions – and a plethora of suppositions.

7. Moray's archaeological complex, Marc Cárdenas, 2019

Then there's the cosmological side. Just how significant was Moray as a ceremonial site or temple for rituals, to pay homage to the revered Pachamama, mark the solstices or receive pilgrimages related to crucial agricultural activities or other astronomical observations? How important was the solar calendar, astronomy and cosmology for the Quechua here? According to scholars John C. Earls and Gabriela Cervantes, eight dates including the equinoxes were all celebrated at pivotal sites such as Pisaq, Quechua administrative center Ollantaytambo, and the Qorikancha sun temple in the city of Cusco.

While the Quechua agricultural calendar was originally based on the growth cycle of maize, given the Inka's [Quechua] intricate ability to interweave cosmological and administrative ordering principles, and their expression in astronomical and calendrical structures, it's to be expected that this arrangement would be instantiated in Moray; key dates in the Inka calendar are marked by specific visual patterns of sun and shade generated all over the terraces,[8] patterns that likely appeared during maize's growth cycle.

Was Moray's construction ever completed? Another question without a definitive answer but it's believed not. Once the Spanish conquest of the Quechua empire was underway, then concluded in 1532, the *mitimaes* likely abandoned the site and returned to their places of origin. Such agricultural sites [and powerhouses] were then largely stigmatized by the Spaniards,[9] either destroyed or simply left to fall into neglect.

While Moray has always been a presence in the lives of inhabitants from the neighboring communities CC Mullak'as-Misminay and CC Kacllaraccay, many 'rediscoveries' include that in 1931 by geologist Robert Shippee and US Navy Lieutenant George R. Johnson in the American Geographical Society-sponsored aerial photography expedition. Thanks to their stunning ethereal images, interest was generated in Moray's story.

It was then re-rediscovered in the 1970s by Australian archaeologist John C. Earls, who first visited the site with Anccoto resident Washington Acurio; to date, Earls has penned numerous papers on Moray. It later became a playground for Washington's grandson and Manuel Acurio, our agronomist at Mil, who, as a child in the 1980s, ran up and over these *muyus* overgrown with weeds with his cousins.

---

8. Inka Cosmology in Moray, John C. Earls and Gabriela Cervantes
9. Moray's archaeological complex, Marc Cárdenas, 2019

• MORAY TODAY

In more recent times, Moray officially entered Peruvian history books when the Ministry of Culture took charge of its conservation in 1990 and since opening to the public in 2008, today it's one of numerous archaeological sites frequented by visitors to Cusco and the Sacred Valley.

Our terraced neighbor, just feet away from Mil, Moray also inspires the menus at Central and Kjolle in Lima. Central's in particular reflects its elevations and ecosystems, the circles themselves, the terraces and microclimates designed in a form that conveys the Andes, its art, its science and technology, its myths.

Moray is a solitary place. Lima and Cusco are heavily visited destinations in Peru that can be easily reached. But arriving in Cusco is one thing, and reaching Moray is quite another. It's far from the city of Cusco and although the common misconception is that it's situated within the Sacred Valley, Moray actually rises over it. But that's okay, we wanted a place where the purity of nature reigns, and where we could forge relationships with the communities who have long been established here.

The connection one has with nature on a daily basis brings us closer to our history and our past in an unknown world. The peace, the feeling of tranquility and safety, of being at one with nature is enjoyable. It's positive. Being in Moray floods one's mind with questions to which we want to find factual answers.

Moray is living heritage: we see the terraces and replicate them and their produce, bringing the past into the present at Mil. It's our interpretation of nature. And, of course, it's a source of daily inspiration for our own agricultural investigations, such as the 2020 harvest of 223 types of tubers from our *chacra* that will catalogue which varieties best survive frost, drought and late blight, undertaken with our partners from the neighboring communities. It's a sign that Moray is starting to come full circle.

SHARING SPACES, WORKING TOGETHER

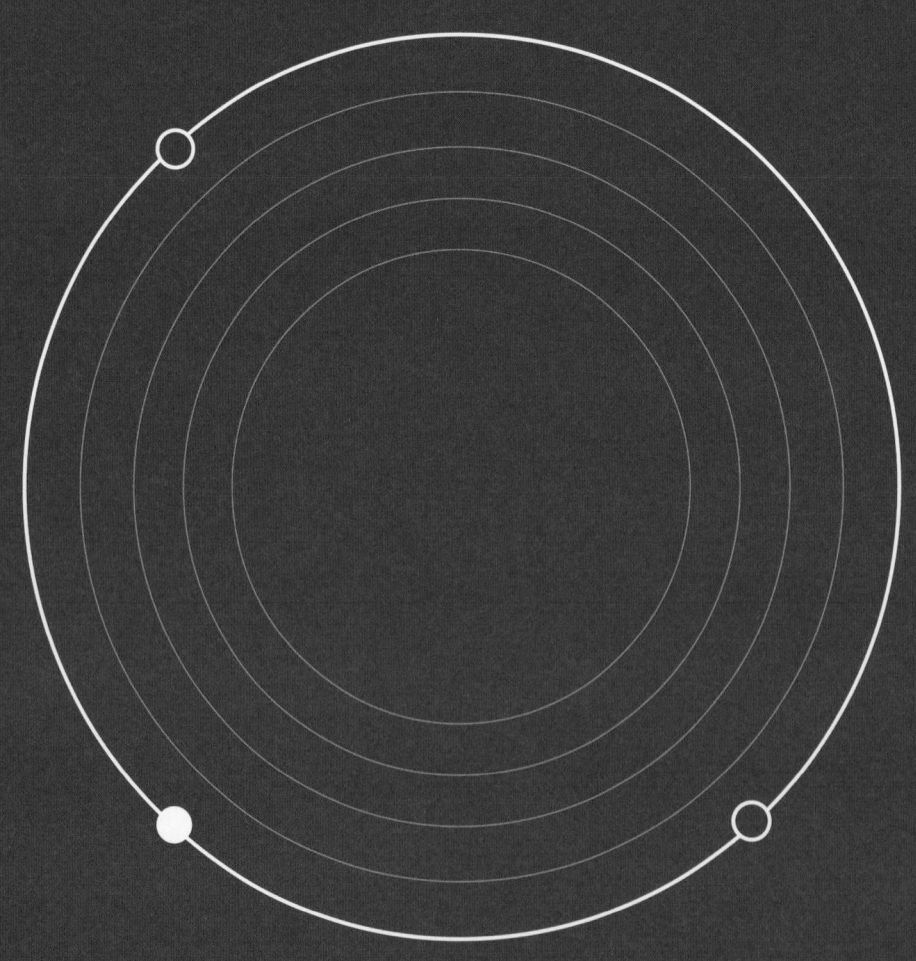

The rural high-altitude villages of CC Kacllaraccay and CC Mullak'as-Misminay represent but two of the numerous small communities bearing Quechua names such as Huatata and Pisaq that are found across the Peruvian Andes, populated for generations by farmers whose dedication to their land ensures their ancestral knowledge provides food for the area.

Together, we share spaces and experiences, and learn from the people of CC Kacllaraccay and CC Mullak'as-Misminay who are largely of Quechua descendancy. And while these small communities are located around 30 miles northwest of Cusco, the notably lengthy 90-minute drive is down to the spiraling roads that weave across the Andes, passing by a tapestry of fields and lakes that form the landscape, undulating at ground level, jagged against the skyline. It is breathtaking in both the aesthetic and physiological senses.

These communities' north is Apu Wañinmarcca, an imposing and mighty force on an already-imposing scene. Not just a geographical reference point, the *apu* (mountain) is also sacred, a spirit that protects the communities. Its story goes like this: Wañinmarcca suffered an attack of the green-eyed monster over the amount of snow that Chicón, a summit on the opposite side of the valley, was covered in. During the night, Wañinmarcca sent its peak to stealthily acquire some powder but, noisy animals woke up Chicón, which caught the pointy mass in the middle of this unsavory act and forced it to stay put – forever. Wañinmarcca is still missing its crest today, while in the lower part of the valley, a curiously small mountain is home to the same flora and fauna as the *apu*. While it's hard to pinpoint at what moment these two villages came to exist, the Wari civilization, which predated the Quechua by around nine centuries, lived in Cusco; continuously inhabited for 3,000 years, it's the Americas' oldest such settlement. It's believed that the Wari (and not the Quechua) first tapped into Maras' Andean salt-water sources to create the district's eminent salt evaporation ponds.

With so much ancestral tradition and history engrained in CC Kacllaraccay and CC Mullak'as-Misminay, it was essential for Mater and Mil to form a relationship that is built on respect and is mutually beneficial. Because whatever Mil's involvement, we need to leave a positive footprint. We didn't come here to mess around, we came here to make a commitment of sharing knowledge and have knowledge shared with us. We wanted to join ranks but in a way that goes beyond the conventional business model so often seen in the Sacred Valley. The context, recognition and research goals were always clear; in addition, Mil needed to be a self-sufficient and sustainable enterprise. The intention was never for communities to work for us, we always wanted to work alongside them and be good neighbors – and the Mil experience needed to reflect all this.

• OPEN DIALOGUE

In order to begin the conversation, Mater's anthropologist Francesco D'Angelo started attending community meetings in CC Kacllaraccay and CC Mullak'as-Misminay in order to express our interest in working together while understanding their necessities, wishes and intentions, and how we could all get closer.

Those initial gatherings allowed Mater to start forging harmonious and inclusive relationships. It was irrelevant to Santiago Pillco, Ceferina Pillco Gutiérrez, Cleto Cusipaucar, Santiago Amau, and other community members that Central and its protagonists had appeared in a Netflix series. What was relevant was their confidence in our word and of our desire to work together, and, slowly but surely, the dialogue began.

Francesco's first visit to CC Kacllaraccay was memorable. After arranging a meeting with the community's then-president Andrés Ayma, the anthropologist went equipped with a rucksack and some notebooks for a day visit – and stayed for two weeks. "Andrés had forgotten to mention the minor detail that it was the community's anniversary and that the patronal festivities were about to begin. I spent a fortnight there, dancing, eating, interviewing Kacllaraccay's residents and drinking *chicha de jora* corn beer with them; that was the beginning," says Francesco.

Of the two communities, CC Kacllaraccay has a smaller population, home to 110 registered residents and land co-proprietors (in 2018, according to Mater research); 74 people live here year round. Located at between 11,810 and 13,125 feet above sea level (asl), its name originates from two Quechua words: *kacllas*, thorn bushes found in abundance in the area, and *raccay*, which translates as a half-built (or partially demolished) house. It divides into three unofficial zones – highlands, the settlement and what is known as 'the slightly lower lands' – spanning 3,847 acres. CC Kacllaraccay was officially recognized as an indigenous community in 1964.

The first language in both villages is Quechua, followed by Spanish; each has a Catholic church and each is led by an eight-member *junta directiva* (directive committee) tasked with addressing situations that may arise and affect its residents. Every decision is taken democratically and each community member is obliged to attend meetings. Other committees specializing in agroforestation, drinking water, electricity, and handicrafts form part of each directive. Not all communities have the same priorities in the Andes. We can't just group them all under a single Andean community umbrella because one is concerned about crops, another wants to engage tourism, while another worries about water shortages.

Barley and potatoes are the agricultural engines driving each community's farmland, although they also grow fava beans, *chuchín* corn, oats, wheat, oca (Oxalis tuberosa) and quinua.

It's not the most diverse array of crops, however, because, unlike other communities close to and in the Sacred Valley, CC Kacllaraccay never formed part of a larger *hacienda* (farm), so farm hands didn't have access to other diverse products they could sow at home. As for other activities, CC Mullak'as-Misminay has built a small cluster of visitor lodgings; in characteristic good humor, there's also now a diner called Dos Mil (two thousand).

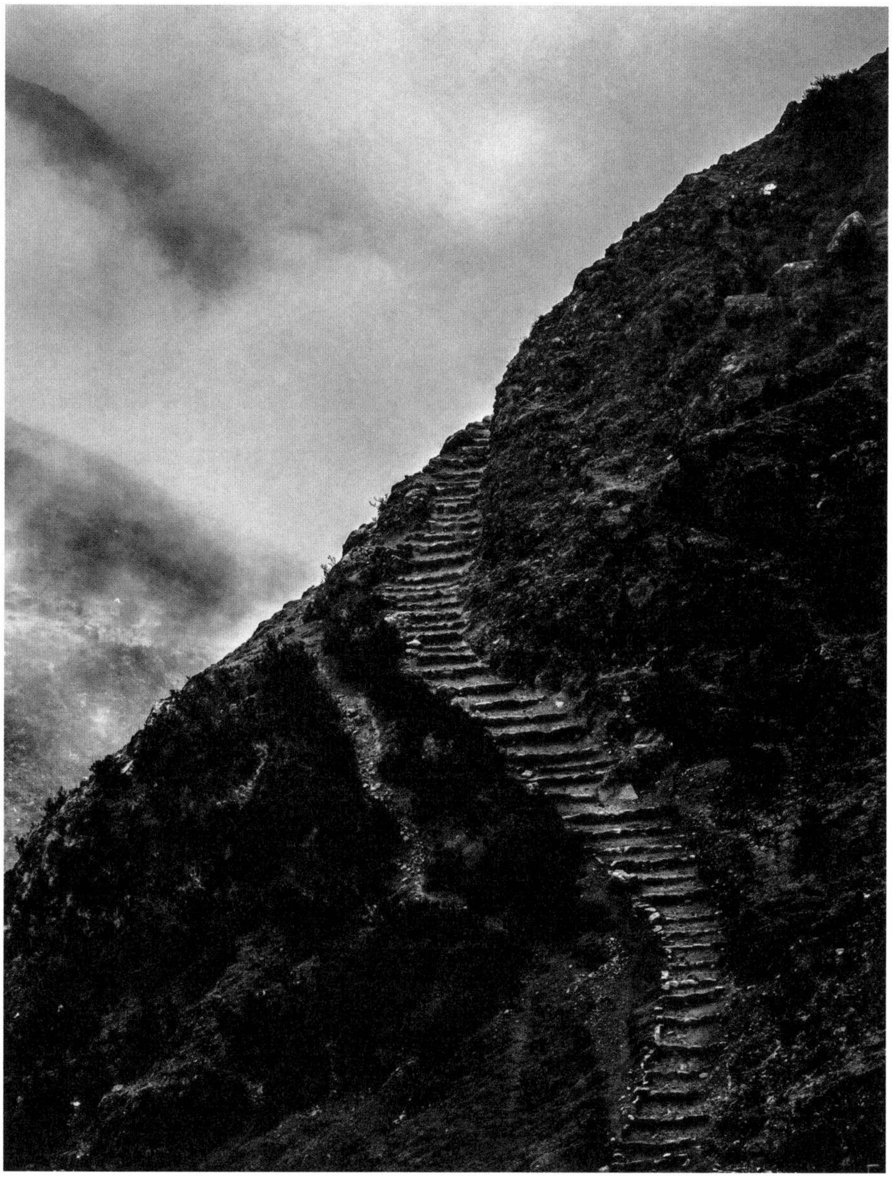

36

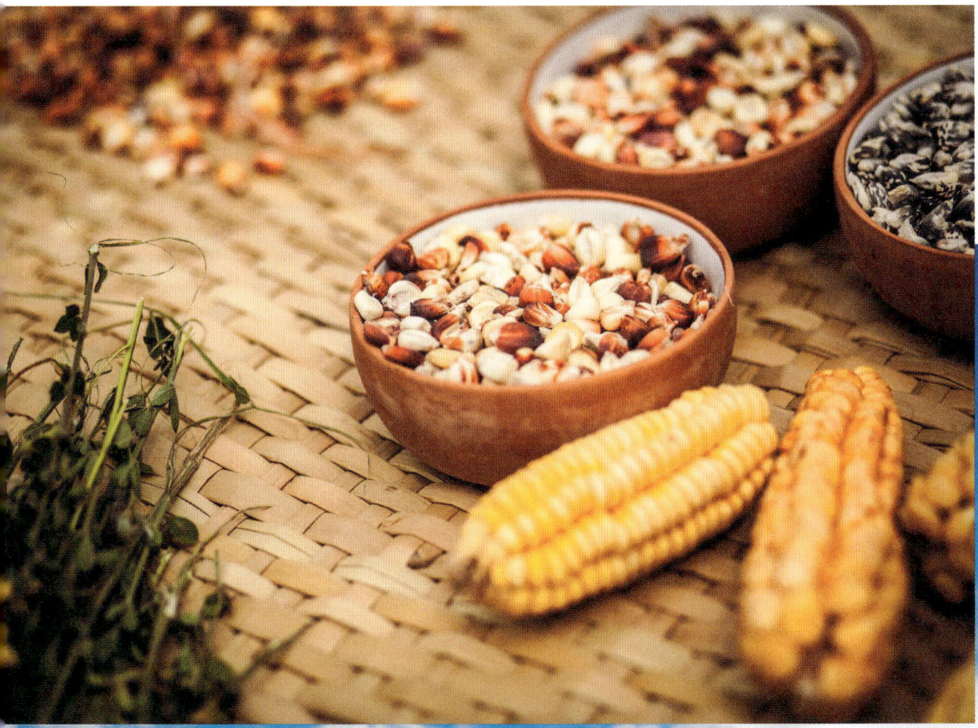

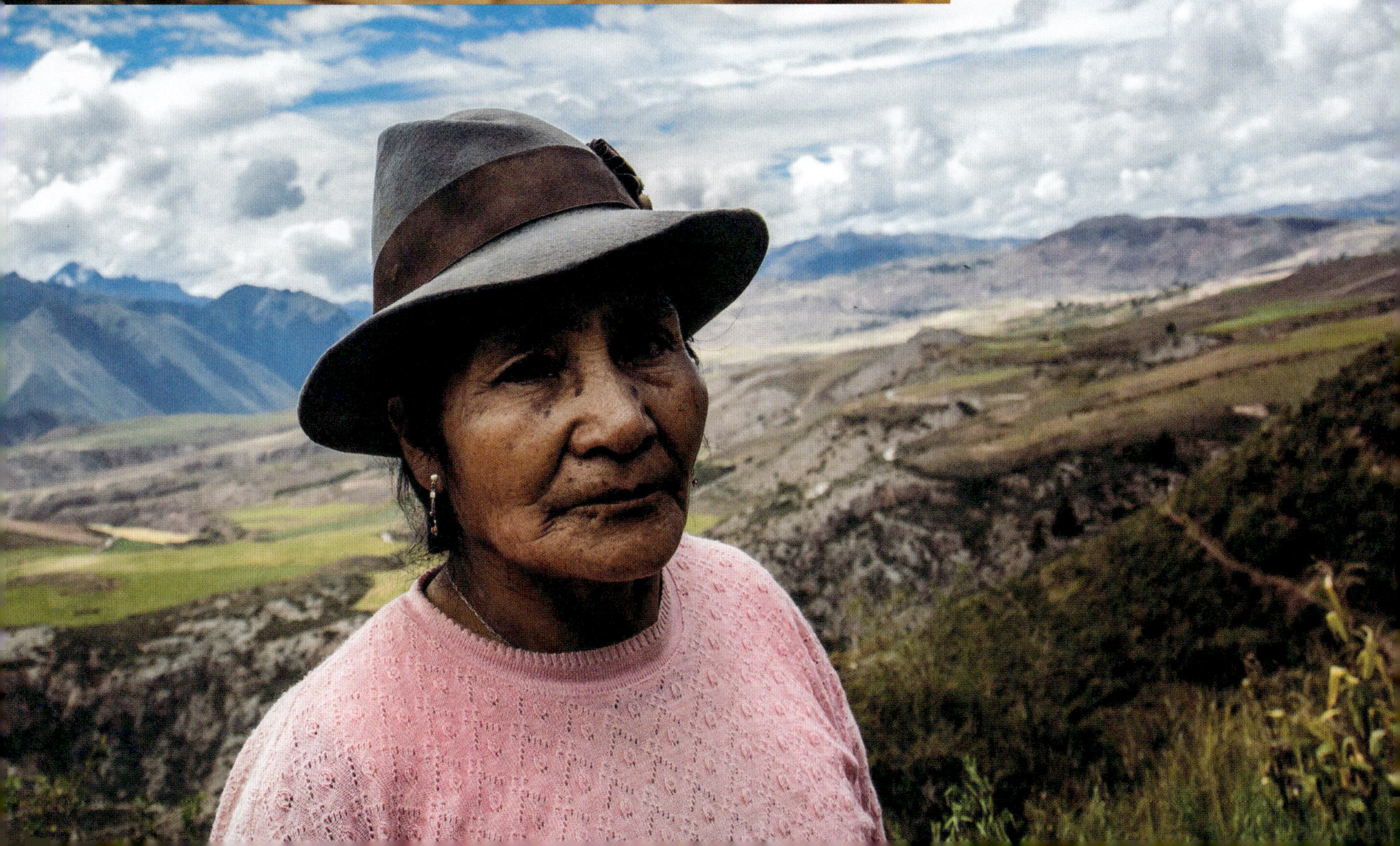

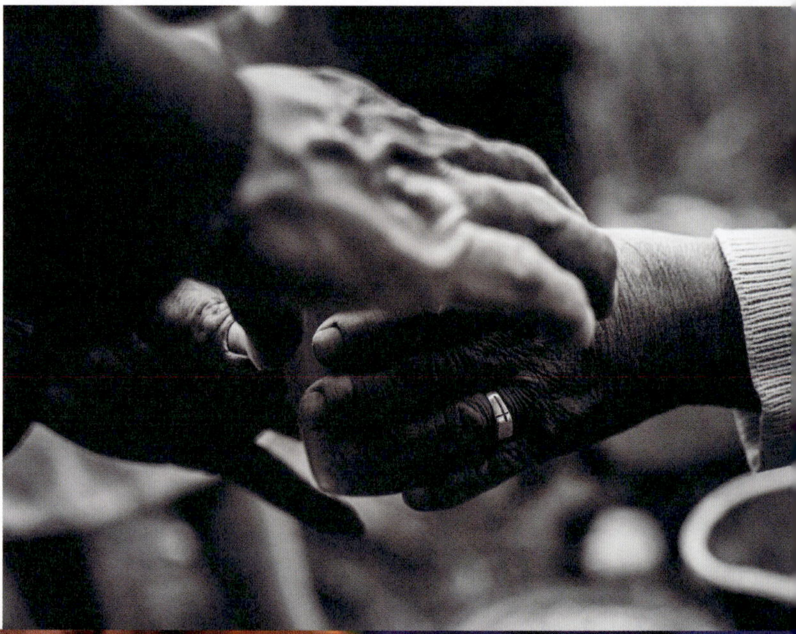

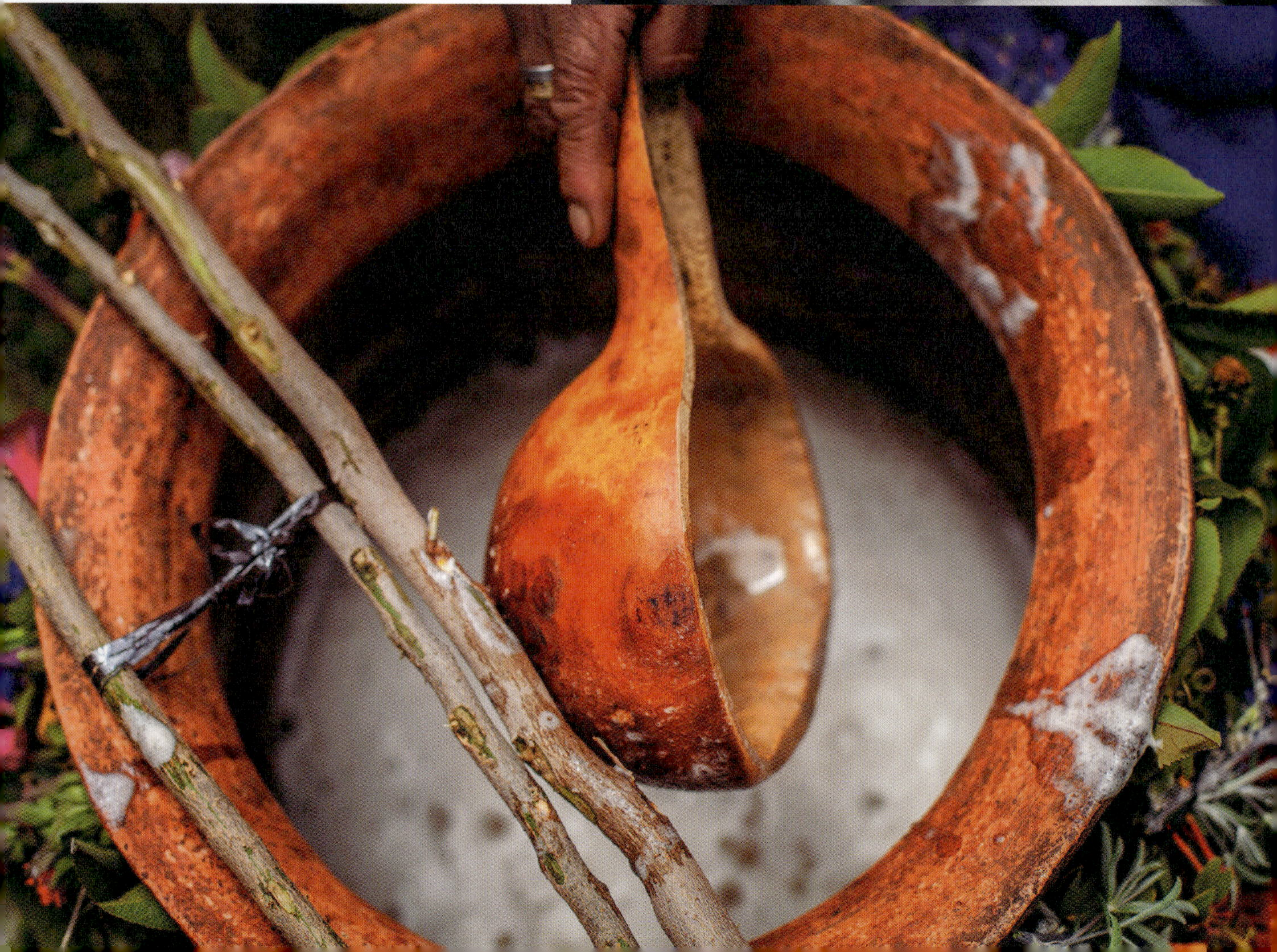

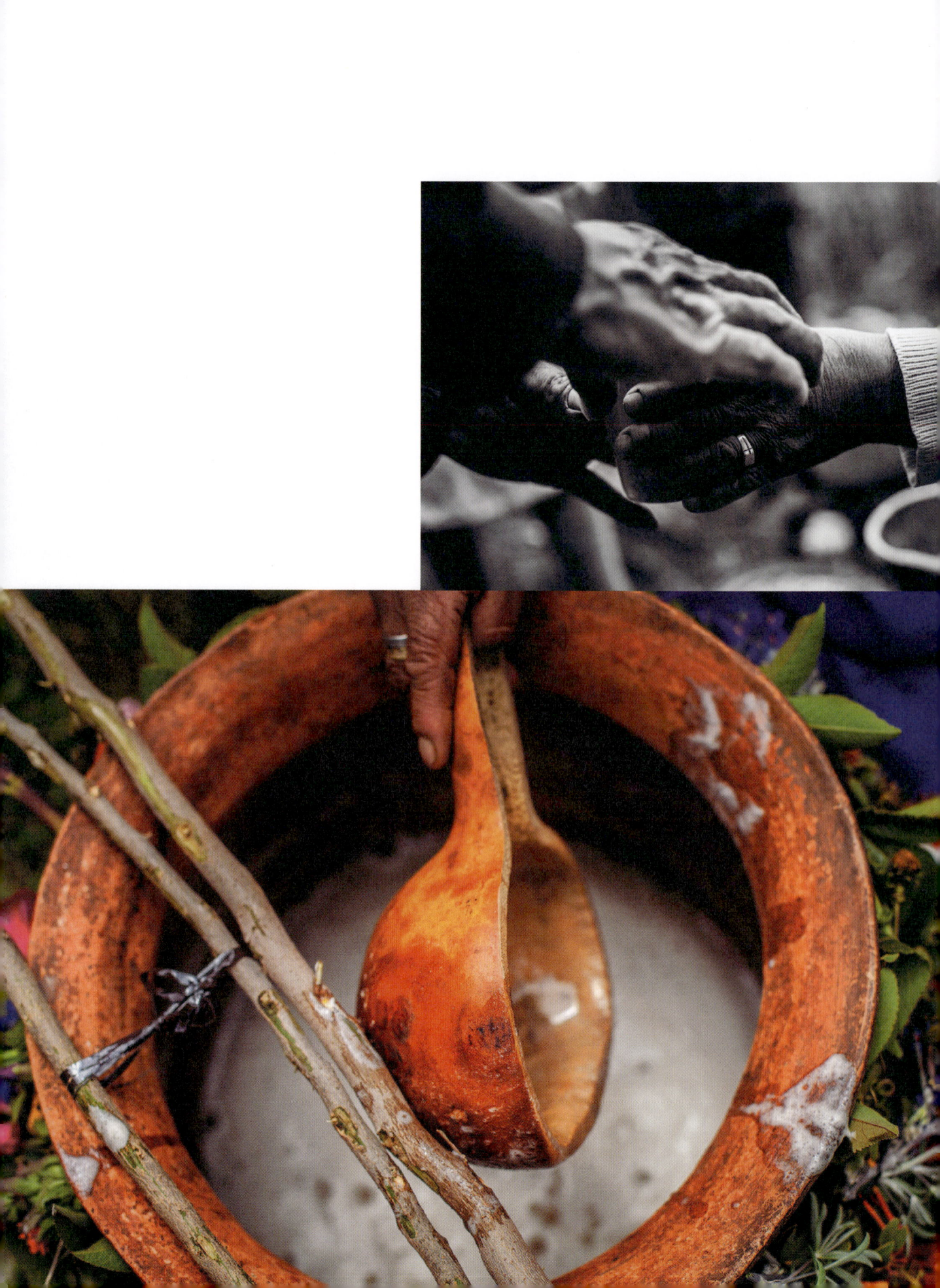

Un poco de chicha? Out in the fields, the working day is always accompanied by a little *chicha de jora*, a beer made with germinated maize designed to keep up energy levels and morale while sowing tuber seeds or harvesting maize, whose consumption is an ancestral ritual in the Andes. Made at home and served by dipping a mug into a large recipient, sip then shake the last few drops into the ground for Pachamama before returning it empty to the *chicha* server to continue the circle, the conversation, the laughter and the welcome break before returning to the fields.

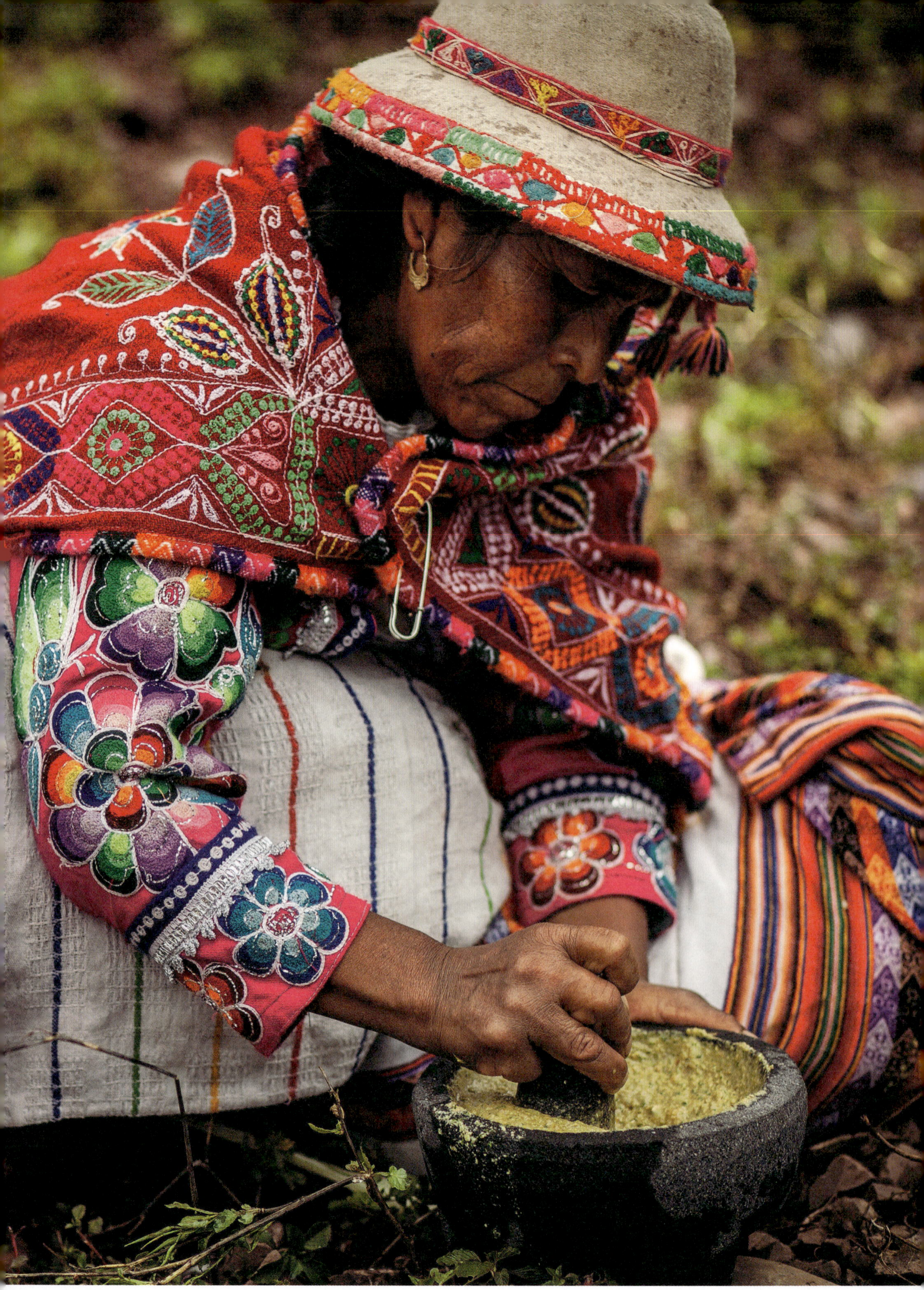

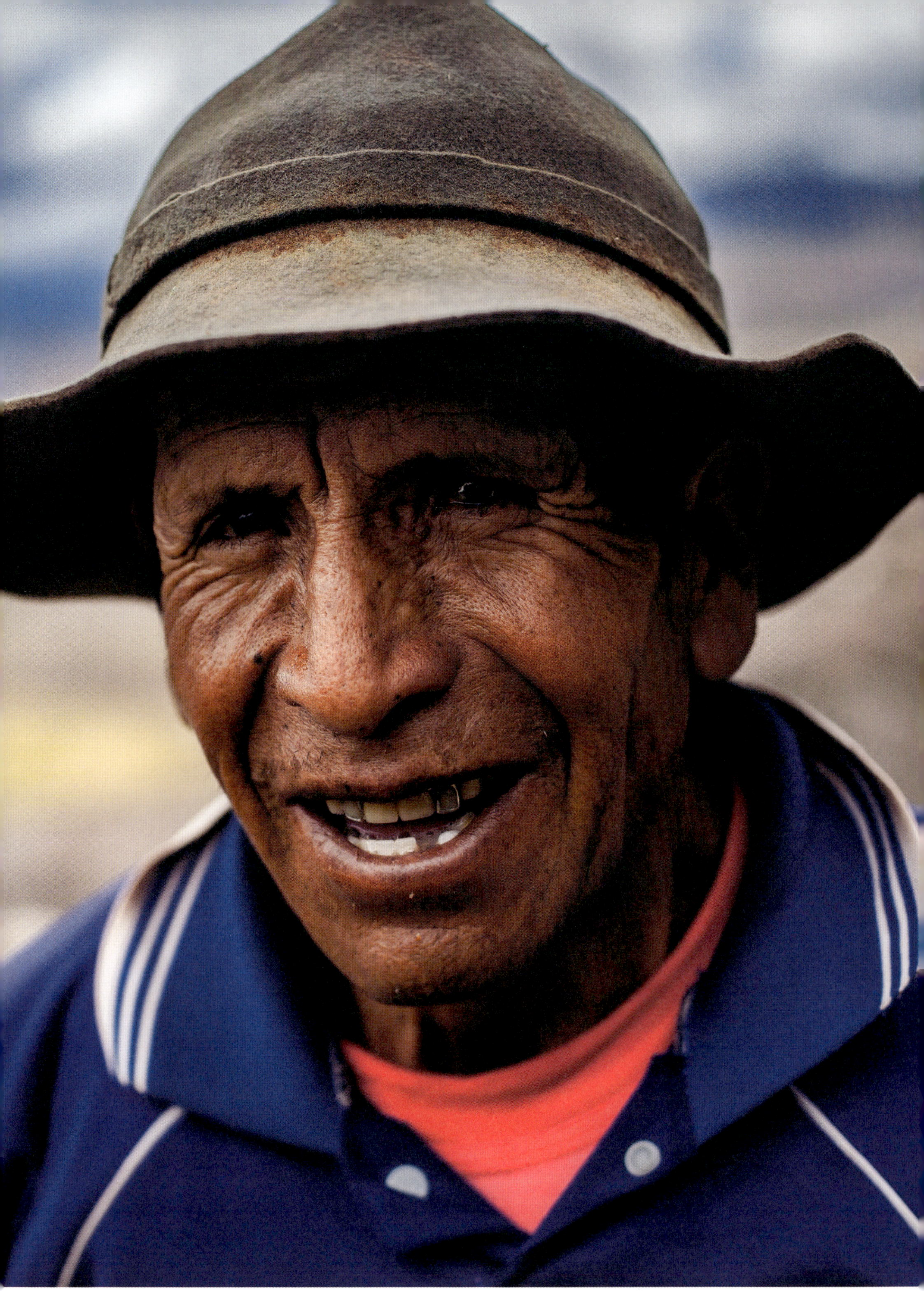

42

- DAY IN THE LIFE

Life revolves around the agrarian calendar, so the day begins early in the communities, at 4.30 or 5 am, at first light, to take donkeys, sheep and cows to pasture. There are no days off or weekends, although *fiestas patronales* (patron saints' holidays) are extremely important and last several days. In CC Kacllaraccay, a member of the community uses the far-reaching loudspeaker to announce the day's activities at dawn, for example, planting trees or gathering *ichu* grass for a perspective arts and cultural project, such as weaving a *khipu* recording device.

Breakfast is taken after this first daily task, a quinua soup, bread, maybe some eggs, then it's off to the fields, to plow, sow, pick, whatever the season demands. Lunch might be eaten at 9 or 10 am, and consists of a large pan of pasta or *chuño* potatoes to be shared out among the workforce, accompanied by *chicha de jora* served out of a large container into a metal mug, that one person drinks from then returns to the *chicha* server who continues the ritual. Each worker brings something edible to share, whether it's *chulpi* corn or *uchucuta* salsa that enliven *chuño*. That's followed up by a *chicha* break at around 1 pm and *merienda* (teatime) at around 3.30 pm, then the race begins to get home before dusk falls, gathering up four-legged wards on the way, before eating dinner, resting then continuing the cycle the following day.

- KEEP TALKING

The dialogue is well and truly open, Mil and our immediate neighbors united in moving forward together across an array of captivating projects. Some of Mil's team members are from the communities, such as salon runner Nery Amau and cook Cirilo Ramsay Casanca, who were both born in CC Mullak'as-Misminay. Meanwhile, members of both communities, such as Santiago Pillco from CC Kacllaraccay, wove and thatched Mil's roof from *ichu* grass in 2017. His wife, Ceferina Pillco Gutiérrez leads the Warmi natural dye workshop while Elba Henrriquez Quispe organises the Sacha textiles workshop; both are from CC Kacllaraccay.

Cleto Cusipaucar is a member of the Immersion team that shares the Mil experience with our visitors on a daily basis. And, in 2019, we joined forces to sow 223 varieties of native potatoes on Mil's farmland to determine which are best produced here, both communities working with our agricultural engineers Manuel Acurio and Marcelo Gonzales Solis. Genetic material from the 2020 harvest will be shared among us, demonstrating a commitment to all our futures.

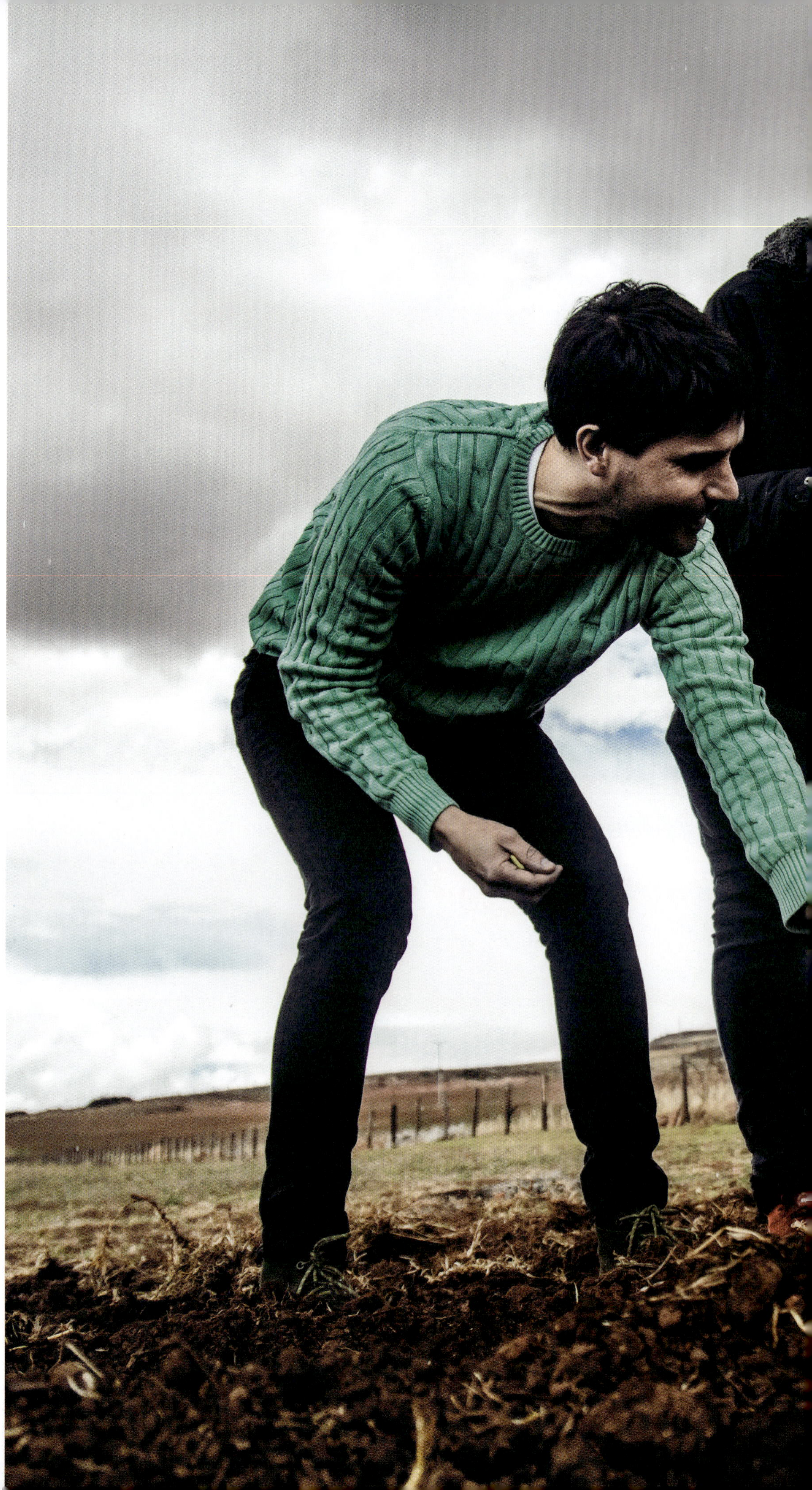

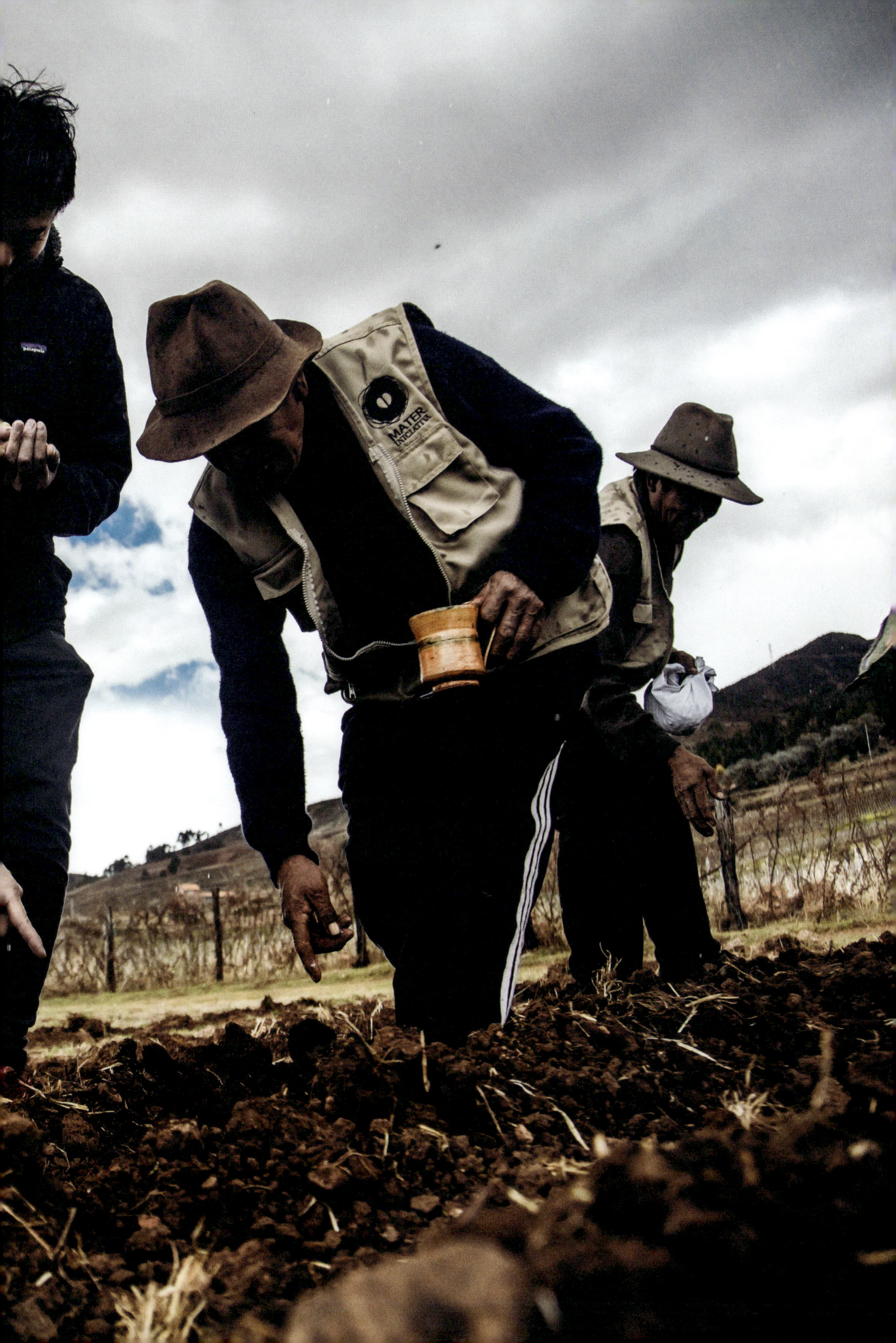
MATER
INICIATIVA

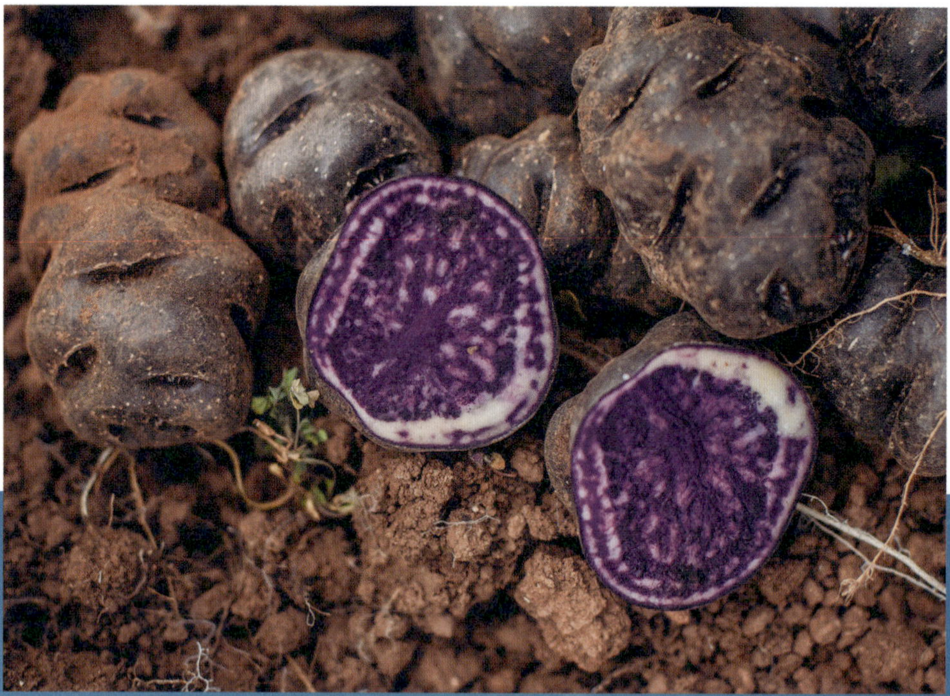

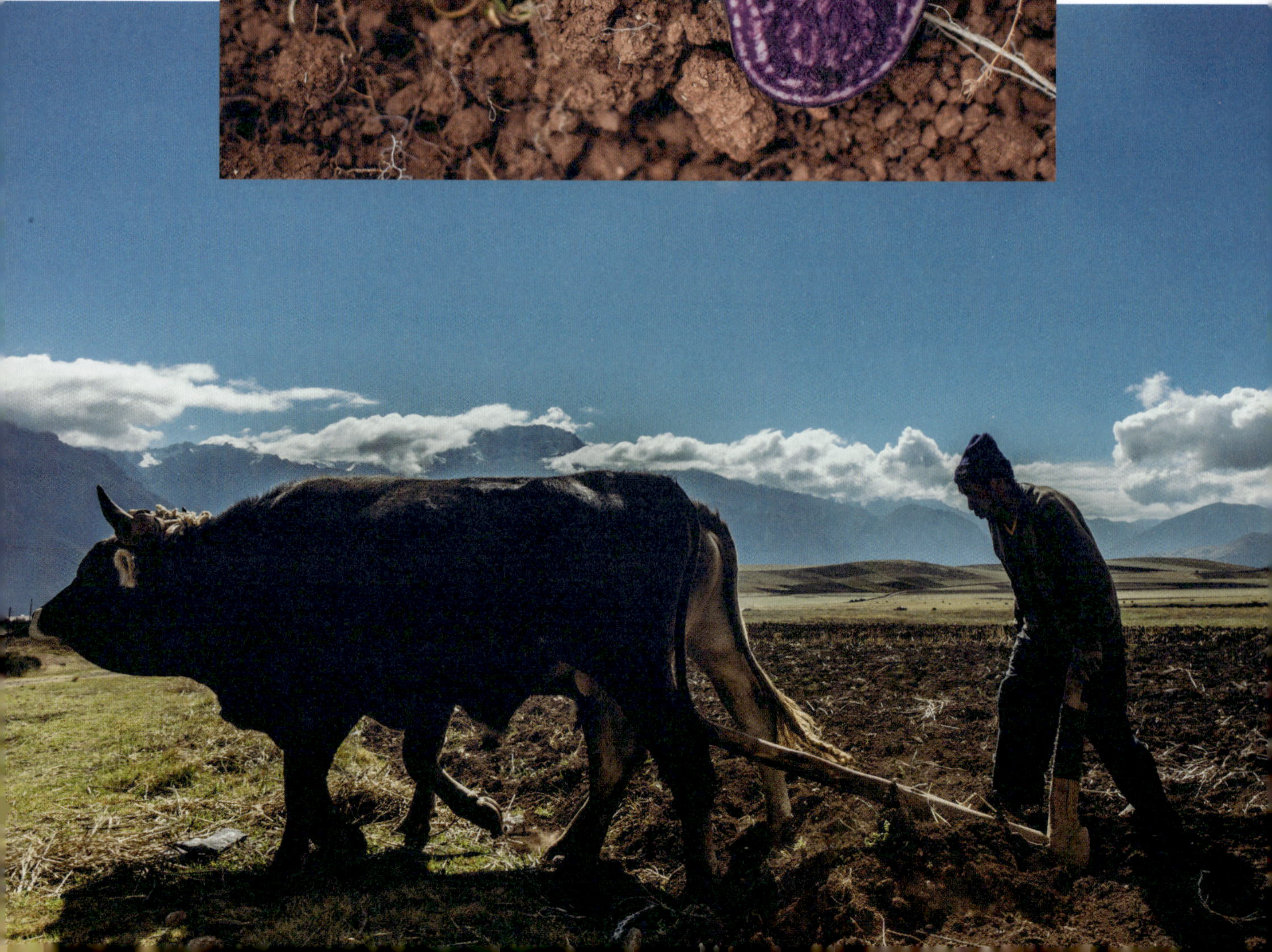

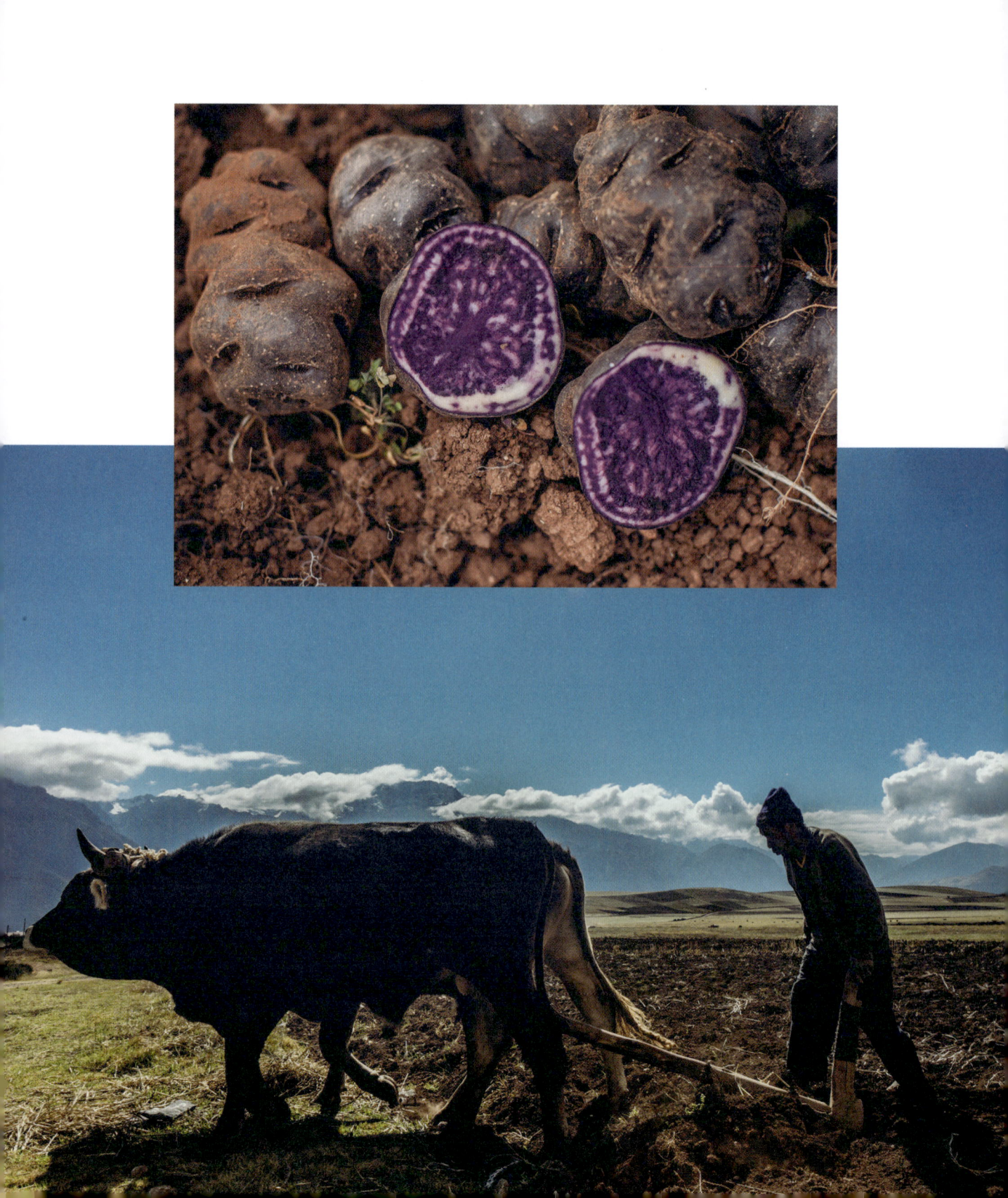

47

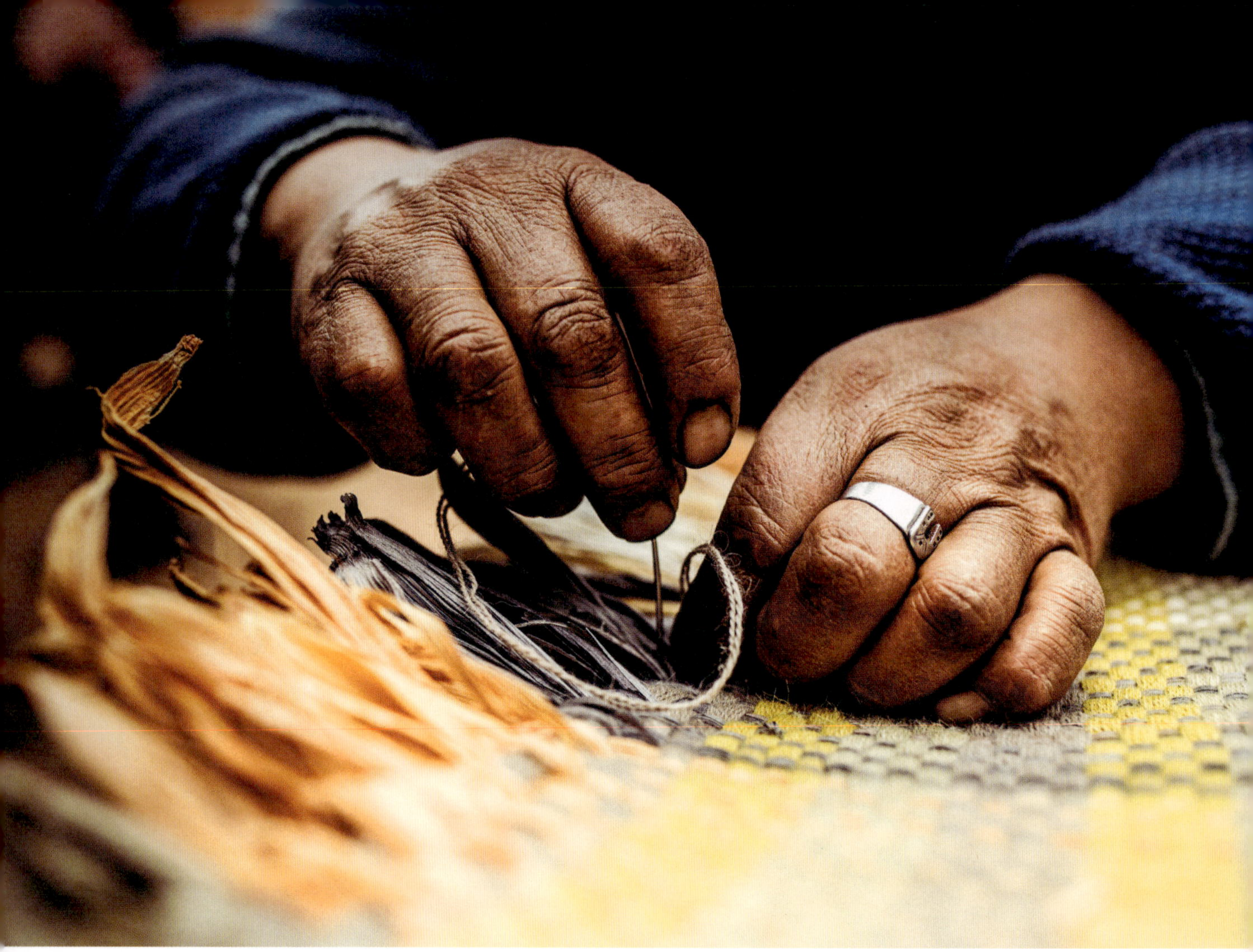

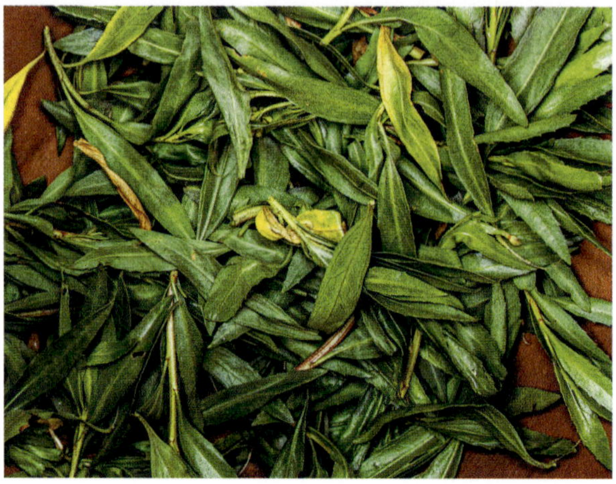

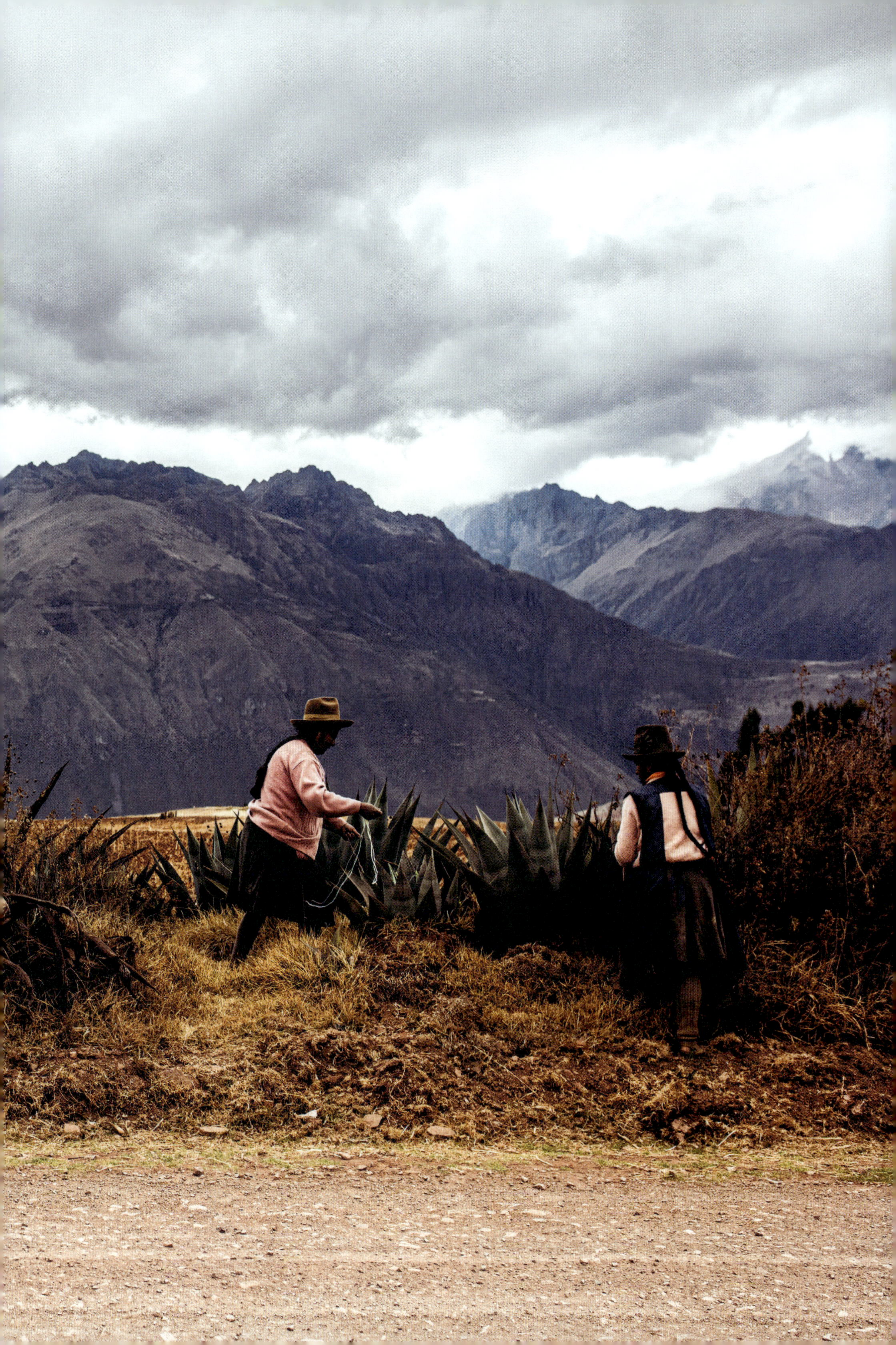

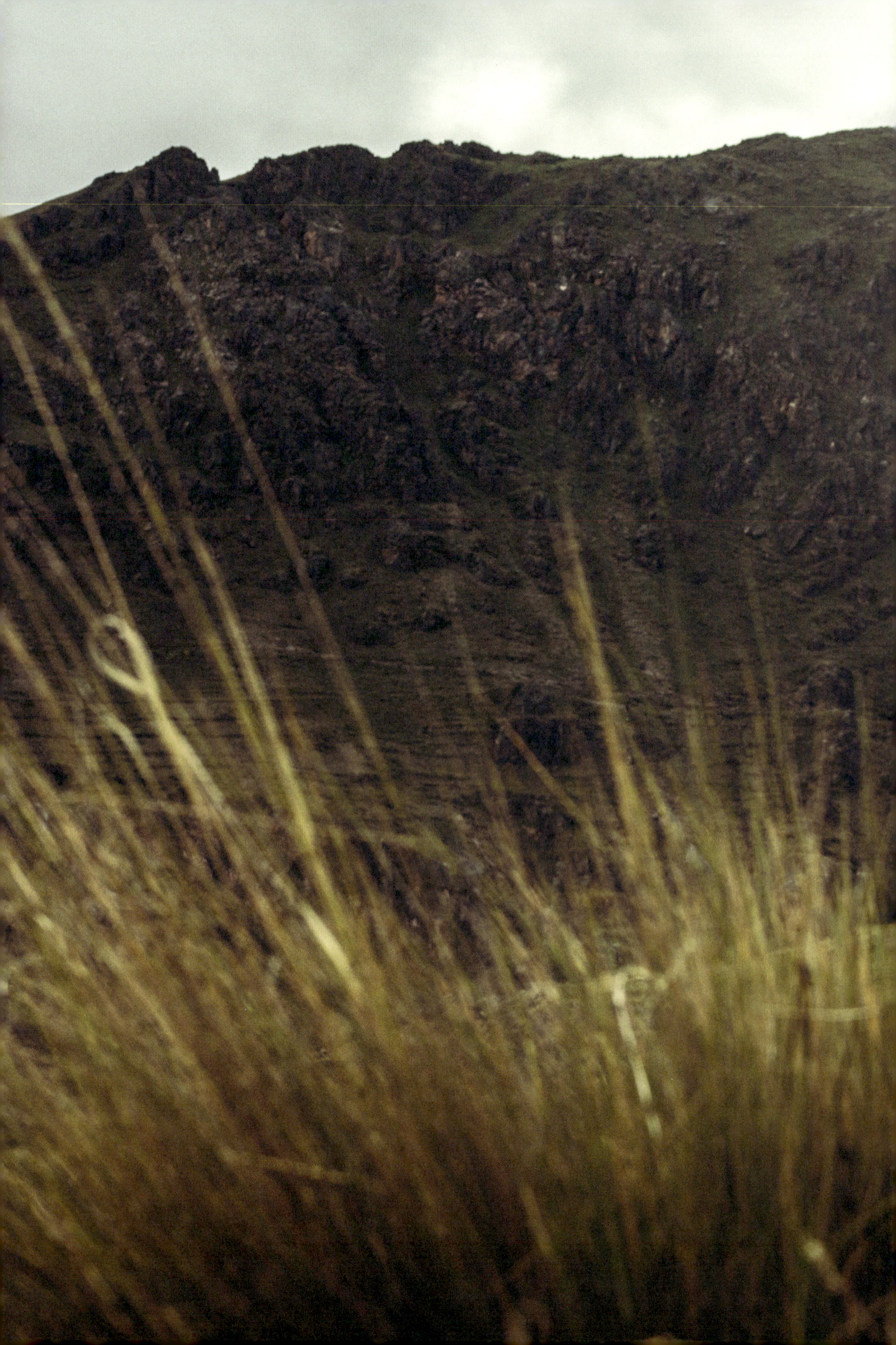

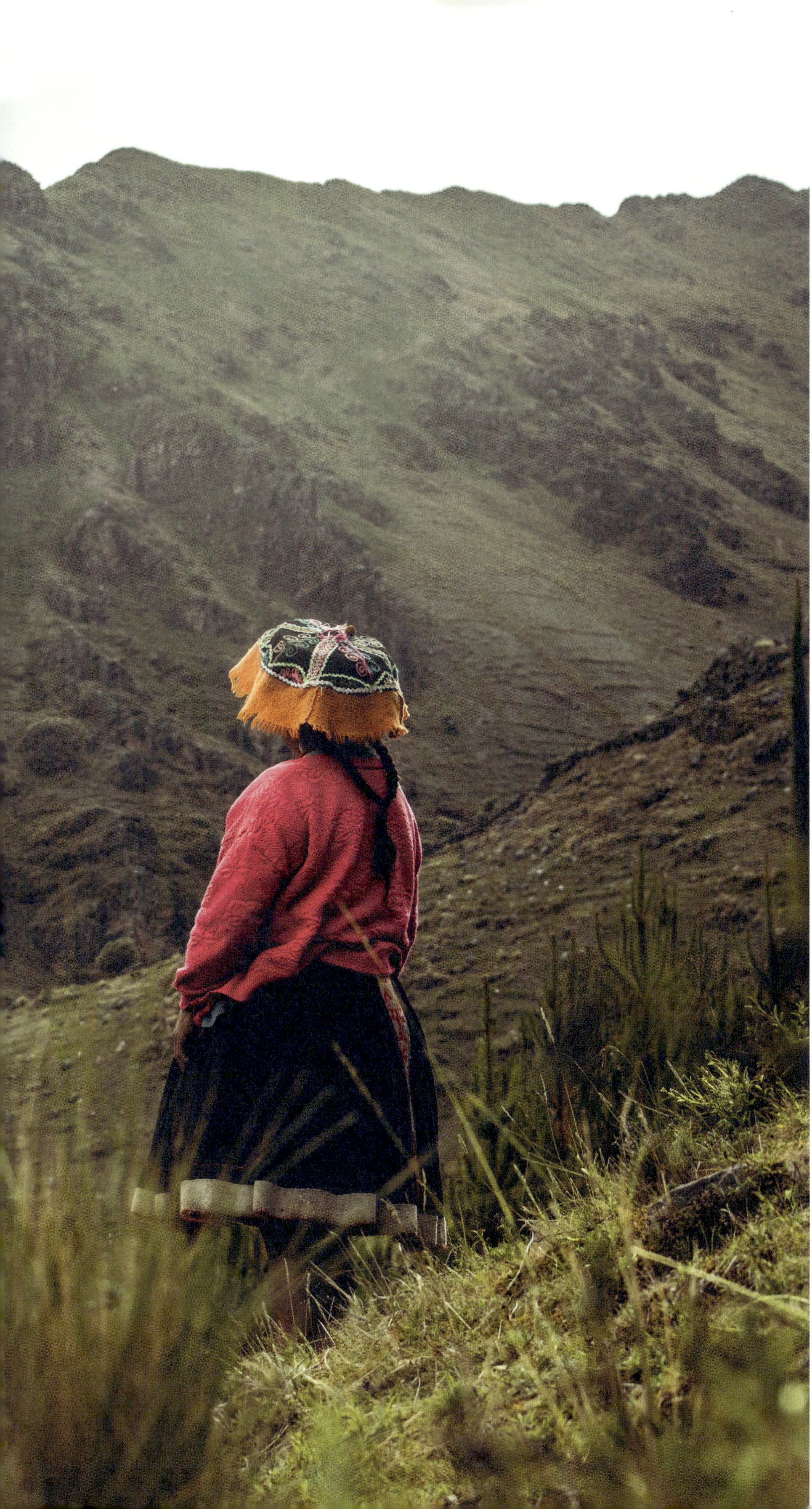

FRANCISCO QUICO MAMANI AND TRINIDAD MAMANI CASCAMAYTA

ORGANIC VEGETABLE AND GUINEA-PIG FARMERS

The natural way

Running a thriving organic farm flourishing with 25 varieties of herbs and vegetables, two greenhouses bursting with cherry tomatoes and warm-clime-loving species including grapes and rocoto chili pepper, an indoor *cuy* (guinea-pig) farm, small diner and even an adorable guest house overlooking Lake Pomacanchi, life paints a rosy and self-sustainable picture for husband and wife Francisco Quico Mamani and Trinidad Mamani Cascamayta. They were the first people who welcomed us to the Andes, when Mil was just a dream.

The intervening years have seen Trini travel to Morelia in Mexico to teach cooking classes on Andean cuisine, filled with joy to share her recipe for a delicious *uchucuta* salsa made from *huacatay* (Tagetes minuta), *sachatomate* (Solanum betaceum), toasted *canchita* corn and *rocoto verde* chili pepper picked from her garden and mashed down in a stone *batán* (mortar), proudly dressed in electrifying Andean finery. But living in Unión Chahuay, Acomayo province, wasn't always so agreeable.

Raised in this small community that lies 12,630 feet above sea level, south of Cusco city and tucked between the lake and the *apus*, meant tough times for her. At the age of 12, Trinidad was sent to work as a child carer and cook for a wealthy family in Calca province. Francisco, her husband, says: "Women have long been held back in our villages. Andean boys went to school and learnt Spanish, but Andean girls pastured animals and spoke mostly Quechua," an attitude that has fortunately changed with the current generation, who is educated and bilingual.

Aged 20, she returned to Unión Chahuay married with two children, Trindad and her young family living in a single room, which quintupled up as kitchen, dining room, bedroom, store room, and guinea-pig quarters, roamed by cats, dogs and ducks. "We all lived together under one roof," says Trinidad.

Besides farming crops such as fava beans and stomping on potatoes to create the freeze-dried *chuño*, the mother of three has long worked as a healthcare representative in Andean communities, trying to eradicate child malnutrition. The couple didn't sell their crops, choosing instead to use *trueque*, a product exchange system, with other communities. But the turning point came when the couple joined Sierra Productiva,

LOCATION
Unión Chahuay,
Acomayo, Cusco

ELEVATION - ECOREGION
12,650 feet
La Puna and High Andes

PRODUCTION CHAIN
Francisco and Trinidad sow, cultivate, harvest and prepare
orders for Sierra Productiva.

SEASONALITY

PLANTING
Tubers and maize: annually
Vegetables: every 3 months
Legumes: monthly

HARVEST
Tubers and maize: annually
Vegetables: every 3 months
Legumes: monthly

Organic agriculture (methods):
organic fertilizers, compost, biol, *laymi* (crop-plot rotation)

CLIENTS
Own consumption
Local market
Restaurants

This project is supported by Sierra Productiva.

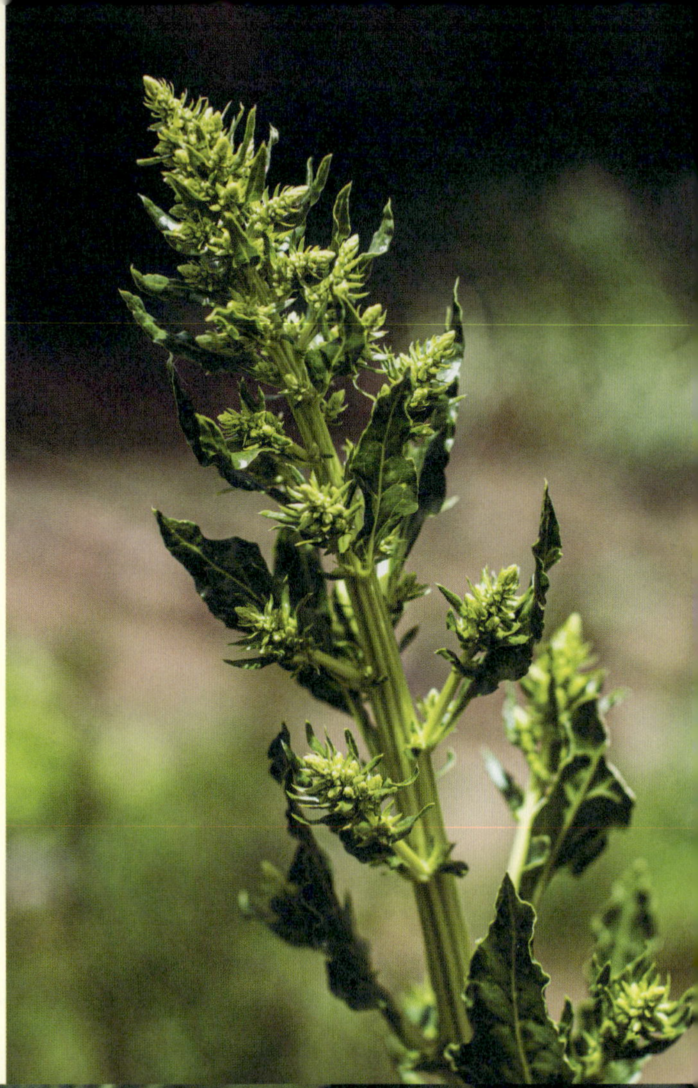
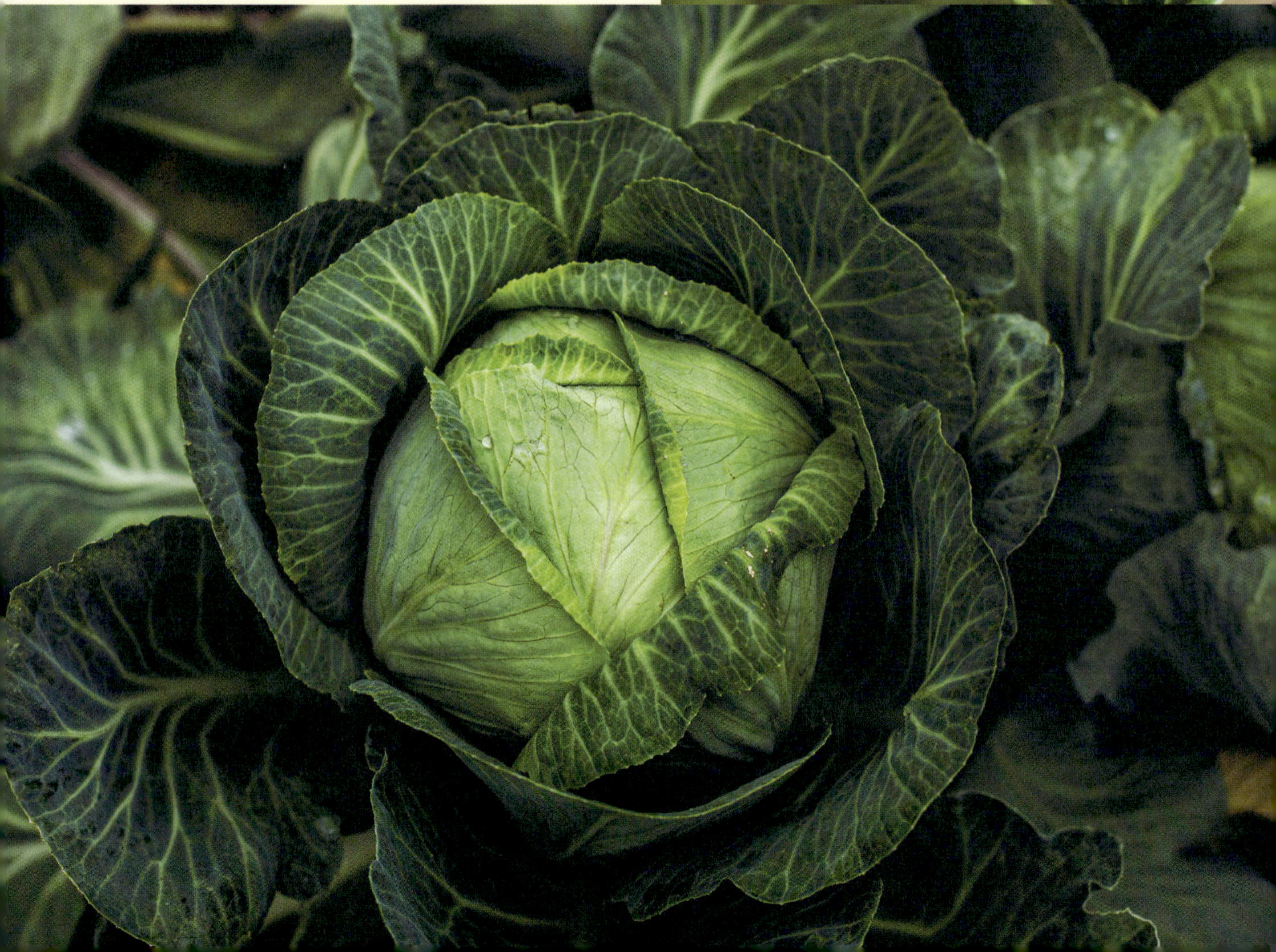

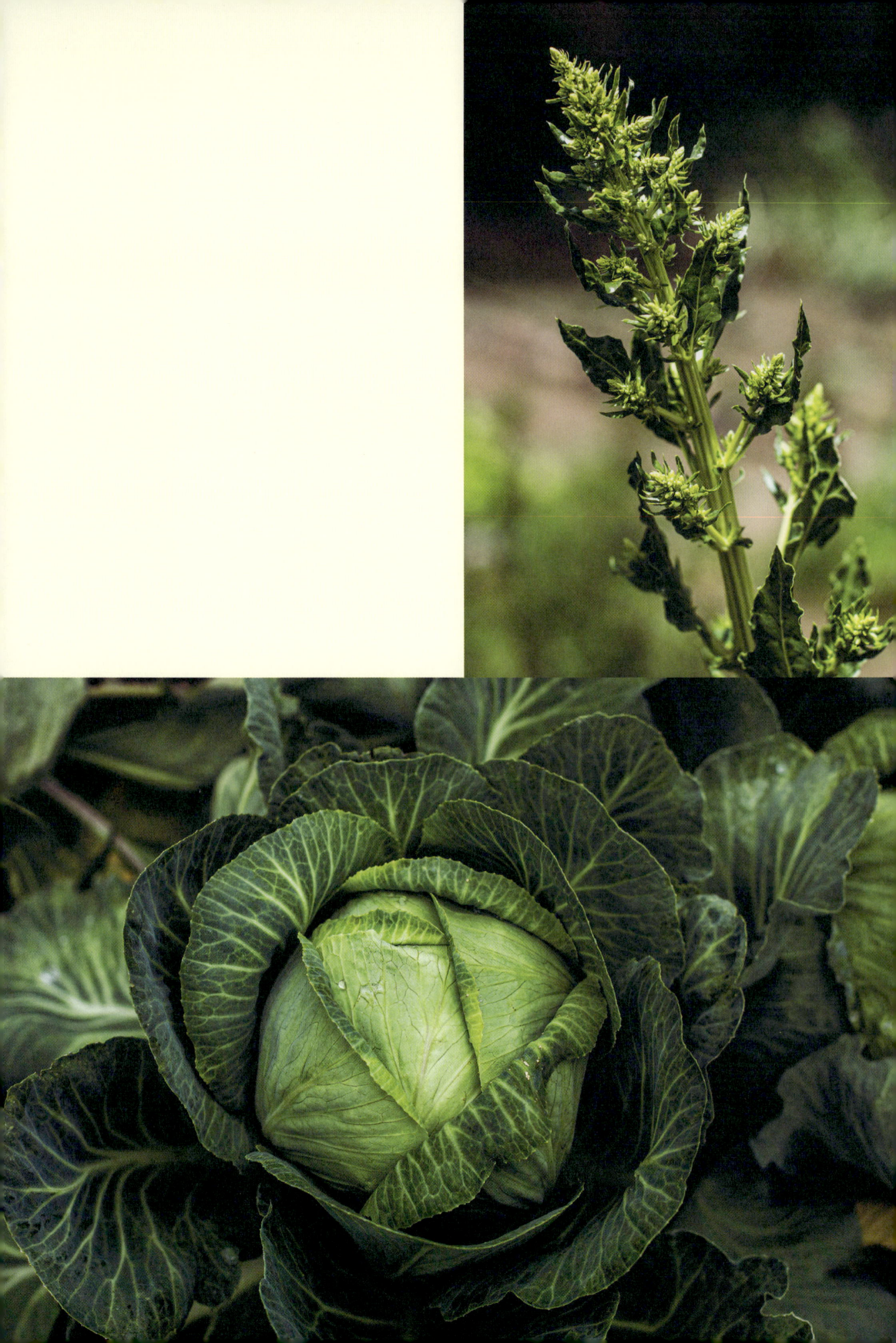

a rural-based non-profit that works inclusively with the Cusco region's small-scale farmers – such as LactoCaneñita in Jilayhua, Yanaoca district – eight years ago and undertook an array of agricultural training courses.

"Not only have we been able to revive the natural way of farming, we've also learned how to cook with new ingredients – and our diet has improved," says Francisco. "Virgilio has given our culture importance, inspired us to sow a greater diversity of plants and helped us to value non-Andean produce such as beet and chard; we once made a beet soup together called *sopa de la laguna azul*." Today, the couple is near totally self-sufficient, only stepping out to purchase rice, salt, oil and sugar from the local store, and nothing gives them greater pleasure than seeing their grandchildren running off to collect organic eggs as soon as they arrive from the city.

Working with the *laymi* soil rotation system and homemade organic bokashi compost made from waste, weeds, cow dung and chicha de jora dregs, enriched by Californian earthworms, Francisco, who takes care of the organic gardens, proudly shows off plants that don't usually grow with such vigor at this elevation or cool temperature, such as lemon, grapes, and *sachatomate*. He also cultivates native Andean plants usually only found in loftier climes, such as *kunuca* (Satureja boliviana), a leaf used by Mil bartender Manuel Contreras, and *muña* (*Minthostachys mollis*), which possesses an array of medicinal properties. "This minty leaf normally only grows between January and April in this area but, because of our farming methods, we can cultivate it year round," he says. "That means our neighbors can buy fresh produce pulled straight from the ground from us every day of the year."

Trinidad, who taught herself Spanish, cares for around 200 guinea pigs, an everyday source of protein in the Andes. She peeps through the windows of the airy farm to check on these anxious little rodents that squeak frantically at the first sign of an intrusion, and points out the most virile male. "We treat them like equals," she says. "They also eat organically and we've even painted their house."

It's been a long haul but the couple refuses to rest on their laurels. "Undertaking all this work isn't just for us but is an example of two farmers, who are proud to wear open-toe sandals and a *chamarra* waistcoat in their fields, and have made progress," says Francisco. "We're proud to be Andean farmers who are finally valued."

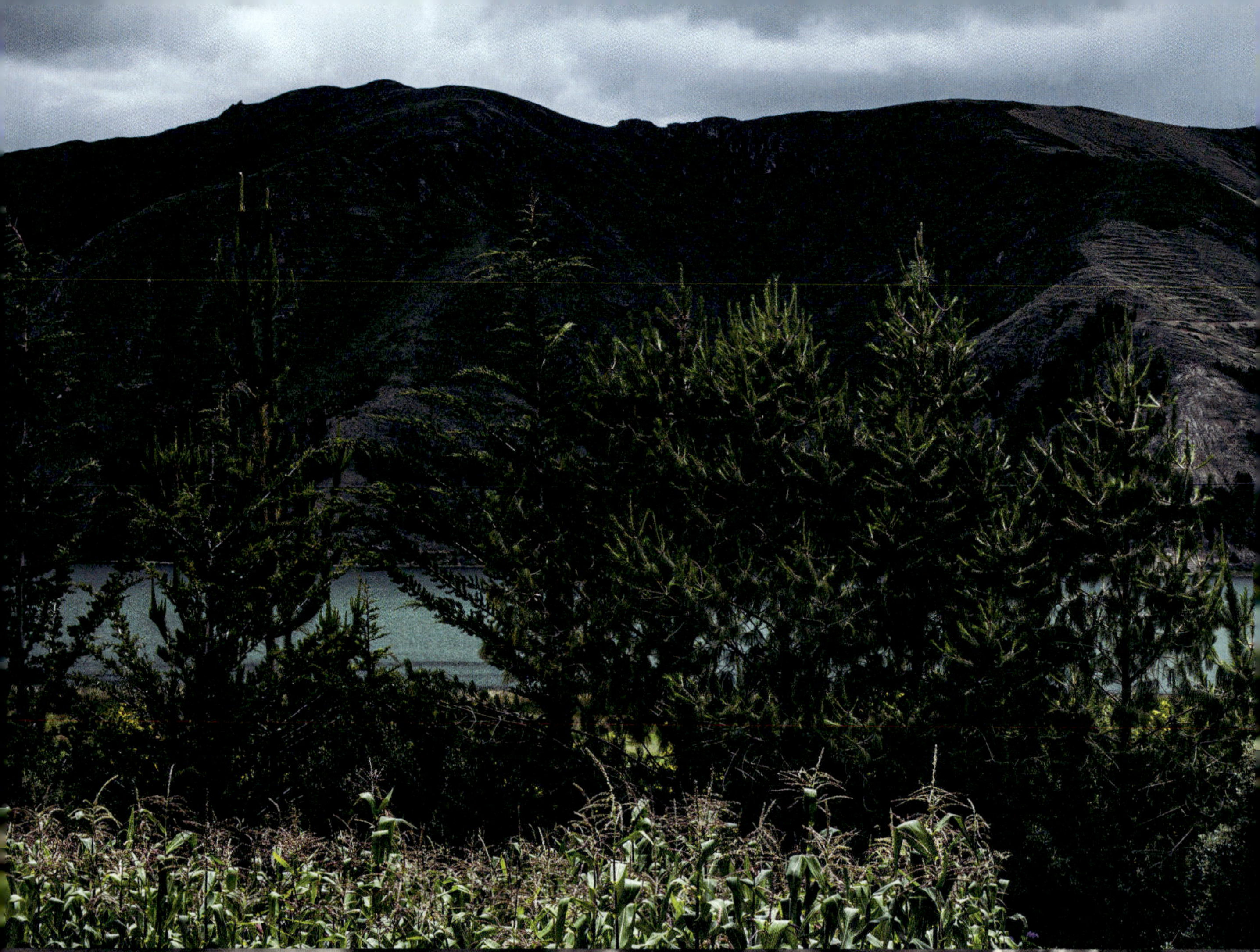
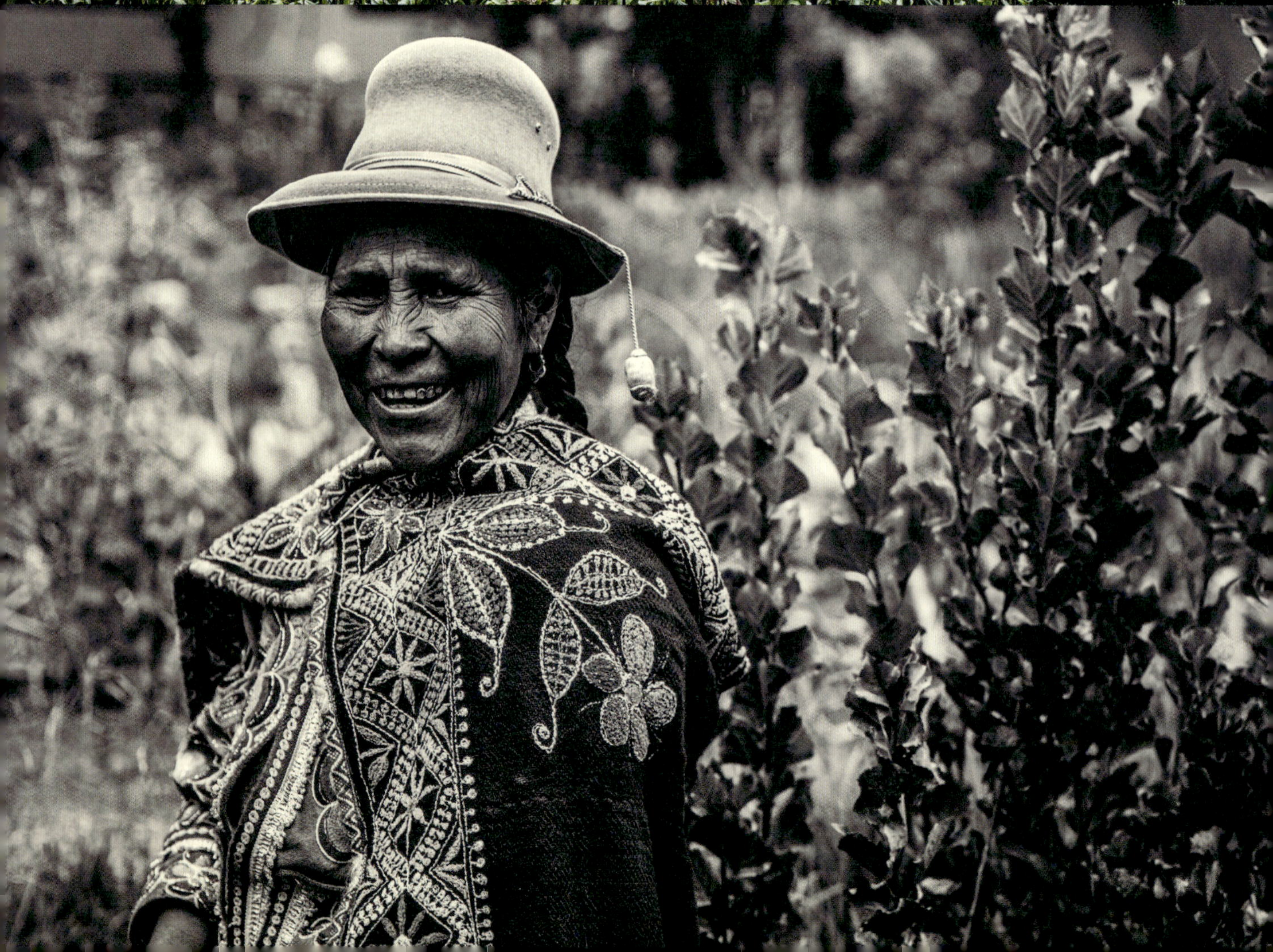

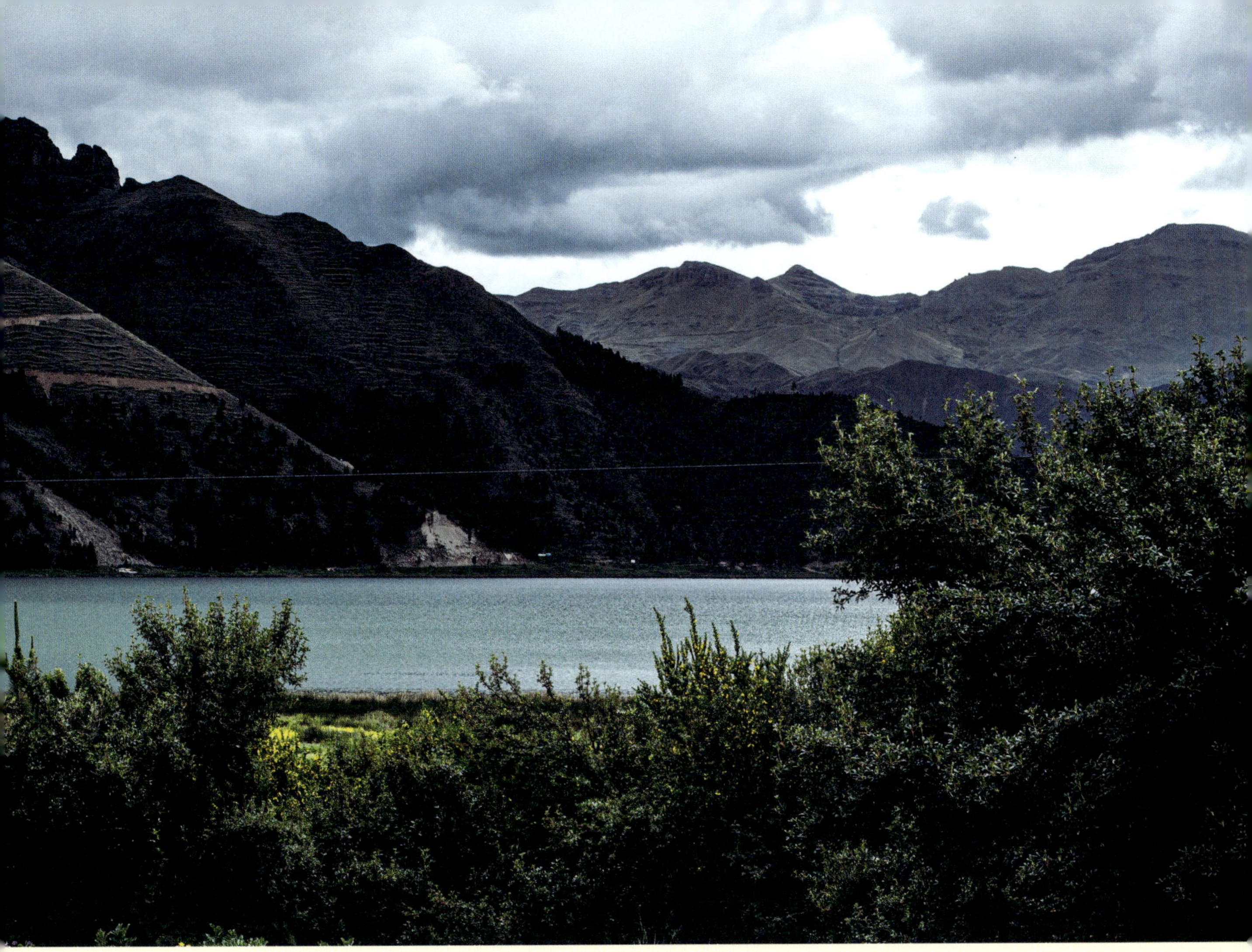

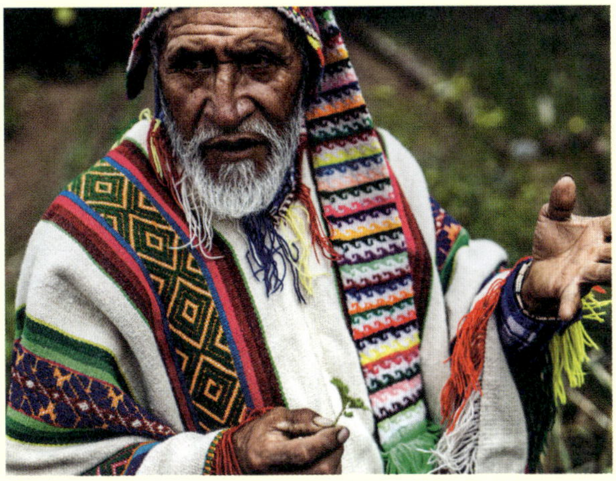

DESTILERÍA ANDINA
LIQUEURS

Lauding Andean liquids

"Chewing on barks and savoring flowers to discover astonishing flavors that can then be captured through distillation means we're creating a new language in Andean spirits," says Haresh Bhojwani of Destilería Andina, the Ollantaytambo-based micro distillery whose liquid speciality is *cañazo* (sugar cane spirit).

While alcohol in the form of *chicha de jora* corn beer has been made in the Andes for thousands of years, *cañazo's* story began when the Spanish conquistadors arrived in what is now Peru five centuries ago armed with, among other tools, copper stills and sugar cane (Saccharum officinarum). Planting this perennial grass throughout the country, top-quality, coastally cultivated cane was a lucrative commodity sent back to Europe, while in the Andes – grown at altitude on inappropriate soil in inappropriate weather conditions then distilled – it integrated into local customs to be used for medicinal and religious purposes. Mothers passed down remedial *compuesto* (botanical extract) recipes to daughters, while shamans used *cañazo* to bless land and undertake spiritual cleansings.

It was a radical career move for former human rights lawyer Haresh to exchange crafting legislation for spirits. Born to Indian parents and raised in the Canary Islands, his professional path led him to Peru to work on creating national parks in the Amazon; in his down time, he'd hang out in Cusco, where he met Joaquín and Ishmael Randall, Destilería Andina's future co-founders. It was their mother's homemade *compuesto* that inspired Matacuy – the distillery's refined and sophisticated version of the Andean digestif *matachancho* – whose 12 botanicals are extracted in *cañazo* then distilled to create a transparent and aromatic liquor.

Together, the trio set up a sustainable business in Ollantaytambo – a small town in the Sacred Valley found at 9,185 feet above sea level (asl) known for its Quechua fortress, sun temple and terminus, trains bound for Machu Picchu – that values ancestral knowledge and generates renewed interest in an Andean elixir whose popularity has dwindled in favor of imported spirits.

Eight of Matacuy's 12 botanicals such as lemongrass and celery are handpicked year round from their organic garden

LOCATION
Ollantaytambo,
Urubamba, Cusco

ELEVATION - ECOREGION
9,150 feet
Dry valleys of the Selva Alta high jungle

PRODUCTION CHAIN
Destilería Andina harvests sugar cane, fermenting the yellow cane for two days and green parts for five days. Initial distillation: heated for eight hours, boiled for two of those hours.
Water is mixed in to yield an alcohol content of 50% ABV.
Second distillation: alcohol content yield of between 70% and 80% ABV.
After resting the distillate for a week, water is added again to reduce the alcohol to 42% ABV.

SEASONALITY

PLANTING
Year round

HARVEST
Sugar cane may be harvested throughout the year with proper irrigation

Plants are harvested after 14-18 months of growth

CLIENTS
Hotels
Restaurants
Cusco and Lima bars
Travelers, tourists

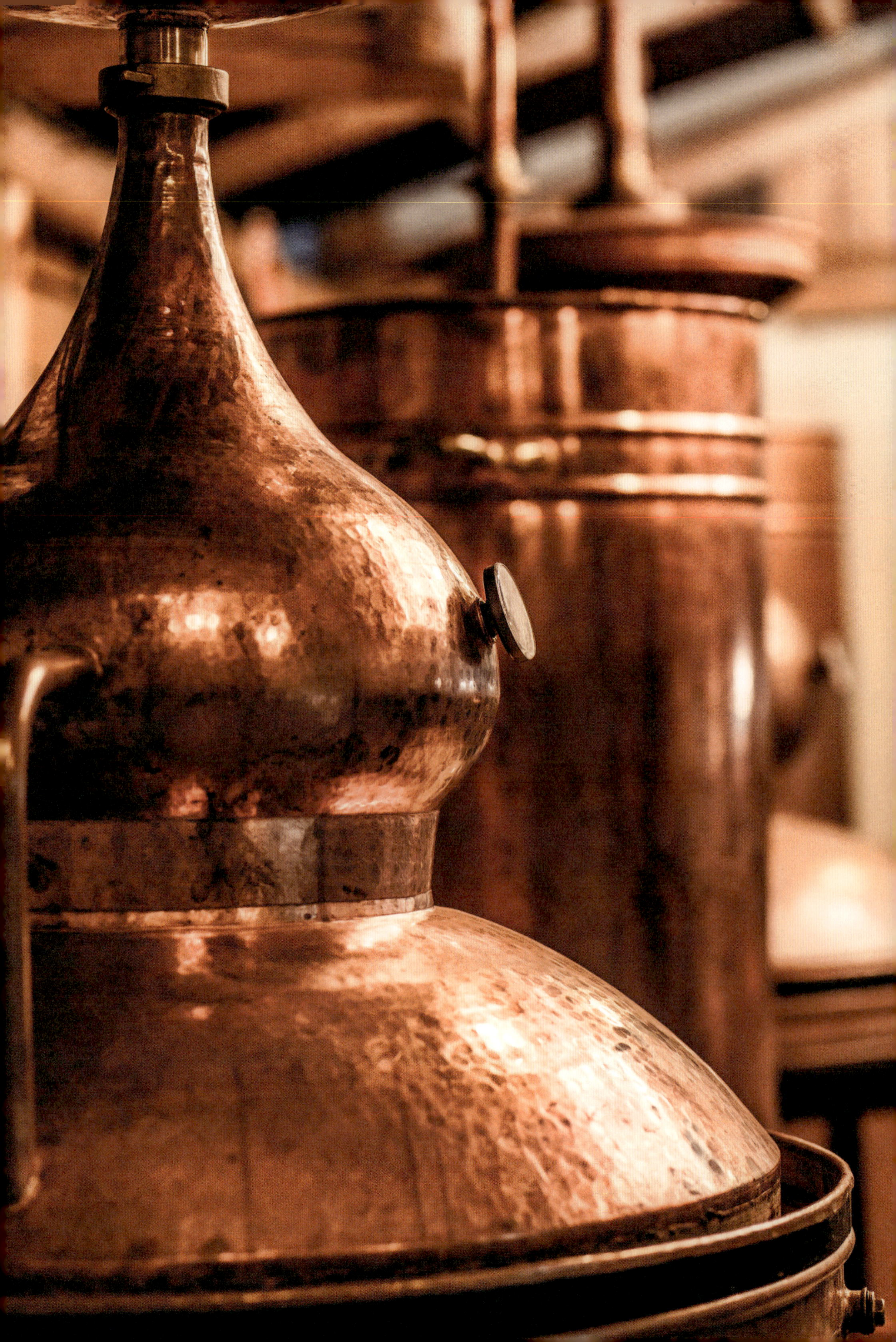

right in front of the distillery, as are those used in the double-distilled *cañazo* Caña Alta, ensuring ingredient availability and flavor purity. The key raw material sugar cane, meanwhile, is sourced from four family-run plantations around the Cusco region, its juices pressed by a water mill advantageously making use of natural elevation before it is fermented and distilled. Chief distiller Haresh says: "Even the sugar cane is special: usually cultivated at sea level in warm climes, it has adapted to grow at 6,600 feet asl, although it takes 18 months rather than the usual six to mature in this imperfect climate. Some canes are 50 years old and while that means their sugar yield is lower, flavor intensity is greater… and even that varies depending on their elevation.

"*Cañazo* is deeply tied to culture in the Andes: it's used for healing and blessings, and is enjoyed at community celebrations. We knew there were traditions in extracting from botanicals – family recipes made with plants plucked from gardens – to create remedies and we believed those traditions would die out if this elixir wasn't preserved."

Age-old agricultural methods are also employed on land that has been tended for thousands of years. Haresh adds: "We sow these fields by hand, they are plowed by a *yunta* (bull yoke) and then irrigated by Quechua-constructed stone canals, using the ancient method of flood irrigation; we also make our own compost. We adhere to the Andean rationale that botanicals hold more value if they're fresh, medicinally speaking. Extracted the day after harvest, that freshness and intensity makes a difference to the final flavor, creating a *compuesto* with distinctive characteristics. The plant spectrum is so broad, and almost none has ever been used to make spirits – that's really exciting."

That diversity inspires Haresh and team, which includes mixologist-turned-distiller André Querol, thanks to the infinite number of botanical combinations to discover. Haresh adds: "*Compuesto* recipes have been handed down through generations of women, a long-spun yarn of knowledge, way before *cañazo* existed. Together, we go foraging in the mountains and they tell us which roots or barks are useful; we catalog and extract in a bid to understand them, and that leads to new recipes." Liquid collaborations are equally stimulating: Destilería Andina has teamed up with potato farmer and agronomist Manuel Choqque Bravo to create a tuber-based liquor and they regularly brainstorm with Cervecería del Valle Sagrado's head brewer Carlos Barroso.

"Take an ear of Andean corn, which isn't traditionally distilled. How would I extract a whole one? If you sample the different parts, they are strange yet complex: the silky top is floury, the outer husks taste like green tea, while the cob is like a sugar lump – and the flavors change if you toast or roast it. Plant diversity in the Andes is so wide and here we are, sitting on the edge doing inherently Peruvian things that have never been done before – and we're only just starting to experiment with all these complex flavors."

The endless possibilities in turn generate innovative mixology. Mil's bartender Manuel Contreras prepares Caña Alta Blue with *tumbo* (banana passionfruit) extract and fermented *mashwa* (Tropaeolum tuberosum) to harmonize with *Preservación*, the first of eight moments in Mil's tasting menu that samples *chuño* (freeze-dried potato), corn, *uchucuta* salsa and *oca* (Oxalis tuberosa).

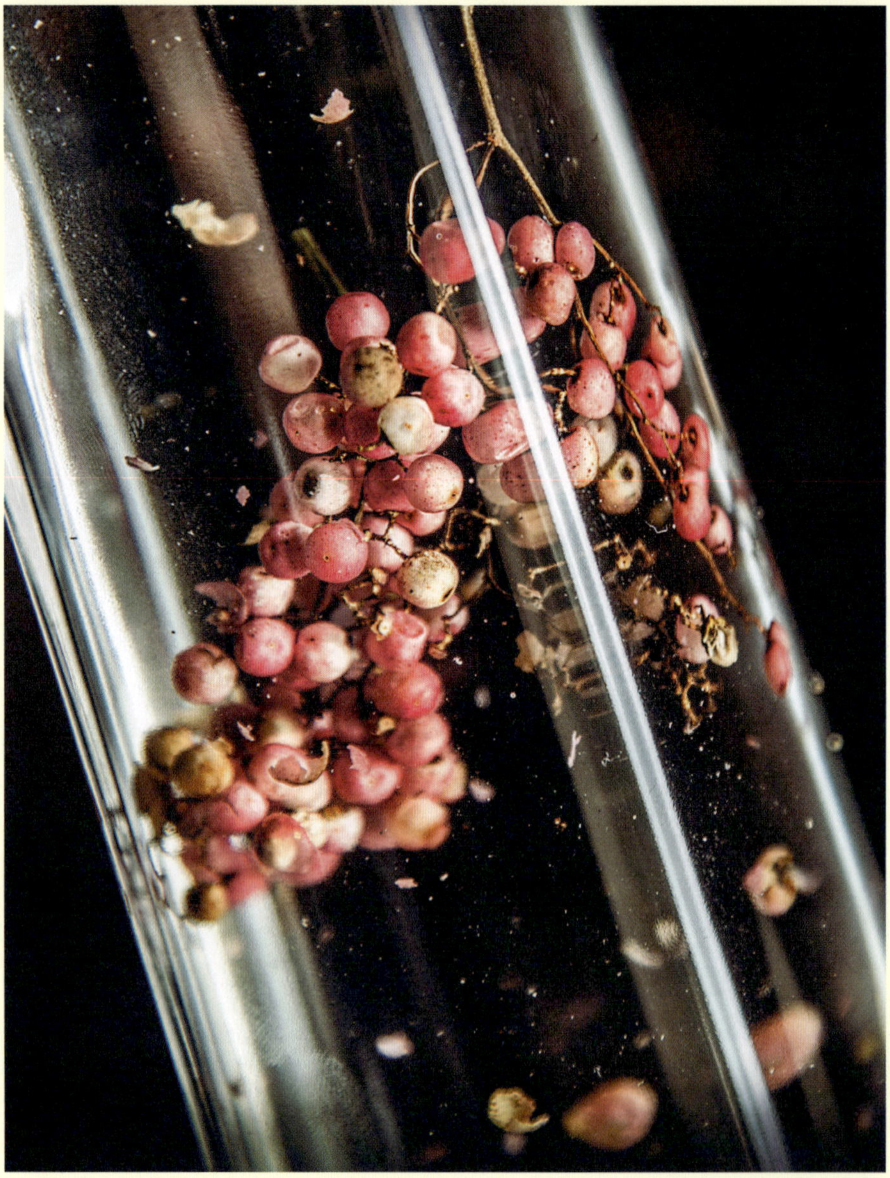

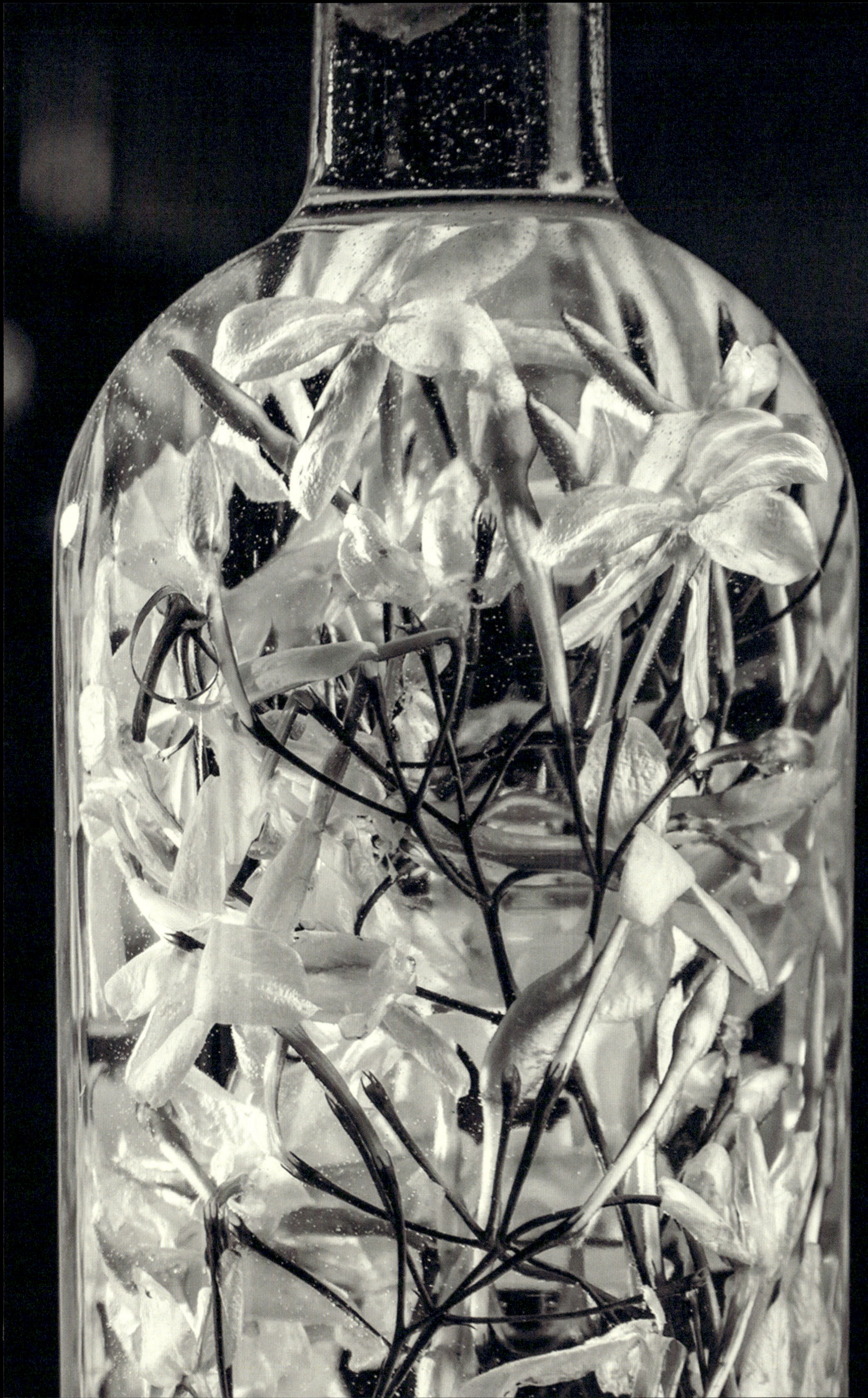

DWIGHT AGUILAR MASÍAS

THREE MONKEYS COFFEE COMPANY

From farm to cup of excellence

"Specialty coffee is my vice. When I get up in the morning, the first thing I do is look at my fermenting beans. Producing coffee is a puzzle – and I love trying to solve it," says Dwight Aguilar Masías.

Today, the third-generation coffee grower is a revered figure in Quillabamba, known for his award-winning, biodynamic Geisha beans sourced from 5,970 feet above sea level that picked up Peru's Cup of Excellence award in 2018.

New growers seek him out for inspiring advice, while baristas come from around the world to harvest and sample his *Coffea arabica* cherries. But it's taken 20 years of onerous elbow grease for Dwight's passion to be recognized.

In 1998, two devastating mudslides destroyed two of his parents' three farms. Forced to look for work in the city of Cusco, Timoteo Aguilar and Berlarmina Masías Zavala left their 16-year-old son in charge of Finca Nueva Alianza, back then a conventionally run plantation near Santa Teresa in La Convención province, located two mountains away from Machu Picchu.

Survival mode kicked in for the home-alone teen: he grew vegetables and kept hens and guinea-pigs for six years in order to make ends meet. "I picked coffee and sold it to co-operatives, but I couldn't afford to hire any farm hands," he says. Barely keeping his head above water for a decade, inevitable low yields meant Dwight started losing faith in coffee – until he visited his cousin Juan's finca in Villa Rica in Cerro de Pasco, Peru's central jungle region.

"I fell in love with his coffee; his cherries matured well and Juan was harvesting more than 40 quintals [one quintal equals 220 lbs] a hectare," he says. Enthused, Dwight returned to Santa Teresa and convinced his father to replant a single hectare of specialty coffee. But, in one of numerous ongoing differences of opinion with Timoteo, Dwight removed – and replanted – 10 times that area. "My dad was furious. He thought I was mad and wasting money." (Even today, despite his son having that prestigious Cup of Excellence award under his belt, Timoteo still says Dwight is crazy.)

LOCATION
Santa Teresa,
La Convención, Cusco

ELEVATION - ECOREGION
5,100–5,600 feet
High jungle forest;
cloud forest

PRODUCTION CHAIN
Dwight harvests by hand, picking the cherries, which then undergo anaerobic fermentation for 28 hours. The fruit covering is removed, the beans washed in water and dried in a chamber with rotating platforms for three days. The coffee is roasted for 14 minutes. That's how it's served at *Three Monkeys* and sold at Mater Sostiene.

SEASONALITY

PLANTING
Newly planted coffee shrubs require three to four years before bearing fruit.

HARVEST
June-August

Organic agriculture (methods):
biol, soil drenching and microorganisms

CLIENTS
Local businesses
Corporate sales
National roasters
Travelers, tourists

Dwight's experimental vision and dedication – clearing old Typica trees one by one with a machete and planting top-quality varieties such as Geisha and Red Bourbon – paid off. In 2014, he and Cusco-based Three Monkeys Coffee Company connected.

Dynamic 20-something baristas Iván Salas, Neto Solórzano and Diego Huillca had set up a dreamers' club for coffee lovers: a space to share ideas, such as a caffeine-focused magazine or a museum dedicated to the black liquid gold. But what united them was the desire to improve the local economy by generating greater value for cherries cultivated by small-scale farmers, of which there are 223,902 in Peru in 2020, according to the International Coffee Organization – then extracting the coffee to prepare outstanding bean-to-cup brews.

They decided to explore Cusco, their local region, the three unbelievably traversing the Andes on a single motorbike with a wisp of a budget to meet growers. The aim was to start a project that would kickstart local coffee culture, improve the economy of *caficultores* – and capture the story behind each cup. "In coffee, there are tears, exploitation, poverty and strength, a narrative that isn't usually told," says Diego, who was Peru's 2016 Latte Art Champion.

"We went to the origin on that initial exploratory journey and while we found a lot of conventional coffee, nothing stood out," adds Neto, a third-generation coffee grower and professional taster. Then, they met Dwight at a fair in Quillabamba. The grower told the Monkeys he was excited about the cherries sourced from a single Geisha plant he'd been gifted in 2012. Intrigued, the trio visited his farm to sample them: "They were exquisite. Sweet, different, intense – we could really foresee the cupping potential."

Dwight became the Monkeys' first 'prototype' grower because they believed his beans weren't just good – they were extraordinary. "In Dwight, we saw and understood his primary passion and that the rest of the world plays second fiddle to him," says Neto. "He thinks about coffee 24 hours a day.

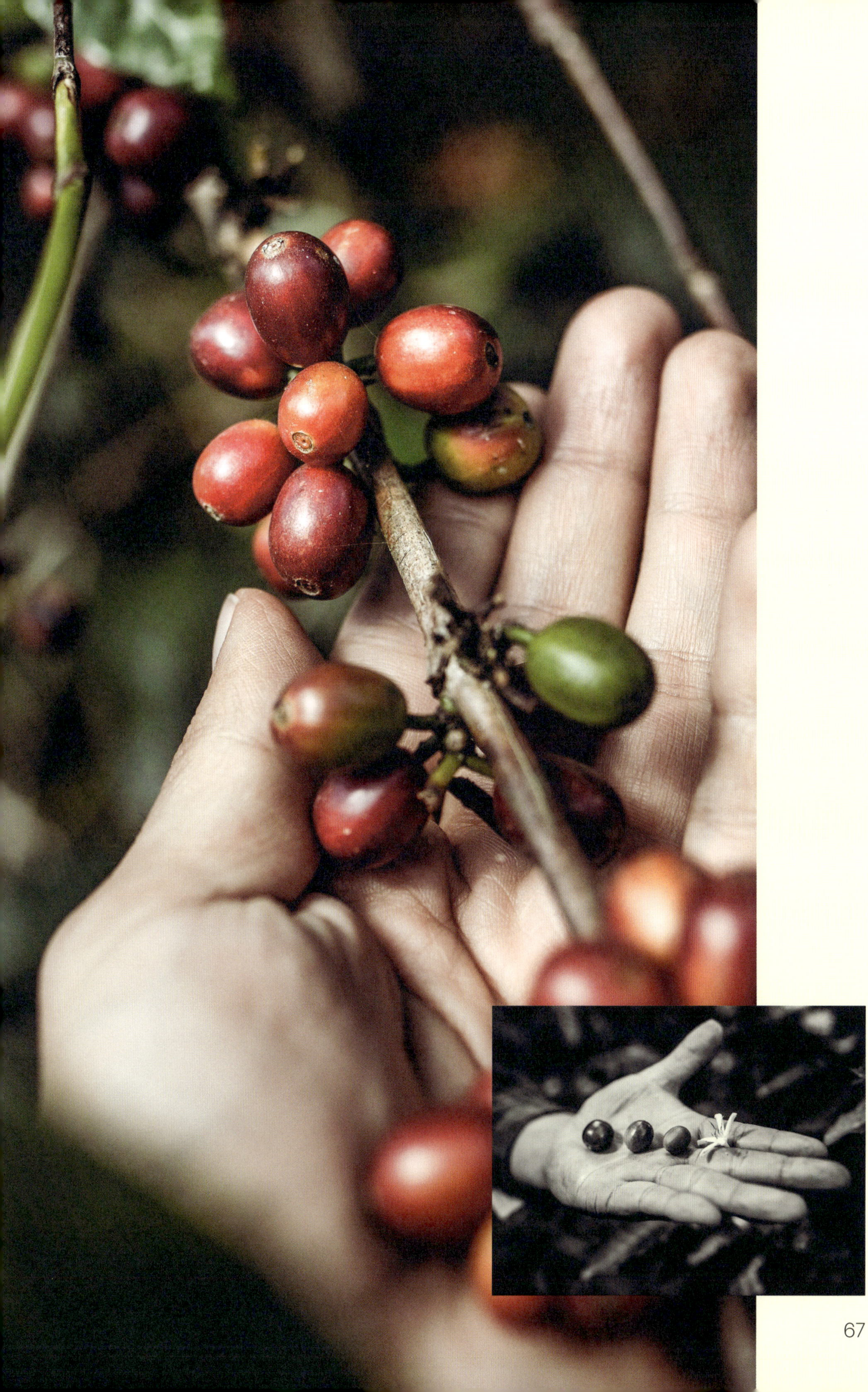

"We look for two things in growers: first, attitude, because without that, it's hard to get going, and second, the ecosystem. His farm is located in the mountains that generate a special microclimate between day and night temperatures, and his shrubs are planted on unique volcanic soils only found in Santa Teresa."

Finetuning these characteristics meant they could create an extraordinary specialty coffee from the world's ninth-largest producer. The Monkeys worked closely alongside Dwight to continue resolving the coffee puzzle. In 2017, they suggested he implement a biodynamic philosophy, which he applied, harvesting at night according to the lunar cycle under a full moon. Dwight also fermented in stainless steel tanks for the first time. Armed with this technical knowledge, passion and dedication, Dwight's Geisha allowed Neto Monkey to nail first place in Peru's 2018 Cup of Excellence competition, the same Geisha beans prepared by Diego Monkey at Mil using the V60 brewing method, when the restaurant first opened.

Dwight maintains a hands-on approach at Finca Nueva Alianza and is slowly branching out: his wife Dyana Mellado Portilla roasts beans at their small plant and café in Huadquiña near Santa Teresa, using their own Dwight Coffee line for brews accompanied by a unique, mountainous canyon panorama. He starts his day with a chilled coffee each morning and sometimes stays up until dawn playing chess.

The Three Monkeys have also propagated their vision: initially collaborating with 15 small coffee growers, today they work alongside 50 and, after deciding to focus on these relationships, only roast beans for Mil, Central in Lima and their own eponymous brand. They recently opened a second mobile coffee shop in Cusco, continue to be Mil's only coffee bean purveyor, and in 2021, picked Geisha, Red Bourbon and Pink Bourbon cherries for the first time from their own farm.

"Coffee remains a puzzle, but there's no single right answer as we simply have more variables to play around with. We can delve deeper into fermentation, topography, post-harvest care; coffee has only recently come to be considered a discipline and is open to exploration for different results," says Diego.

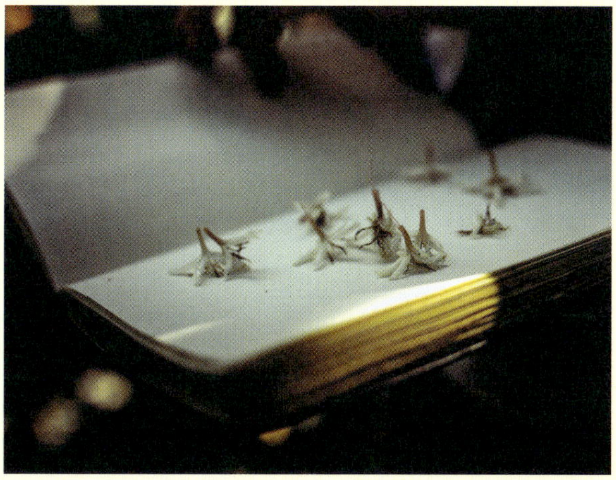

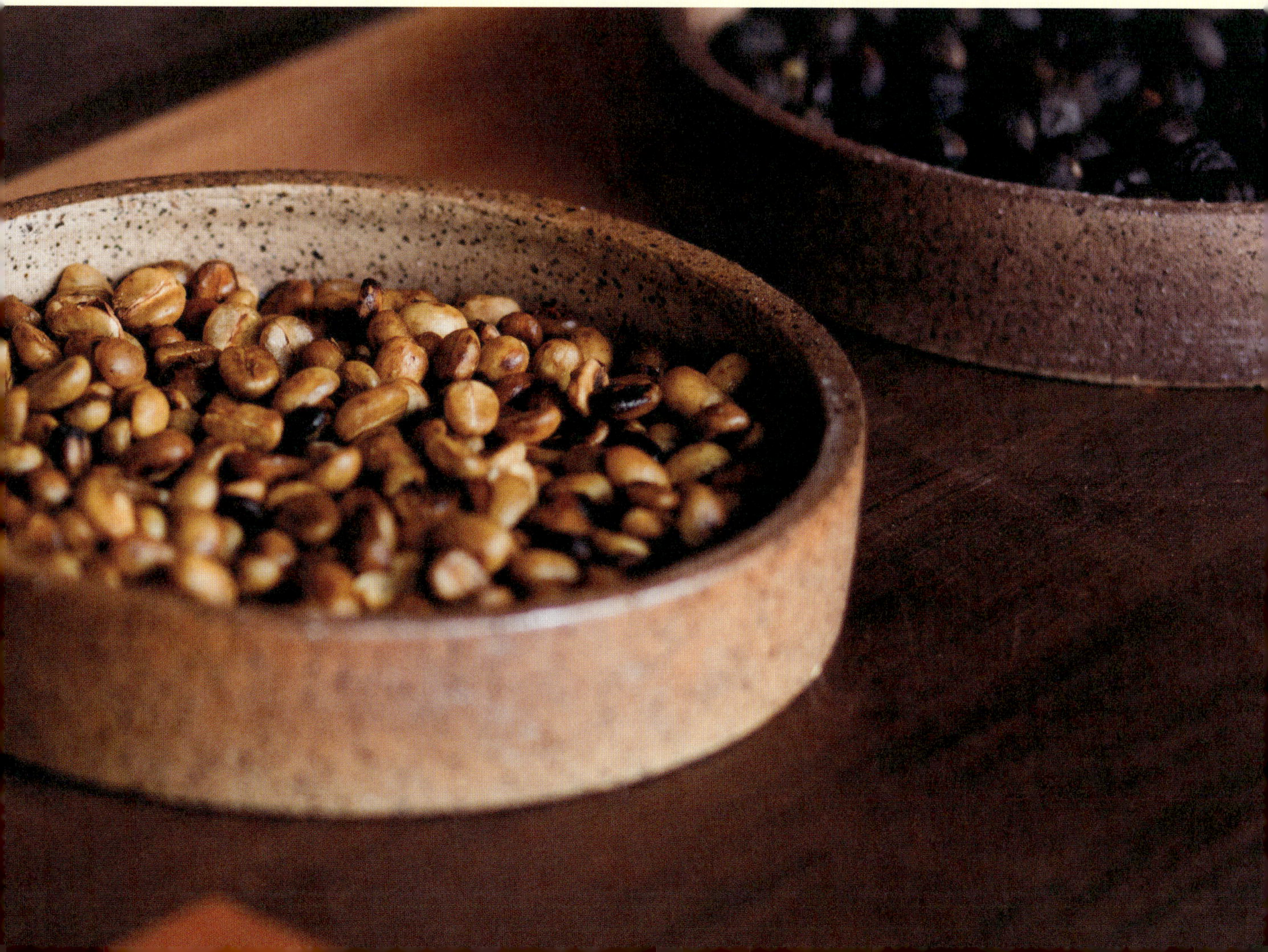

MANUEL CHOQQUE BRAVO
AGRICULTURAL ENGINEER, TUBER FARMER

Potatoes are a way of life

"Native potatoes mean everything to me. I eat them every day. Thanks to tubers, I have a degree in agronomy. I learn from them and they represent everything. Health. Satisfaction. Happiness – but also heartache. They're a way of life."

Manuel Choqque Bravo was born in Huatata, a small village located 12,270 feet above sea level, the highest point between the city of Cusco and the Sacred Valley, in the district of Chinchero, and tubers were always going to shape his future. Son of an innovative third-generation potato farmer, his father Augusto was sought out by agronomists keen to learn more about the diverse varieties he created through cross-pollination, favoring these radical tubers with bumpy hard-to-peel surfaces and vibrant violet flesh – rarely seen in local markets – over standard starchy white ones. The family fields were Manuel's playground, lobbing tubers around like balls, scaring his sisters with *puma maqui* and *pusi qachun waqachi* – the first named after the shape of a puma's paw, the other meaning 'make your daughter-in-law weep' – and building *huatia* ovens out of adobe clods. "Potatoes were the cell phone of our day," he says.

Having already followed in his father's innovative footsteps by experimenting with manual cross-pollination, merging genetic material between two potato varieties, as a teen, Manuel was determined to formalize his education and study agronomy. "But, I didn't learn that much that first year in college!" he says. Regardless, he was soon boosting diversity by improving genetics and nutrients and, following graduation, started working at Peru's National Institute of Agricultural Innovation (INIA) to specialize in potatoes, the world's fourth-most important food source.

Manual cross-pollination in an open-air lab (his garden) located next door to Huatata's small church is just as delicate as the work of a chef – and he only has the opportunity to do so once a year. Painstakingly removing a flower's five stamens with soft-ended tweezers, Manuel places them into a small paper envelope, shaking it to remove pollen, then rubs a second plant's stigma into the cream-colored dust.

Patience and dedication pay off: since 2014, Manuel has created 90 brand-new native-derived potato varieties that

LOCATION
Huatata,
Chinchero, Cusco

ELEVATION - ECOREGION
12,150 feet
Mountain pastures

PRODUCTION CHAIN
Manuel sows, cultivates and harvests. Late harvest: sun-dried 20-30 days.
For distillation: heated the first time with water, the second time with pure distilled water.
Heated to 149°F (65°C), then rested. Juice is extracted. Heated to 95°F (35°C) to reactivate
fermentation, then continues fermenting in tanks for five months.

SEASONALITY

PLANTING
November-December

HARVEST
Tubers: May-June
Fermentations: August-September

Organic agriculture (methods):
crop rotation, application of cinnamon
and horsetail extracts

CLIENTS
Hotels
Restaurants
Travelers – tourists

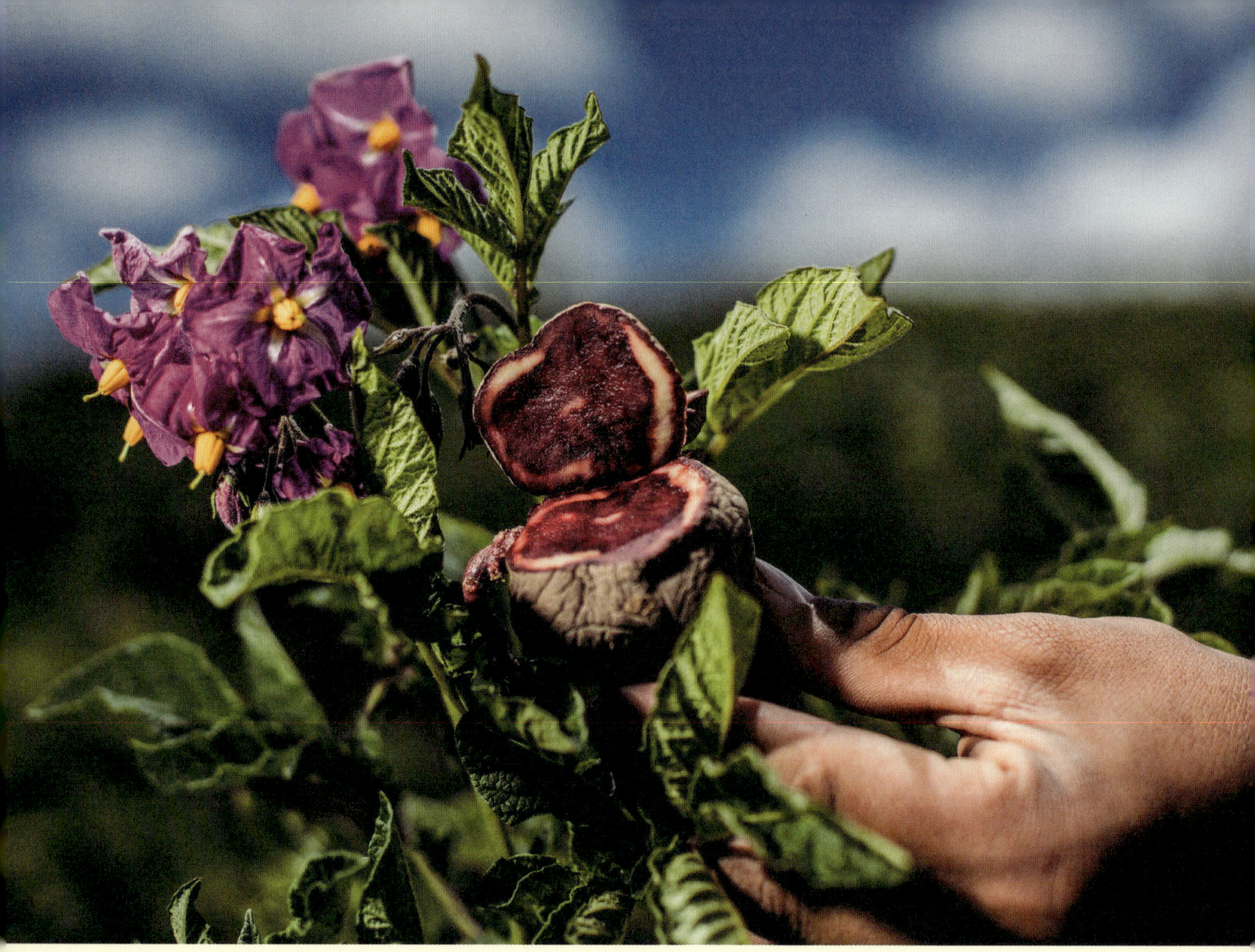

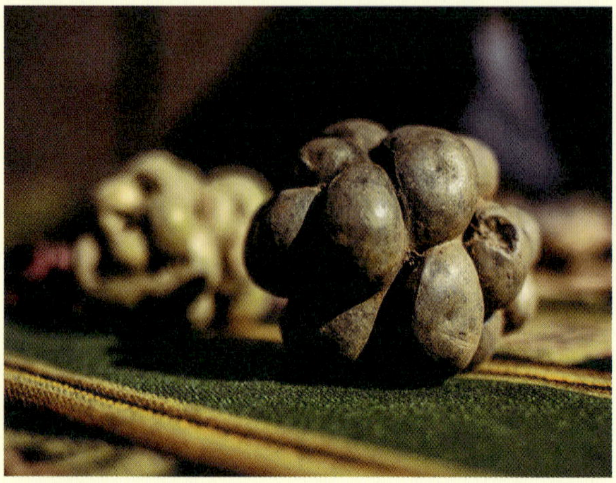

paint a palette of vibrant amethyst, blushing pink and intense orange, and he's showing little sign of slowing down when it comes to creating originals. "I've got 2,000 seedlings right now, and who knows how many new potato plants those will eventually yield? Maybe 50." he says. "The objective, however, is always the same. New varieties need to be multi-functional and well pigmented like berries – the more intense, the better – so they reach their potential in antioxidants and nutrients."

The story behind how we met Manuel reflects the same persistent patience he puts into manual cross-pollination. After reading an article in a local paper about Mil's imminent opening, his interest piqued by the fact it would also house Mater's regional headquarters, Manuel called Central in Lima, not once but several times over the coming months, to offer us his tubers.

Malena and I visited him at home, and besides selling *mashwa* (Tropaeolum tuberosum) and *oca* (Oxalis tuberosa) to Mil, he also donated 55 native potato varieties that were sown on our experimental farm in 2018.

Manuel says: "I contributed because it's not very common to see native forms and colors in the region, so it was an opportunity to rescue historical varieties that still have a future. It was an interesting trial to see how they'd adapt, given that Huatata's microclimate is different to Moray's, which has poorer soils, less rain and lower elevation."

His donation was the first step in creating a gateway for Mil and the communities to sow 223 native varieties donated by INIA in 2019, an agricultural exchange program led by our agronomists Manuel Acurio and Marcelo Gonzales Solis that rescues ancestral knowledge while regenerating local biodiversity. Manuel says: "While it's important to revive traditional practices and knowledge, working with Mil means that the restaurant's cooks learn more about agriculture, and can give the diverse world of root vegetables the value they deserve. And, there's nothing like seeing the splendor of diversity when a potato field is flowering… apart from harvesting them."

Naturally, the potato pioneer has a favorite (the same as Pía's) and in a bid to blaze new trails, found an innovative use for Oxalis tuberosa – not a potato, but still a tuber. "*Oca* is so diverse and complex: you can use its flowers, stalk and leaves as well as the tuber itself. I started fermenting yellow and black *ocas* with yeasts used in winemaking to create an Andean alcohol; today, the white, rosé and red O-Tuber line of beverages, which have around 12 percent alcohol, form part of Mater Sostiene's product portfolio. Plus, I've been experimenting with orange *oca* to make a sparkling fermented drink as well as distilling it in a collaboration with Destilería Andina."

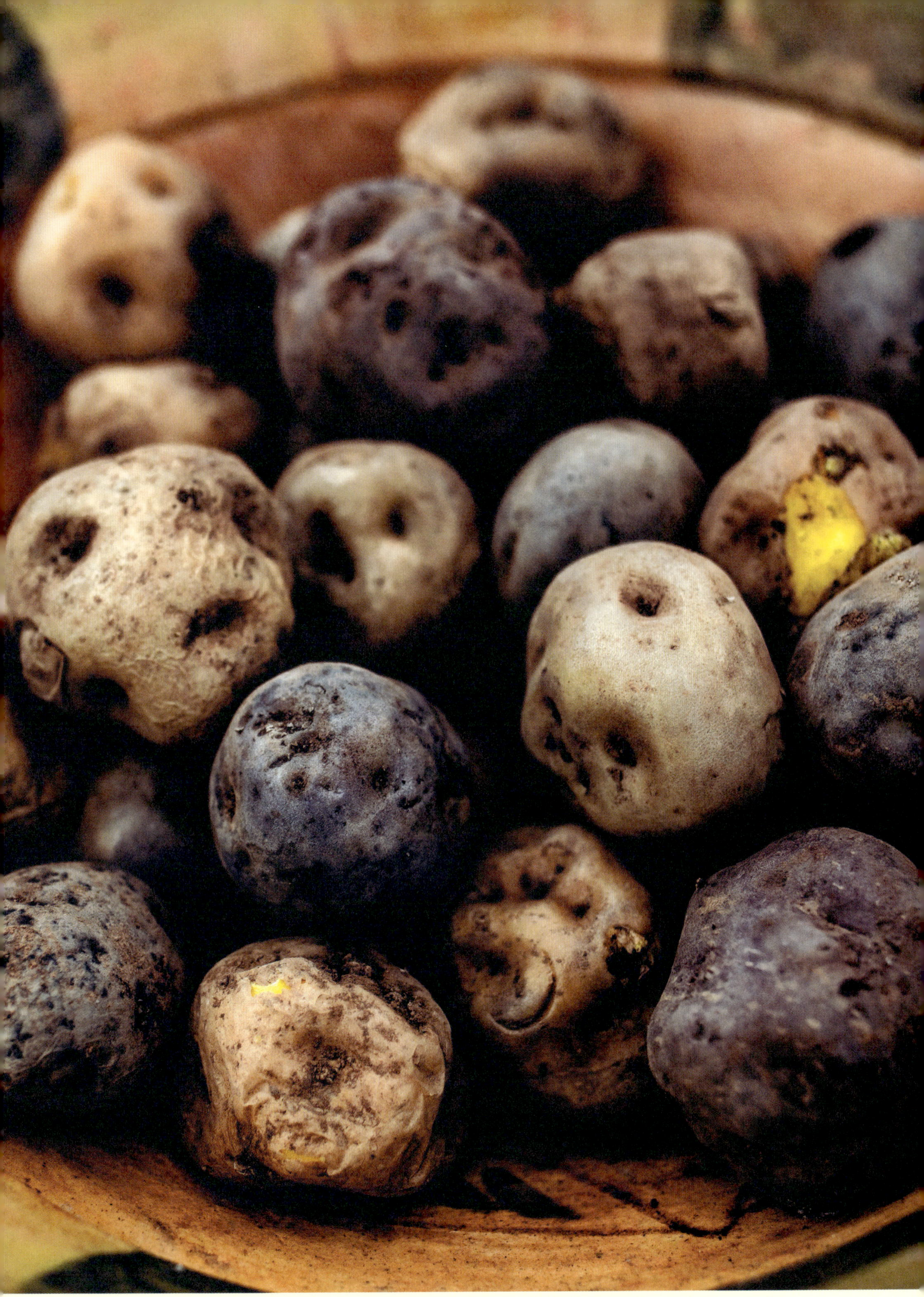

ANDEA
MINERAL WATER

The journey

It takes 2,628,000 minutes for a single drop of rain water to trickle 5,049 feet through Apu Pachatusan (in Quechua, Pachatusan means 'the one that sustains the world') in Cusco's Picol mountain range.

To say it 'trickles' over the course of 43,800 hours is an exorbitant exaggeration of speed. When rain penetrates Pachatusan's peak at 15,885 feet above sea level (asl), usually between the region's rainy season November through March, it takes the most infinitesimal of navigational approaches to drip, drip, drop its way for 1,825 days, absorbing minerals such as calcium and magnesium as it crisscrosses down through the craggy behemoth to reach an underground passage at 11,155 feet.

At the rate of one lone drip filtering through 250-million-year old Andean sandstone's sedimentary fractured rock faults for 60 months is reflective of geological time: to put it lightly, mighty laborious work.

Accustomed to making pilsner and other styles of beer, Cusco-based brewer José Casafranca was keen to bottle a mineral water with health benefits. It took him a lifetime contemplating the reason his grandfather, a *cusqueño* farmer, lived to a remarkable 107, and 13 years to find the ideal source, which takes five years to come to fruition as Agua Andea.

"My *abuelo* Camilo Bozo Bozo was lucid, healthy and never got sick: I'm convinced it was due to his daily routine. As he worked in the fields [in open-toe sandals], his feet were often cold. So, at night, Camilo would heat up water that he fetched from a mountain spring, pour it into a glass bottle and place it in bed to warm up his feet. He'd start his day the following morning drinking that same tepid water in a *mate* (infusion) with herbs. Personally, I put his fantastic health down to that spring, whose origin was the same as Tambomachay [a sacred Quechua site devoted to H_2O located around three miles from the city of Cusco]," says José, one of Agua Andea's five co-founders.

Following 13 years (or around 6,832,800 minutes) of analyzing an array of waters sourced from mountain springs around the region, José finally sampled one that met his criteria with respect to the health benefits that his grandfather enjoyed. Andea's pH of 8.2 means it has notable alkaline levels

LOCATION
Mount Picol,
San Jerónimo, Cusco

ELEVATION - ECOREGION
11,150 feet
Mountain pastures

PRODUCTION CHAIN
Andea draws the water from a 2,625-feet tunnel inside Mount Picol.
The water is purified then bottled.

SEASONALITY

PLANTING
Year round

HARVEST
Year round

CLIENTES
Restaurants
Cusco and Lima Hotels

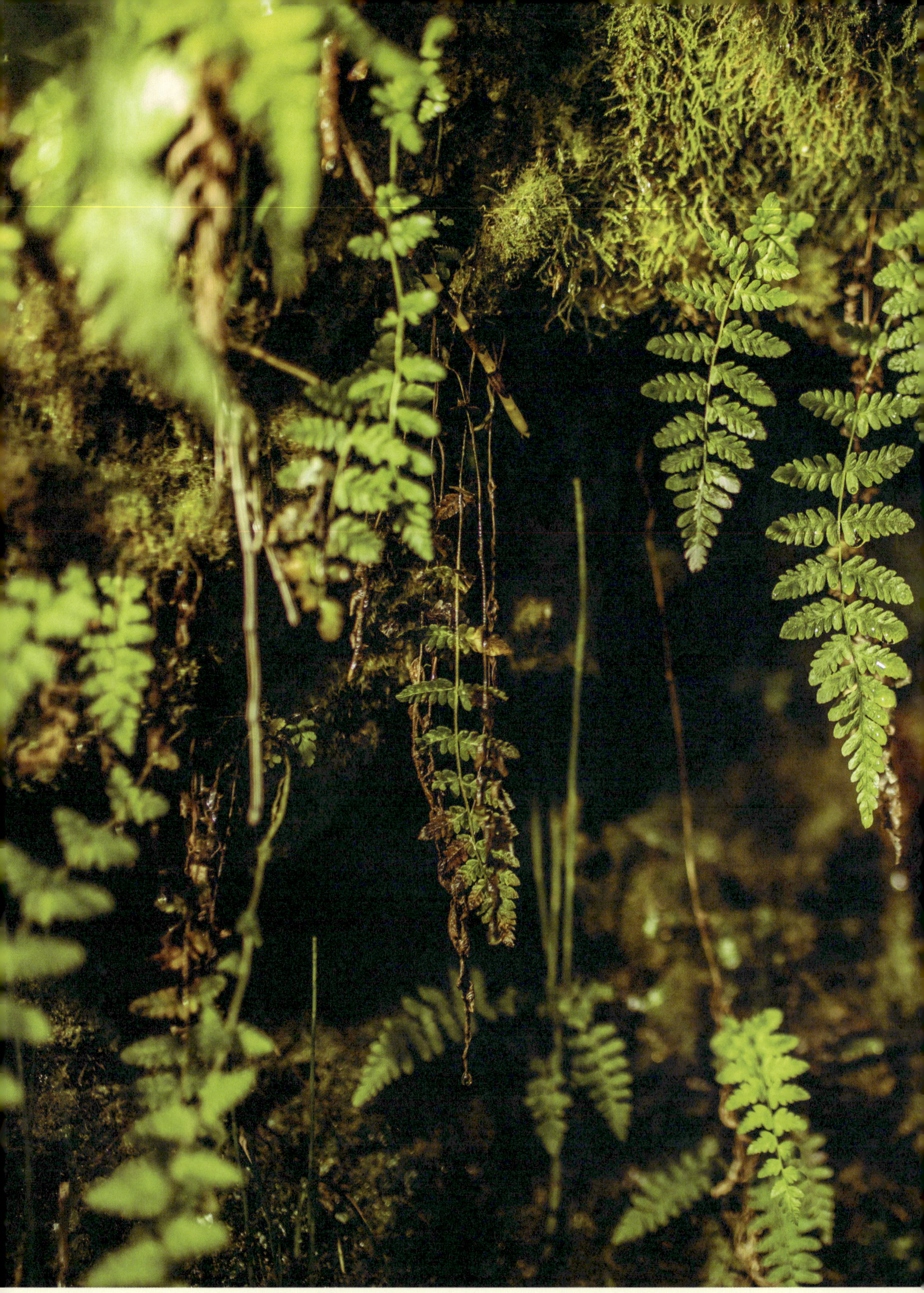

as well as bicarbonates, while it also contains trace quantities of calcium, magnesium, and potassium, minerals that proffer its drinkers benefits similar to what Camilo enjoyed.

Sustainability forms part of Andea's mission: the apothecary-style sparkling water bottles are reuseable, while product information is printed directly onto the glass. The company is also due to phase out plastic bottles over the next three years, and is working with the local municipality to plant one million new trees in the San Jerónimo district where the bottling plant is based.

79

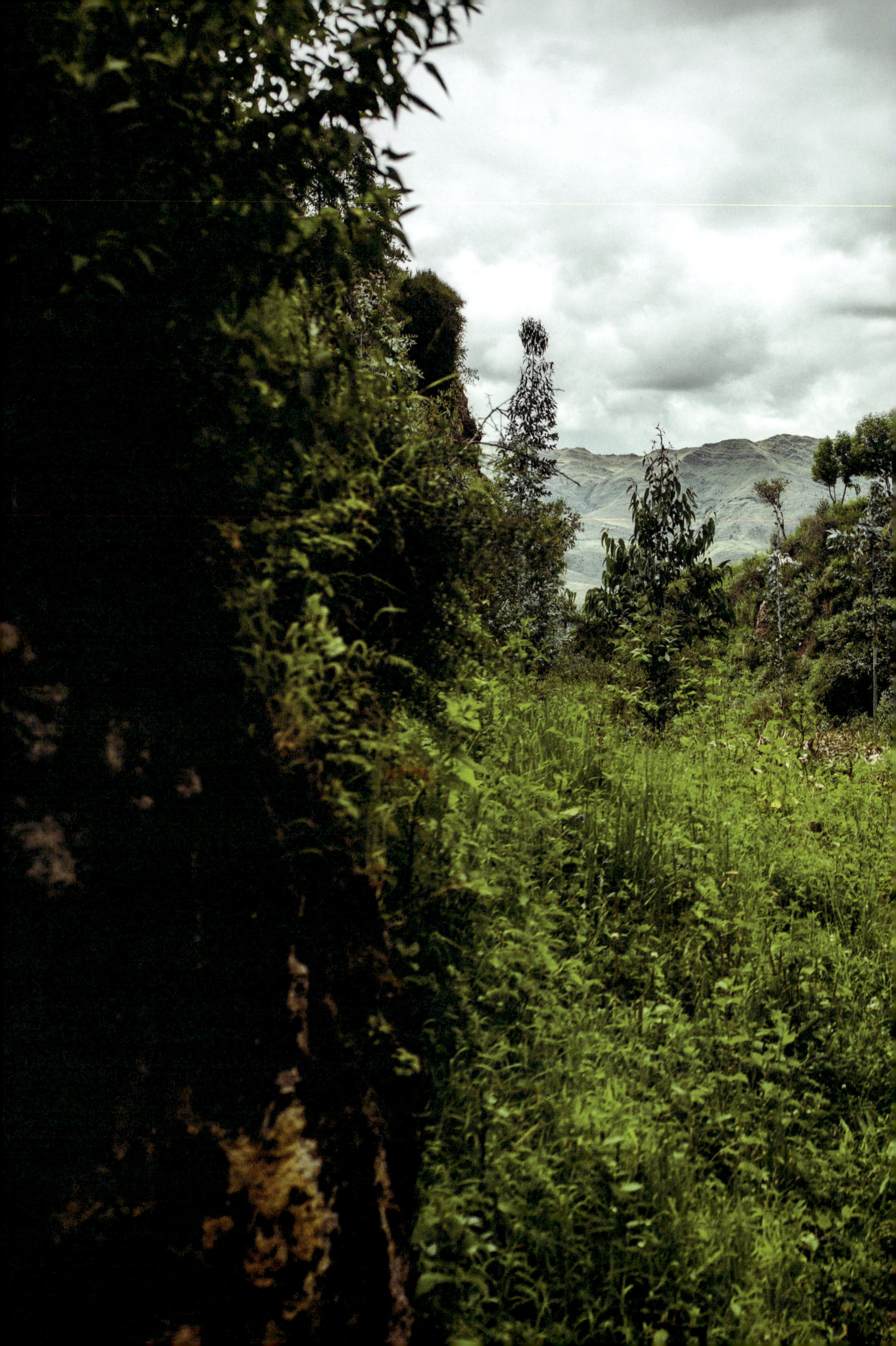

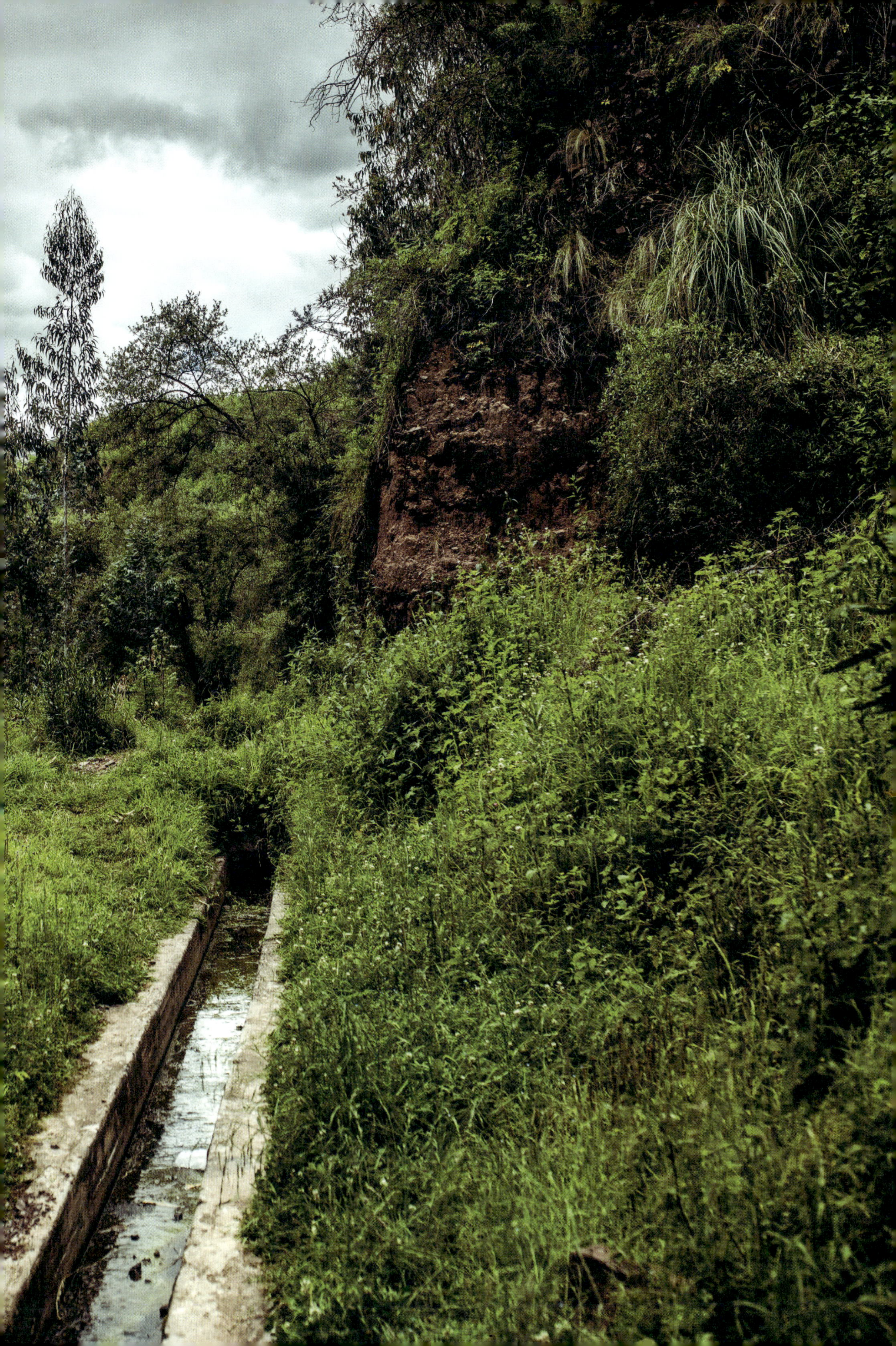

ORQUIMIEL
WOMEN'S APICULTURE ASSOCIATION

A hive of queen bees

This story of female empowerment in the subtropical Andes brings together a diverse group that was ready to beat sexist adversity. How did these women of varying ages from different communities overcome this hurdle? By replicating the daily activities of their flying wards and joining forces as beekeepers harvesting honey as the Orquimiel association.

Reaching the small community of Lucmabamba, where Orquimiel's store and plant is based, isn't straightforward. The drive from the Sacred Valley to Santa Teresa district in La Convención province takes you up and over the 14,107-feet Abra Malaga pass then down into subtropical vegetation, mango and banana trees lining the road, in a flash, a magnificent and almost surreal topographical contrast in 90 minutes. Looking at a map, those 180-degree zigzags seem unbelievable; in fact, danger threatens to spring from every rock face along the road between Ollantaytambo and Santa Teresa, with landslides, mudslides and vision-altering fog par for the course during the rainy season. From Santa Teresa, Lucmabamba is a bumpy, winding drive back up into the mountains at 7,215 feet above sea level (asl), and while distant, it's not totally remote – it's one of many small villages peppering the well-trodden Inca Trail. Coffee grower Dwight Aguilar Masías' plantation is also near, on the western side of the Río Vilcanota river.

A catastrophic landslide in 1998 prompted by El Niño, followed by inevitable subsequent flooding of lands around that part of the tributary, devastated Santa Teresa; a disaster that had a knock-on effect on the surrounding communities. Much of the town was buried under mud and boulders, including the bridge connecting it to Abra Malaga and the Sacred Valley, cutting off Santa Teresa and its even more rural neighbors from the world. The area's recovery became a high priority for non-profits such as CarePeru, which eventually provided a small group of potential beekeepers with the necessary tools to found Orquimiel in 2010.

While 30-year-old Laura Góngora Ccohua is the association's current president, her 53-year-old aunt René Mora Roque was one of the founding members; both moved to the community to get married. Housewife René worked breeding guinea

LOCATION
Lucmabamba,
La Convención, Cusco

ELEVATION - ECOREGION
6,550 feet
High jungle forest;
cloud forest

CADENA DE PRODUCCIÓN

Orquimiel uses smoke to keep bees away when approaching the hives and harvesting the honey. The honey is collected from all the hives during the same time, distinguishing between the two production elevations, and jarred. They have also developed honey infused with medicinal roots and honey with kunuca, an aromatic herb. Both types of honeys are sold.

SEASONALITY

SIEMBRA
Year round

HARVEST
First: May-June
Second: September

Organic agriculture (methods):
Honey extraction from hives, no additives.

CLIENTS
Local market
Fairs
Travelers, tourists, thanks to its location on the Machu Picchu trail

This project is supported by CarePeru and Senasa.

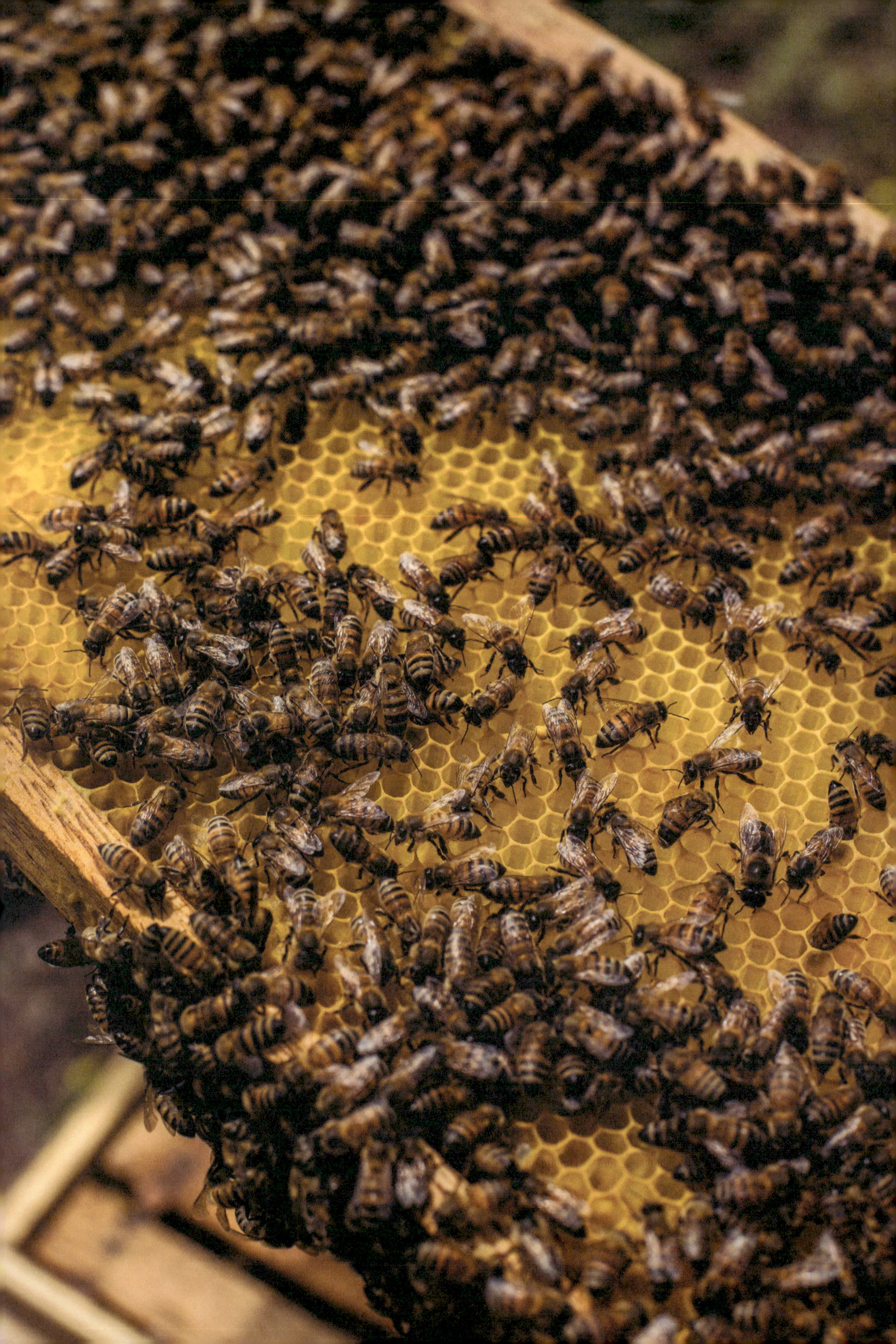

pig and cultivating coffee and Hass avocado on the family farm, but she never earned a wage until she started caring for bee colonies at the age of 42; her husband's chauvinistic attitude didn't allow it.

"I hardly used to earn anything because my husband would give me money to run our home. Now that I harvest and process honey, I earn at least as much as him and, thanks to our pots, not only has that machismo attitude subsided but the way we live, what we eat, our health and even the clothes we wear have changed for the better," she says.

René seized the opportunity to train in apiculture and, in order to set up an association, encouraged her female friends, family and neighbors to join so as to reach the required 15-member minimum – and Orquimiel dawned.

Every year, 25 enthusiastic beekeepers aged between 24 and 75, from five communities, harvest around 18,500 lbs of raw golden liquid from hives housed in peaceful elevated meadows, processing two pure honeys as well as spin-offs such as *hidromiel* (mead), coca leaf-infused honey and *polimiel*, which is mixed with pollen. Together, the Orquimiel ladies bottle this antioxidant-rich extract at a small plant under the same roof as the wood-and-stone roadside store they built, also collectively, which buzzes to life during the biannual extraction periods.

The 325 hives are tucked away from the relatively humming lane that runs through Lucmabamba, in meadows abundant in vegetation such as the white and violet orchids after which the association is named. Honey's aroma, color and taste depends on the type of flora bees patronize, for example, passionfruit, wild pacay, corn and mountain aniseed grow within a two-mile radius of those hives at 8,530 feet asl and their honey is light and bright in color. However, the flowers on citrus trees such as lime and grapefruit, along with coffee blossom and the same wild pacay that grow 1,970 feet further down the mountain define a darker, more intense end product.

Orquimiel's two pure honeys are visibly distinct and taste different precisely because of the floral influences of their respective elevations. Besides sampling them at the association's store, visitors can also try them at René's petite tasting room in a wooden cabin beside her home; Mater Sostiene sells both as *Miel de Altura* (Altitude Honey).

Besides economically empowering these 25 worker bees (all female, just like nature), working in apiculture has also boosted self-esteem, according to mother-of-two Laura. "I used to be shy and quiet, but the beekeeping training I've received has helped me to express myself better. I've learned how to sell our honey – and I'm no longer timid."

Collaborating with bees to make honey isn't without its challenges. Orquimiel started out harvesting three times a year but climate change in the form of prolonged weather systems has reduced it to two over the past decade. And, while the apiculturists take extreme care to keep their fields free from contamination, the reality is that acquiring organic certification is beyond the association's means for the time being. But, with their ever-growing strength as individuals and ability to stick together as a collective, no hurdle seems insurmountable – with the bees flying by their side.

"We've learned to be a team," says Laura, "not just uniting to physically work together as an association but also supporting each other on a personal level. We don't have healthcare plans, so if one of us gets sick, we organize fundraisers to help pay for medication."

René adds: "Honey has changed my life as it supports me in many ways. We need to encourage other women to stand up for themselves and earn their own income. There's no reason why we should watch men earn all the money."

86

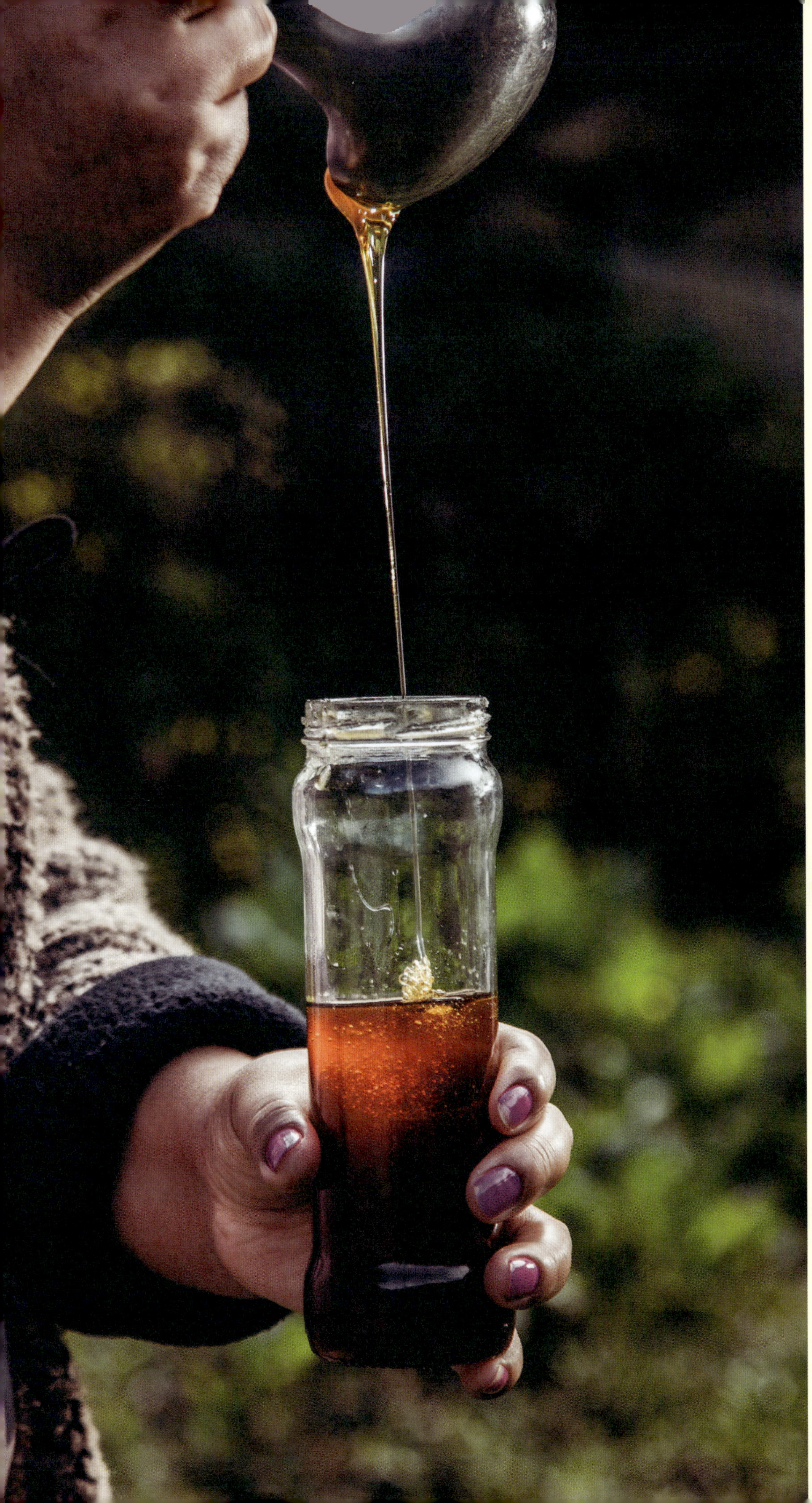

TRACING ORIGINS

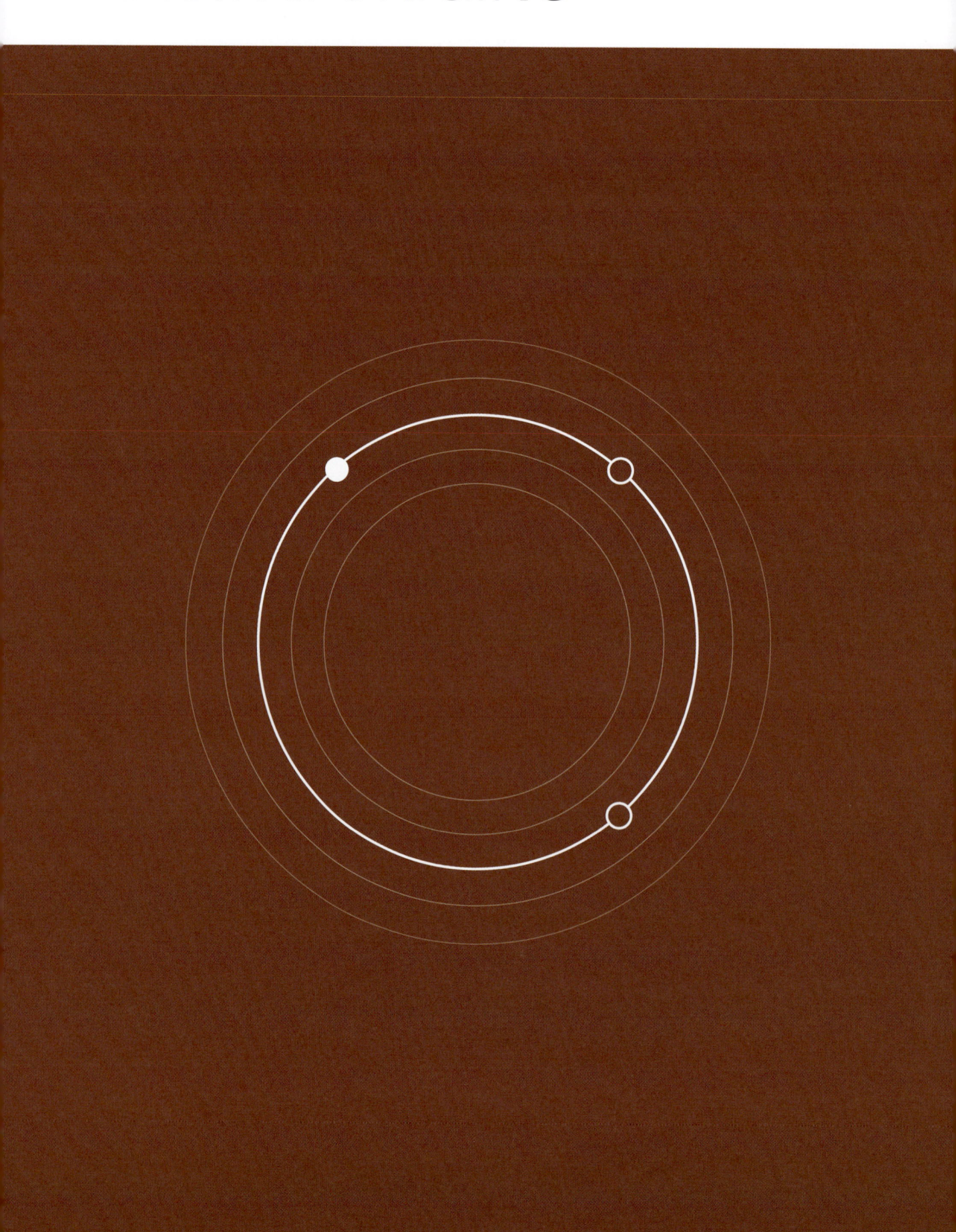

A seed floats on air currents until it falls serendipitously to the ground and germinates, its stalk firming up into a trunk, before blooming and yielding fruit. That's how Mater has grown since its rather spontaneous propagation in 2013, when my sister Malena started out cataloguing the botany of Peruvian products and I prepared dishes with *cushuro* Andean algae (Nostoc sphaericum), *kiwicha* (Amaranthus caudatus) and *chaco* edible clay. Together, we nourished the restaurant's philosophy while reviving the value and identity of these little-known products and mapping their traceability, methodically meeting farmers, producers and gatherers – sharing their narratives at Central.

From a simple notion eight years ago, we cultivated that unknown seed into our interdisciplinary research organization, and while it is so much further advanced than what we envisaged then, Mater is an organic work in progress that has an effortless ability to blur lines and seamlessly blend ideas together, and bring these thoughts into being.

In a nutshell, Mater interprets Peru's cultural and biodiversity in our gastronomic concepts while supporting producers, their products and processes.

A non-profit, today Mater is the backbone to all our projects, a deep-rooted tree with a sturdy core that has grown interdisciplinary branches that go beyond food, because creativity goes beyond devising recipes or displaying exceptional culinary techniques; sharing the context and tradition of every component that goes into each dish is as significant as the dish itself.

Including archeologists, bartenders, biologists, anthropologists, agronomists, designers, chefs, sommeliers, artists and students of various disciplines among its numbers – both transitory and long-term – the people who drive Mater forward with their artistic, scientific, academic and cultural ideas and collaborations ensure that gastronomic trunk has branched into many divergent yet linked disciplines to start telling new stories.

Think of Mater as a singular tree, but one that produces multiple fruits, vegetables, botanicals and grains from an array of ecosystems. Each branch yields a different crop – *tumbo* (Passiflora tripartita) on one, cacao (Theobroma cacao) on another, and *mashwa* (Tropaeolum tuberosum) on yet another – and each of their fruits ripen, falling to the ground, dispersing seeds that germinate to spawn a new sapling that will bear as-yet-unknown fruits, populating a garden of diverse Mater projects that take shape as academic papers, dishs, beverages, handcrafted textiles or artwork.

After living and working outside of Peru for a decade, I opened Central with the aim of devising a new narrative about what was happening in Peru, about gastronomical diversity and riches, and its potential. The turning point came when I decided my kitchen needed to prioritize Peruvian ingredients – thanks to its rich and varied geography, Peru possesses 84 of the world's 117 life zones [IUCN for UNESCO, prepared by Miklos D.F. Udvardy, 1975], and 28 of its 32 identified climates – but it wasn't until I started consulting for a restaurant in Cusco in 2013 that I realized it was, in fact, easy to access the origin of some truly incredible ingredients. One day I said to Malena, 'let's explore Peru'. There wasn't a budget or corporate office that could send us somewhere, simply my intuition sensing the need to nourish Central by gleaning greater knowledge of Peru's products and producers and for Central to develop its own language in order to share our culture. Male was just as curious as I was, and so with Pía, Mater's culinary director, the three of us took off on our first expedition to the Andes.

"Looking back, it seems crazy that we simply left for Cusco," says Malena. "After qualifying as a doctor, then living in the US and working in a medical laboratory, I'd returned to Peru around the same time as Virgilio and changed my professional direction to work in nutrition. When he suggested this trip, I was happy to leave my comfort zone to travel and meet producers. Equipped with notebooks and cameras, we went off in search of unique places, ready to listen to fantastic stories and learn about the history and contexts about the food chain that Virgilio would later share on Central's first *Mater Elevations* menu."

The fact that our professional paths had themselves been divergent – doctor and cook – has only ever complemented Mater. Fortuitously, our two worlds collided then merged – analytical and ordered versus creativity and boundary pushing, yet both efficient and meticulous – on that initial adventure.

Malena says: "Visiting producers around the Cusco region proved to be easier than we'd imagined. One of our first contacts was Sierra Productiva, a non-profit that works with tiny smallholders; they introduced us to Francisco Quico Mamani and Trinidad Mamani Cascamayta, a charming couple who grows organic herbs and vegetables and raises *cuy* (guinea pig). The Andean world proved to be so diverse – even within the same communities – a spectrum of undervalued ecosystems, and we quickly realized we could make diverse disciplines visible by bringing together nature, cultures, the environment and gastronomy."

The Andean landscapes started to make sense, both culturally and gastronomically, and we saw we could become a source of information with regards to food, education, raising awareness and sharing knowledge, designing culinary experiences instilled with values such as connectivity between nature and humans, cultural identity and respect for the environment.

We started recording our visits to this mega, borderless diversity, blogging what we learnt about, say, *tarwi* (Lupinus mutabilis) or *cabuya* (Agave sisalana), noting botanical information then experimenting with this bean or cactus in the kitchen until it was ready for its story to unfold on the plate. And together, we realized that the same object – an herb, a tree, a fruit – can be read in many ways. Mater had taken root.

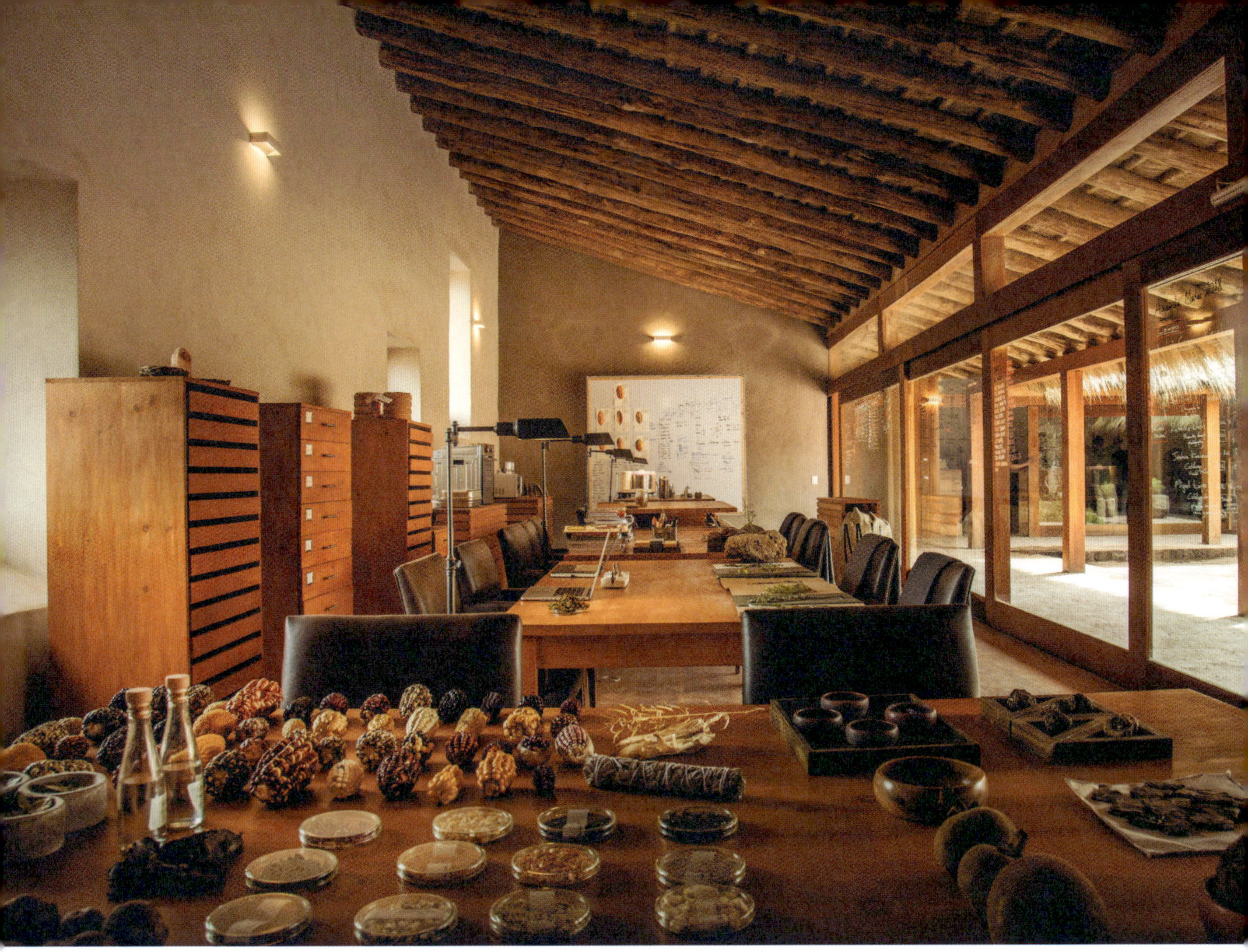

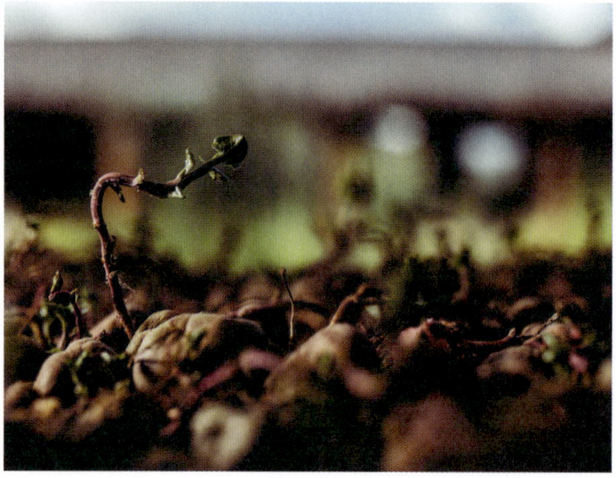

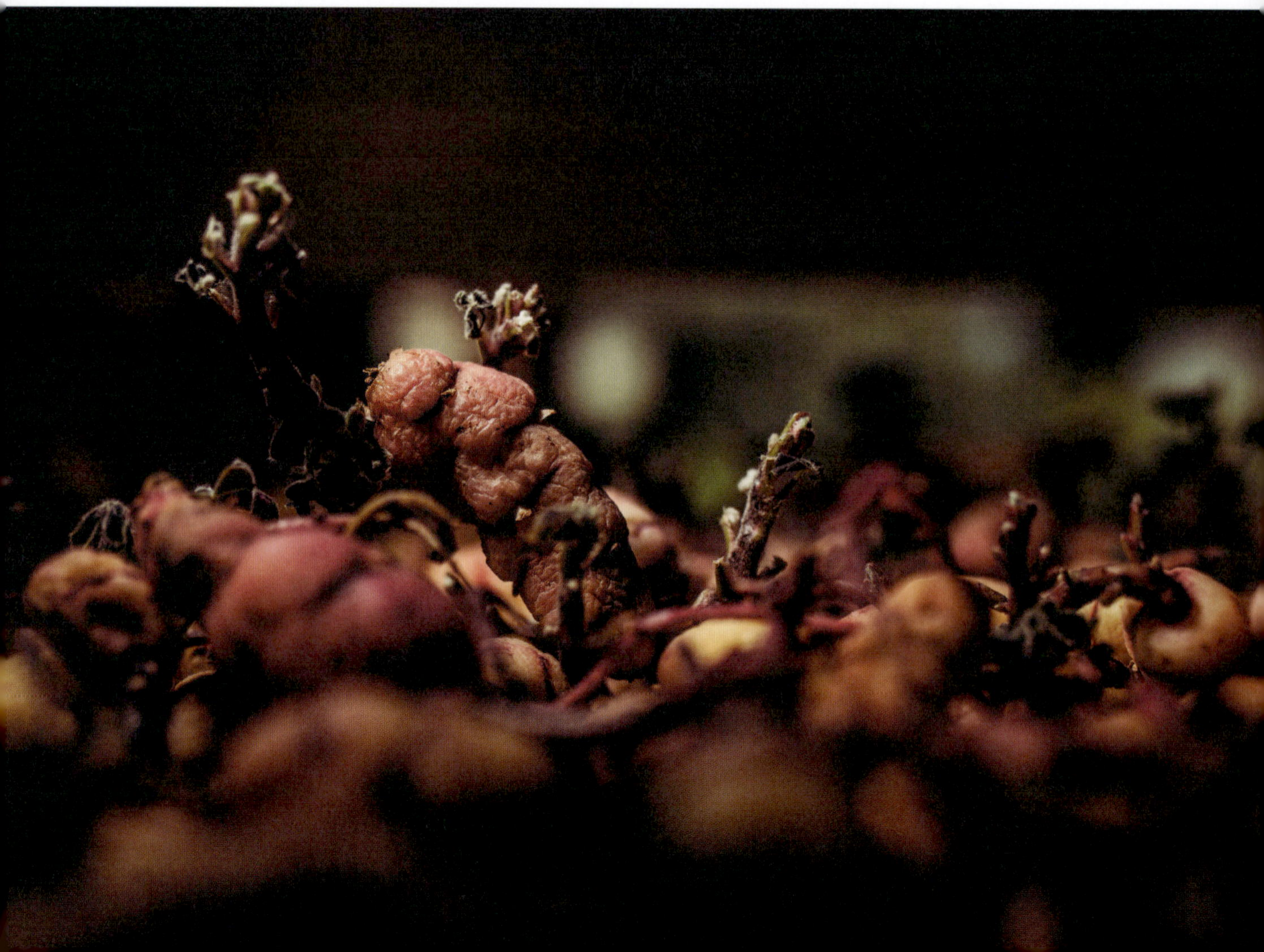

93

94

An interdisciplinary research organization that is the backbone to all our restaurants and projects, Mater interprets Peru's cultural diversity and biodiversity in our gastronomic concepts while supporting producers, their products and processes. Think of Mater as a tree that yields citrus, berries, tubers, herbs and corn from an array of Andean ecosystems, whose fruits then seed and grow into as-yet-unknown saplings. Those tiny trees are our diverse projects that will soon take shape as academic papers, dishes, beverages, handcrafted textiles or artwork.

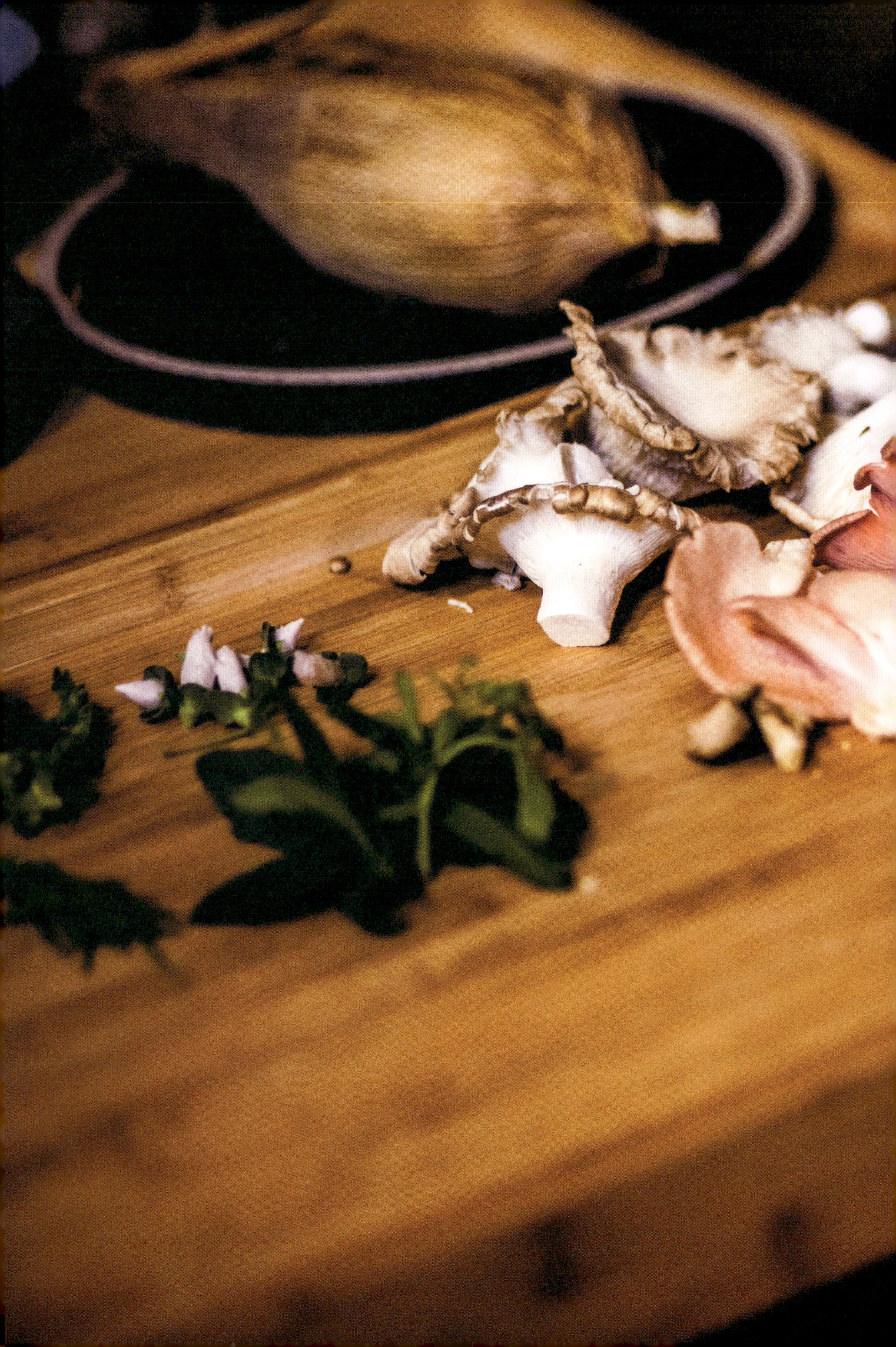

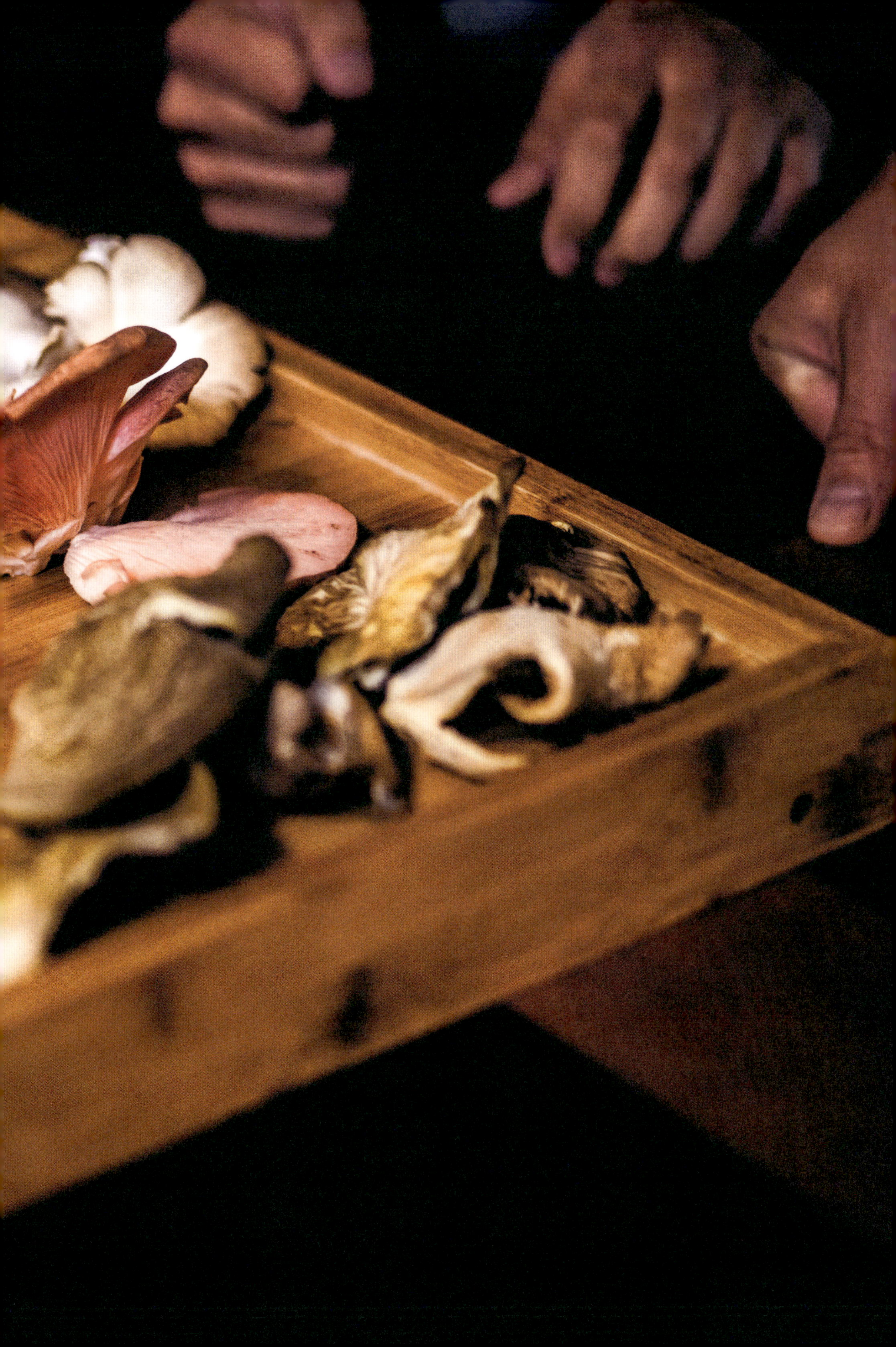

• HEART AND SOUL

Seven years on, Mater is our essence, our heart and soul. Extending far beyond the biological research arm we conceived of cataloguing botanical species sourced from Peru's life zones – and it continues to do so, for example, we published the first edition of *Catálogo Mater – 30 especies para Central* (*Mater Catalogue – 30 Species for Central*) book in 2019 – Mater is a synonym of our philosophy.

While Mater emerged from Central's needs, today the interdisciplinary research organization is the nucleus, the parent nerve center. The beating heart behind everything we do, Mater doesn't just pump culinary and cultural blood into Mil, Kjolle, Mayo and Central, but wherever we go, sowing the seeds in the Andes, the high jungle and the Amazon, from the northern mangroves to the southern coasts. Mater has transcended our restaurants, acquiring tools to connect people, connecting us with our different cultures, motivating us to continue learning. Mater encourages us to ask questions – and seek answers.

While *Central* the book (2016) was our first foray outside of a restaurant context that discussed cooking with Peru's ecosystems, opening Mil in 2018 marked the start of Mater's decentralization. Mil became our first regional headquarters, fortuitously in the area where we dreamt up Mater.

And where Central and Kjolle have transcended the philosophy of a local, Peruvian focus with regard to ingredient origin and traceability, Mil takes that concept a step further – it is ultra local, strictly drawing from an Andean snapshot that focuses on the Cusco region and the Sacred Valley.

Today, Mater has centers in Moray near Cusco and at Casa Tupac in Lima, home to Kjolle, Central and Mayo bar following a 2017 move from Miraflores to Barranco (the days of Malena hot-desking in any available corner of the restaurant are now a distant memory) and while there are budgets, Mater remains a non-profit. With Malena as co-director, Pía as culinary director and myself as director, the team has grown exponentially to include 22 members – and it continues evolving.

From time to time, Mater brings together groups from professional fields so diverse, it seems impossible that there could be any kind of cohesion of thoughts on a subject. But Momento, Mater's sporadic inter-disciplinary gatherings, has connected scientists and artists, such as North American neurosurgeon Atom Sarkar with Argentine chef Narda Lepes, Peruvian linguist Roberto Zariquiey, Indian biologist Varun Swamy and Gael Almeida, the Mexican senior director for Latin America at the National Geographic Society, among others, to share ideas, cultural knowledge and gastronomy, a blurring of lines that invites us all to take stock and revisit our surroundings.

Constructing bridges between the worlds of art and Mil has really taken shape since 2018, given that Mater's art and cultural projects director Verónica Tabja weaves social, sustainable, gastronomical and environmental elements into each new artistic project, always preserving traditional techniques and practices while interpreting biodiversity from a creative perspective.

99

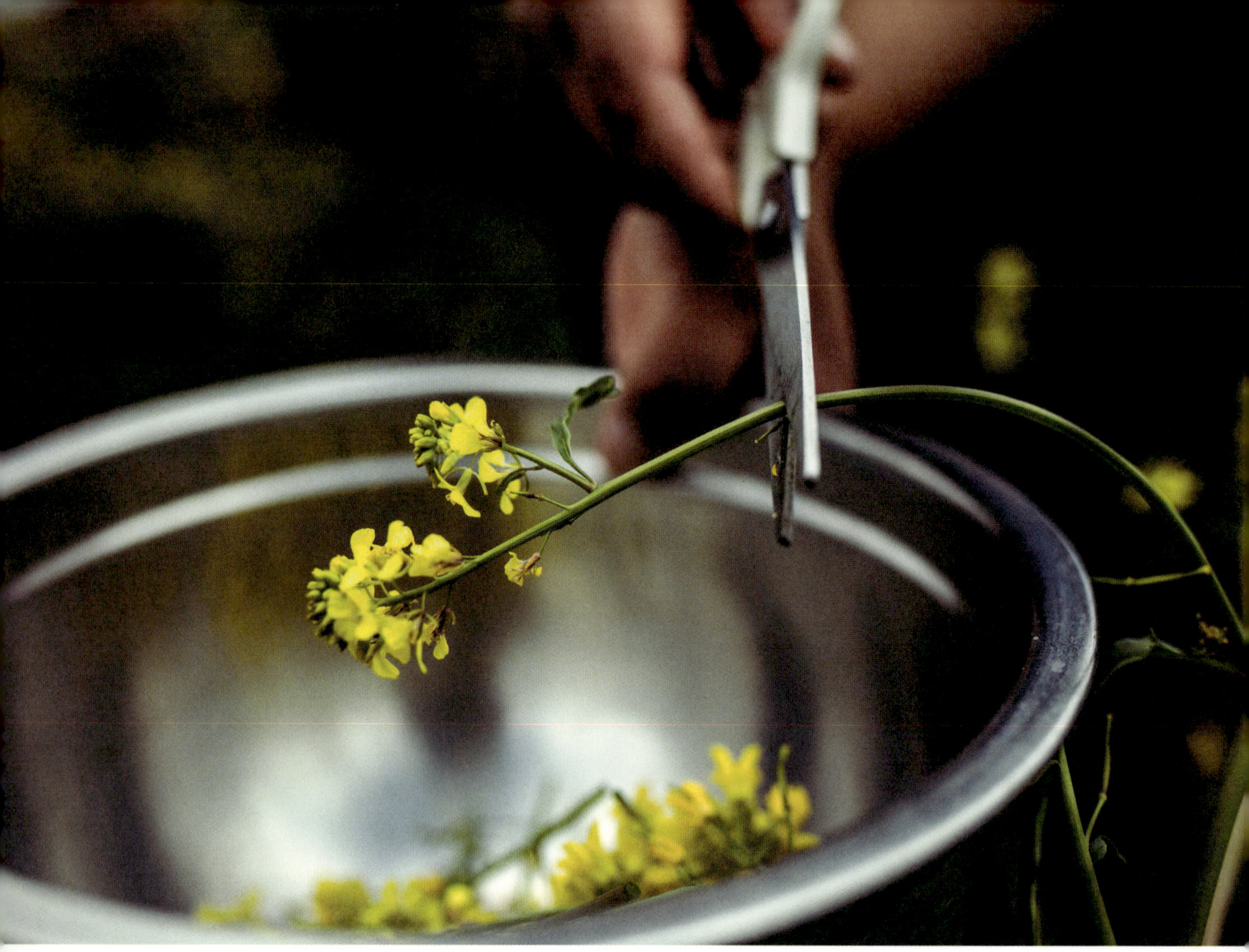

Wildflowers, roots, seeds, and leaves that heal, refresh, soothe, perfume, tint, an Andean apothecary that's integral in shaping and feeding its habitat. A kaleidoscope of petals bloom while roots are quenched during the rainy season's downpours. With every sunbeam, fronds gain energy and strength. Aromatic, bitter, fresh or simply tasting of the very earth it is plucked from, plant life is integral to the Andes and its communities.

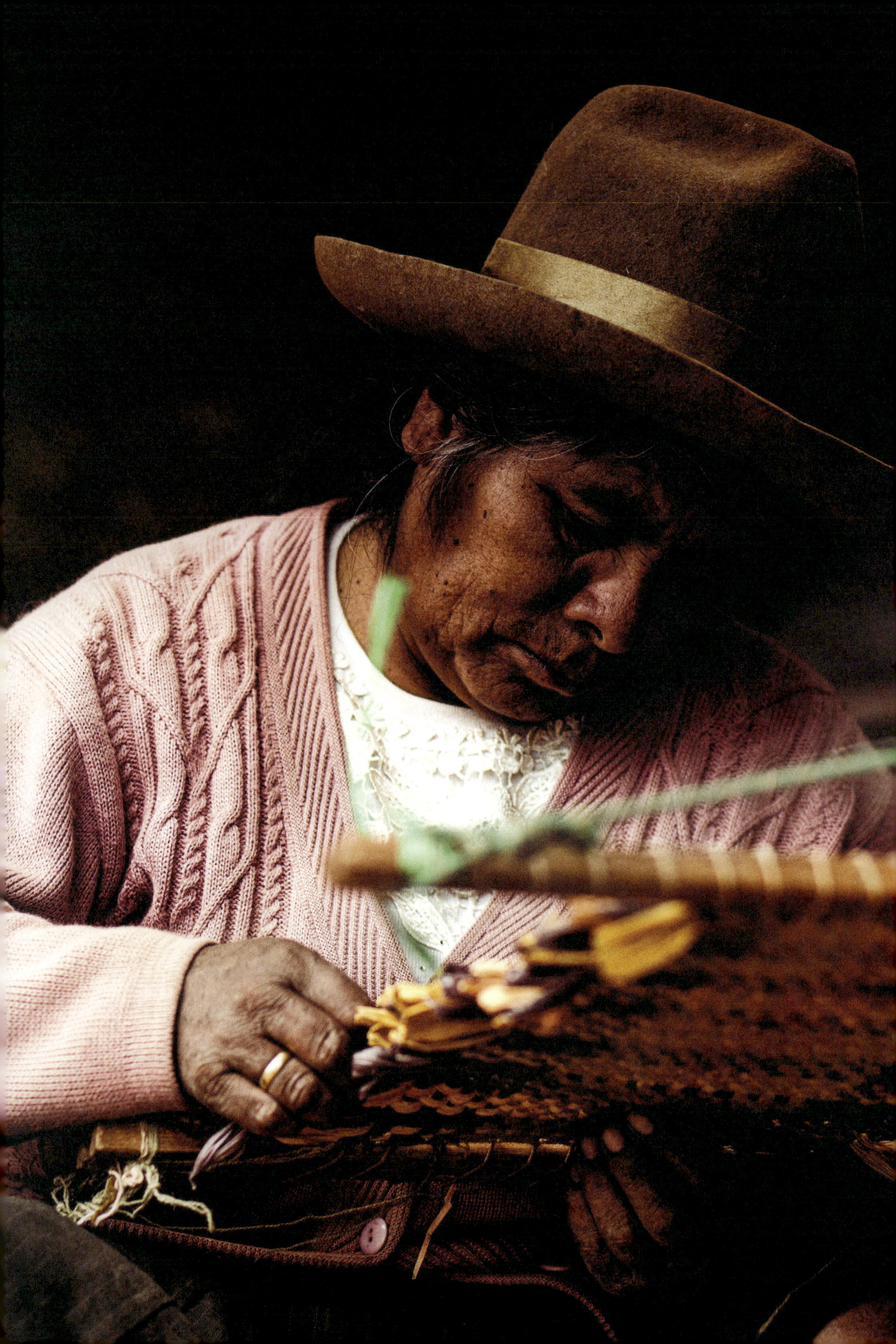

Take Warmi, a women-only collective based in CC Kacllaraccay. That project came to fruition when Italian textile designer Giulia Pompilij took up an artist-in-residence posting at Mil and met Ceferina Pillco Gutiérrez. This intercultural meeting of minds led them to share their respective academic and ancestral perspectives on dyeing techniques and together they began revealing the plant life ecosystem that surrounds Mil. Besides empowering 20 women from CC Kacllaraccay, today Warmi lends renewed value to traditional artforms, encouraging its members to interpret everyday objects through fresh eyes to create sustainable products, such as hand-dyed alpaca yarns.

To ensure continuity across this and other ventures, we set up Mater Sostiene, a platform that displays the results of projects developed between the communities, visiting artists and local artisans: Warmi's wools; the Sacha collective's table runners woven with corn husks and hand-dyed yarns; honey harvested from different elevations by the Orquimiel women's association; chocolate handcrafted with *cacao chuncho* sourced from the APA Vallecito association by Mil's in-house chocolatier Nilver Melgarejo; the O-Tuber alcoholic beverage made from oca (Oxalis tuberosa) fermented by agronomist and potato farmer Manuel Choqque Bravo; Q'aqe, a bitter distilled from 28 Andean roots, herbs, seeds and wildflowers by bartender Manuel Conteras; Espíritu Mil, a spirited collaboration with Destilería Andina; or Dwight Aguilar Masías' Red Bourbon beans roasted by Three Monkeys Coffee Company.

Through Mater Sostiene we can share our Andean landscape that has been replicated, gathered, fermented, bottled, roasted, woven or shaped, and sales finance Mater's activities so these vital projects continue flourishing. These products are also researched further and supported by Mater I-A, which brings ideas and applications to life by developing then communicating these new concepts.

But perhaps one of Mater's most meaningful functions at Mil has been connecting us with our neighbors at CC Kacllaraccay and CC Mullak'as-Misminay, because whatever Mil does, it must be mutually beneficial – and it has to create a legacy.

This is how Mater metaphorically and literally sows seeds. Concepts take root, connecting ingredients, ecosystems and people, cultivating innovation, research and knowledge to reach new levels, always a work in progress, forever widening the circle, always with an interdisciplinary philosophy.

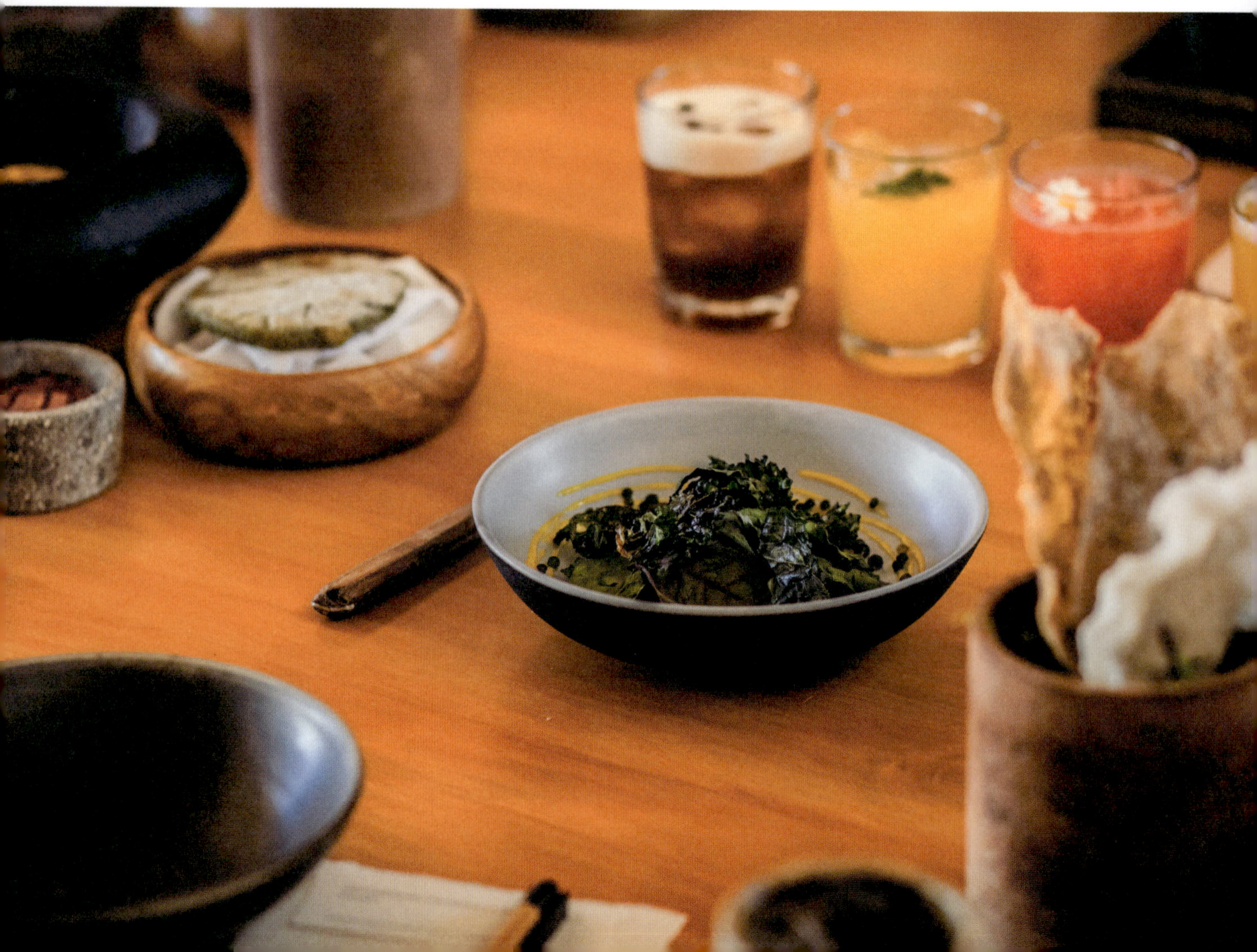

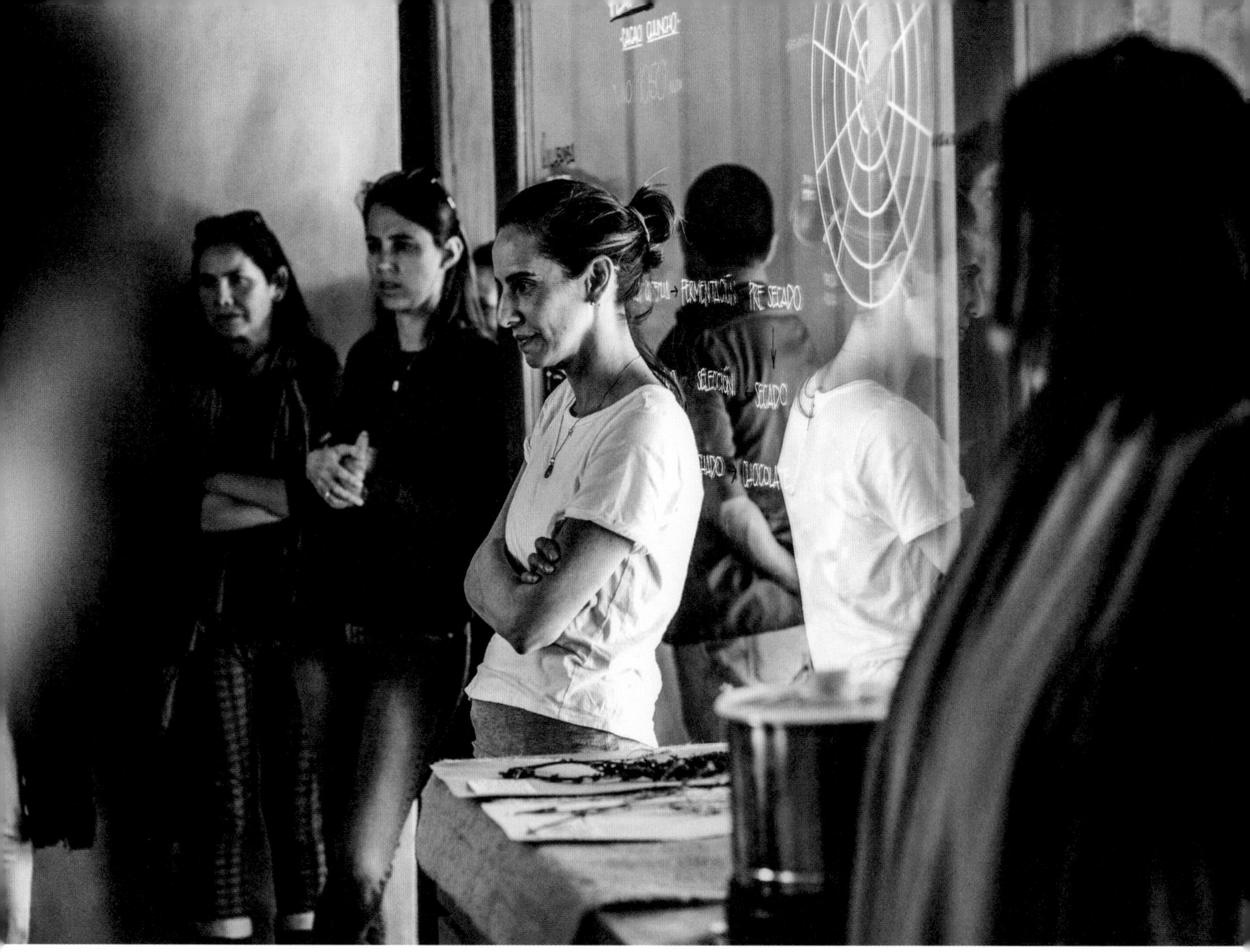
PRE SECADO
SECADO

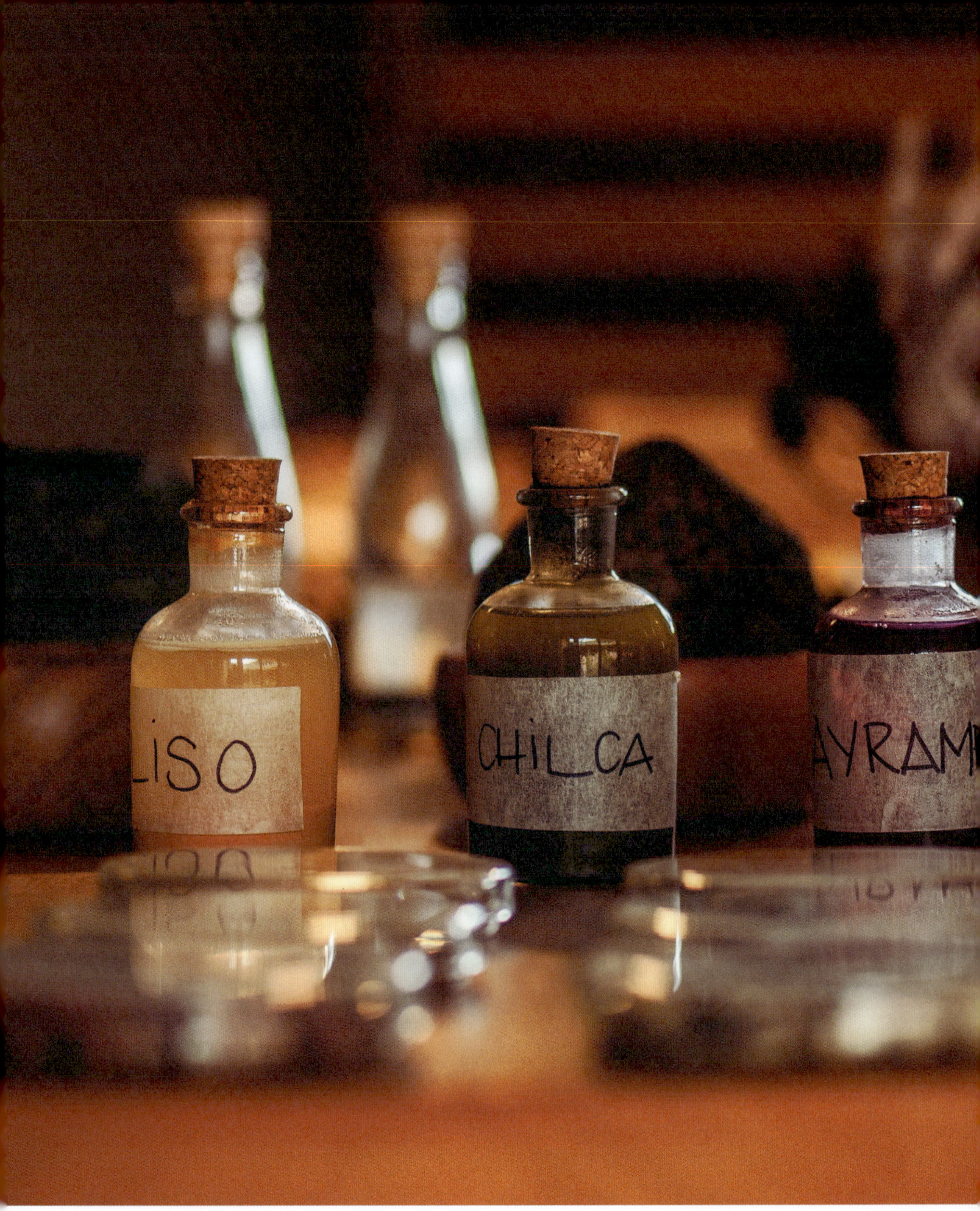
LISO
CHILCA
AYRAM

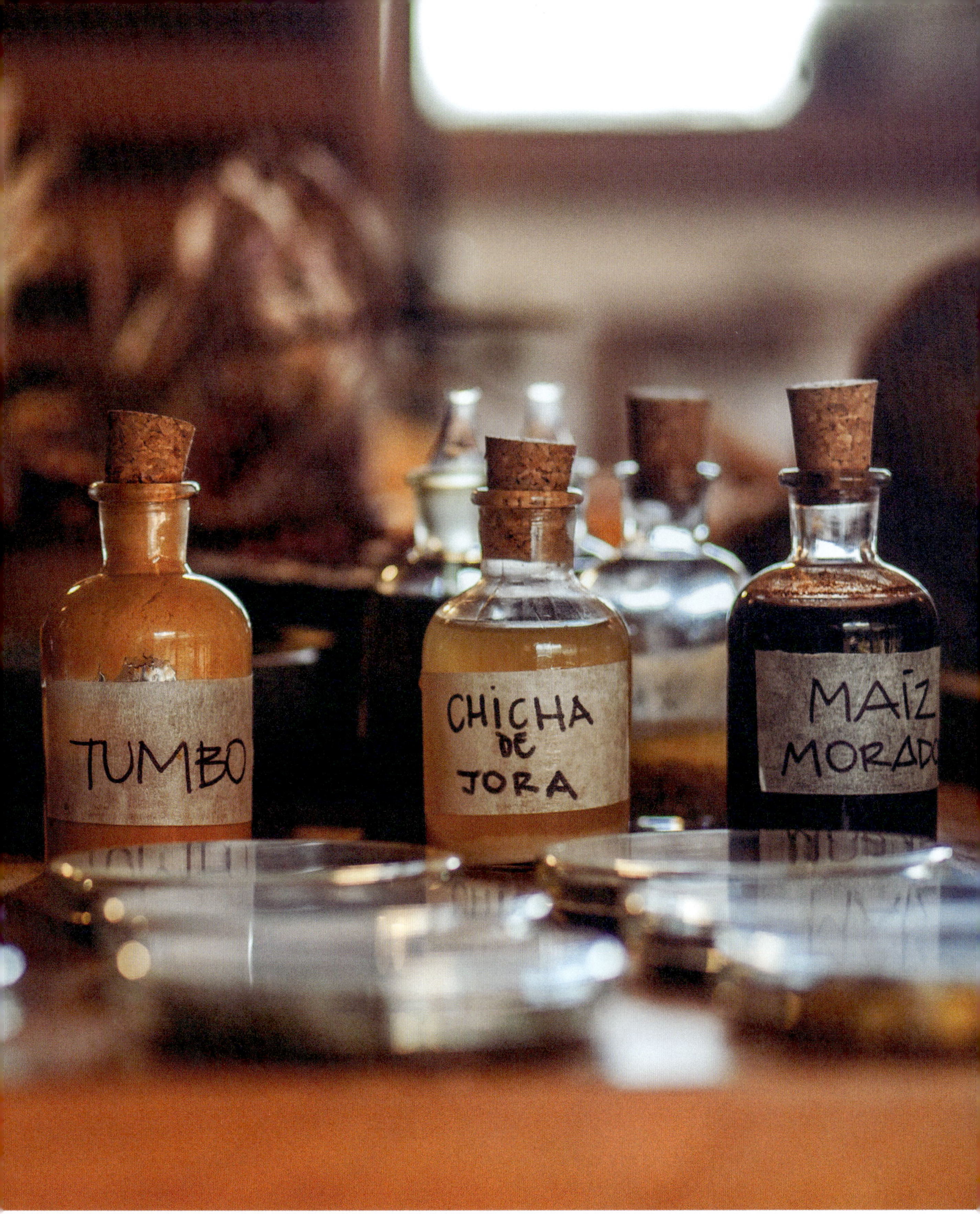
TUMBO
CHICHA
DE
JORA
MAÏZ
MORADO

To Be Funded
Rebecca Wolf
SALA MIL
M2 Marco
M3 Juan Diego / Willy
M5 Marco
M6 Marco / Willy
M7 Sharon
M8 Sharon

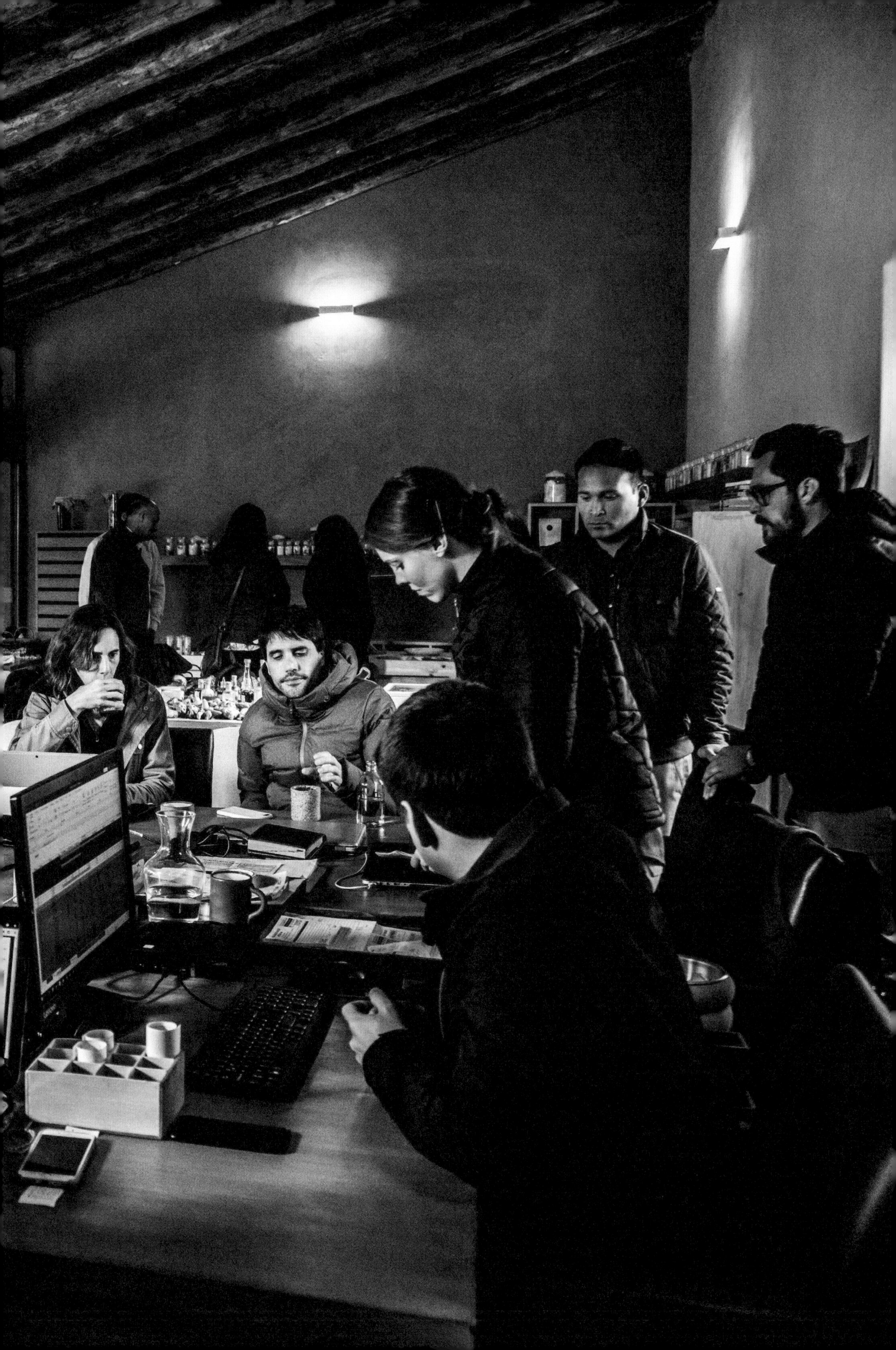

Interpreting the past today, with future vision

VIRGILIO MARTÍNEZ
Chef at Mil, director of Mater

> "Loving food doesn't just mean eating great meals. Respecting ingredients is as important as enjoying them, and every moment we prepare at Mil has to open a portal, tell a story…"

The 11,706-feet elevation is hard at Mil. It hits you as soon as you arrive. Located next to Moray in the high-altitude *puna* plateau, the weather can be blazing hot during the day and extremely raw at night. This is difficult and inhospitable territory. I'm acclimated but making decisions such as devising the menu or sowing seeds on our experimental farm, and not having enough oxygen to thread together thoughts, can prove challenging.

It's a long way, literally and figuratively, from the days when I aspired, first, to become a pro skateboarder, then buckled down to study law in Lima. The former was going pretty well until a few accidents put an end to that career, and as far as law, the truth is, I never felt comfortable in or enjoyed academia; I was more inspired by sporting, physical and artistic disciplines.

My mom is an architect and artist. She sculpts, paints and makes ceramics, and became an interior designer later in life. Her side of the family is bohemian in nature, which is the path I was eventually drawn to. Feeling constrained by Lima, and after dropping out of law school, I thought cooking would open up the possibility to travel and that I'd easily find work around the world.

It wasn't until I stood inside a professional kitchen that I experienced both excitement and fear in this physical and artisanal work, work that I enjoyed. Whether it was handling a knife or cleaning vegetables, I liked working with my hands and interacting with a team. I never imagined just how much. The very first time I stepped inside the kitchen of an haute-cuisine restaurant, I knew that was where I wanted to be, in a place where food had a profound sense of purpose.

- ADDING TO PERU'S NARRATIVE

I was looking to add to the narrative about Peru when I opened Central. I wanted to focus on diversity, the country's potential and nature as well as cultural aspects, building upon Gastón Acurio's inclusive culinary movement that had already begun to communicate the greatness of our territory, the breadth of our products and celebrate the value of traditional cooking techniques. Sharing the context and tradition of every component that goes into each dish therefore became as significant as the dish itself to me.

Through Mater, our biological and cultural research center, I began exploring my country, which possesses 84 of the world's 117 life zones. I met farmers and producers, hearing the stories behind their ingredients (at times new to me), investigating then recording a plant's botany, experimenting in my test kitchen until I was ready to unfold a story on the plate. With my sister Malena and head chef Pía, my future wife, the three of us visited Piura in the north, Madre de Dios in the Amazon, Arequipa in the south and Cusco in the Andes, learning the importance of *chicha de jora* corn beer for Andean communities, what breeders fed *cuy* (guinea pig), wondering why vegetables such as beet – historically cultivated in low-lying lands – were planted at elevation, why certain clay was edible… Together, we realized that a single species – a grain, an herb, a tree, a root or a fruit – can be meaningfully read in many ways.

- RECIPROCAL RELATIONSHIPS

Gastronomy doesn't just revolve around Lima. We started decentralizing because everything that happens in Central happens across Peru first. It's important to have an eye in other places, a responsible eye, and a connection with the people so we can sow together, harvest together, work together and have a cordial and mutually beneficial relationship.

When the opportunity arose to open a restaurant in the Andes, I immediately saw *mil* (a thousand) reasons to grasp it: the unique location – a few feet away from Moray, the 15th-century Quechua-built agricultural research center enshrouded in science, technology and history – getting to know and work alongside members of the indigenous rural communities (CC) that neighbor these remarkable concentric formations, and the singular chance to exclusively cook with products sourced from one single region. Through our efforts in Moray, CC Kacllaraccay, CC Mullak'as-Misminay and the Sacred Valley, a series of interdisciplinary projects from textile weaving to scholarly archeological research has since unfolded… and continues to do so because, for us, cooking is merely one of many points of contact where everything here comes together, adjusting, harmonizing and evolving.

Mil interprets the past in the present, and each interpretation has an ephemeral nature. But it's also a vision of the future, always considering its possible effects on the communities. That's why we took a respectful approach to forging relationships with members of CC Kacllaraccay and CC Mullak'as-Misminay (because we are the outsiders), first understanding their needs before inviting them to work alongside us on our experimental farm, sharing each other's agricultural knowledge, reintroducing diversity in the form of native Andean potatoes, an organic herb garden or a near-forgotten ancestral culinary technique, then taking the fruits of that diversity to the restaurant's kitchen then the dining room. Working together is mutually beneficial.

As for its name, Mil translates as a *thousand* but we bandy the word about a lot: 'I've got *mil* things to do,' 'there are *mil* products to choose from, 'there are mil things outside…' And, we often say tres *mil*, cuatro *mil* (three thousand, four thousand) when referring to elevated ecosystems and altitudes in this region; I've used this word in my notes many, many times. It's solid.

- **RESPECT FOR INGREDIENTS**

Loving food doesn't just mean eating great meals. Respecting ingredients is as important as enjoying them, and every moment we prepare at Mil has to open a portal, tell a story, take you to the farmer and the place it was cultivated, paying tribute to how that person and their community eat cuy, *tarwi* (Lupinus mutabilis) or *chuño* (freeze-dried potato) and appreciating the handcrafted ceramic dishware it's served on. When products such as *Paria* cheese or bunches of pot marigold (Calendula officinalis) arrive at our door early in the morning, we immediately prep them... but the less intervention in the kitchen, the better.

Each of Mil's eight moments are windows to products and practices, which could be as simple as using an herb we've recently come across but communities have always known and used for infusions, for medicinal purposes or in cooking: *huacatay* (Tagetes minuta) lends aromas to the huatia adobe-brick oven while harvested quinua stems are used as tinder. Ingredient availability can change from one day to the next, which keeps us, the cooks, on our toes, and the landscape also transforms with the changeable weather, an intense rainstorm cascading down without any notice, clouds concealing the surrounding peaks. All this forms part of the challenging charm of running a one-of-a-kind restaurant and interdisciplinary research center located at high elevation in the mountains.

Every ingredient we gather, cook, infuse, hydrate, macerate, bottle and plate at Mil is a platform for Mater, embracing Mater's mission by taking innovation, research and knowledge to new levels. Perhaps our greatest achievement here is in the land itself, connecting with those who work the fields every single day. Like sister restaurant Central, Mil is compelled to create a legacy of creativity, sustainability, collaboration and cultural respect.

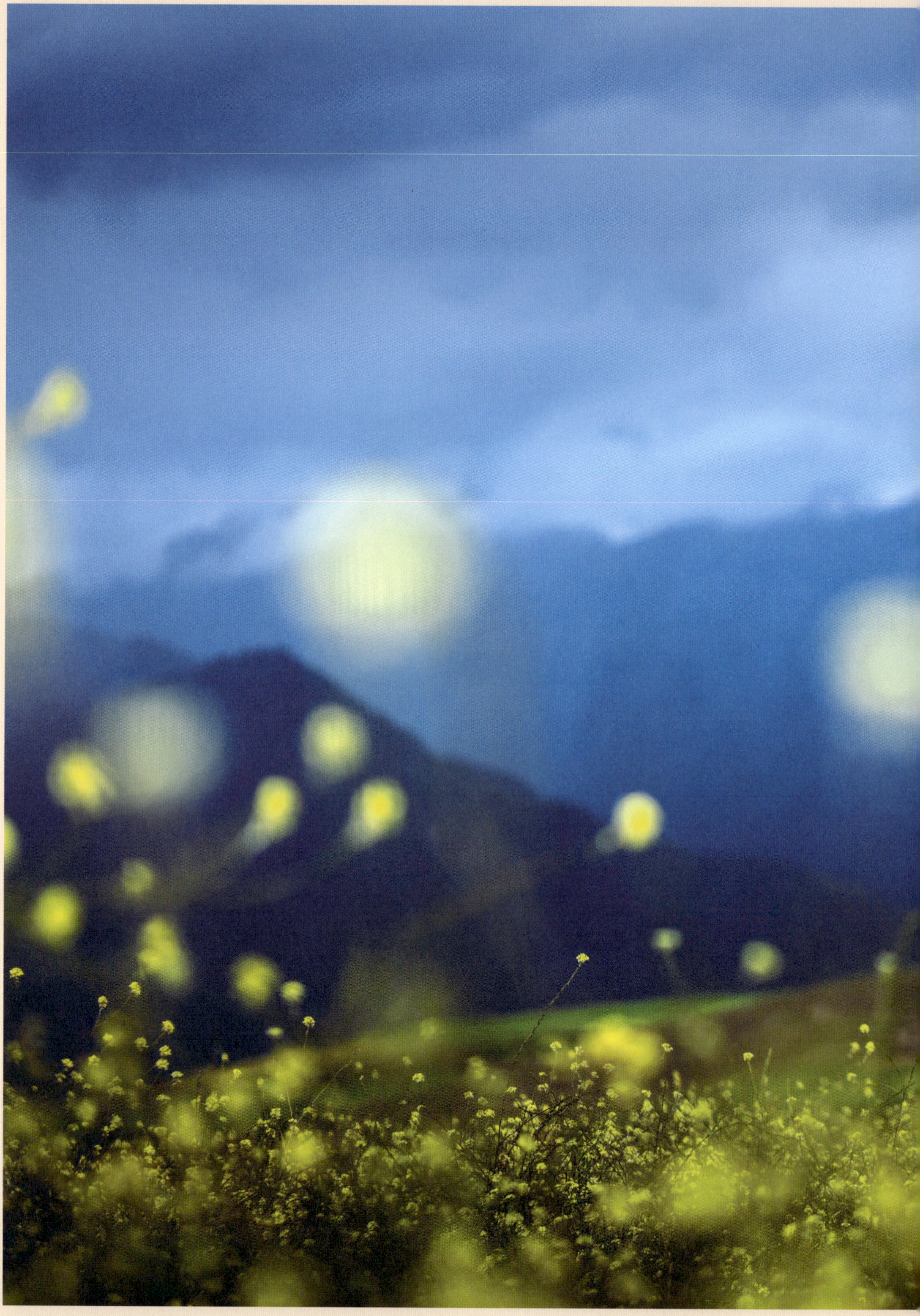

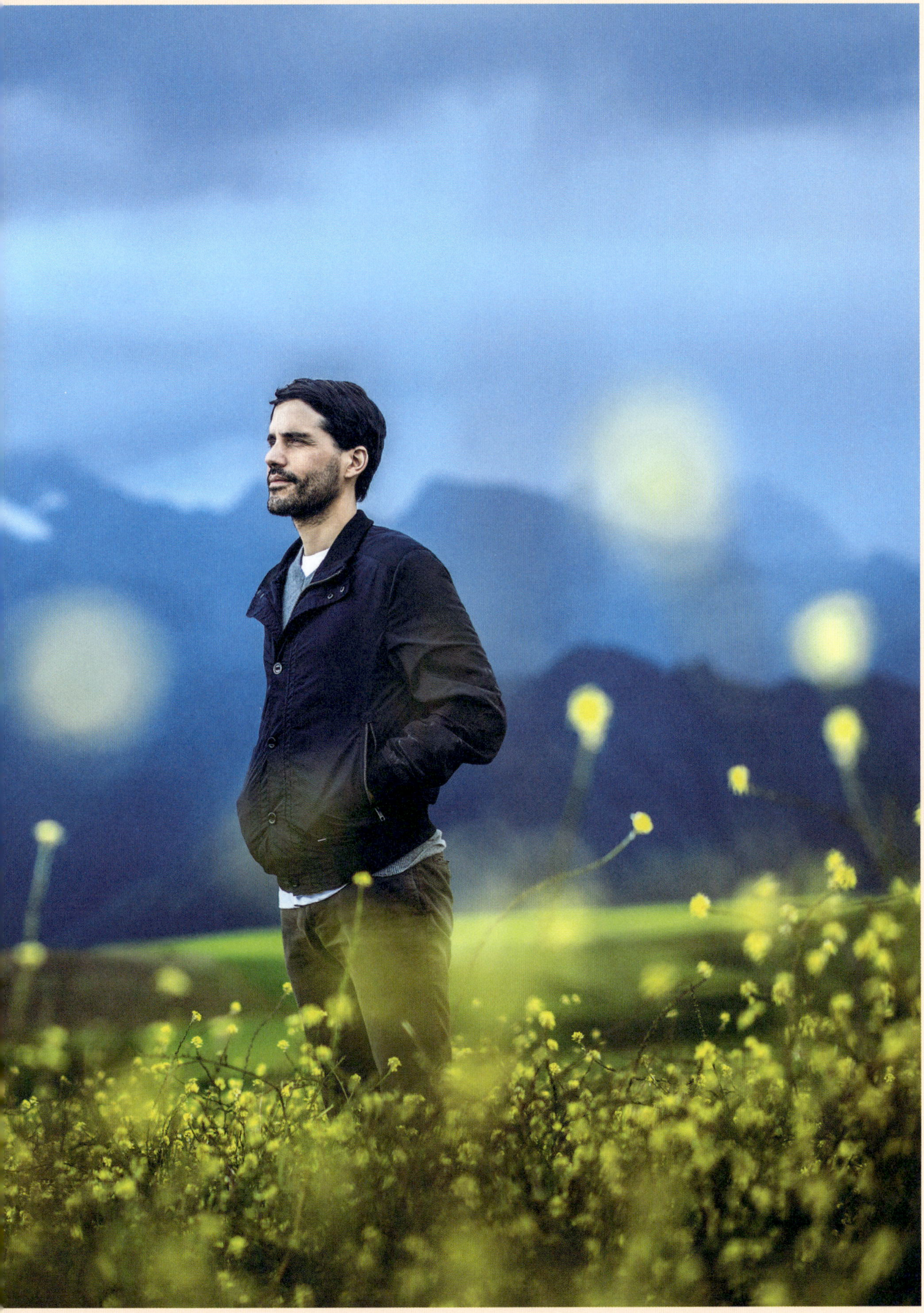

Creating living laboratories

VERÓNICA TABJA
Director of art and cultural projects, Mater

When Italian designer Giulia Pompilij shared her textile expertise with women from CC Kacllaraccay, who reciprocated with their botanical knowledge, having her join their group to gather Andean plants then dyeing yarns together, little did they imagine that the future Warmi collective would be selected to show at Peru's most prestigious artisanal crafts fair.

Cindy Valdez's Mater collaboration, however, was literally down to earth. The Berlin-based Peruvian product designer dug up an array of distinctive clays that form the Andes' ecosystems. A second artist, sculptor Valeria Figueroa, picked up Cindy's clay-catalog baton to help set up T'uru Maki (Quechua for clay hands), a ceramics workshop for women from CC Mullak'as-Misminay, to shape handcrafted dishware that reflects Mil's environs.

These are some of Mater's creative collaborations curated by Verónica Tabja, who, as director of our art and cultural projects, weaves social, sustainable, gastronomical and environmental pillars into each venture, implementing the research organization's interdisciplinary philosophy while reviving recognition of traditional skills.

A Lima-born nutritionist whose cold-pressed juice business works directly with organic fruit farmers, Mater projects start with Verónica propagating a tiny seed, as if she were working on Mil's patch of farmland. "We sow something that grows and expands to create new layers and circles. The value behind Mater's artistic and cultural projects is preserving traditional techniques and practices while interpreting biodiversity from a creative point of view. We're currently in a critical stage of loss because so much is being diluted and lost down the generations, but these projects can help sustain, transmit and reevaluate, which are extremely important."

When it comes to choosing Mater's collaborations, Verónica draws from her own interdisciplinary background to give life to projects that spark curiosity, rather than sticking to inflexible guidelines. "I go with artists who take inspiration from nature to learn about materials, ingredients and techniques, and who have an affinity to connect with Mater and its surroundings," she says.

One such project saw Warmi and sister weaving collective Sacha collaborate with Mater artists-in-residence Alejandra Ortiz de Zevallos and architect Constanza Gainza, who took *ichu*, the tufty, pale-yellow Andean grass traditionally used to create interactive knot-records and thatched roofs, to construct an interactive 39-foot by 39-foot *khipu*, commissioned for

Lima's MALI art museum. "That first day, learning how to braid *ichu*, then playing around to thread in Warmi hand-dyed yarns, simply flowed. It was a living laboratory," she says.

Given that Warmi (Quechua for women) was the debut symbiotic collaboration undertaken with a community that forged a path for future projects, the natural dyes workshop is Verónica's first Mater love. "It was a whole new universe to discover," she says. "Having this energetic group of women make the most of their potential and create a nucleus buoyed by overlapping projects with Sacha and the *khipu* has been wonderful."

Warmi's color palette is inspired by the shifting hues seen on Apu Wañinmarcca mountain, replicating in the alpaca wool nature's shades as they appear during the rainy and dry seasons. Earthy tones prevail, and the captivating range of yarns changes depending on the time of year. In Warmi's case, the end purpose of these plants is to create textiles, but interpretations vary depending on who is looking at plants, according to Verónica. "These botanicals could be used for medicinal purposes, for cooking or as fibers for knitting. That's a metaphor for Mater that helps us understand its interdisciplinary nature."

Her favorite Warmi hue is sourced from the *checche* plant, whose fruits look like blueberries. She says: "It's hard to obtain blue from nature, plus these berries are only available for one month of the year, which makes this color exclusive. This blue is really fun; women play around with it and use it to paint their lips."

Being on the ground in CC Kacllaraccay means getting drawn into the activity at hand, which could mean gathering plants growing within the community's vicinity or dyeing wool, stirring yarns with leaves or flowers around a large pot over an outdoor fire. "One of the most riveting tasks is *la madeja*, unraveling a large skein of wool to create smaller balls, separating threads by crossing your arms over each other very fast. It looks like a dance – I love watching it, although it's tiring if you actually do it!" she says.

Mater's artistic projects often develop to take on a life of their own, overlapping to create additional contexts generated by fresh ideas. Cindy took clay samples sourced from CC Kacllaraccay to Berlin, incorporating them into *Migration of Matter*, her thesis project that overlaps technology with ancestral tradition and globalization. At T'uru Maki, Valeria and the ceramics collective are fine-tuning techniques to create dishware that will be used to plate Mil's eight-moment tasting menu. And, a year after the Warmi textile workshops began, their hand-dyed alpaca yarns are set to be used in a capsule collection created by a leading Peruvian women's wear designer.

From botanicals to liquids: the Andes in a glass

MANUEL CONTRERAS
Bartender, beverages
(Andean ingredients) researcher

"Foraging isn't easy. We might walk for 10 hours at 15,000 feet above sea level (asl) from CC Huama-Chuquibamba and back to find plants and… I feel so small, like we're literally nothing. But, I do have to say, it's marvelous to feel like a tiny insect at that altitude."

Manuel Contreras' career as a bartender and beverages researcher at Mil bears certain similarities to his childhood, when he played at botanist with his father collecting wildflowers, roots and leaves, carousing among maize and coffee crops on the family farm. Raised in Peru's northern highlands, Morero in the Cajamarca region, the village's very location straddled both the mountains and the Amazon, yet Manuel didn't realize the relevance his upbringing would play until a cocktail-making course piqued his curiosity later in life.

Moving to Peru's capital aged 16 to live with older siblings, Manuel worked in a *cebichería* restaurant for four years to pay for college. Two years into an administration degree, he had a change of heart and enrolled on a bartending course focusing on Andean and Amazonian ingredients. Joining his worlds together, it became his epiphany. "The majority of ingredients was so familiar, my childhood flashed by and I recalled my dad saying, 'you can find a lot of essential plants in the mountains'. I started thinking about what I could do with them, and that was the moment when I found my calling," he says.

On Mondays, his day off, our knowledge-thirsty bartender combs the Sacred Valley's mountains, in solitude or with Mil co-workers such as cook Alex Siwar, to unearth botanicals to which he can give fresh attention. His curiosity knows no limits: "I recently found a small-leafed bitter plant but I didn't know what it was. I went to Urubamba Market the following Wednesday at 5:30am to ask sisters Catalina and Hilda Quispe – foragers who gather then sell Andean roots, leaves and flowers – what it might be. Their traditional knowledge, which they apply medicinally as well as in their daily lives by preparing *mates* (hot infusions), is so important and without it I couldn't experiment with beverages." Naturally, the most enriching foraging voyages of discovery are made with those who know, the Quispe sisters.

An hour's drive from Urubamba in Calca province, CC Huama-Chuquibamba surpasses Mil's altitude, clocking in at 12,460 feet asl. Born and raised in this elevated village, Hilda and Catalina take these altitude extremes ever further, trekking up the Pongo Pata mountain in flat, open-toe sandals [rural footwear usually worn to work in the fields] to gather plants twice weekly, tapping into expertise passed down from their foremothers, their infectious laughter reverberating around the mountains.

Fortunately their knowledge is reaching the younger generations, given that Hilda's daughter Yolanda and grandson Gabriel join her on foraging missions. The day's provisions are wrapped inside colorful *llicllas* (shoulder cloths) and include hot water for *mate*, leaves or flowers gathered then and there in the moment, and a saucepan filled with *chuño sacta*, a soup made with *moraya* and *chuño* (two types of freeze-dried potatoes), as well as *tarwi* (Lupinus mutabilis), *muña* and *cushuro* (Nostoc sphaericum). Manuel uses the latter two, respectively a type of mint and a spherical Andean algae, in hand-crafted, non-alcoholic beverages at Mil.

When joining the Quispe sisters on foraging expeditions, he religiously makes tasting notes of herbs, leaves, roots and flowers, considering their health benefits, aromas, flavors, textures, what each botanical is traditionally used for, whether it's aromatic, bitter or used for dyeing textiles, always assessing its potential. He collects obsessively, carefully hoeing a whole plant out of the soil before popping the roots or leaves into a bottle of *cañazo* (sugar cane spirit) to extract its properties over several days, weeks or even months.

This impassioned curiosity led Manuel to create Q'aqe, a bitter digestif inspired by botanicals that only grow in the Andes. Made from 28 roots, herbs, seeds and wildflowers infused in *cañazo*, Q'aqe's profile goes beyond classic drinks descriptors such as citrus fruits or berries. "One root is bitter, one tastes like stone and another reminds me of a damp forest, for example – Andean aromas and flavors can be hard to describe," he says.

But what truly inspires Manuel, and every concoction he creates, is discovering the environment and its botany. "Being surrounded by mountains, learning the traditions communities adhere to, the moments I share and finding ingredients. Whether they are roots, leaves or flowers, the ingredients themselves are more important than recipes; they are totally unique."

As for that small-leafed bitter plant he didn't recognize, Hilda and Catalina could instantly put a name to it: Manuel now uses *ñuto raqui* (Lycopodiaceae) in infusions.

Cooking under the sky

PÍA LEÓN
Culinary director at Mil

While Central in Lima shares the stories behind products from Peru's diverse ecosystems via a multitude of elevations, Mil is Virgilio's specifically Andean response, sourcing seasonal ingredients to create a narrative about one ultra-local, multi-layered region. Giving renewed value and a fresh perspective of the Cusco region and Sacred Valley's abundant high-altitude pantry while interpreting Andean culinary tradition and sustainability are my core responsibilities.

After a decade leading Central's team, I worked simultaneously on opening both our Andean project as well as my Lima-based restaurant Kjolle to transfer the workings and knowledge from an urban kitchen with four walls and a roof to breath-taking (literally, for those not accustomed to 11,705 feet) heights in the Andes. The challenges are numerous, the shared rewards between Mil, Mater and the communities, countless.

The vision behind Mil, Mater's first regional base outside of Lima, has always been inspired by Moray and its historical function as an experimental agricultural station, which in a single location traverses the mountain range's subtropical zones to its frigid peaks from between 3,935 and 14,765 feet above sea level (asl). It's essential to understand how our neighboring communities cultivate the likes of *mashwa* (Tropaeolum tuberosum), how they prepare it and whether there's a ceremonial reason before integrating that into a dish. A single ingredient can be interpreted in a multitude of ways.

When we devised the concept behind Mil's first *High-Altitude Ecosystems* tasting menu, there were a thousand combinations. But logic dictated that we should start with traceable products from origins that Mater had already catalogued: each moment would be dedicated to a single product to honor it properly.

With Mil's team, led by operational chefs Alonso Cárdenas and Franz López Chávez, we started with the most familiar, which allowed us to continue researching and experimenting with new products. From there, we chose what to feature in each moment, for example, *chullpi, piscoronto and kculli* – three varieties of maize – in *Diversity of Corn* and chocolate in *Huatia of Cacao*.

Relatively brief in the grand scheme of global tasting menus due to the reality of eating (and digesting) at this elevation, each of Mil's eight moments embraces three or four dishes served on hand-crafted or carved stone dishware – all of which might allude to culinary techniques and traditions – in the middle of the table to be shared family style. The concept defines a community experience, savoring products our neighbors cultivate or craft such as *kañiwa* (Chenopodium pallidicaule), *oca* (Oxalis tuberosa) and *Paria* fresh cow's cheese. Take the aforementioned fourth moment, *Diversity of Corn*: snap off a piece of a violet *piscoronto* maize and dip it into a purée blended with *huacatay* (Tagetes minuta), *chincho* (Tagetes elliptica) and corn. It's so vibrant, the colors fascinate me – that's definitely my favorite moment.

As you eat, you can play around: spooning lamb tartare on top of crunchy, purple quinua and spreading on a little *chirimoya* (Annona cherimola) is fun! And it's edifying, deliberately lively so it commands your attention. *High-Altitude Ecosystems* is simply bursting with textures, colors and flavors.

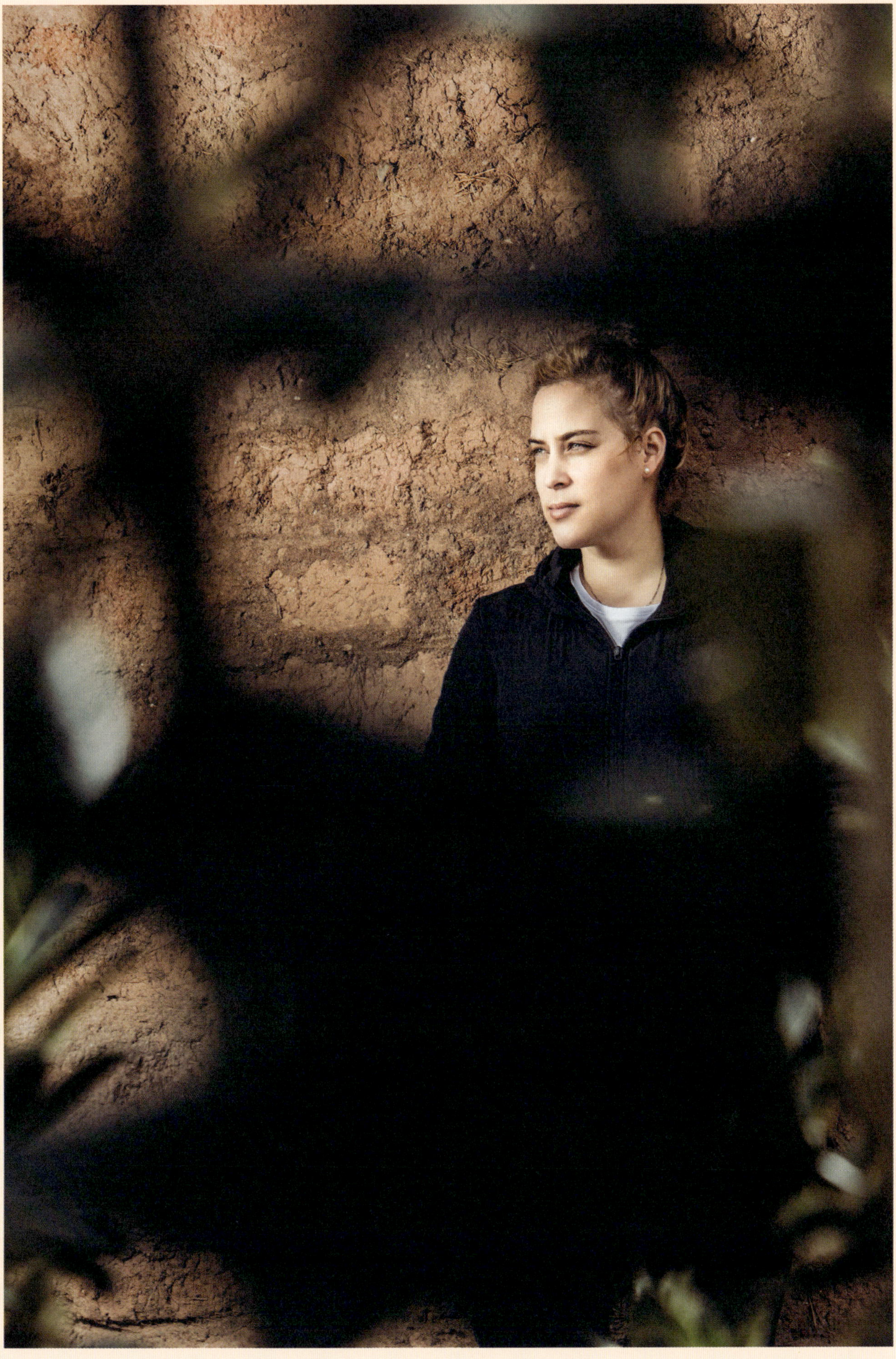

"Sustainability in terms of provisions and waste is core to Mil's daily functions due to its remote location: we recycle water, for example, which is in short supply here. Besides cooking our allocated portion of root vegetables cultivated on Mil's farmland, the kitchen team cuts salad leaves and vegetables from our organic garden when needed, using every last piece of foliage and stalk."

Besides taking inspiration from and drawing attention to carefully sourced yet often unappreciated Andean ingredients, it is also our way of paying tribute to the CC Kacllaraccay and CC Mullak'as-Misiminay communities, who share midday meals together after a morning tending the fields.

Any given day can witness intense levels of both sunshine and rainfall, clinging clouds lifting to blithely reveal the Andes. These unpredictable weather fronts are also a source of inspiration. Adapting to the seasons motivates me because we're in continual motion and the routine is always surprising – looking for solutions is the entertaining aspect to working in the Sacred Valley.

Logistics is the greatest challenge to running our elevated mountain restaurant and while Mil's immediate surroundings include a wealth of wild herbs and flowers as well as riches cultivated at both our experimental farm and organic garden, acquiring products means being highly organized. But when planning goes out the window for reasons beyond our control, such as a thunderstorm knocking out power, I shift my efficiency and creativity into overdrive.

While we source herbs such as *huacatay*, *chincho* and *muña* (Minthostachys mollis) from Mil and around Moray, they are only available for short periods. But if the *muña* runs out, it isn't a problem – we'll adapt and gather another aromatic leaf to switch in. Thinking on our feet means we're continually on a learning curve.

Sustainability in terms of provisions and waste is core to Mil's daily functions due to its remote location: we recycle water, for example, which is in short supply here. Besides cooking our allocated portion of root vegetables cultivated on Mil's farmland, the kitchen team cuts salad leaves and vegetables from our organic garden when needed, using every last piece of foliage and stalk. Whatever the origin, we work with everything that comes out of the ground for both staff meals and the restaurant, and making good use of quinua leaves and stems, for example, so there's no waste. We also produce bokashi compost from restaurant waste, which goes straight back into the organic garden.

Contrary to expectations, the indoor kitchen isn't jam-packed with the latest high-tech gadgets. We try to keep things basic and only work with what's indispensable, such as fridges and mixers, in order to reduce energy use, not rely too much on technology and adhere as closely as we can to ancestral traditions.

Respecting Andean culinary customs means incorporating traditional preparation techniques, often in a second, outdoor kitchen under the sky. One ancestral technique we've adopted is natural dehydrating, leaving oca (my favorite Andean ingredient) and *mashwa* out in the sun to concentrate their sugar levels; we also dry *muña* and *chincho* as well as chili peppers, but in the shade, which better preserves their aromatic and organoleptic properties. *Ch'arki* (from which the word jerky is derived) is another renowned Andean preparation, salt-curing proteins such as alpaca, llama and lamb.

One of the Andes' most fundamental preservation methods is freeze-drying tubers to be consumed months, even years, after harvesting. First exposed to sun, small potatoes are blanketed under dried grass at extreme elevation for a few nights, following a thawing and freezing pattern for three nights. Barefoot, farmers squash them to remove most of the skin before placing them in nets and submerging them into shallow river or lake waters repeatedly for a week; this laborious technique that requires dedication produces the white *moraya*. *Chuño*, black in color due to its prolonged oxidation, doesn't have any contact with water, repeating the thaw-and-freeze cycle for longer. Once dried, we mill it into flour, plus *chuño* also forms part of *Preservation*, the menu's first moment.

Like Moray's terraces, Mil's moments follow the circle of life, using ingredients in their entirety, but I also hope Mil's future enjoys a full circle of life, as well – certainly if our son is someone to go by. We often talk to Cristóbal about the mountains and took him to Mil for the first time when he was three. He grabbed a hoe and started making holes in the earth, playing at building a *huatia*. Being here is real, and it's impossible not to be inspired.

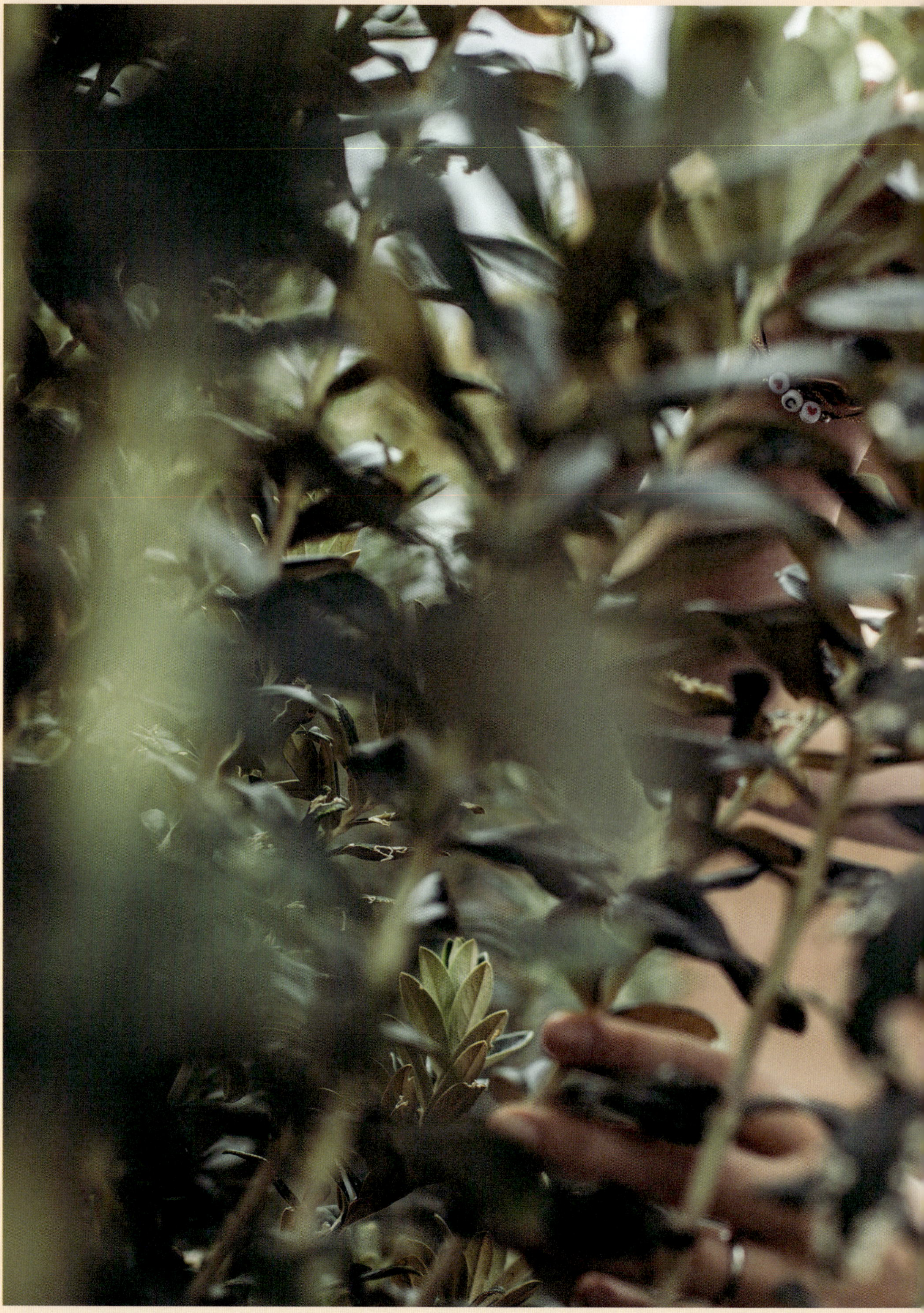

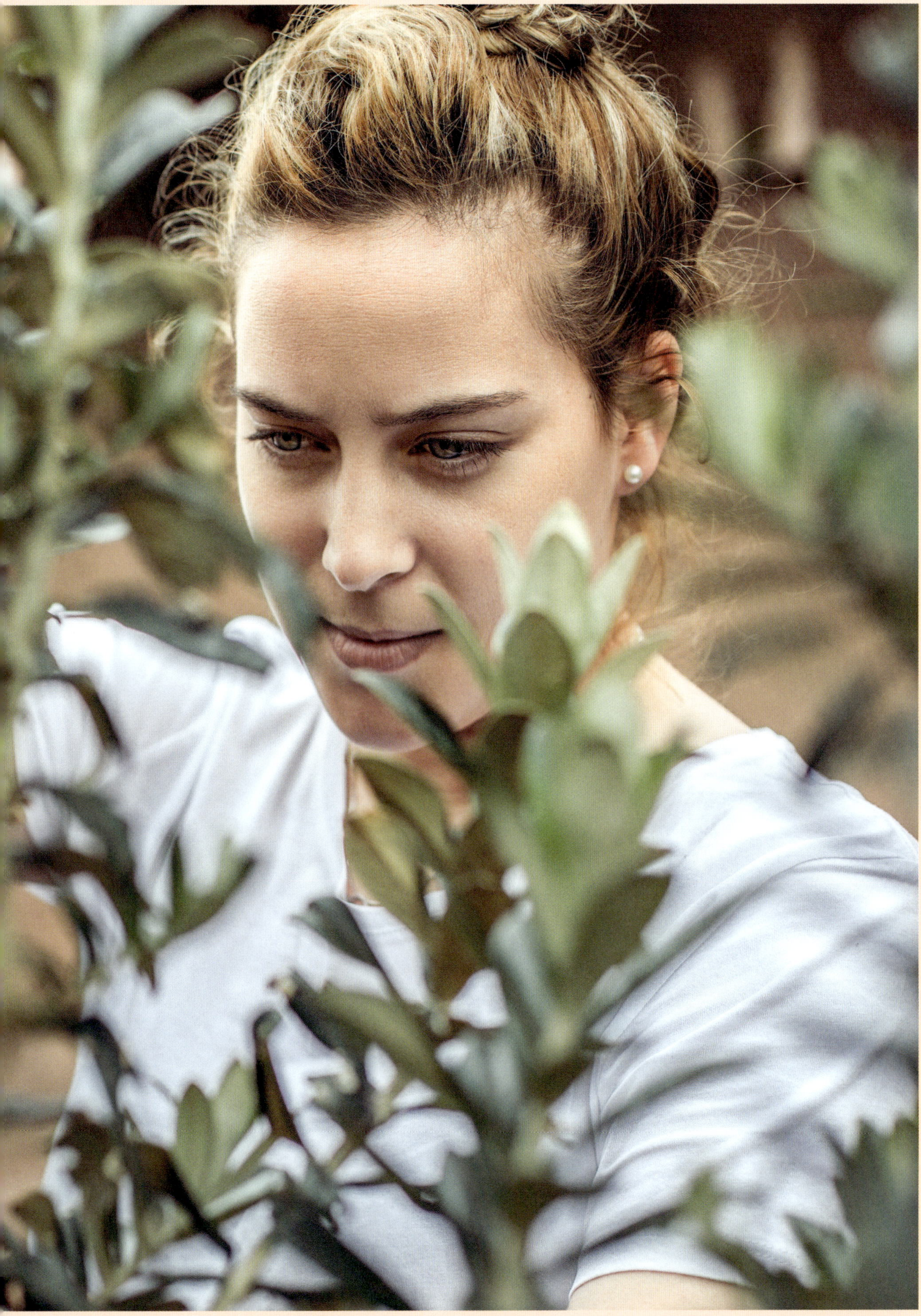

AN ANDEAN PLACE

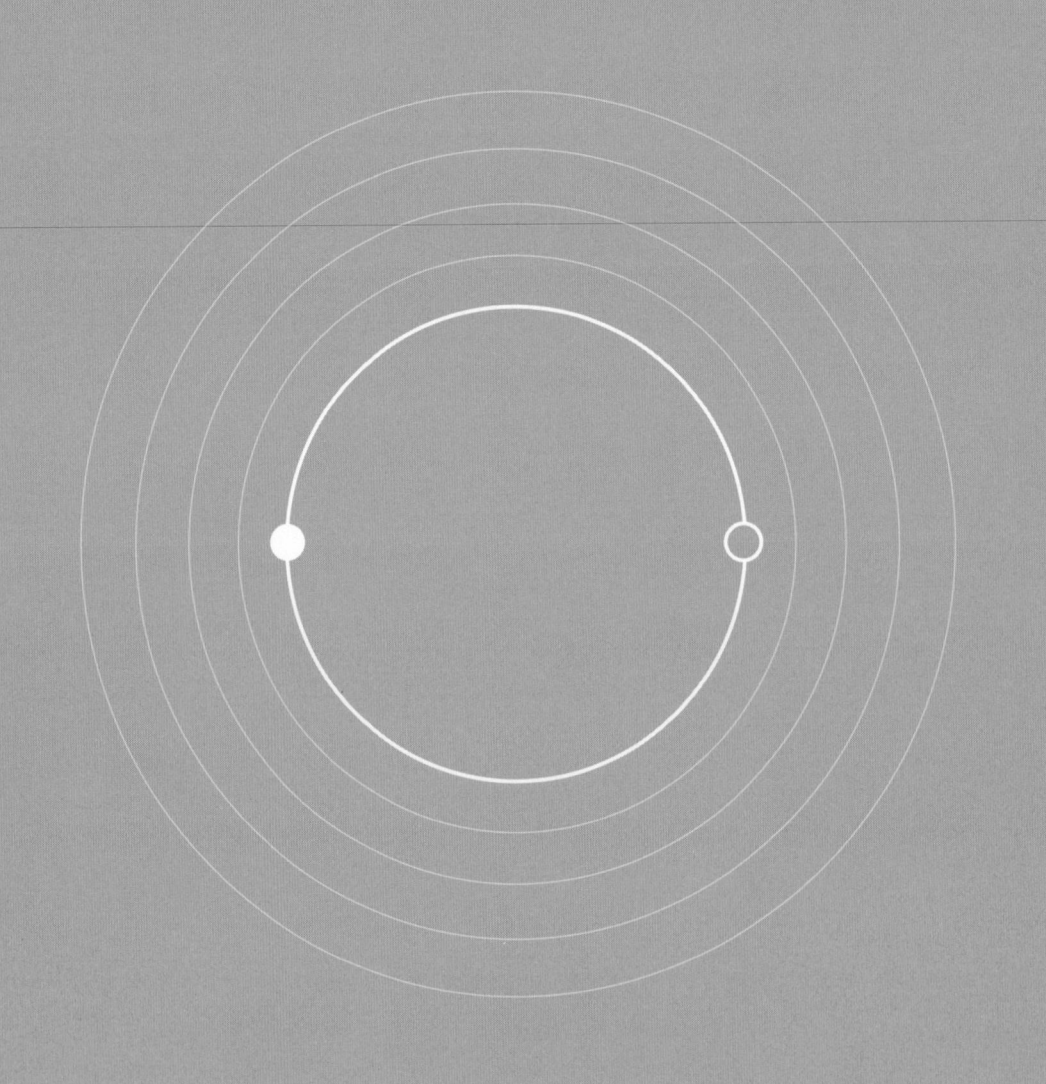

In an aerial image, the adobe walls and handwoven thatched roof of Mil effortlessly blend into the expansive Andean panorama. Drawing from this very landscape, with its intriguing palettes of texture and color, ensured the materials and techniques employed in Mil's construction seamlessly integrated with the Andean geography and ecosystems, restoring a sense of time and place, an homage to heritage.

The property already existed at the threshold of Moray's concentric terraces, so Lima-based architect Rafael Freyre was tasked with refurbishing the 30-year-old colonial-style building that has previously served as both a vicuña breeding facility and an events space. The objective was to create an authentic and sustainable Andean home for Mil that welcomes inclusivity, not just in honoring the landscape by using materials sourced within a two mile-radius of the Quechua agricultural experimental station, but also celebrating local culture and artisanal traditions. To accomplish this, the first tasks involved removing the industrial paint and cement covering the adobe brick walls, replacing the colonial-style red ceramic tile roof with traditional Andean thatch and converting the central courtyard and its pond into a welcoming patio and garden.

Thatching with *ichu*, a tufty feather grass that only grows in the high plateau and whose fibers become stiffer with increasing elevations, required patience given that it can only be harvested once it takes on yellow tones in the dry season. But the process revived a traditional and sustainable roofing technique seldom seen in the 21st-century Andes.

Rafael says: "Resurrecting this craft and choosing this species was our way of evoking the collective consciousness of the past and transforming it for the future." Members of both CC Kacllaraccay and CC Mullak'as-Misminay harvested ichu in June, leaving its roots so it grows back the following year, before weaving and knotting grassy bunches into a tightly compacted, waterproof, 7,530 feet^2 covering; that project took two months.

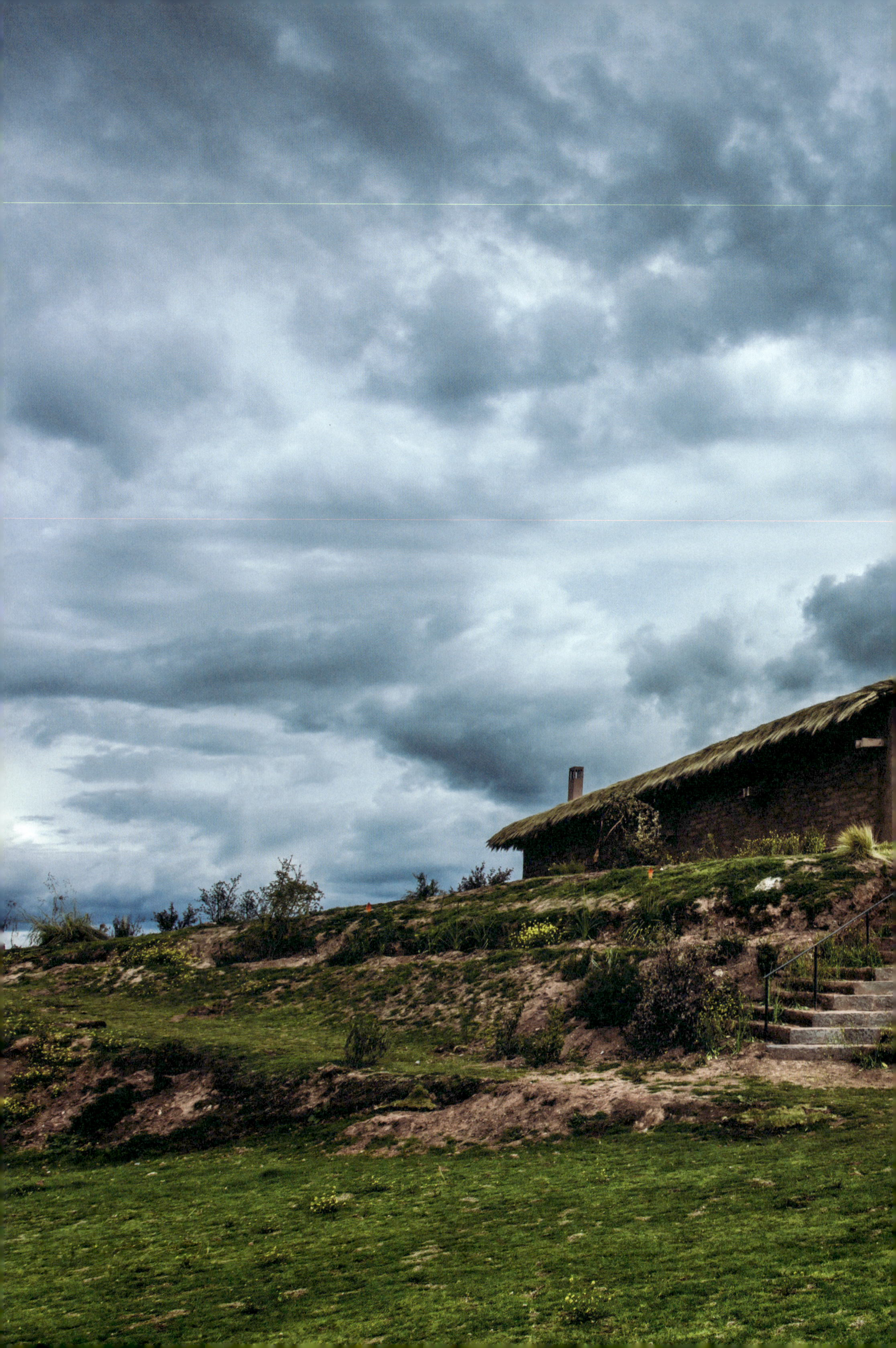

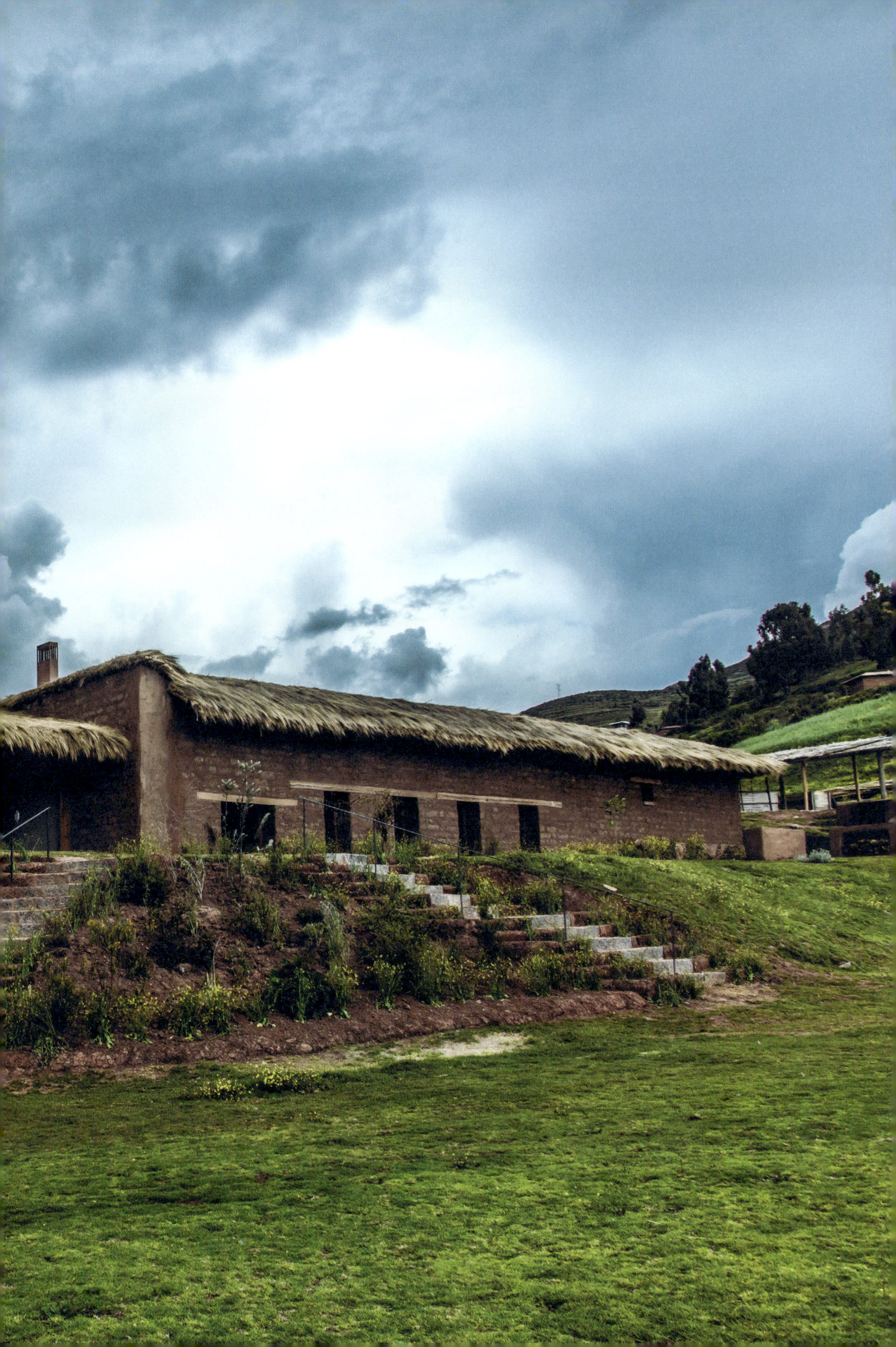

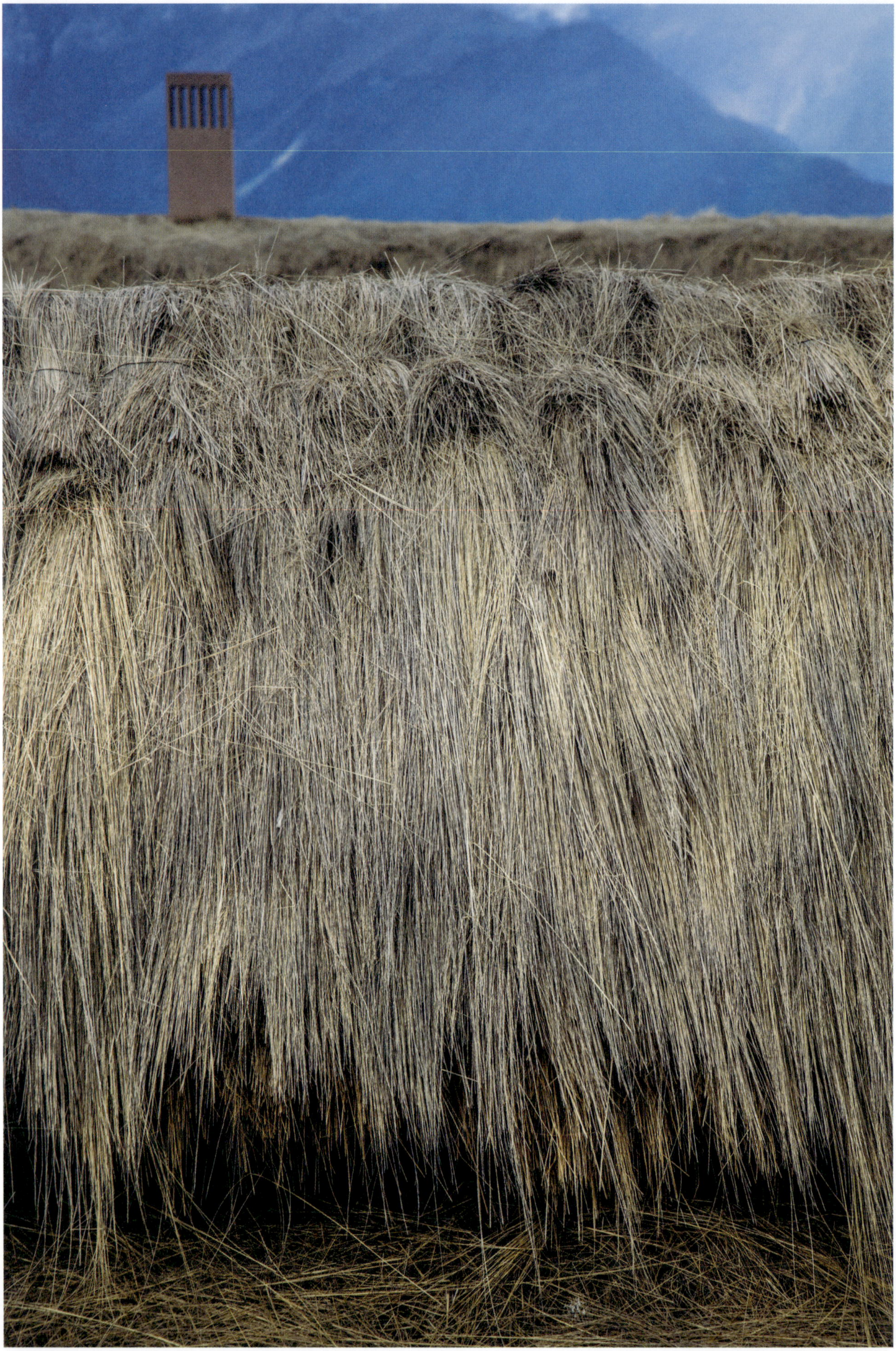

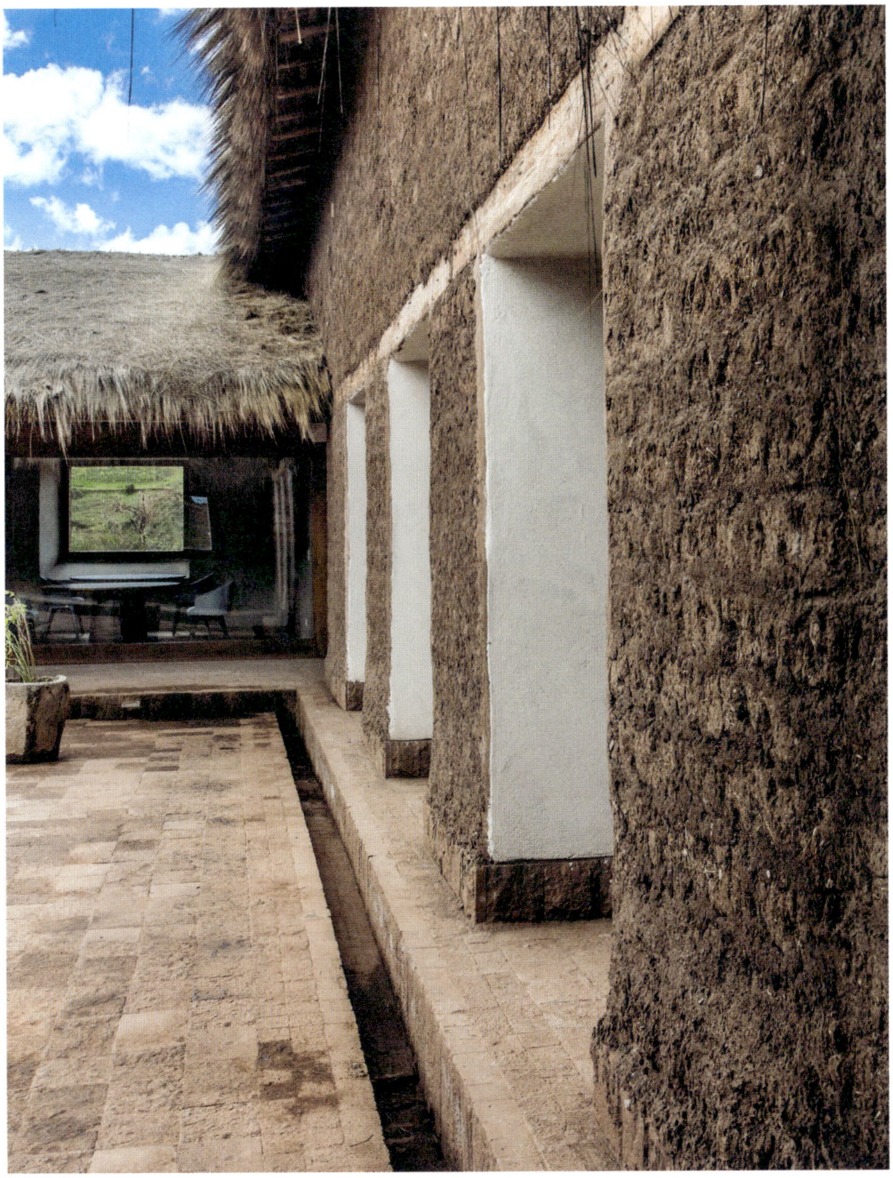

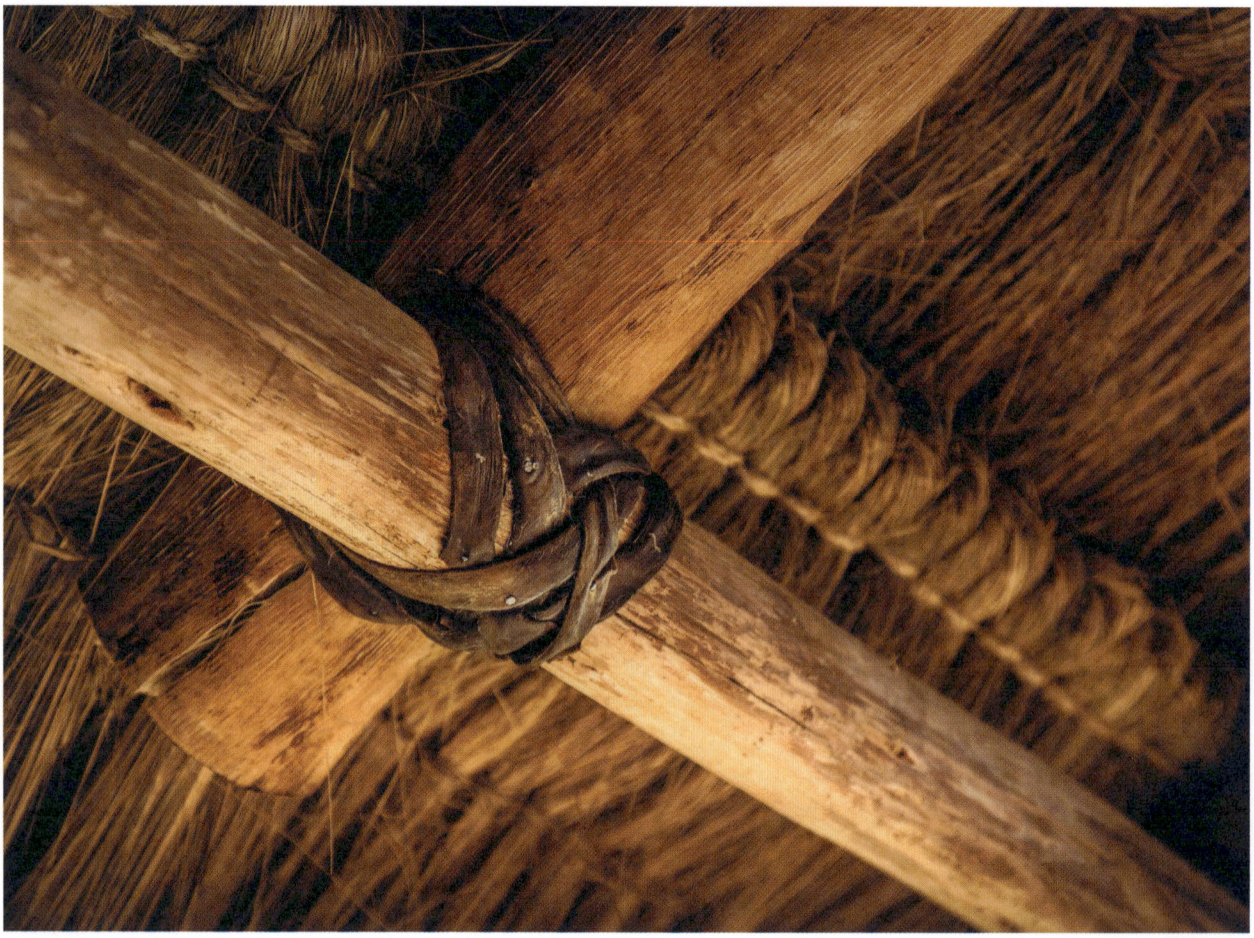

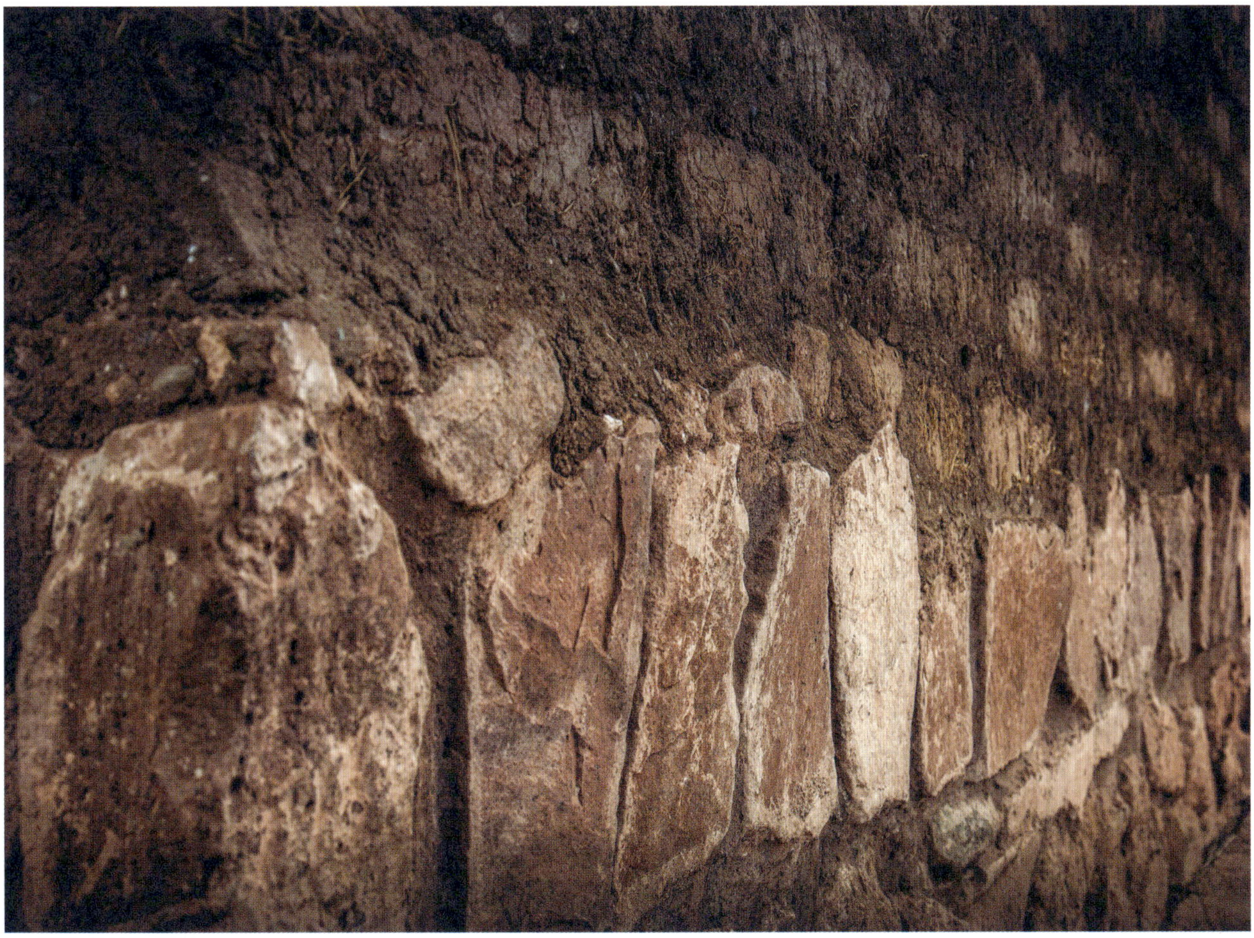

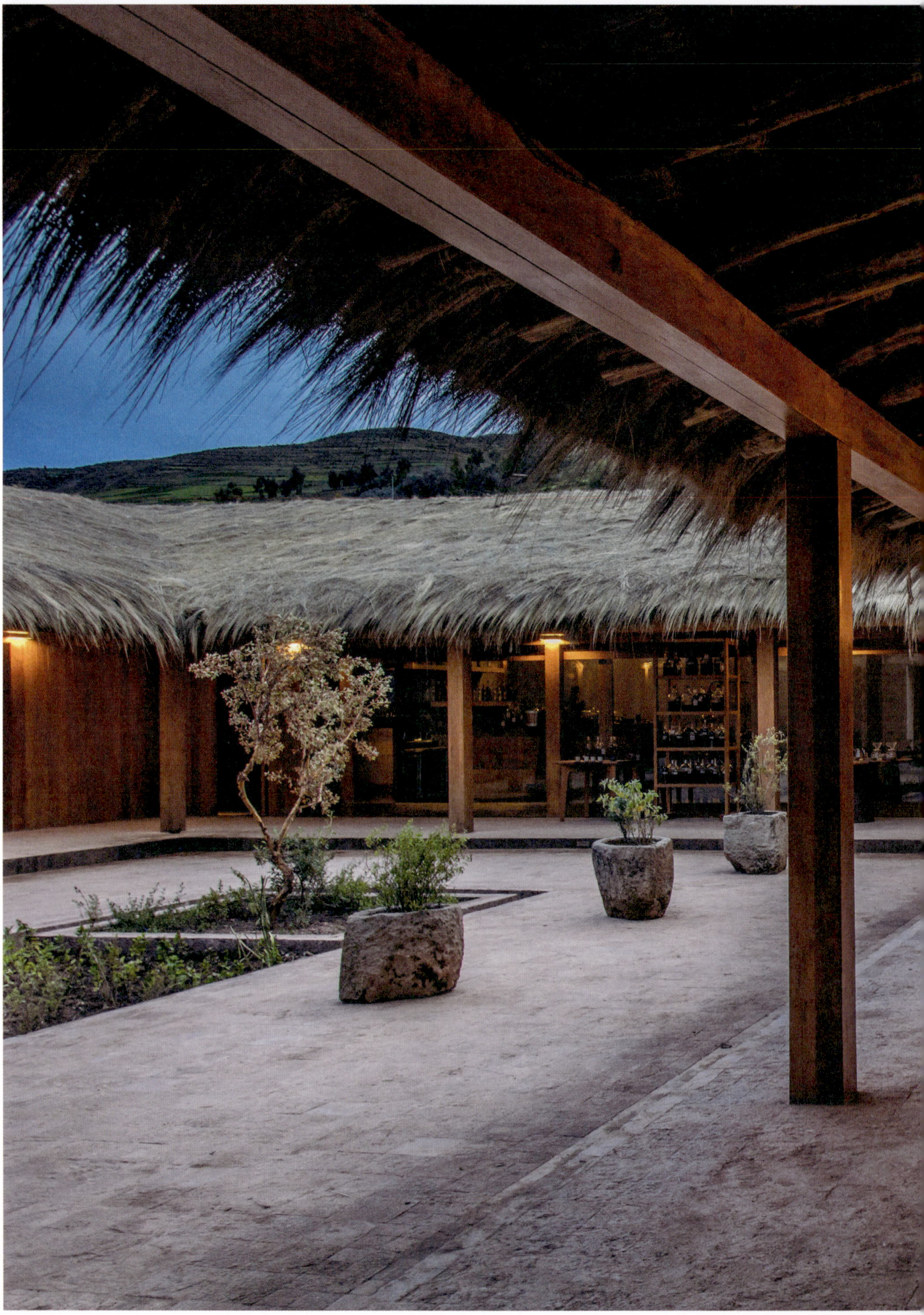

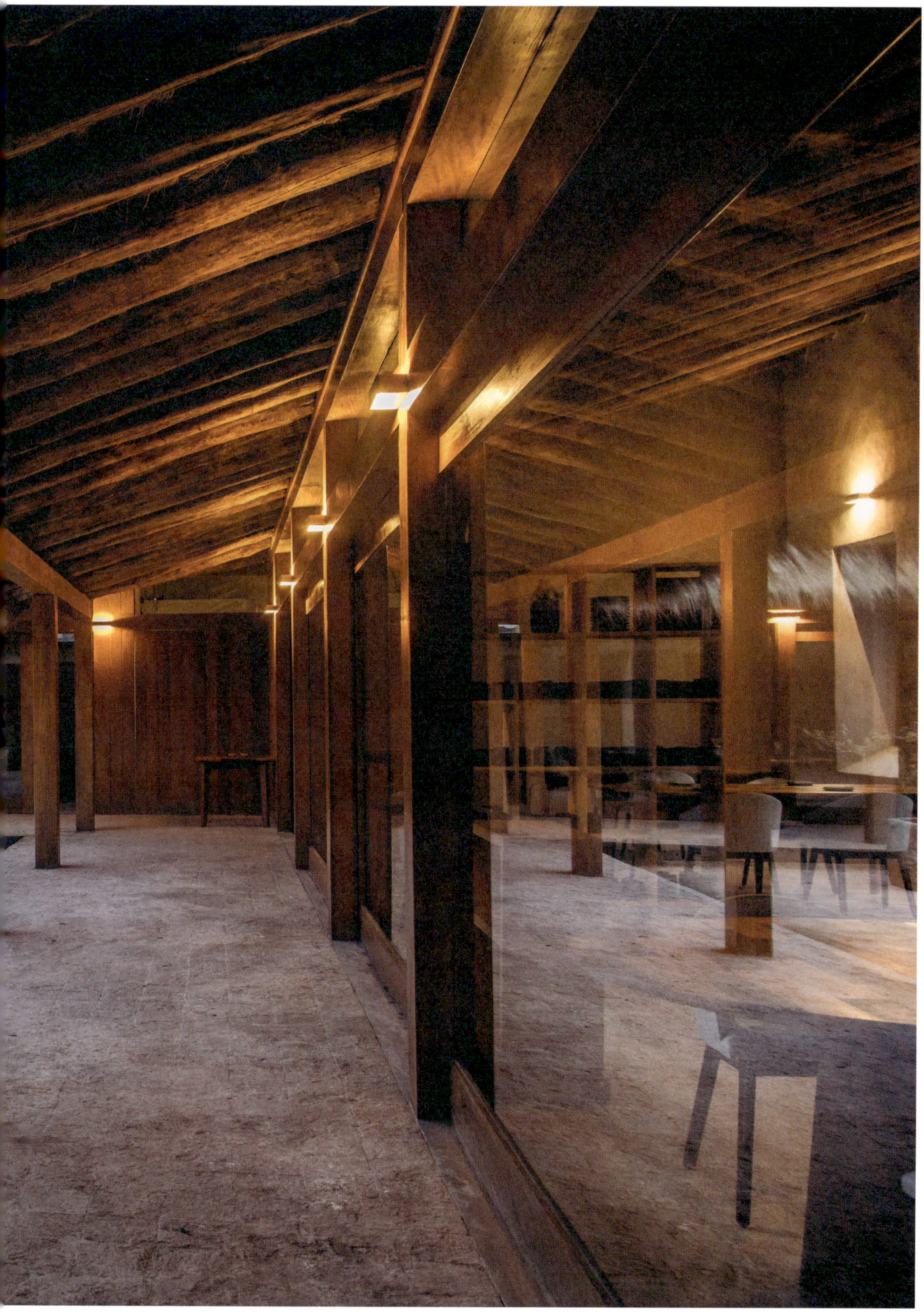

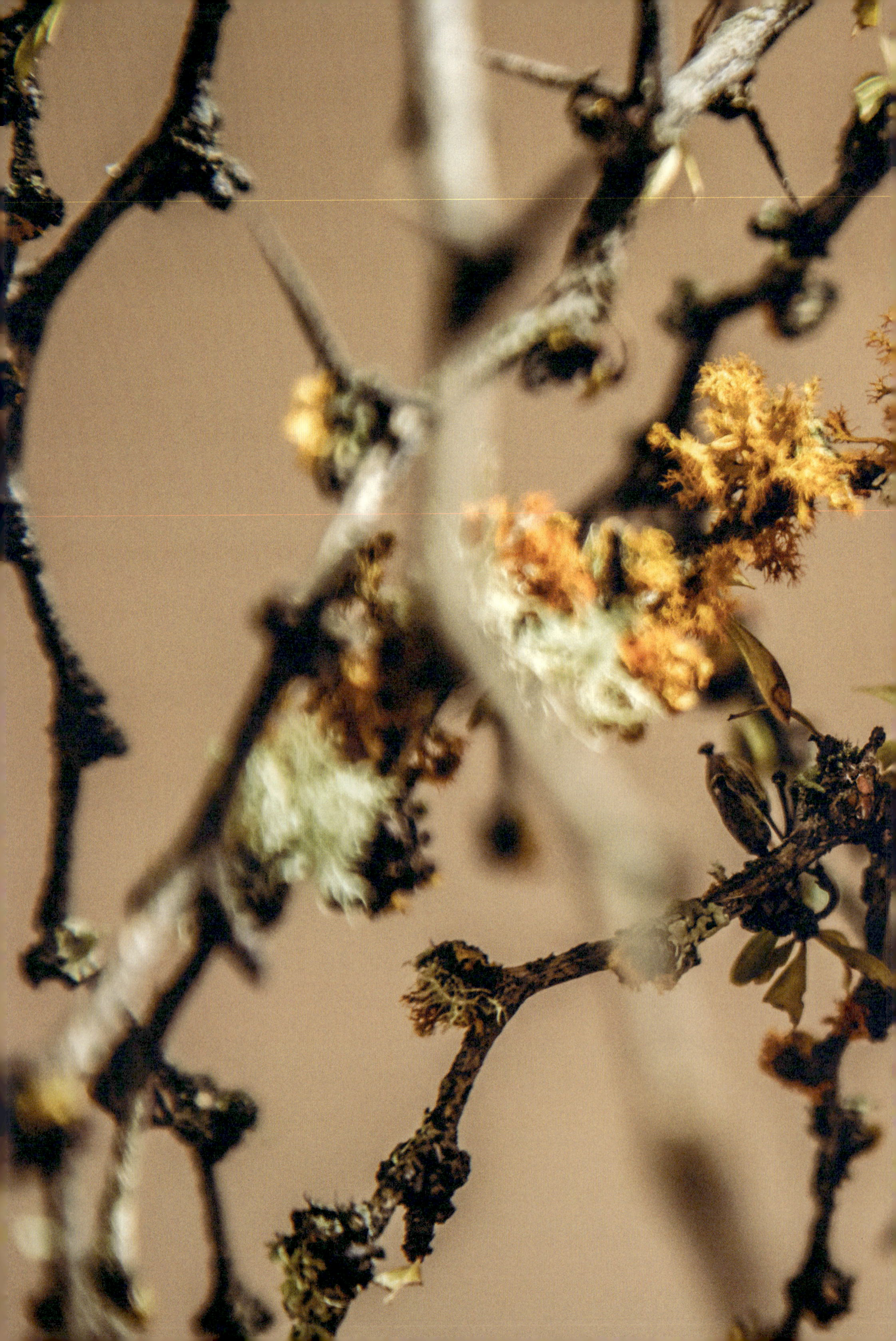

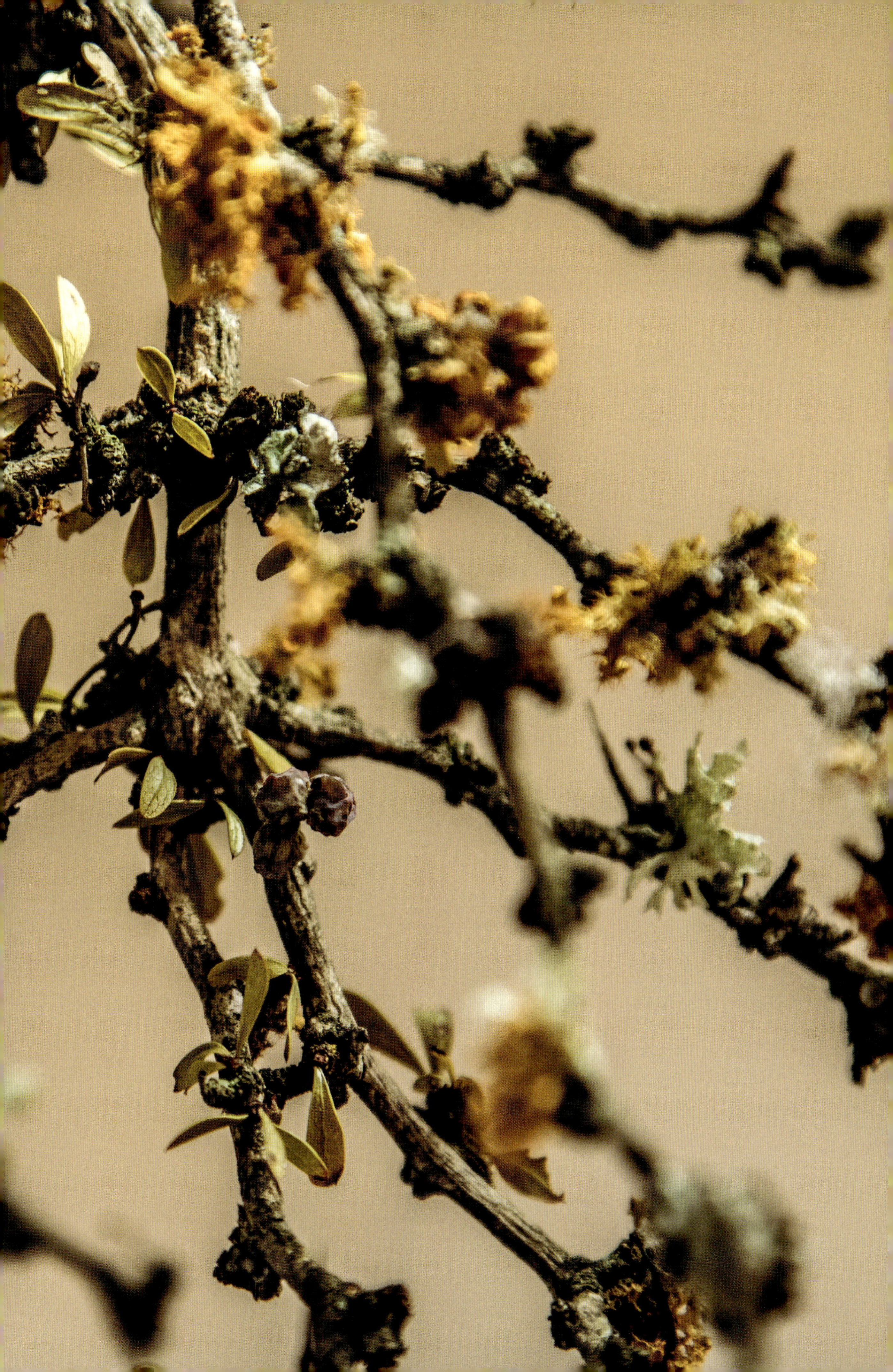

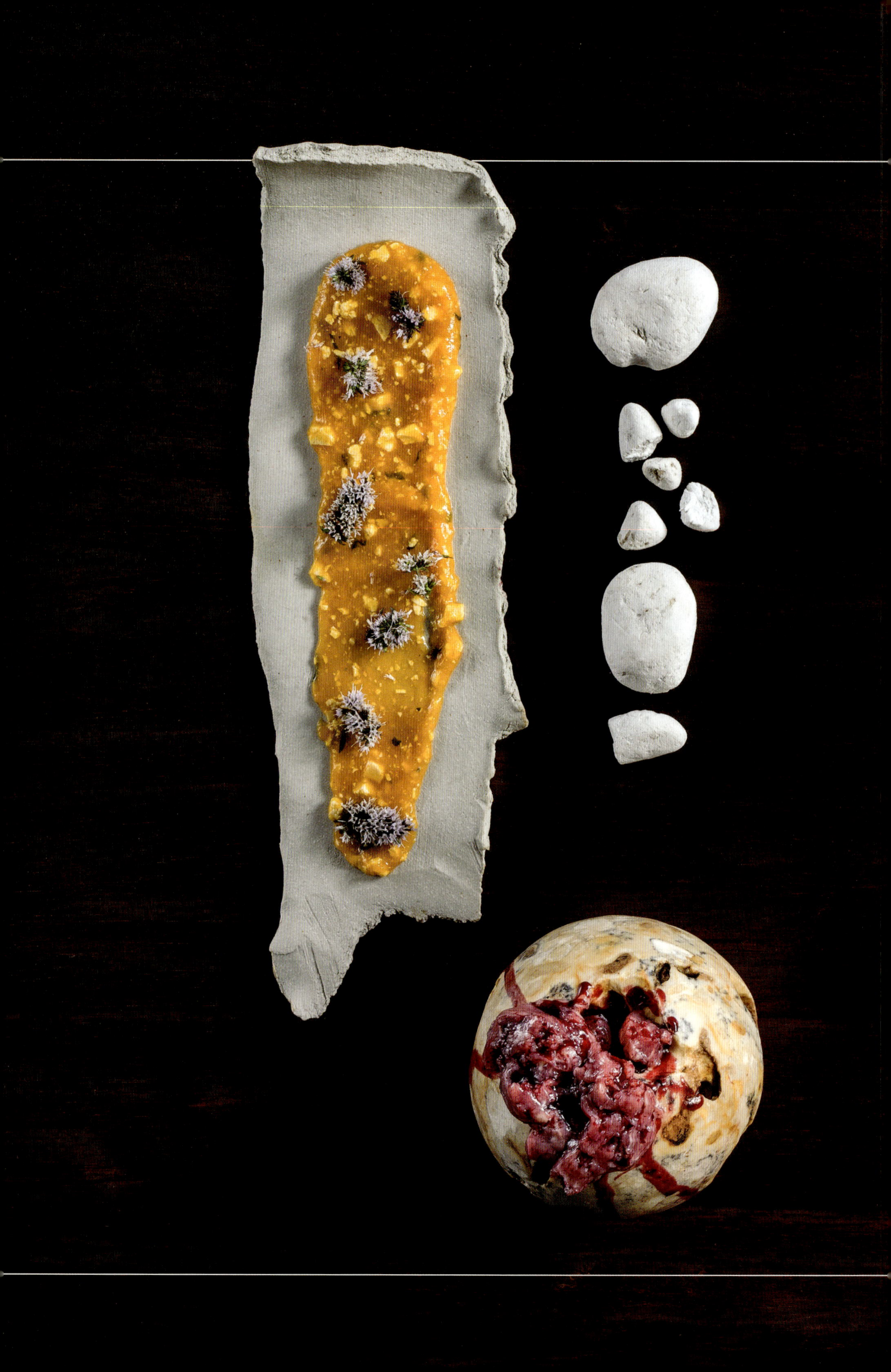

METHOD

SACHATOMATE (TAMARILLO) UCHUCUTA

SACHATOMATES (TAMARILLOS), 5
YELLOW CHILI PEPPER PASTE, 30 g
PARIA CHEESE, 20 g
HUACATAY LEAVES, 30 g
CHINCHO LEAVES, 30 g
RAW CANE SUGAR, 30 g
MARAS SALT, TO TASTE
SACHA INCHI SEED OIL, 40 mL

- Remove the stems and cut the tamarillos in half, arrange on a baking sheet, add oil and salt. Bake at 220°C (430°F) for 20 minutes. Remove from the oven, remove skins and press through a chinois to make a smooth purée. Set aside.
- Measure out the ingredients and mix in an Andean mortar until blended.

CORN PURÉE

PISCORONTO CORN (PURPLE), 1 kg
CHULLPI CORN (YELLOW), 1 kg
KCULLI CORN (RED), 1 kg
PARAQAY CORN (WHITE), 1 kg
RED ONION, 20 g
PEELED GARLIC, 5 g
CORN OIL, 30 ml
WATER, AS NEEDED

- Dice the garlic and onion into small cubes. Remove the fresh corn kernels from the Piscoronto, Chullpi, Kculli and Paraqay and transfer each variety into a separate bowl as each will be cooked separately.
- In a heavy-bottomed saucepan, sauté the garlic and onion in corn oil and sweat over low heat for 8 minutes until the onions are transparent, then add one single variety of kernels. Repeat this process, separately cooking each type of corn. Add water to cover the corn in each pot and cook over low heat for 1 hour. Remove from heat and cool. Separately process each variety of corn in water in the same way.
- Use a little of the cooking liquid to process each individual corn variety in a blender or food processor. Pass the purée through a strainer so it's smooth and homogenous. To make this step easier, work while the kernels are still warm. Refrigerate the finished purée.
- Each variety of corn offers a different color in our recipes.

CORN CAKE

PARAQAY CORN PURÉE, 500 g
YELLOW CHILI PEPPER PASTE, 60 g
KAÑIWA POWDER, 40 g
KIWICHA POWDER, 40 g
EGG, 10 g
CABUYA SYRUP, 20 ml
MARAS SALT, 5 g
UNSALTED BUTTER, 30 g

- Preheat the convection oven to 185°C (365°F).
- Line the bottom of a buttered 5 cm deep 40 x 60 cm baking pan with parchment paper.
- Measure out all the ingredients into a large bowl and mix well, then transfer the mixture into the baking pan and bake for 55 minutes. Remove from the oven and allow to cool at room temperature. Turn out and remove the paper.
- Slice the corn cake into 2 x 2 x 2 cm cubes. Use a culinary torch to brown the top of the corn cake, thin the cabuya syrup with a little water and drizzle over the top. Set aside.
- To serve hot, heat up the little cakes in a combi-oven for 3 minutes and serve on the dishware of your choice.

ELDERBERRY BUTTER

UNSALTED BUTTER, CREAMED, 250 g
FRESH ELDERBERRY, 80 g
CABUYA SYRUP, 50 ml
OLLUCO EXTRACT, 30 ml
MARAS SALT, 5 g

- Leave the butter at room temperature for three hours so it becomes smooth and creamy.
- Measure out all the ingredients into a deep bowl and, using food prep gloves, combine well until the butter is partially emulsified, which will create a different visual presentation. The fruit will start to break up in the process. Refrigerate.
- Before serving, transfer the butter and broken elderberries to small ramekins, and level the tops with a spatula.

COCA LEAF CHAPLA (TORTILLA-STYLE BREAD) FILLED WITH OCA

COCA DOUGH

WHEAT FLOUR, 100 g
WHEAT FLOUR, 100 g
WATER, 120 ml
COCA LEAF FLOUR, 20 g
SACHA INCHI SEED OIL, 3 ml
MARAS SALT, 3 g

- Combine all the ingredients in a deep bowl, knead 8 minutes, then wrap dough in plastic wrap and refrigerate for 1 hour.
- Bake.

1.

PRESERVATION

Chuño
Corn
Uchucuta
Oca

PARA 4 PERSONAS

OCA FILLING

OCAS, 400 g
HONEY, 20 ml
MARAS SALT, 30 g

- Preheat a convection oven on mixed function with 100% humidity to 250°C (480°F).
- Carefully wash and dry the ocas, then lay a bed of salt on a baking pan and arrange the ocas on top. Cook in preheated oven for 40 minutes, check they are cooked al dente, remove and let them cool slowly.
- Place the cooked ocas in a deep bowl, and use a pestle to make a rustic mash, adding honey and salt to taste. Refrigerate.

CHAPLA

COCA DOUGH, 200 g
OCA FILLING, 180 g
WHEAT FLOUR, 50 g

- Heat a griddle or heavy frying pan over medium heat.
- Measure out 4 coca leaf dough balls of 40 gr each, set aside.
- Use a rolling pin to roll out the ball into 15-cm diameter discs, then place 40 gr of oca filling in the middle of each. With your hands, gather the edges of the dough and close them at the top to form a sealed ball, removing excess dough and reserving for later use. Cover the balls in plastic wrap.
- For serving, cover each filled ball with wheat flour, place on a clean and dry table and gently press down on them with your hands to form 10-cm diameter tortilla-style breads. Cook on the griddle or in a heavy-based frying pan for 5 minutes on each side.
- To serve, use dishware covered with a light piece of fabric.

MORAYA CRACKERS

MORAYA, 500 g
WATER, 1 l
MARAS SALT, TO TASTE
SACHA INCHI SEED OIL, 1 l

- Grate the moraya and sieve.
- Preheat the oven to 80°C (175°F). Line a baking tray with a silicone mat.
- In a heavy frying pan, hydrate the moraya powder with water, simmer and stir over medium heat for 30 minutes until it becomes a sticky and shiny dough.
- On the silicone mat roll out the dough until it is 5mm thick. Dehydrate the dough sheets in the oven for at least 6 hours.
- Remove the dehydrated moraya sheets, mist with water and then refrigerate uncovered overnight.
- Heat the oil in a heavy-bottomed pan until it reaches 200°C (390°F). Remove the moraya sheets from the fridge and cut into 5x5 cm pieces, fry quickly until they double in size, remove, drain on paper towels, then salt to taste.

CHUÑO CRACKER

CHUÑO, 300 g
WATER, 1 l
MARAS SALT, TO TASTE
LINSEED OIL, 1 l

- Grate the chuño then sieve.
- Preheat the oven to 80°C (175°F). Cover a baking tray with a silicone mat.
- In a heavy-based frying pan, hydrate the chuño powder with water, simmer and stir at medium heat for 1 hour 15 minutes, until it becomes a sticky and shiny dough.
- On the silicone mat roll out the dough until it is 5mm thick. Dehydrate the sheets in the oven for at least 6 hours.
- Remove the dehydrated chuño sheets, mist with water, then leave uncovered in the refrigerator overnight.
- Heat up the oil in a heavy-bottomed pan to 200°C (390°F). Remove the chuño sheets from the fridge and cut into 5x5 cm pieces, fry them quickly until they double in size, remove and drain on paper towels, then salt to taste.
- To serve, use a 10-cm deep bowl, fill it with whole morayas and chuños, then arrange the chuño and moraya crackers vertically in the bowl.

FINISH AND PRESENTATION

- To serve, start with the little corn cakes, continue with the coca chapla filled with oca accompanied with elderberry butter, then present the moraya and chuño crackers with sachatomate uchucuta.

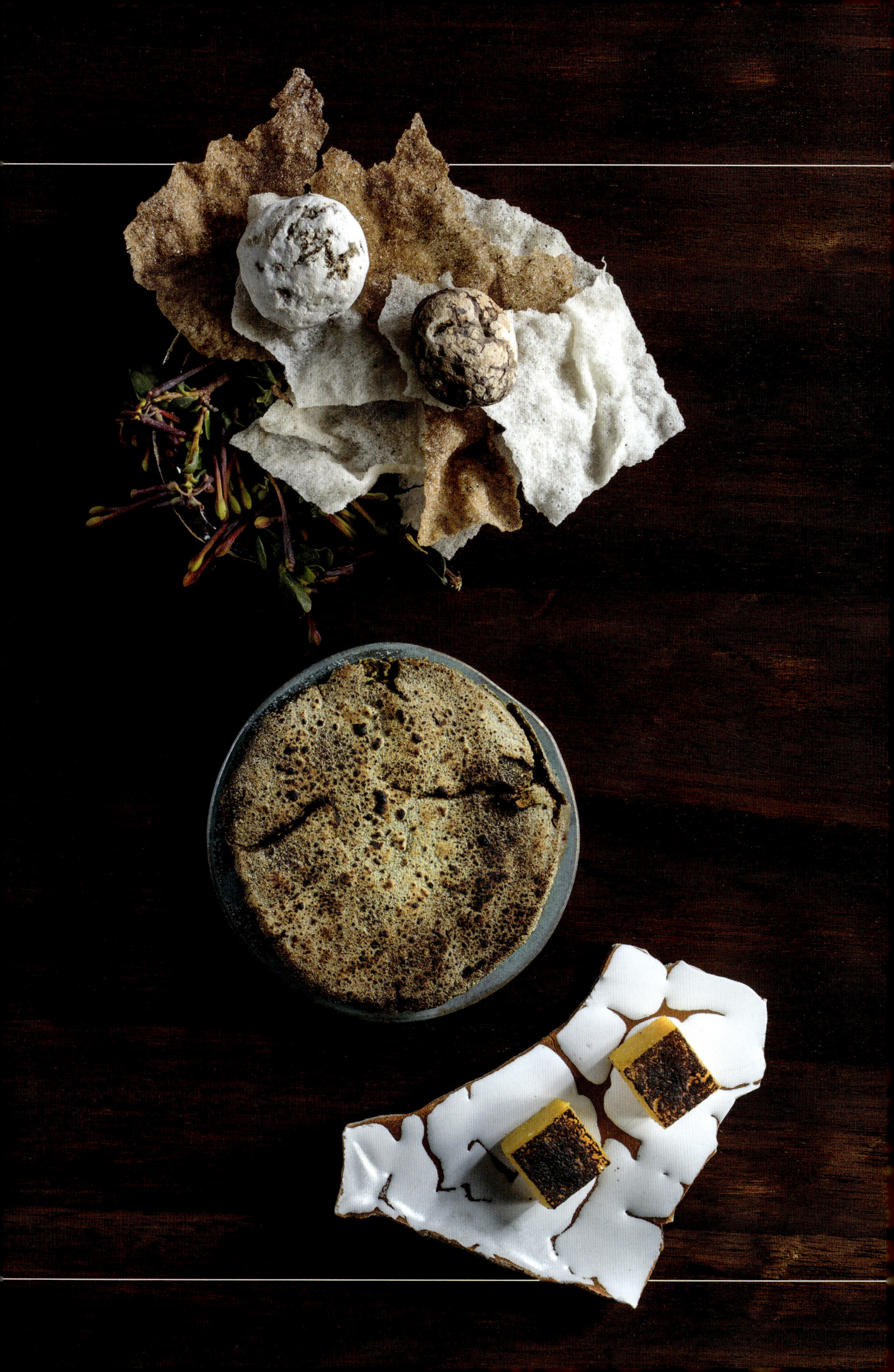

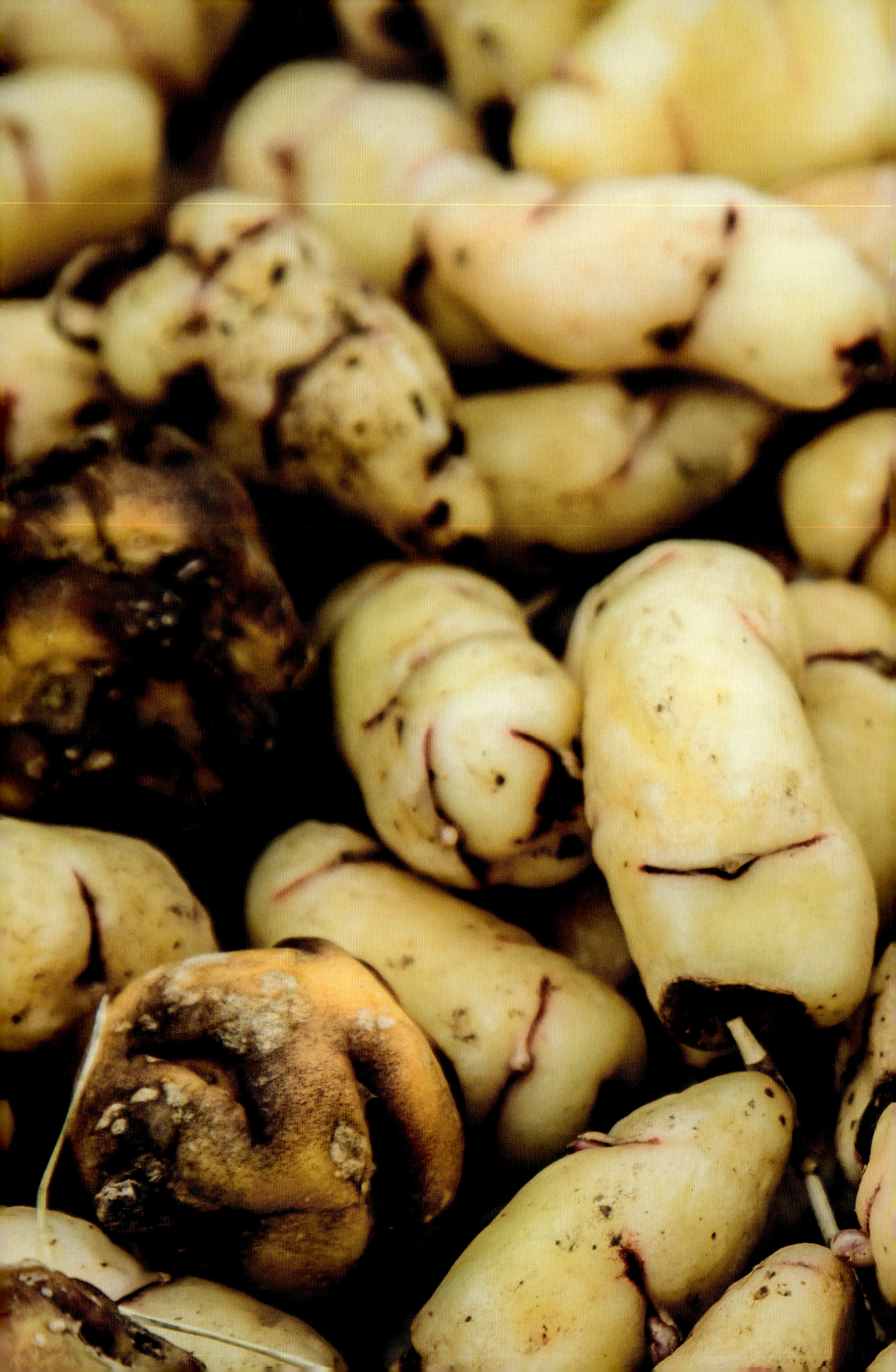

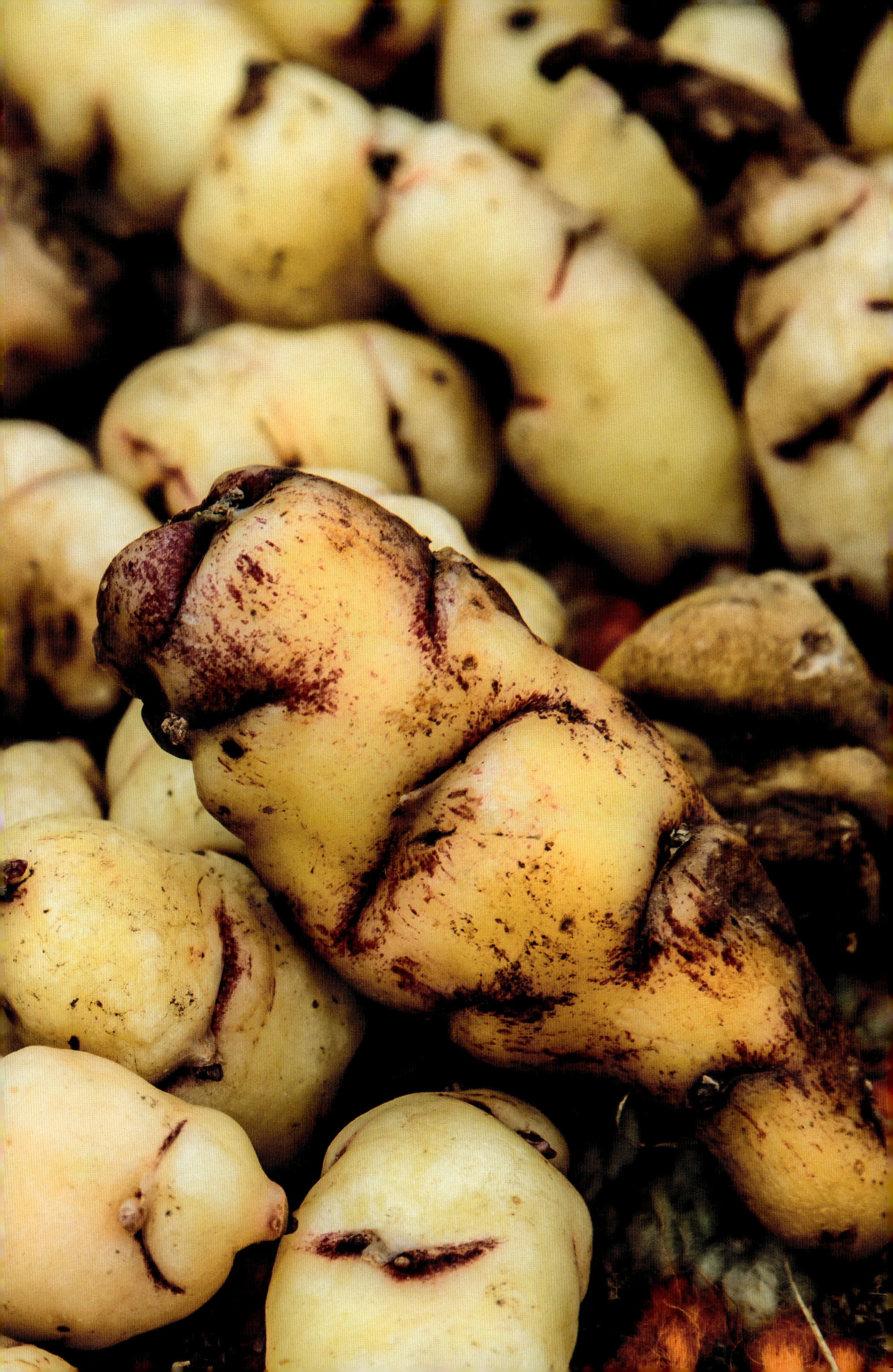

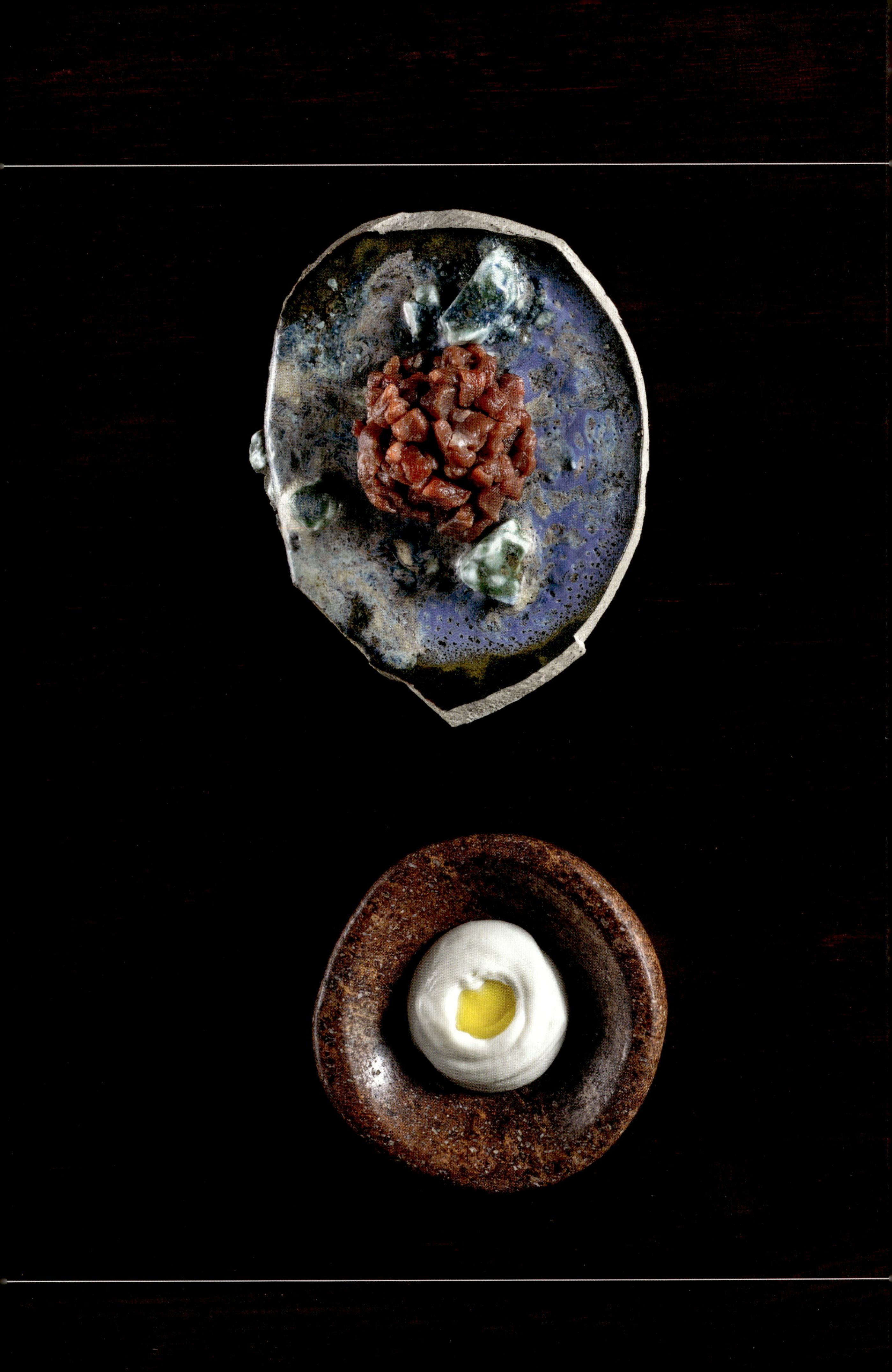

METHOD

CHIRIMOYA (CUSTARD APPLE) CREAM
QUINUA MILK

QUINUA FLOUR, 100 g
WATER, 350 ml

- In a deep pot, bring the water to a boil, sprinkle in the quinua flour and stir briskly with a balloon whisk. Cook for 20 minutes until it thickens to a heavy cream. Pass the mixture through a fine strainer and set aside.

CHIRIMOYA (CUSTARD APPLE) CREAM

CHIRIMOYA, 400 g
QUINUA MILK, 50 ml
CREAM CHEESE, 10 g
MARAS SALT, TO TASTE

- Wash and peel the chirimoya, carefully removing the seeds, then remove and refrigerate the pulp for 1 hour to ensure the final cream doesn't oxidise.
- In a blender, add all the ingredients and process until you obtain a delicious and smooth cream. Season with salt to taste.
- Serve on dishware suitable for sharing.

GARDEN SALAD
CABUYA NECTAR (AGAVE AMERICANA L)

CABUYA HEART, 5 kg
WATER, 1 l
DRIED CABUYA LEAVES (FIBROUS), 5 u

- Take a 5-liter container and make 5-mm holes in its base, then place a bed of cabuya leaves inside to act as a colander. Prepare a press that fits into our container to extract the nectar.
- Preheat the oven to 180°C (360°F).
- Wash the cabuya heart, place on a baking sheet and bake in the oven for 30 minutes until its sugars caramelize.
- Remove the cabuya from the oven and slice into small pieces, then transfer to water for 3 hours.
- In our container, add the cabuya pieces and press to extract the cabuya nectar.
- Pour the extracted nectar into a saucepan and reduce over medium heat until it's syrupy. Allow to cool then refrigerate.

CABUYA VINAIGRETTE

RED ONION, 250 g
GARLIC, 10 g
CORN OIL, 100 ml
CABUYA NECTAR, 150 ml
CORN VINEGAR, 80 ml
MARAS SALT, TO TAST

- Wash and finely dice the onion and garlic. In a deep saucepan, add 20 ml of corn oil, the finely chopped onion and garlic, cook on low heat for around 20 minutes until they are well caramelized. When they reach this point, add half the cabuya syrup and all the corn vinegar, reduce until it becomes a creamy, heavy paste, then refrigerate.
- In a blender, add the refrigerated paste and emulsify by drizzling in the remaining corn oil and cabuya nectar.

CARAMELIZED ONION

RED ONION, 100 g
WATER, 150 ml
RAW CANE SUGAR, 150 g
CHIA OIL, 500 ml

- With a mandoline, slice fine feathers from the red onion, then set aside.
- Make a simple syrup by heating the water and raw cane sugar in a saucepan until the sugar dissolves completely. Cool and set aside.
- Submerge the feathered onion into the simple syrup and steep for 3 hours in a vacuum-sealed bag, otherwise steep the onions in the syrup for 45 minutes at room temperature. Strain well and dry on a paper towel.
- Fry the onions at 140°C (285°F) until they are golden and crunchy, drain and set aside on paper towels.

2.

ANDES PLATEAU

Cabuya
Lamb
Kañiwa
White quinua

FOR 4 PEOPLE

GARDEN LEAVES

RED LEAF LETTUCE, 120 g
GREEN SORREL, 80 g
RED SORREL, 80 g
BABY SPINACH, 50 g
CABUYA VINAIGRETTE, 40 ml
CHIA OIL, 10 ml
CARAMELIZED ONION, 20 g
KIWICHA LEAVES, 50 g
QUINUA LEAVES, 50 g
HUACATAY LEAVES, 20 g
HUAMANRRIPA LEAVES, 20 g
MUÑA LEAVES, 20 g
CEDRÓN (LEMON VERBENA) LEAVES, 20 g
MARAS SALT, TO TASTE

- In a large, deep bowl, mix all the ingredients, cleaned and cut to the same size, season with salt to taste, corn oil and cabuya vinaigrette.
- To serve, place the salad on the dishware, sprinkle our caramelized onion on top and garnish with elderflowers.

KAÑIWA CRACKER

COOKED KAÑIWA, 50 g
KAÑIWA FLOUR, 30 g
WHEAT FLOUR, 30 g
AVOCADO OIL, 5 ml
CORN OIL, 500 ml
MARAS SALT, TO TASTE
WATER, AS NEEDED

- Cooked kañiwa: in a saucepan, bring water to boil then add the kañiwa and stir. Cook for 15 minutes over low heat, then strain and return to the pan for 10 minutes. Allow to cool.
- Place all the measured ingredients in a bowl, season and add water until it forms a tight dough.
- On an oiled work surface – to keep our dough from sticking – roll out the dough to a 3 mm-thick sheet, cut isosceles triangles with two sides of 8 cm and a 3 cm base. Let the dough dry on the work surface for 15 minutes.
- Heat the oil to 170°C (340°F), fry our kañiwa dough triangles on both sides until they are crunchy, remove and drain on paper towels, set aside.
- To serve, use dishware decorated with seasonal leaves.

LAMB TARTARE

LAMB LOIN, 200 g
CABUYA VINAIGRETTE (SEE RECIPE), 50 ml
CITRONETTE, 10 ml
FIELD MUSTARD FLOWERS, 5 g
MARAS SALT, TO TASTE

- Cure the loin for 1 hour in Maras salt, then chop.
- Season with the salt, cabuya vinaigrette and citronette. To serve, use dishware of choice and decorate with field mustard flowers.

FINISH AND PRESENTATION

Start with the kañiwa crackers then the lamb tartare, the chirimoya cream and finally the garden salad.

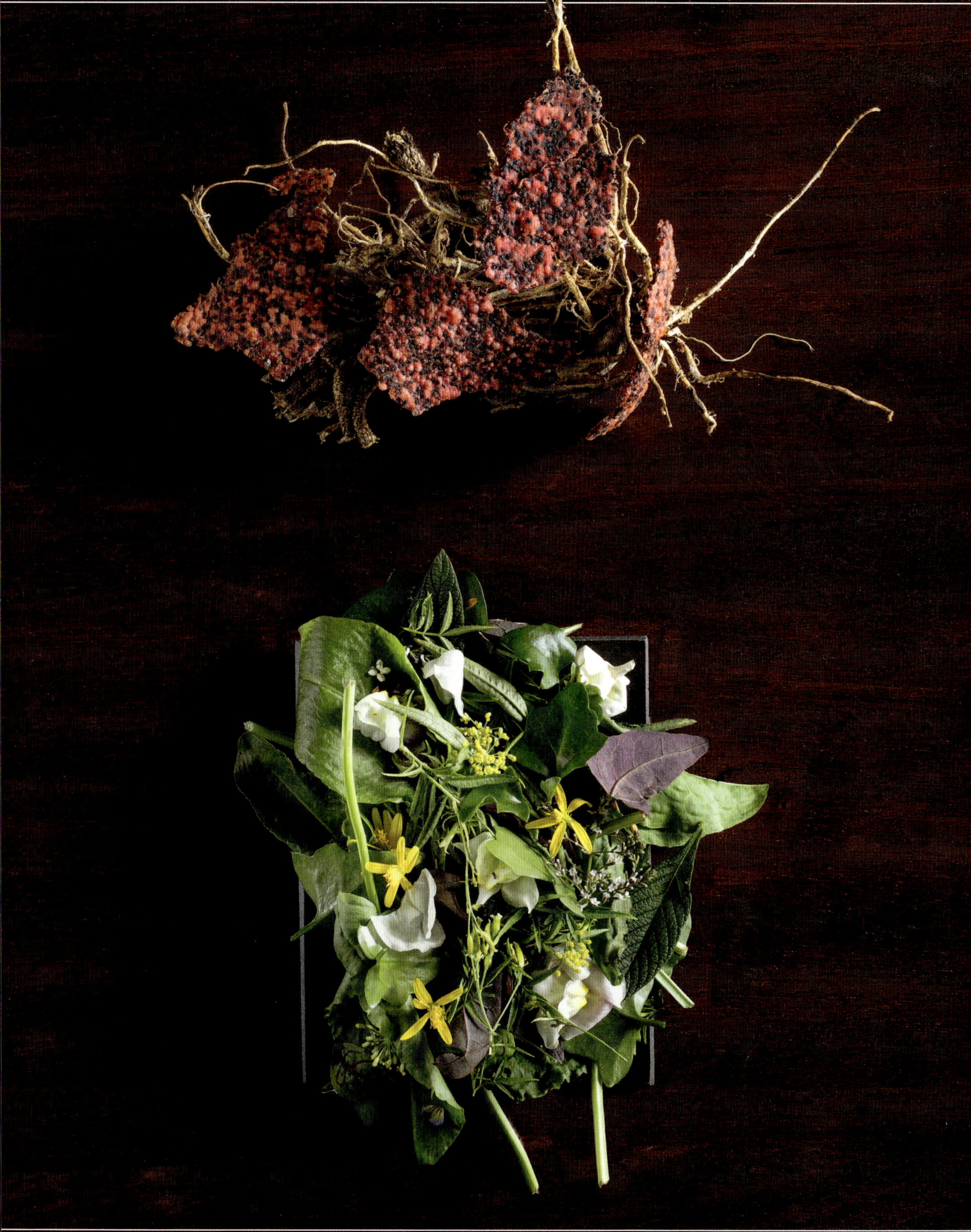

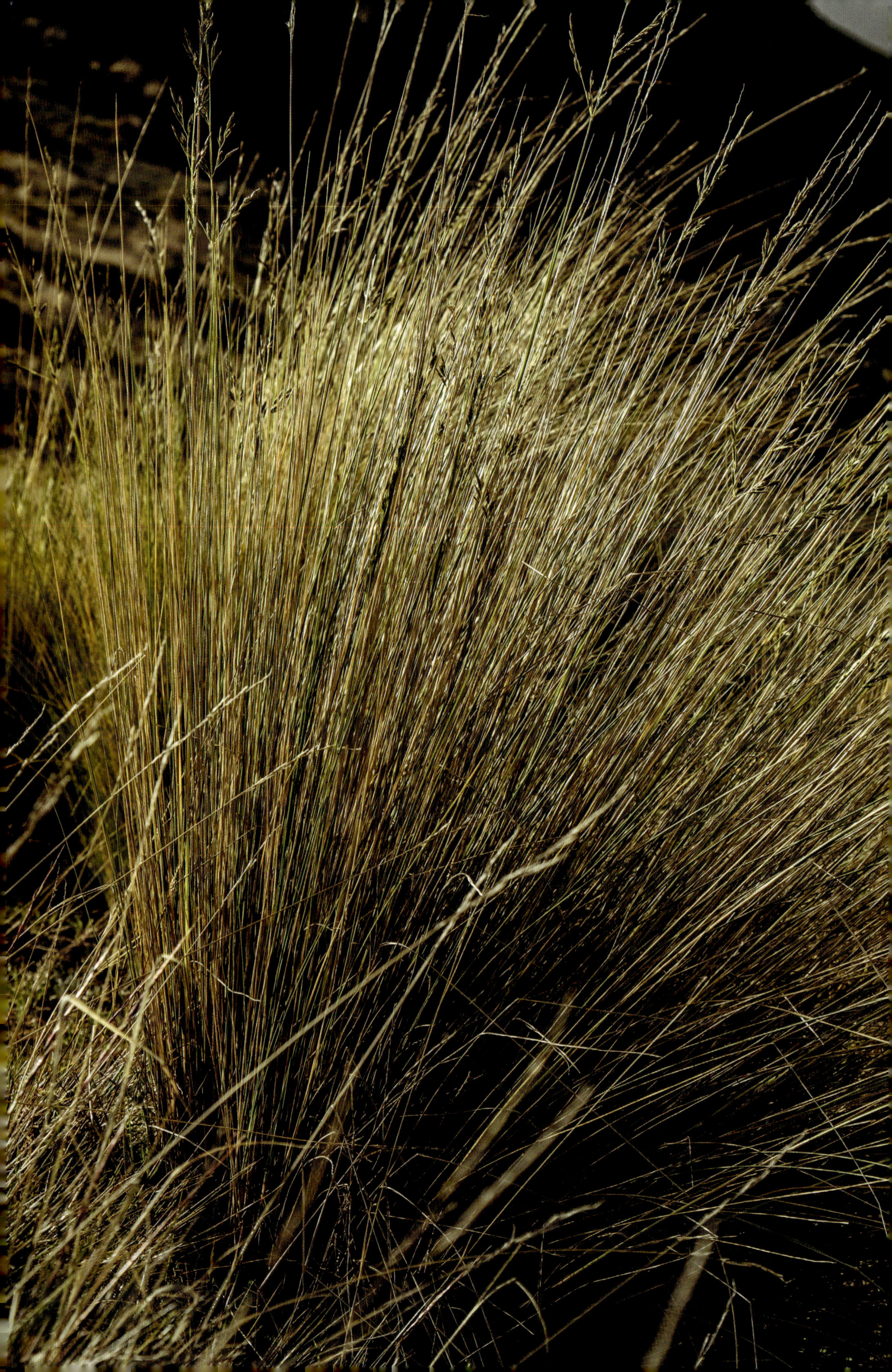

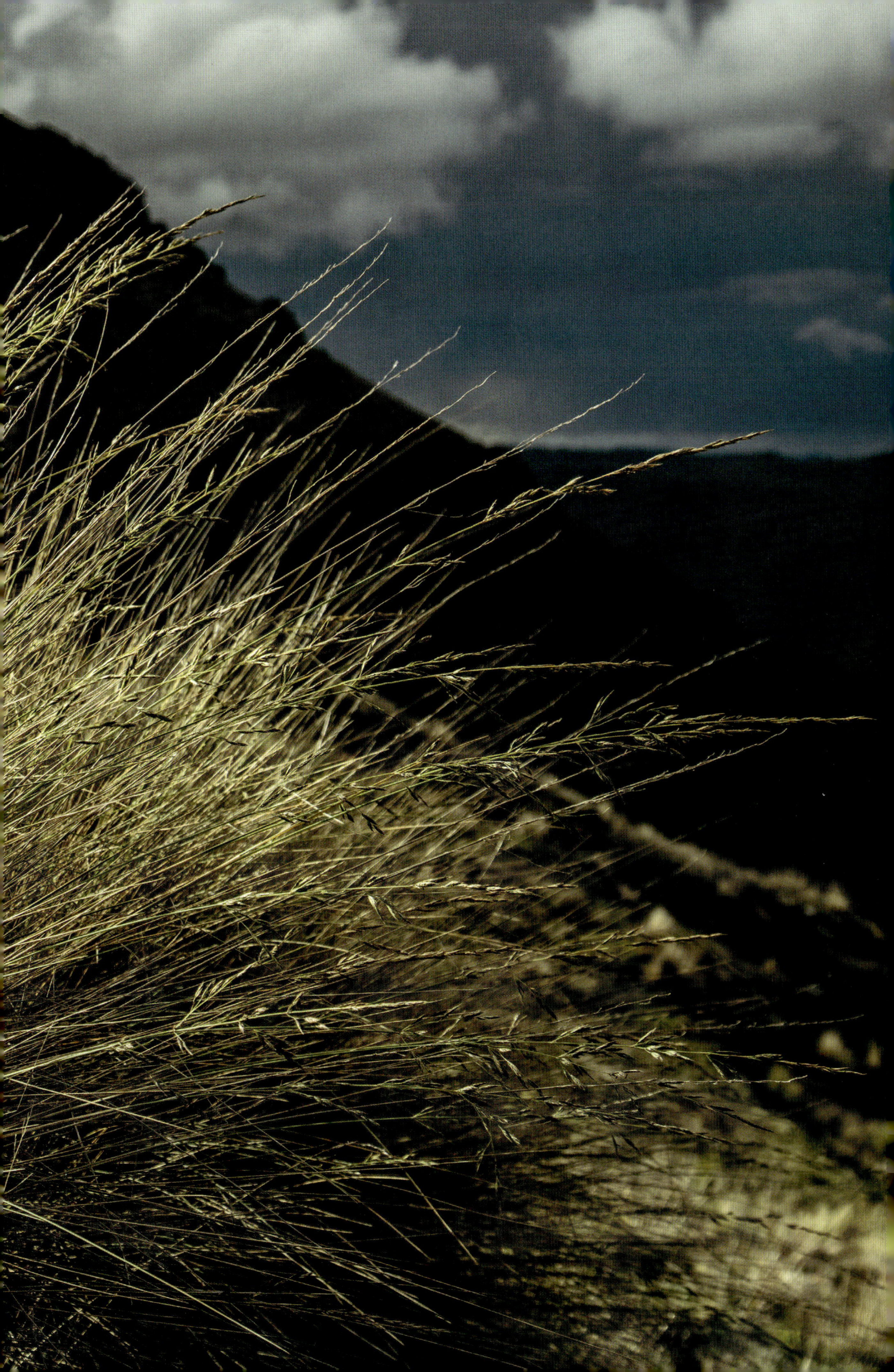

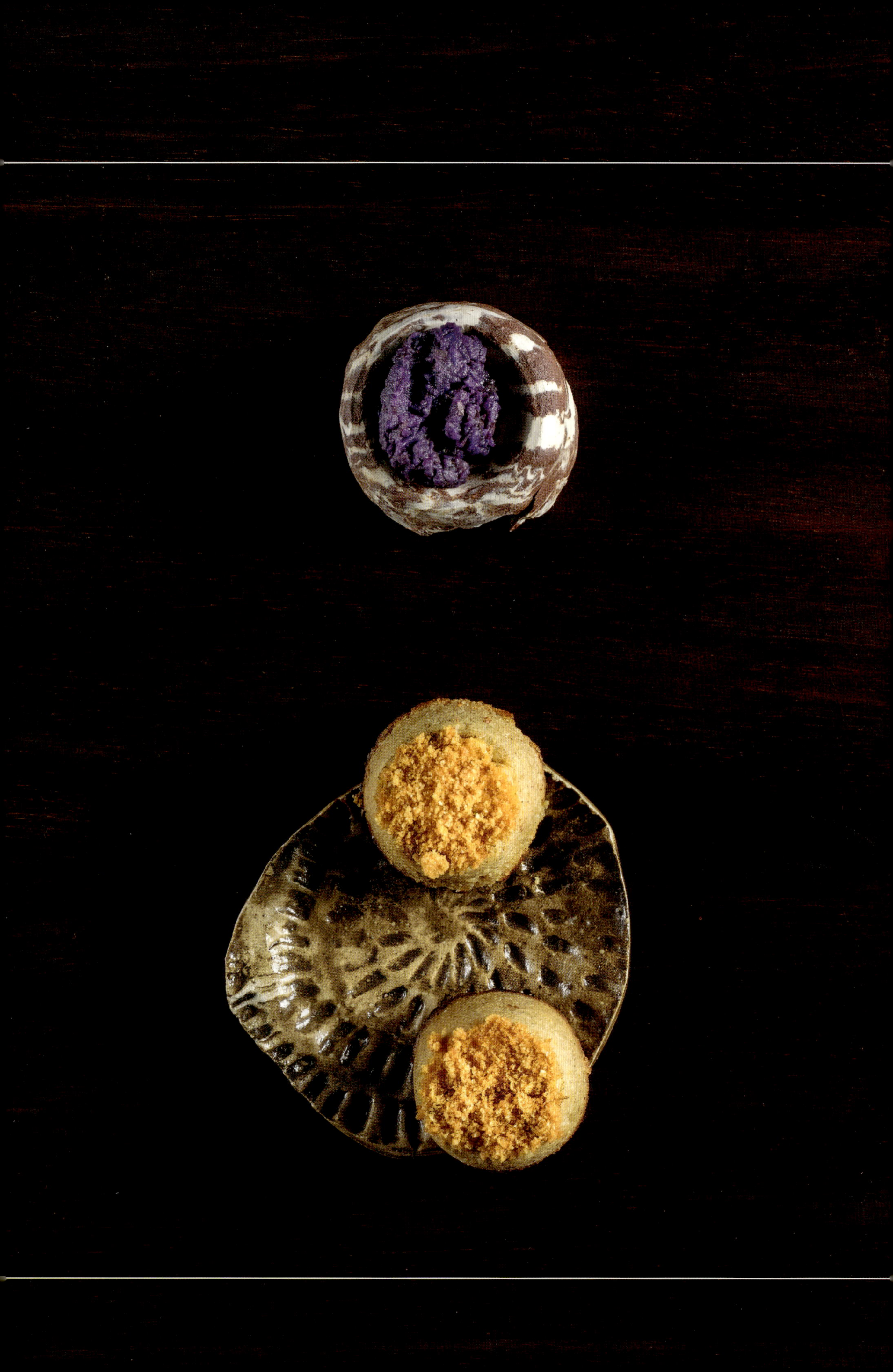

METHOD

TARWI CAKE

GROUND TARWI, 160 g
WHOLE TARWI, 44 g
QUINUA FLOUR, 44 g
FRESH MILK, 20 ml
RAW CANE SUGAR, 25 g
MARAS SALT, TO TASTE
PORK LARD FOR GREASING MOLDS, 15 g

- Preheat the combi-oven to 170°C (340°F) and place the molds in the oven to heat up. Mix all the ingredients except the whole tarwi and place the mixture into a pastry bag. Remove the molds from the oven and grease with pork lard, arrange the whole tarwi at the base and pipe the batter on top of that.
- Arrange the molds on a baking sheet and bake at 170°C (340°F) for 35 minutes, remove the cakes from their molds and return to the oven for another 15 minutes at 180°C (360°F) with 30% fast-dry setting. Set aside.

PORK BACON

PORK BACON, 680 g
RAW CANE SUGAR, 20 g
MARAS SALT, 20 g

- Clean and section the pork, removing blood, season and place in cooking bags. Steam at 79°C (175°F) for 16 hours. Remove the bacon from the bags and discard the cooking juices. Shred the meat and mix it with the collagen and the fat, place the mixture inside deep trays or baking pans overnight. Divide into four portions and set aside.

3.

ANDEAN FOREST

Tarwi
Pork
Avocado
Rocoto

FOR 4 PEOPLE

ANDEAN POTATOES IN CITRUS EXTRACT

NATIVE POTATOES, 30 g
WILD ANDEAN STRAWBERRY VINEGAR, 5 ml
AVOCADO OIL, 10 g
CHINCHO LEAVES, 25 g
HUACATAY LEAVES, 25 g
MARAS SALT, TO TASTE

- Very finely chop the potatoes, then the chincho and huacatay leaves. Place them all into a bowl, season with salt, wild Andean strawberry vinegar and corn oil. Transfer to piping bags and set aside.

LECHE DE TIGRE

YELLOW CHILI PASTE, 100 g
RED ONION, 20 g
CELERY, 10 g
GARLIC, 2 g
GINGER, 2 g
CHINCHO LEAVES, 10 g
LEMON JUICE, 50 ml
MARAS SALT, TO TASTE

- Measure out all the ingredients into the food processor workbowl and pulse to extract aromas, strain and season if necessary. Set aside.

TARWI SALAD

WHOLE TARWI, 160 g
RED ONION, 5 g
RED, GREEN AND YELLOW ROCOTO CHILIS, 20 g
LECHE DE TIGRE, 60 ml
AVOCADO, 80 g
MARAS SALT, TO TASTE

- To serve, place a little of the avocado cream and on top of that the tarwi that's already seasoned with salt and leche de tigre, then place on top the mixture of red onion and red, green and yellow rocoto, all diced into very small and fine cubes, season with leche de tigre and salt, then distribute evenly. Finish with a good layer of leche de tigre that covers the whole surface of the preparation.

FINISH AND PRESENTATION

- Sear bacon on a griddle by pressing down and portion into 80 gr trimmed rectangles. Cover the bacon with the Andean potatoes with citrus extract and serve. Dress the tarwi salad in a bowl with leche de tigre. Additionally, heat the tarwi cake and serve one per person.

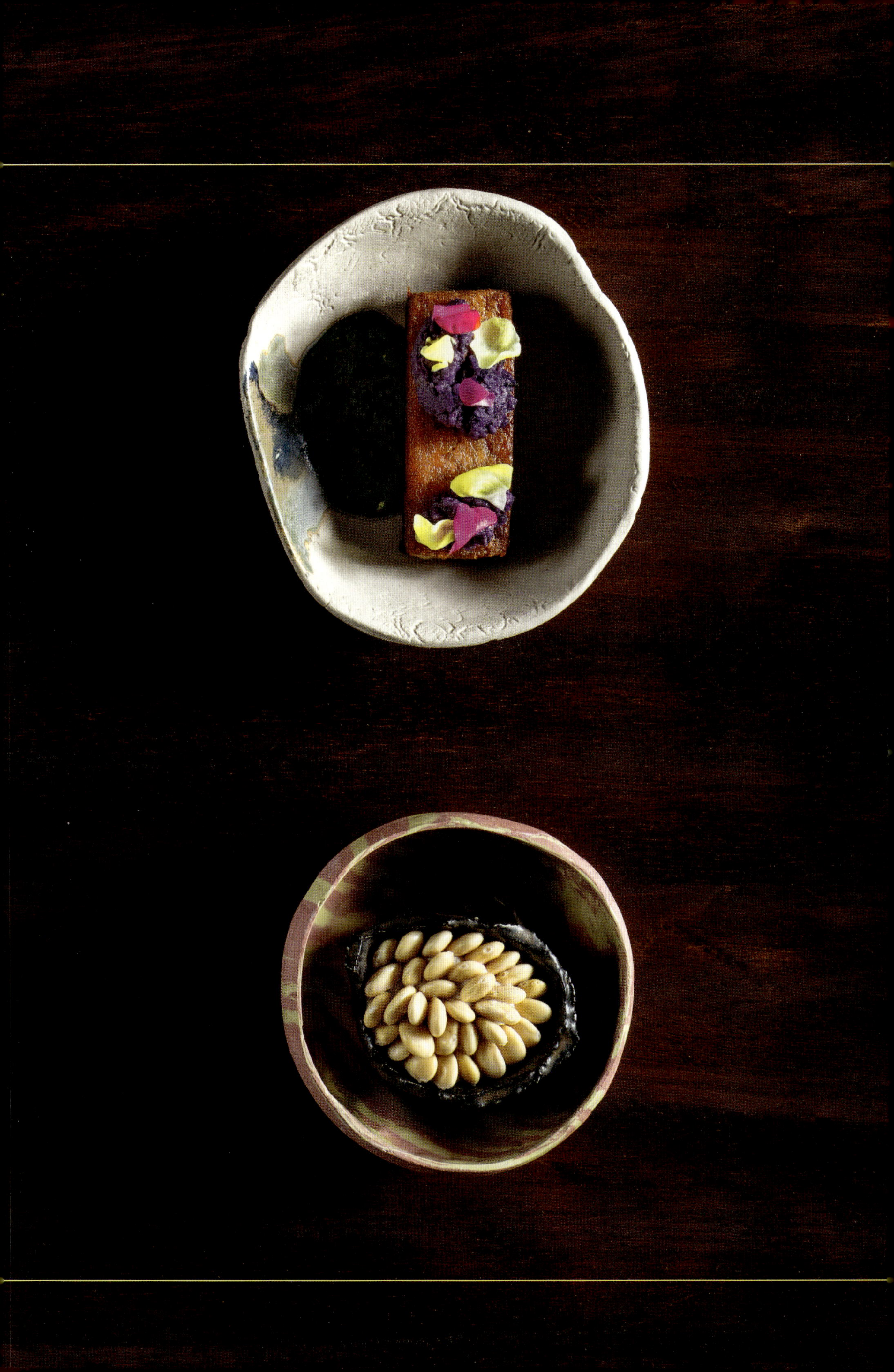

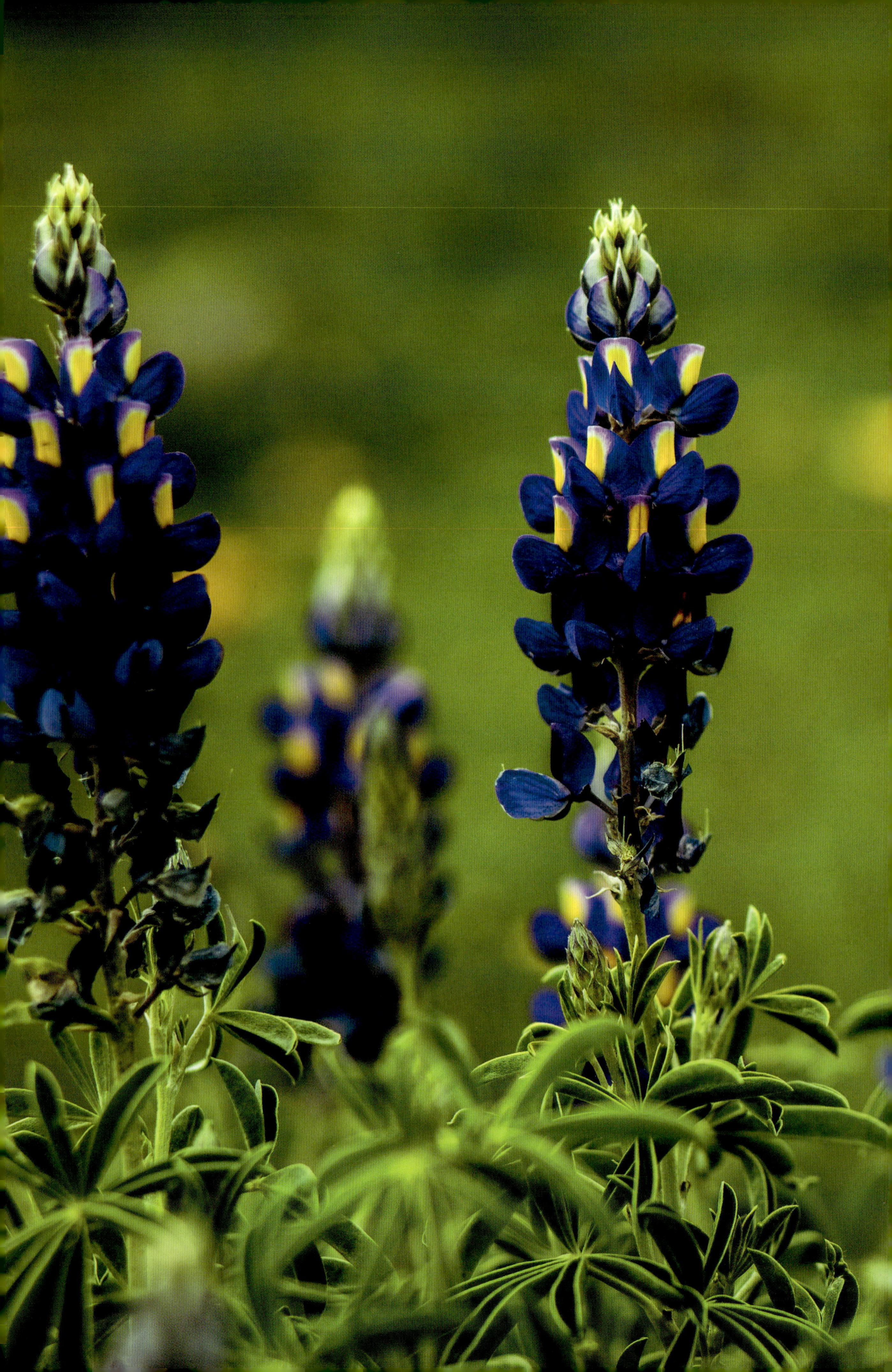

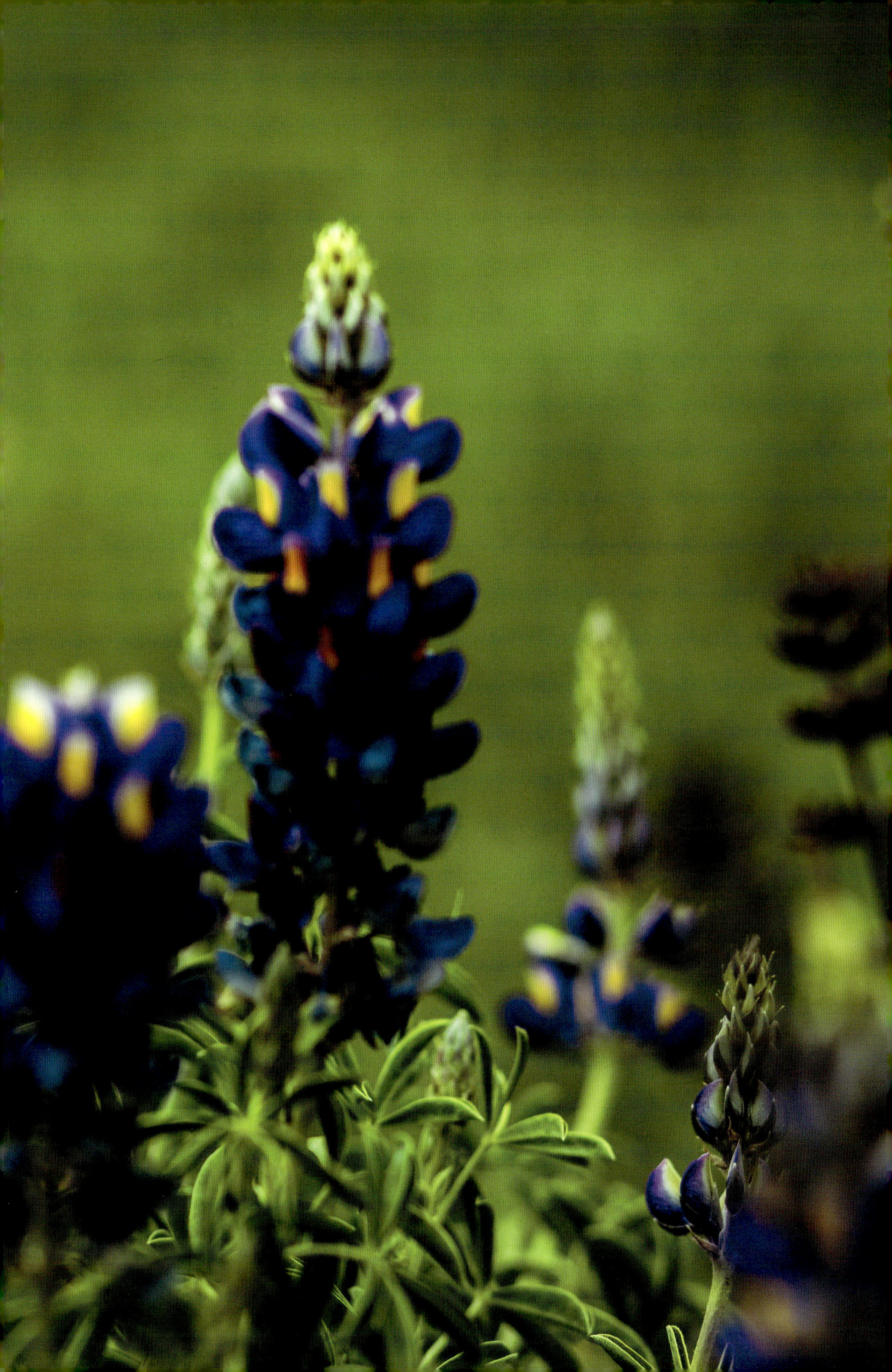

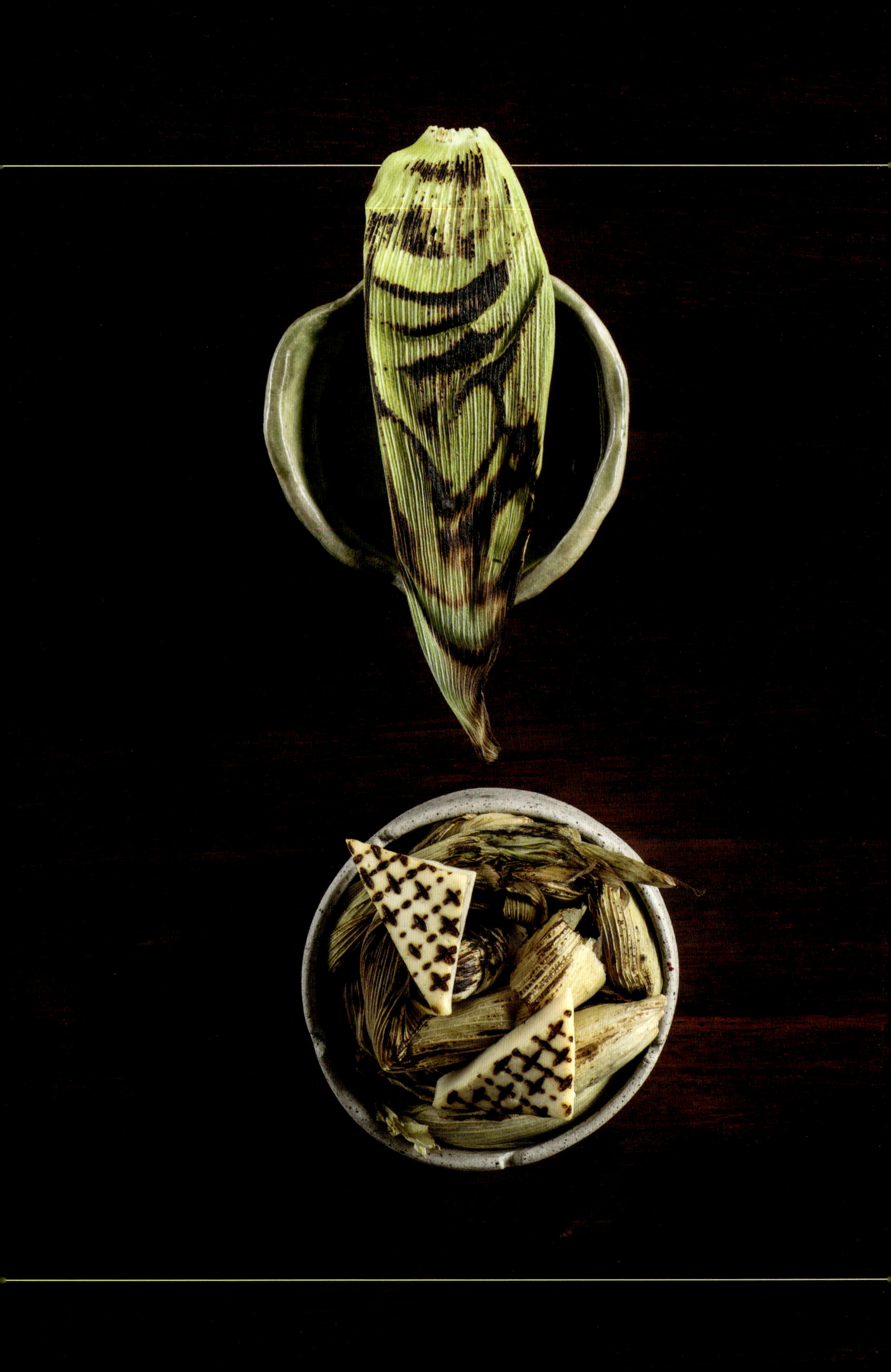

METHOD

CREAMED CORN

PARAQAY CORN PURÉE, 280 g
RAW CANE SUGAR, 15 g
KAÑIWA LEAVES, 25 g
CHIJCHIPA LEAVES, 25 g
MARAS SALT, TO TASTE

- Blanch the kañiwa and chijchipa leaves in boiling water for 1 minute, then immerse in ice water to cool quickly. Mix with a food processor and reserve.
- Place all the ingredients in a processor to make a smooth and uniform cream, set aside.

PISCORONTO CORN CRACKER (VIOLET)

PISCORONTO CORN PURÉE, 100 g
MORAYA STARCH, 90 g
TAPIOCA STARCH, 20 g
WATER, 400 ml
HONEY, 20 g
LINSEED OIL FOR FRYING, 0,5 l
MARAS SALT, TO TASTE

- Measure out all the ingredients and add to a heavy-bottomed saucepan. Simmer for around 35 minutes, stirring continually.
- Roll out the dough onto silpats or silicone mats, then place in a dehydrator for 6 hours at 63°C (145°F). Remove from the dehydrator and hydrate by sprinkling water across the rolled-out sheet, then refrigerate for 12 hours.
- Heat linseed oil to 200°C (390°F), cut the sheets into small slices and fry. Remove and drain on paper towels. Season to taste.

CHULLPI CORN CRACKER (YELLOW)

CHULLPI CORN PURÉE, 100 g
MORAYA STARCH, 90 g
TAPIOCA STARCH, 20 g
WATER, 400 ml
HONEY, 20 g
LINSEED OIL FOR FRYING, 0,5 l
MARAS SALT, TO TASTE

- Measure out all the ingredients and add to a heavy-bottomed saucepan. Simmer for around 35 minutes, stirring continually.
- Roll out the dough onto silpats or silicone mats, then place in a dehydrator for 6 hours at 63°C (145°F). Remove from the dehydrator and hydrate by sprinkling water across the rolled-out sheet, then refrigerate for 12 hours.
- Heat linseed oil to 200°C (390°F), cut the sheets into small slices and fry. Remove and drain on paper towels. Season to taste.

4.

DIVERSITY OF CORN

Piscoronto corn
Kculli and white corn
Kañiwa

FOR 4 PEOPLE

KCULLI CORN CRACKER (RED)

KCULLI CORN PURÉ, 100 g
MORAYA STARCH, 90 g
TAPIOCA STARCH, 20 g
WATER, 400 ml
HONEY, 20 g
LINSEED OIL FOR FRYING, 0,5 l
MARAS SALT, TO TASTE

- Measure out all the ingredients and add to a heavy-bottomed saucepan. Simmer for around 35 minutes, stirring continually.
- Roll out the dough onto silpats or silicone mats, then place in a dehydrator for 6 hours at 63°C (145°F). Remove from the dehydrator and hydrate by sprinkling water across the rolled-out sheet, then refrigerate for 12 hours.
- Heat linseed oil to 200°C (390°F), cut the sheets into small slices and fry. Remove and drain on paper towels. Season to taste.

FINISH AND PRESENTATION

- Arrange three differently colored crackers, one atop the other. Add the creamed corn to a bowl. Serve together.

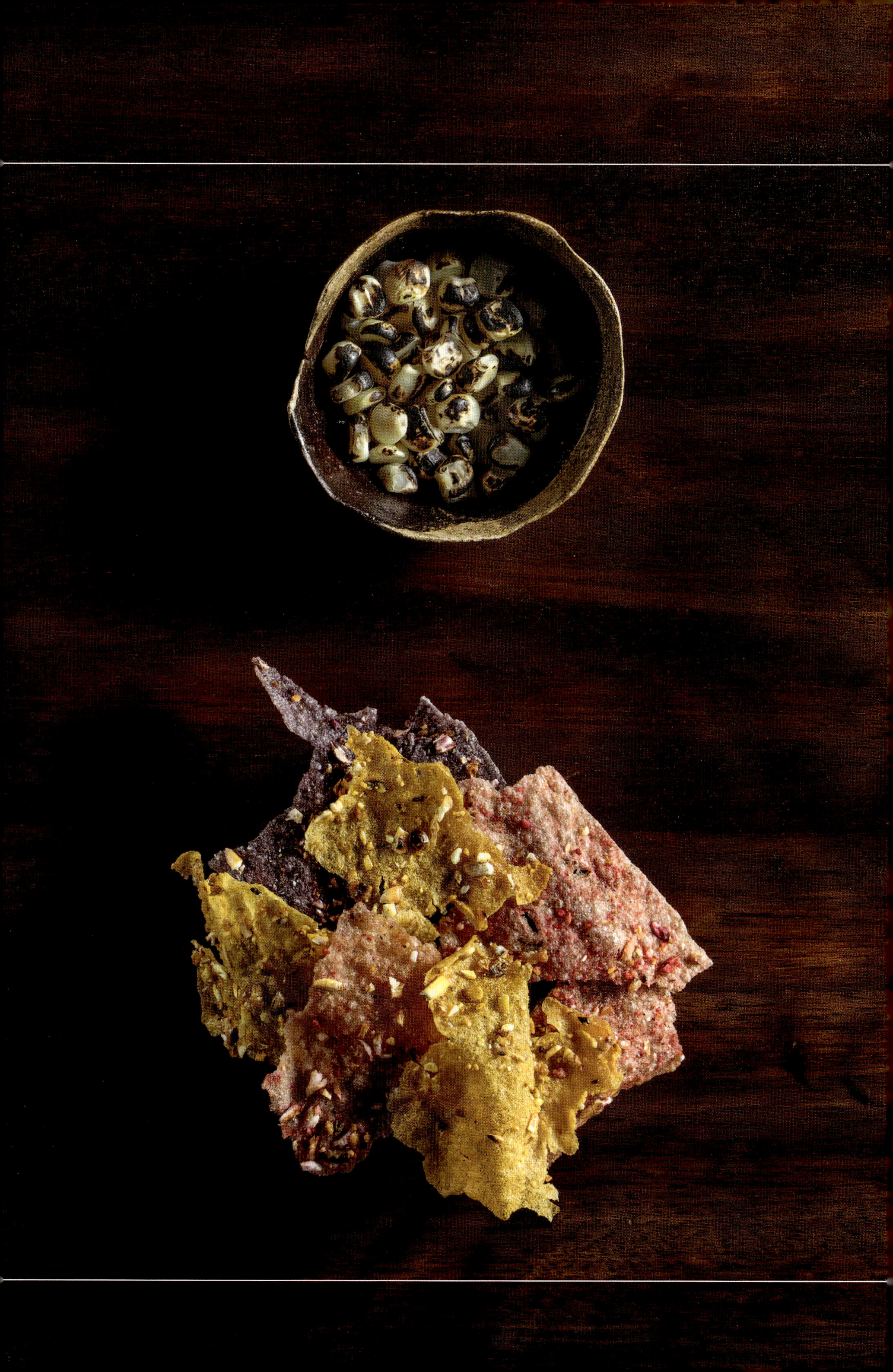

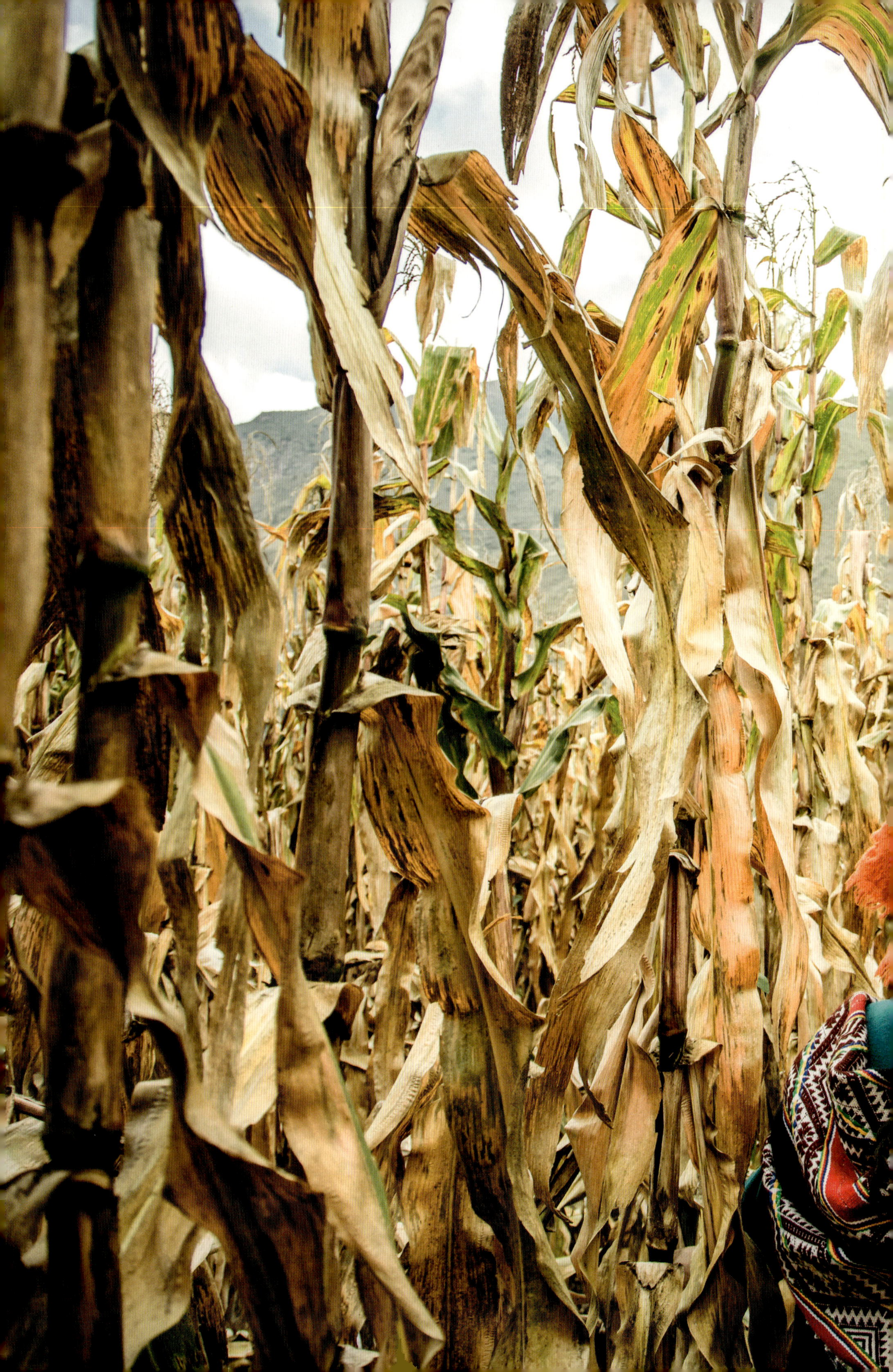

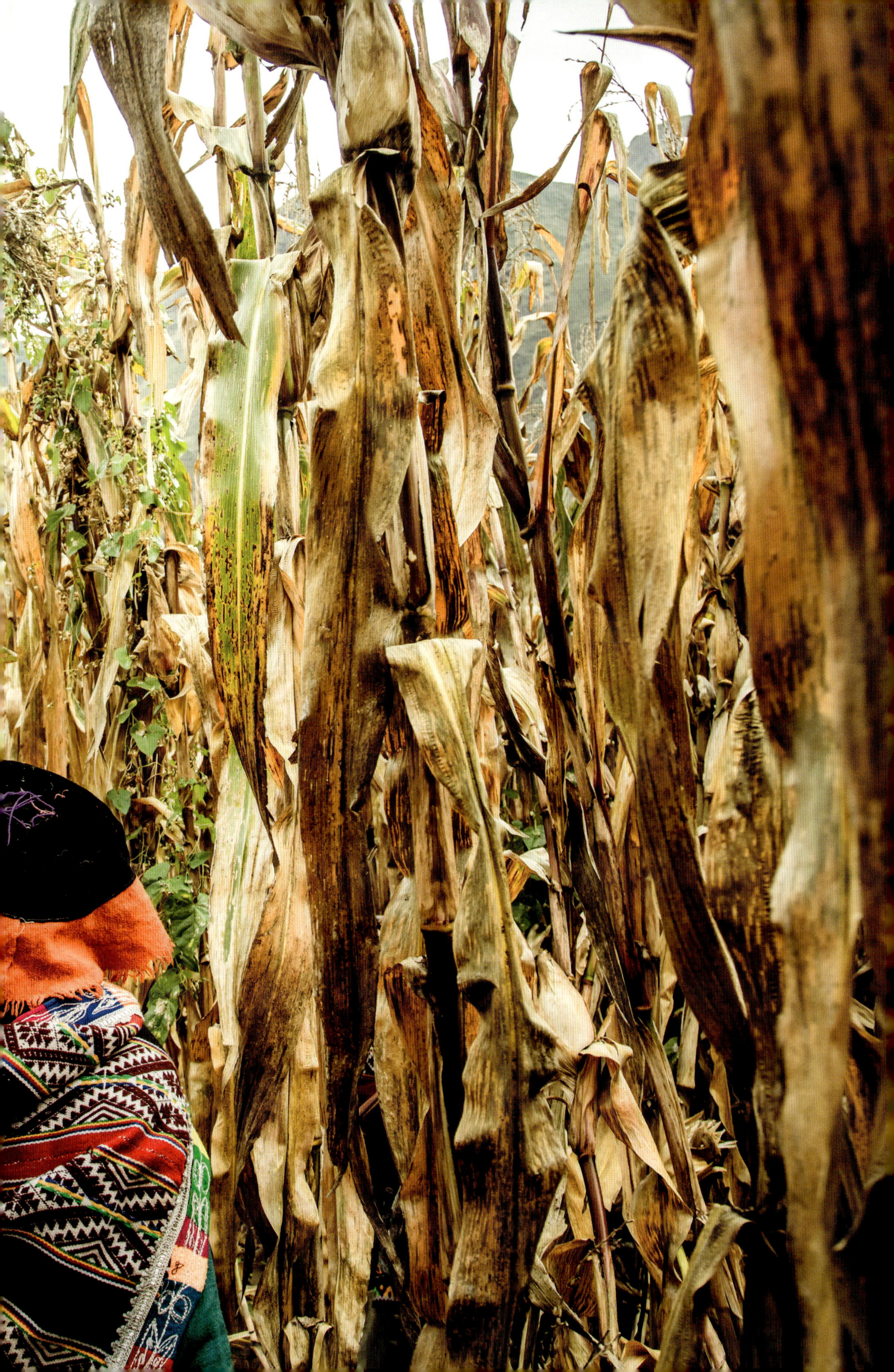

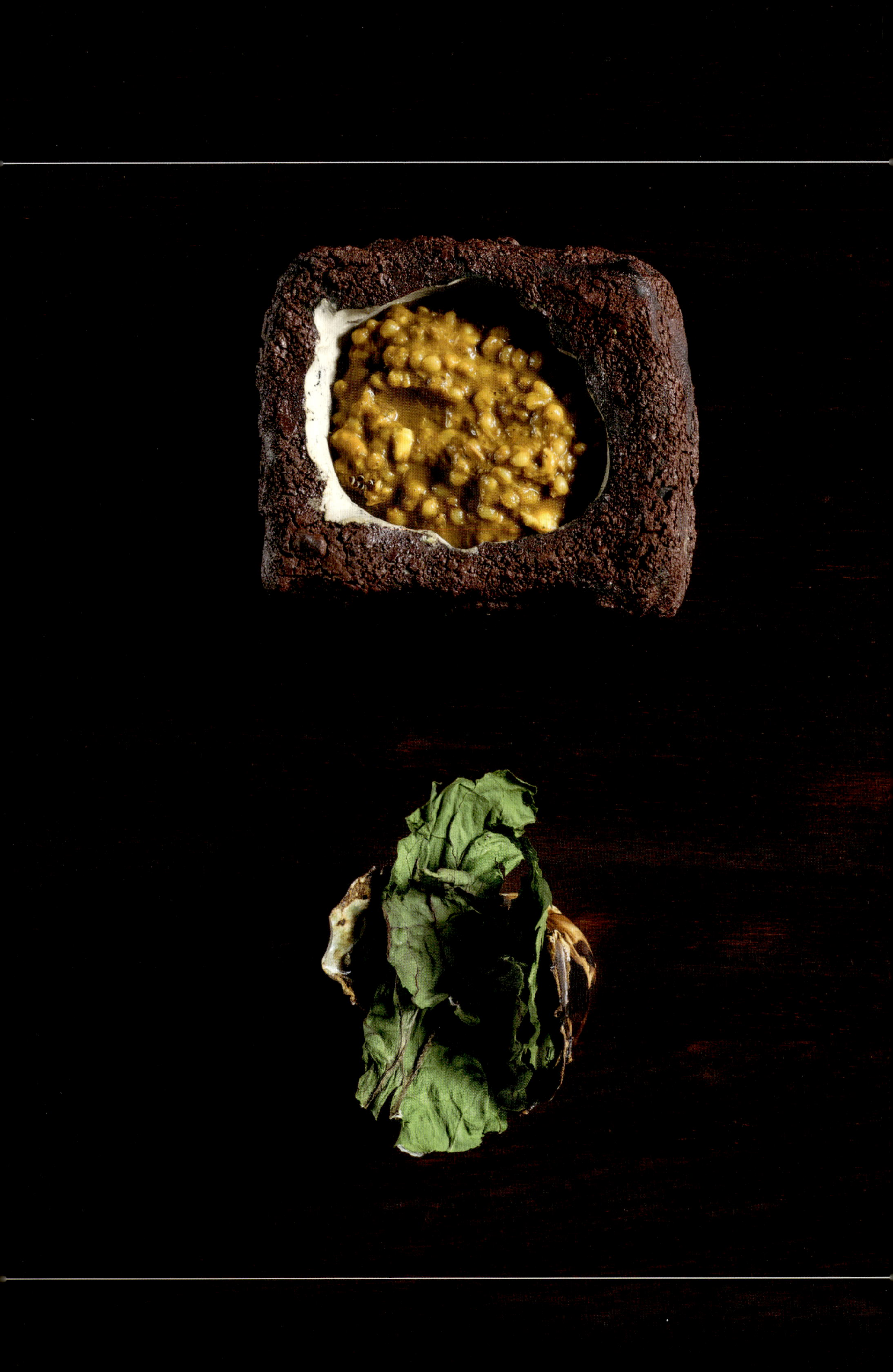

METHOD

DUCK STEW

SMALL WHOLE DUCK, 750 g
RED ONION, 250 g
SACHATOMATE, 200 g
CELERY, 50 g
LEEK, 50 g
YELLOW CHILI PASTE, 100 g
GARLIC, 5 g
CHINCHO LEAVES, 10 g
HUACATAY LEAVES, 10 g
CHICHA DE JORA CORN BEER, 150 ml
WHEAT BRAN, 150 g
ANDEAN CHEESE, 20 g
DUCK FAT, 10 g
MARAS SALT, TO TASTE

- Clean the duck, separating the carcass, legs and magret. Set aside the magret for serving. Slice the vegetables thinly and oven roast with the carcass at 250°C (480°F) until they caramelize. Sear the legs and wings in a large, heavy stock pot, then remove from the pan and reserve.
- Transfer the roasted vegetables to the stock pot along with the chicha de jora and reduce until the alcohol has evaporated. Add the yellow chili paste and simmer for 20 more minutes, then return the seared duck pieces to the pot along with the roasted carcass, cover with water and add the chincho and huacatay leaves. Cook for 16 hours.
- Allow to cool then carefully remove the pieces of duck; wings and legs. Pick off and reserve the meat in a vacuum bag, discarding the bones, cartilage and skin. Process in a processor the rest of the sauce with the vegetables, sieve through a very fine colander and set aside.

5.

EXTREME ALTITUDE

Duck
Black quinua
Cushuro
Chincho leaves

FOR 4 PEOPLE

TART SACHATOMATE (TAMARILLO) SAUCE

BASE DRESSING, 150 g
SACHATOMATE PURÉE, 100 g
YELLOW CHILI PASTE, 20 g
WHITE VINEGAR, 30 ml
VEGETABLE STOCK, 300 mL
RAW CANE SUGAR, 20 g
MARAS SALT, TO TASTE

- Add the base dressing, white vinegar and vegetable stock to a saucepan, reduce until it thickens to a paste, then use a food processor or blender to mix until it's a smooth, heavy cream. In a processor, add the base dressing, the sachatomate purée and sugar, and yellow chili paste, process until it becomes a smooth and dense yellow sauce. Set aside.

SALAD FOR DUCK

RED QUINUA, 160 g
BLACK QUINUA, 80 g
FIELD MUSTARD LEAVES, 40 g
MASHWA LEAVES, 30 g
CUSHURO 40 g
AYRAMPO CRUMBLE, 10 g

- Separately cook the two types of quinua in boiling water for 30 minutes, drain, cool and set aside.
- Remove and discard stems from the leaves, wash well and dry thoroughly then fry them in plenty of oil.

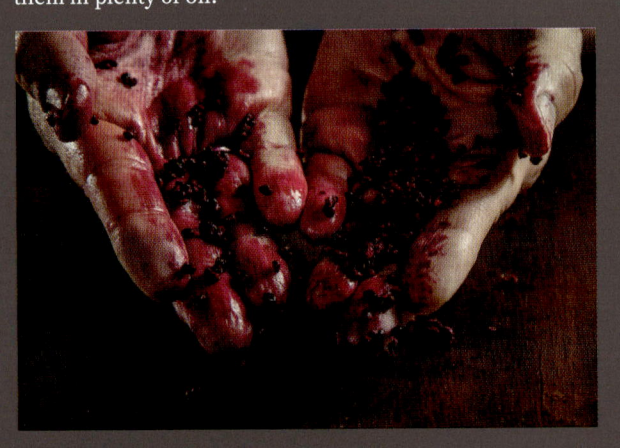

FINISH AND PRESENTATION

- Serve a portion of duck stew in a deep dish and garnish with seasonal flower petals. Sprinkle the cushuro and ayrampo crumble over the salad, then dress with the tart sachatomate sauce and serve as the side dish.

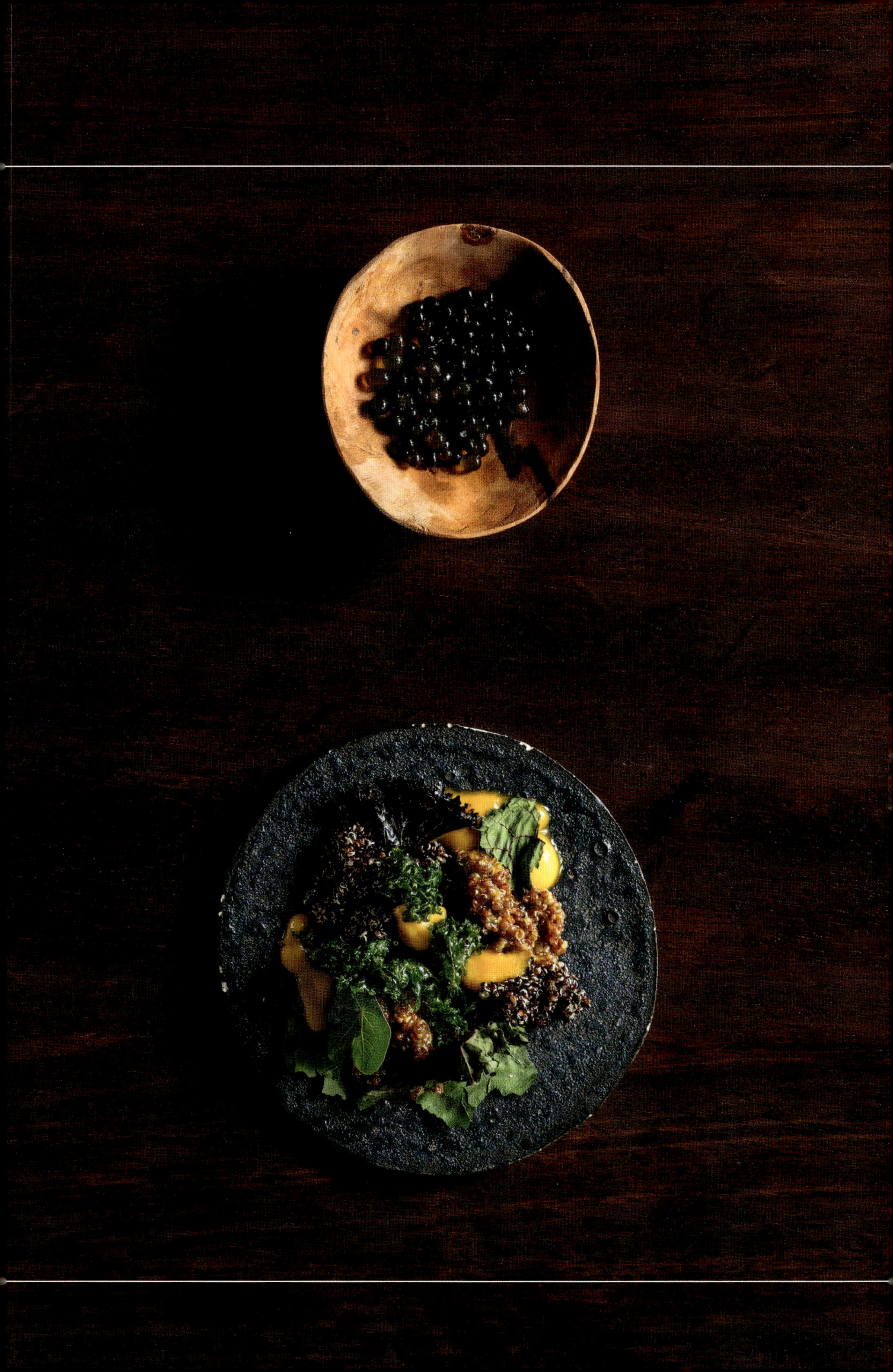

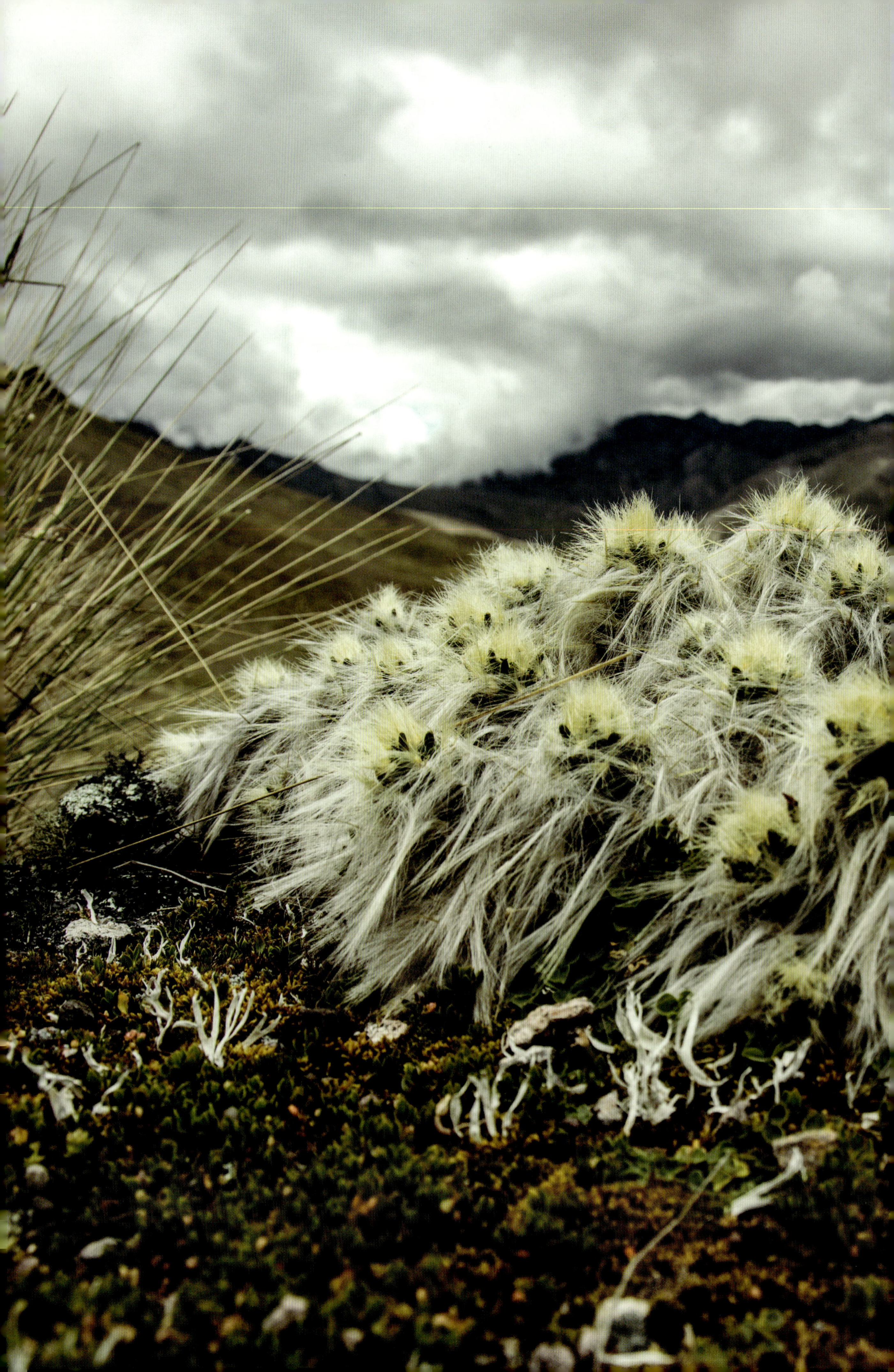

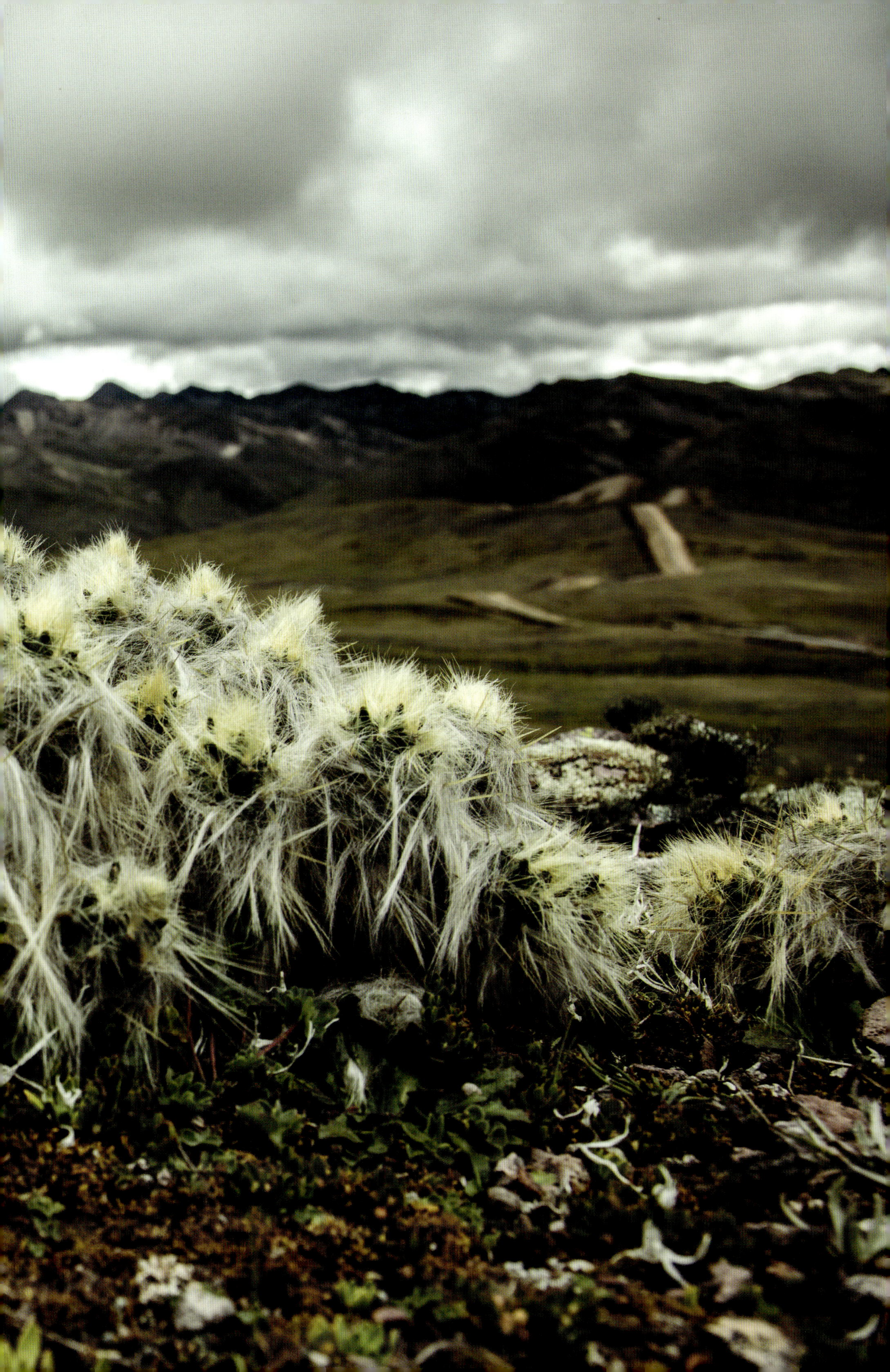

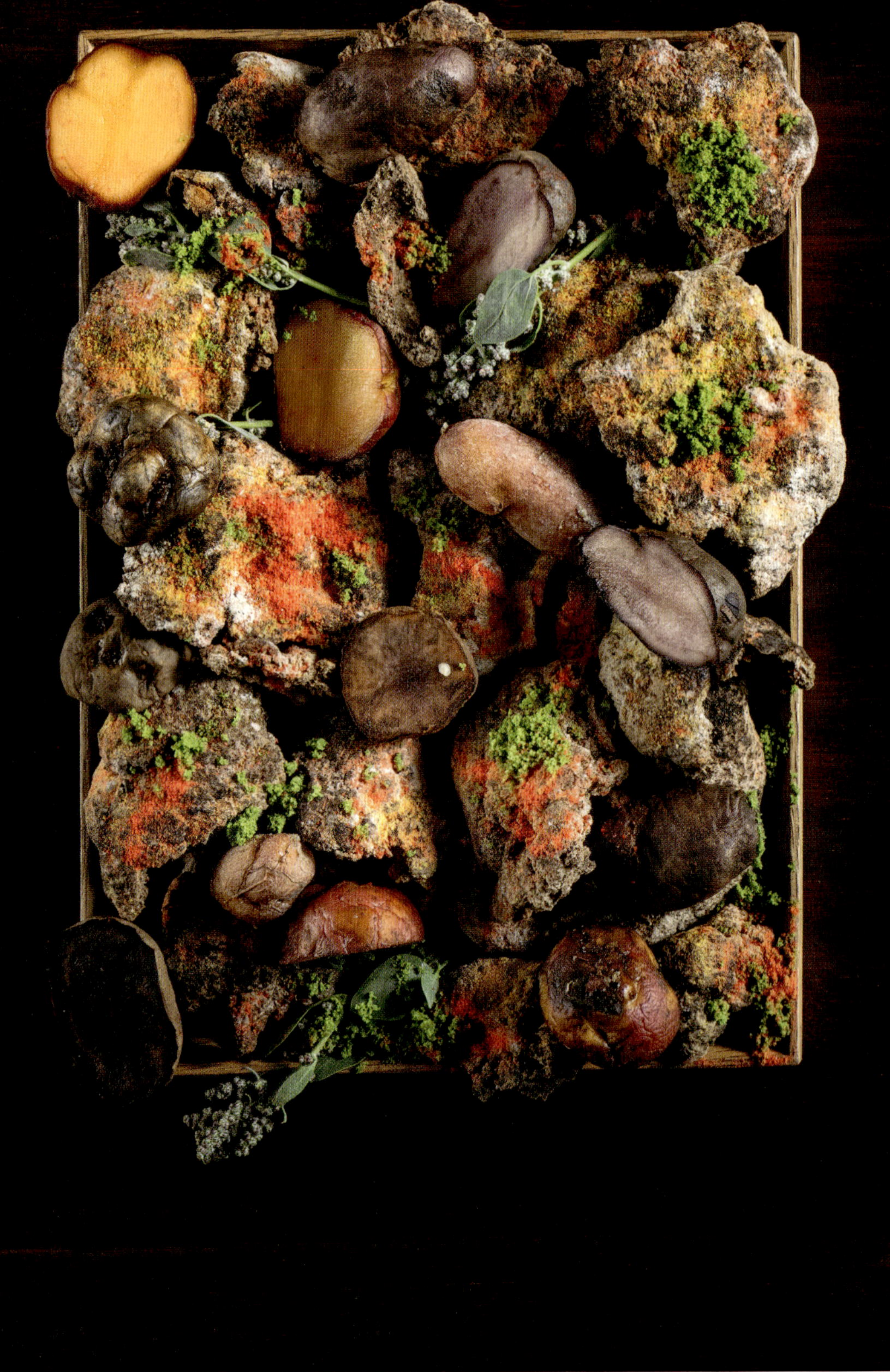

METHOD

CHACO CLAY, MARAS SALT, COCA LEAVES

MARAS SALT, 160 g
COCA LEAF FLOUR, 10 g
CHACO CLAY, 50 g
EGG WHITE, 50 ml
WATER, 45 ml
OCAS, 3
MASHWAS, 4
NATIVE POTATOES, 5

- Preheat the oven to 180°C (355°F). In a bowl mix the salt, the clay, coca leaf flour, egg whites and water.
- Evenly spread a 2.5 cm layer of the clay dough into an ovenproof bowl. Place the ocas, mashwas and native potatoes on top and cover them with the rest of the dough. Bake for 40 minutes.
- Remove from the oven and carefully lift up the baked clay top with a kitchen knife. Serve the tubers.

6.

CENTRAL ANDES

Native potatoes
Chaco clay
Chincho leaves

FOR 4 PEOPLE

ANDEAN CHILI BASE

ROCOTO CHILI, 70 g
YELLOW CHILI, 30 g
RED ONION, 50 g
GARLIC, 10 g
AVOCADO OIL, 15 ml
MARAS SALT, to taste
ANDEAN POTATOES, 200 g

- Clean the rocoto and yellow chilis, removing properly seeds and ribs. Finely dice all the vegetables and sauté them in a heavy-bottomed saucepan until well caramelized. Set aside.

GREEN UCHUCUTA

CHILI BASE, 120 g
HUACATAY LEAVES, 30 g
CHINCHO LEAVES, 20 g
CHULLPI CORN, 10 g
MARAS SALT, TO TASTE
PARIA CHEESE, 10 g

- Sautée the chincho and huacatay in a pan, transfer to a processor with the chili base, chullpi kernels, water and paria cheese. Process until dense and creamy, season with salt and set aside.

FINISH AND PRESENTATION

- Remove the clay from the oven and carefully cut the top off to reveal the potatoes, then replace the top to keep the potatoes hot until ready to serve. Serve the potatoes with green uchucuta sauce on the side.

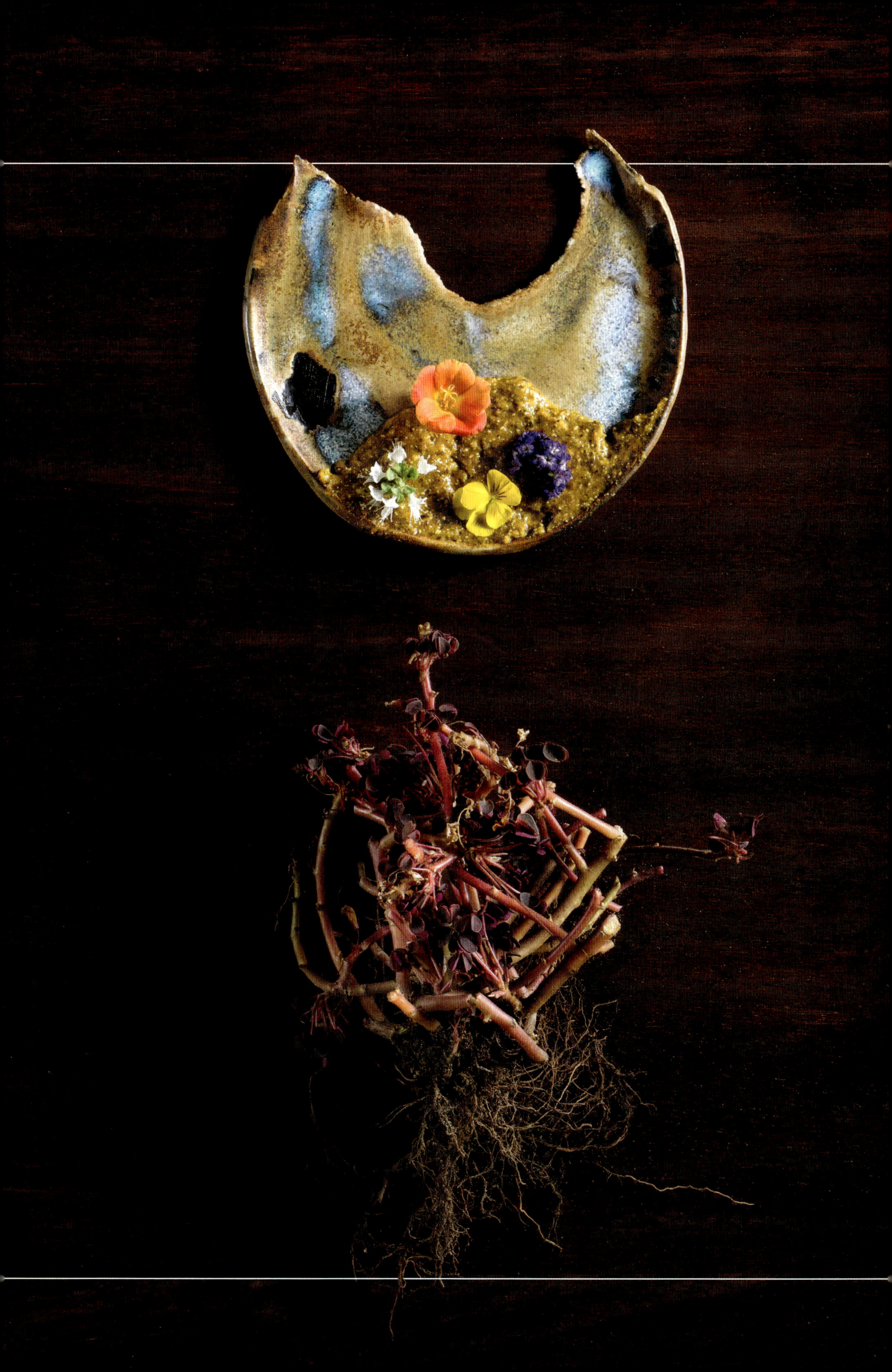

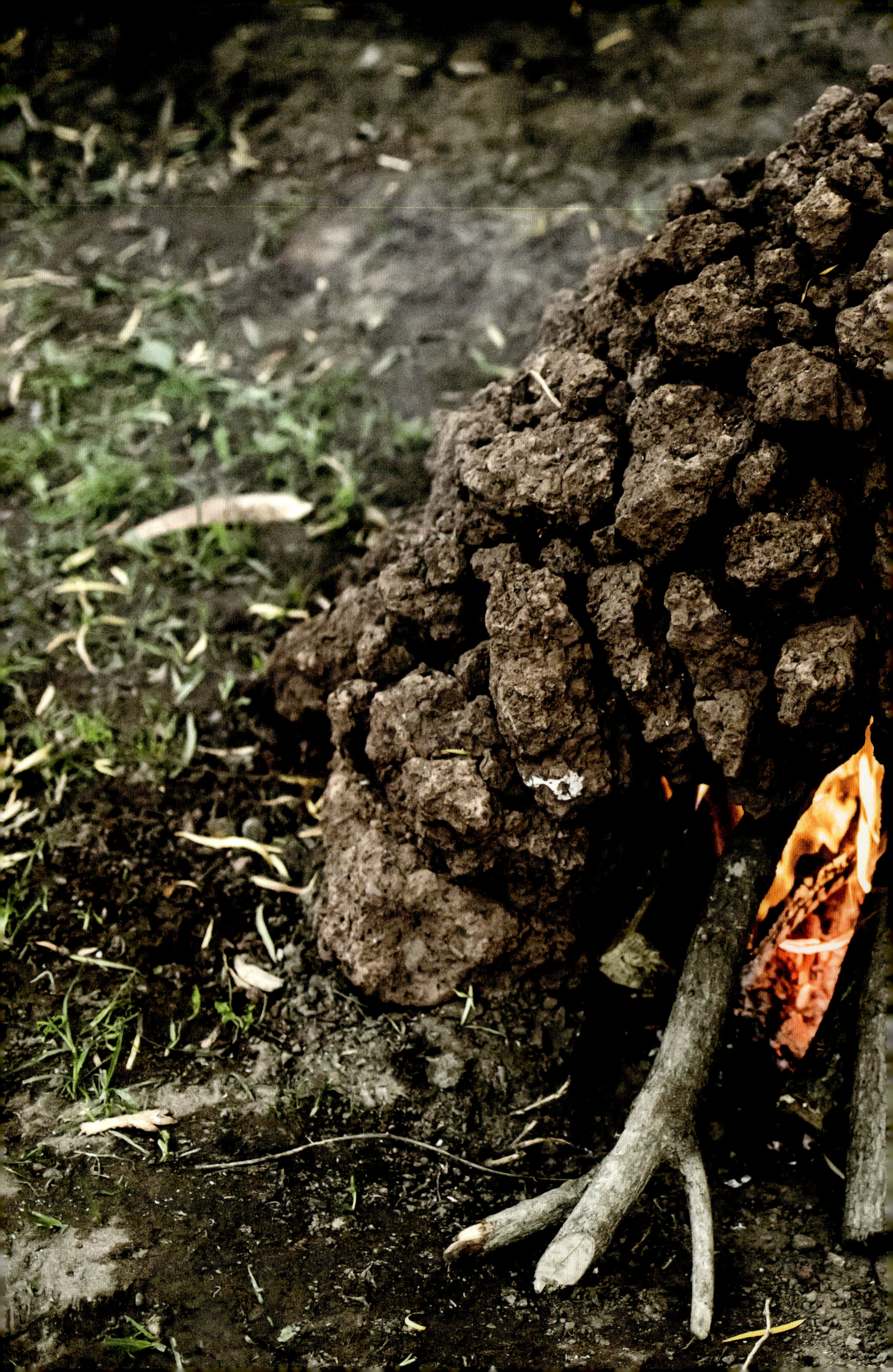

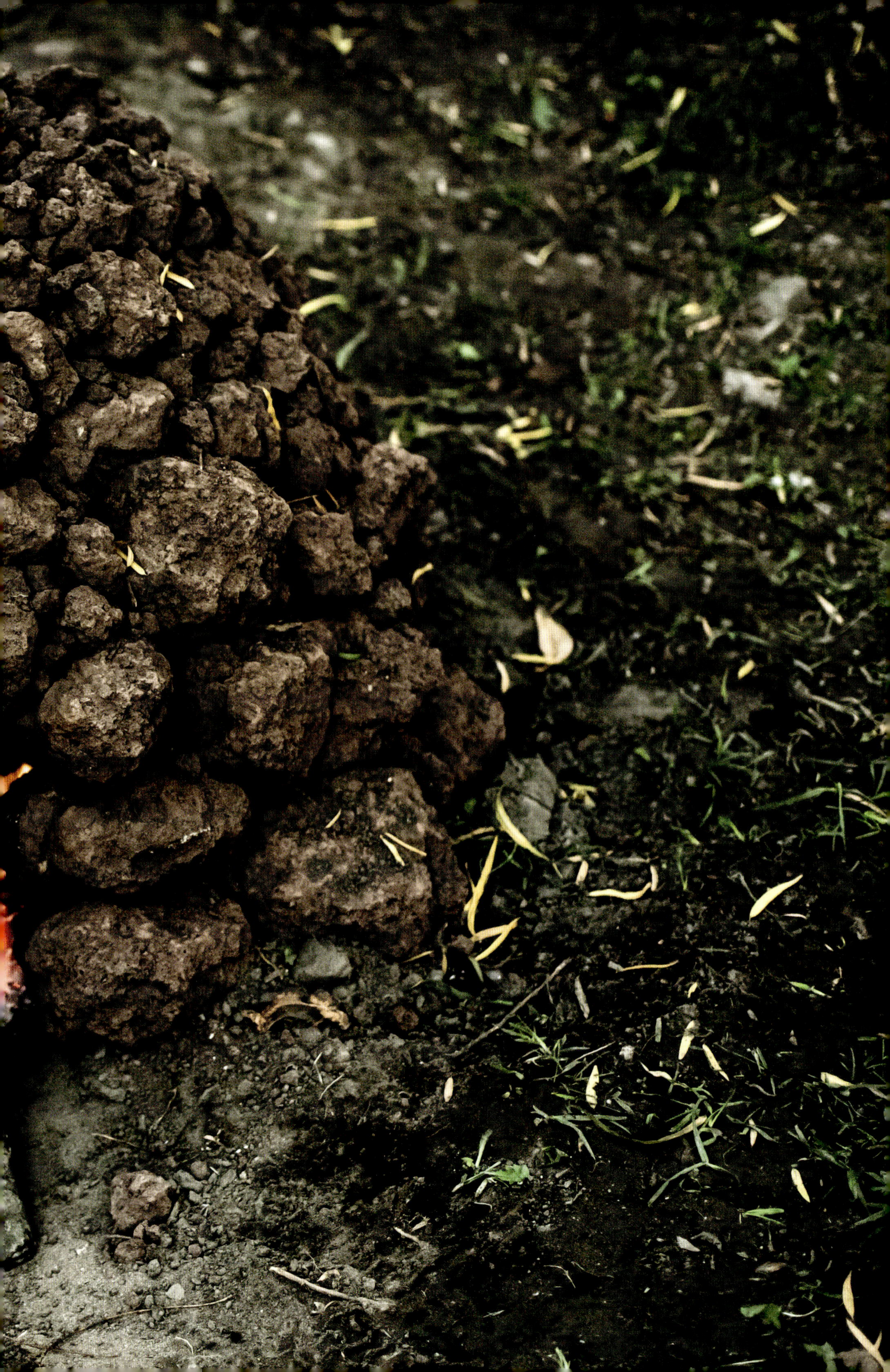

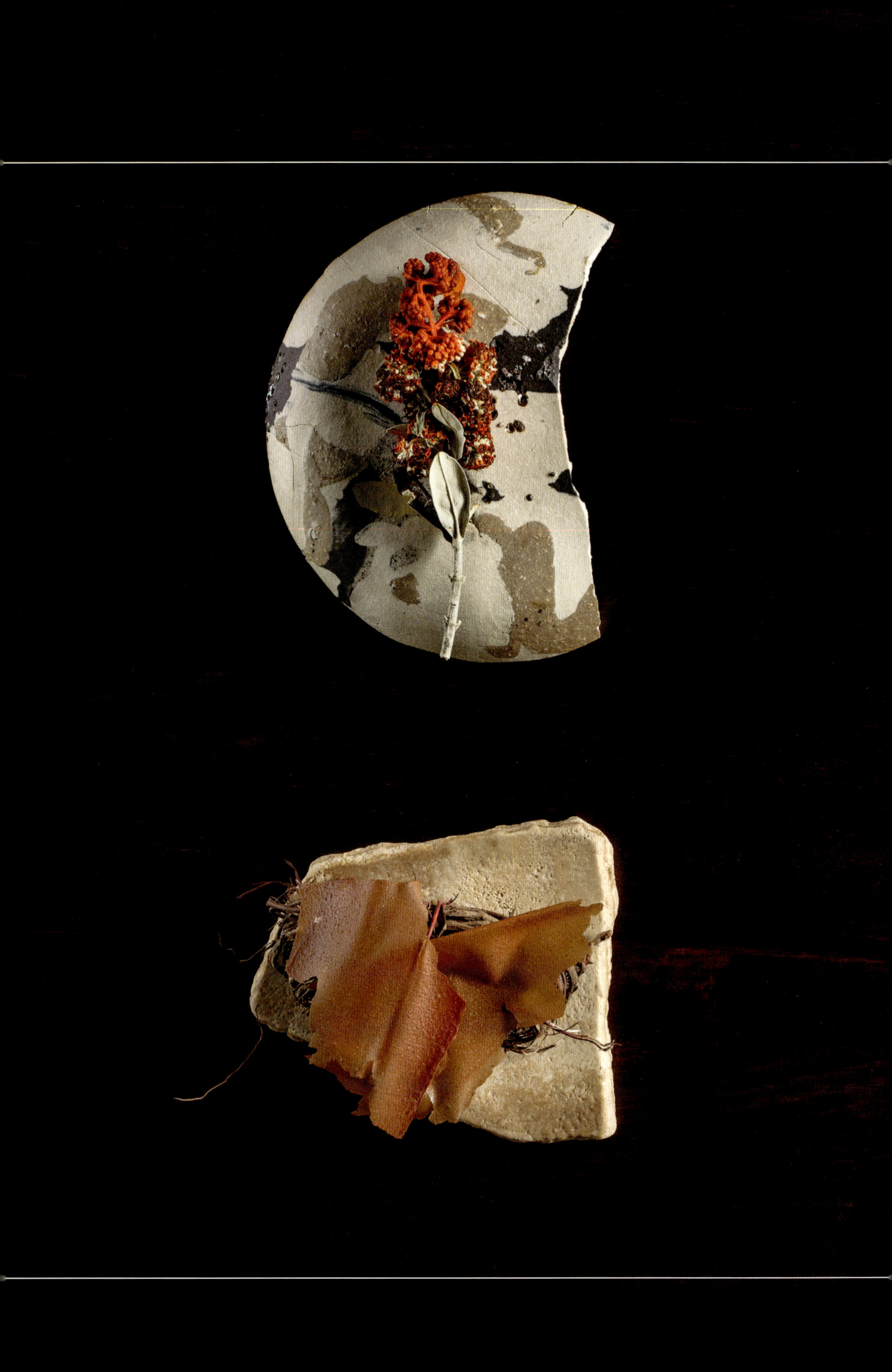

METHOD

KJOLLE CREAM

KJOLLE FLOWERS, 10 g
MORAYA STARCH, 40 g
CREAM, 20 ml
WHOLE MILK, 100 ml
RAW CANE SUGAR, 30 g

- In a saucepan on a low heat, infuse the cream and the whole milk with the kjolle flowers to extract their color, strain and return the liquid to the saucepan, mix in the moraya starch and cook for 5 minutes. Set aside.
- Transfer the preparation to a blender, sweeten with the raw cane sugar and blend until the mixture becomes a light and smooth cream. Set aside.

7.

FROZEN CORDILLERA

Muña
Banana passionfruit
Kjolle

FOR 4 PEOPLE

TUMBO AND HUACATAY GRANITA

TUMBO, 2 kg
SPINACH, 120 g
HUACATAY LEAVES, 40 g
SIMPLE SYRUP, 50 ml

- Tumbo juice: slice the tumbos in half and use a knife to remove the pulp. Pulse in a food processor to separate the seeds from the pulp, then strain through a very fine chinois. Set aside around 500 ml of extracted tumbo juice.
- Blanch the spinach and huacatay leaves in boiling water, then transfer immediately to an ice bath to cool. Use your hands to wring out the excess water.
- Transfer all the ingredients to a food processor, process at high speed, then strain the mixture through a very fine chinois. Transfer and seal in vacuum bags and freeze overnight.
- For serving, remove the granita from the freezer and use a fork to scrape it into very fine crystals. Keep in the freezer until serving.

FINISH AND PRESENTATION

- In a freezing cold stone bowl, pour a large dot of kjolle cream then a smaller one of yoghurt, and on top of those the tumbo and huacatay granita, and finally add 3 muña leaves.

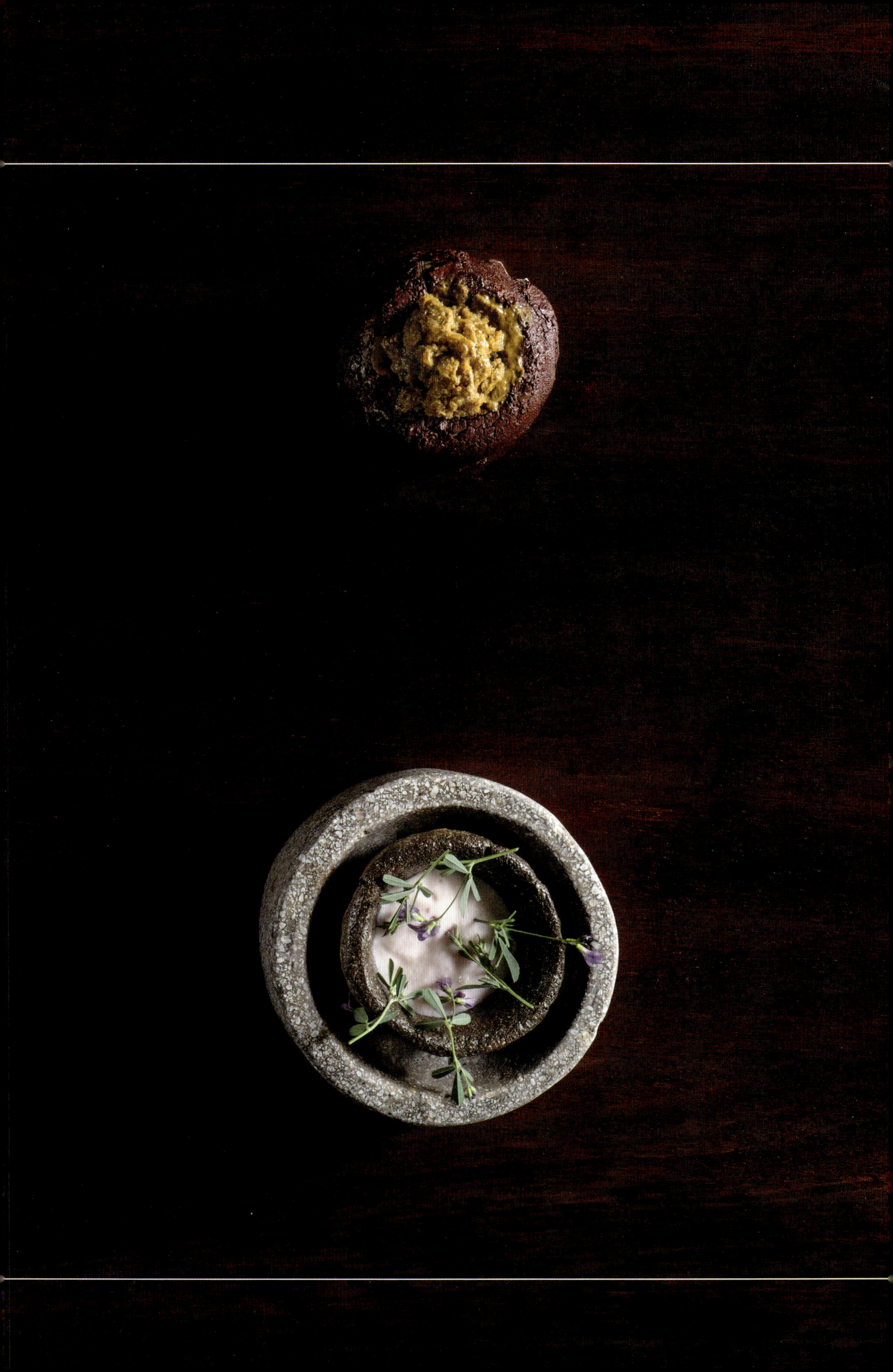

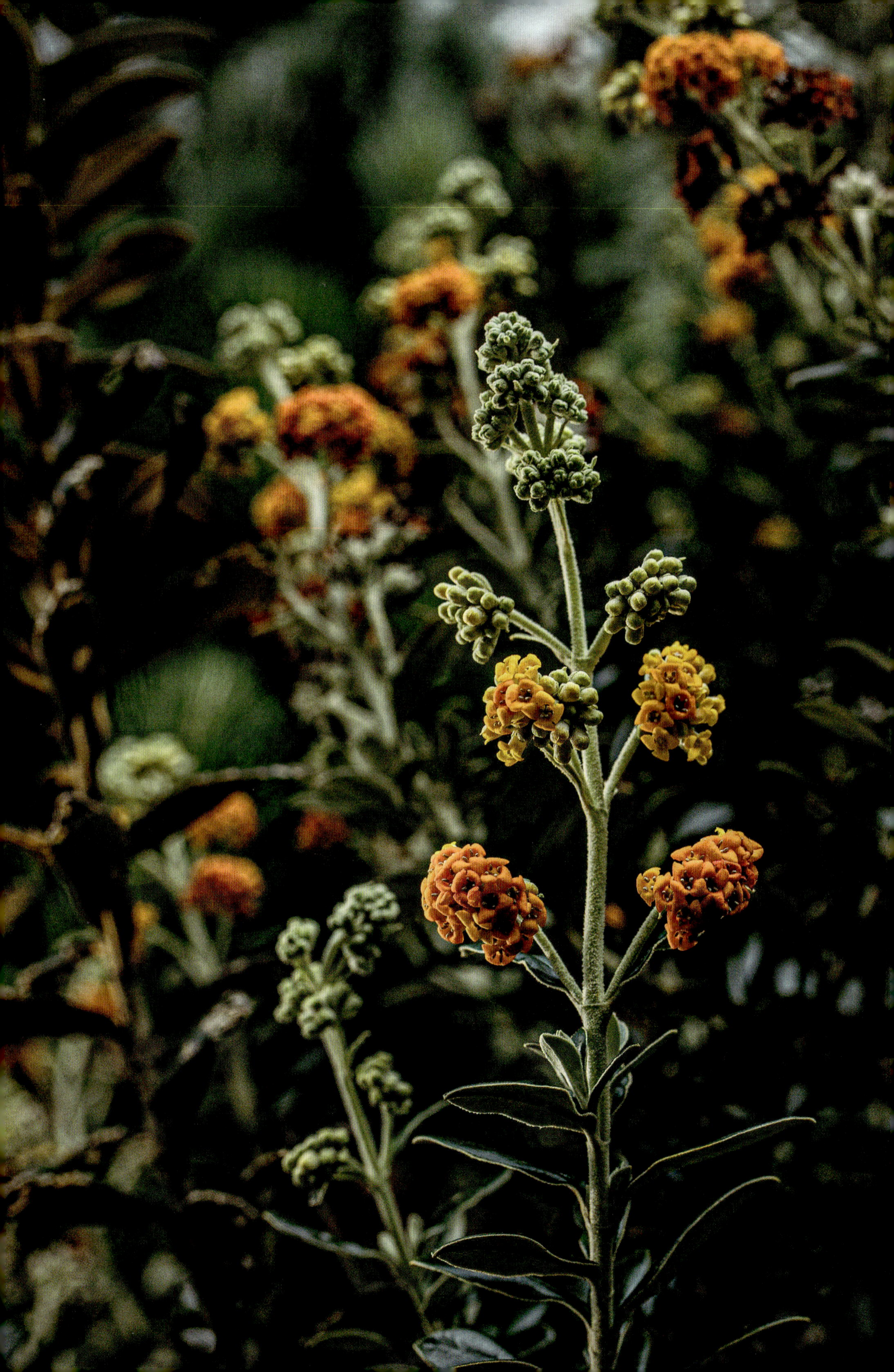

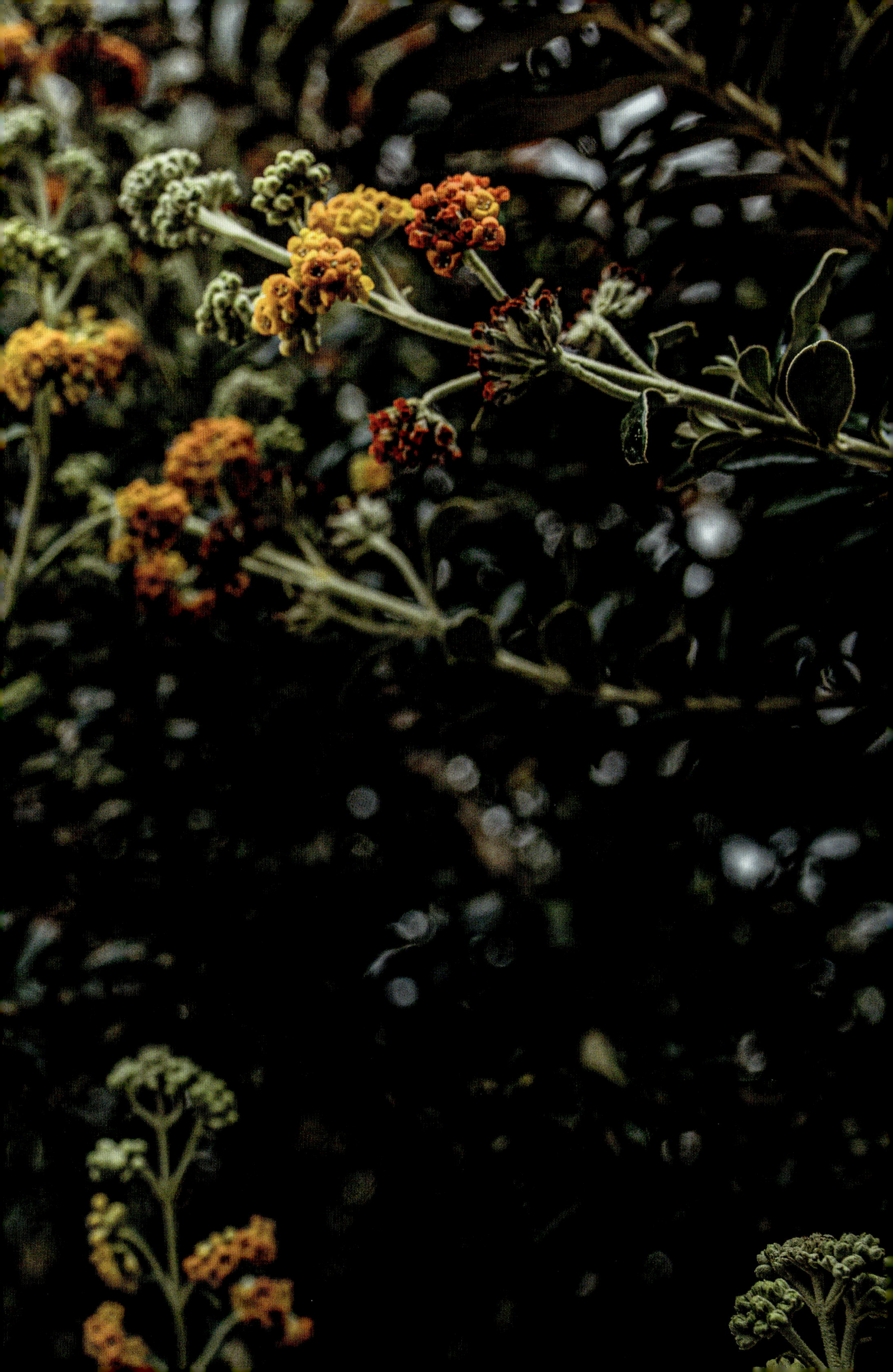

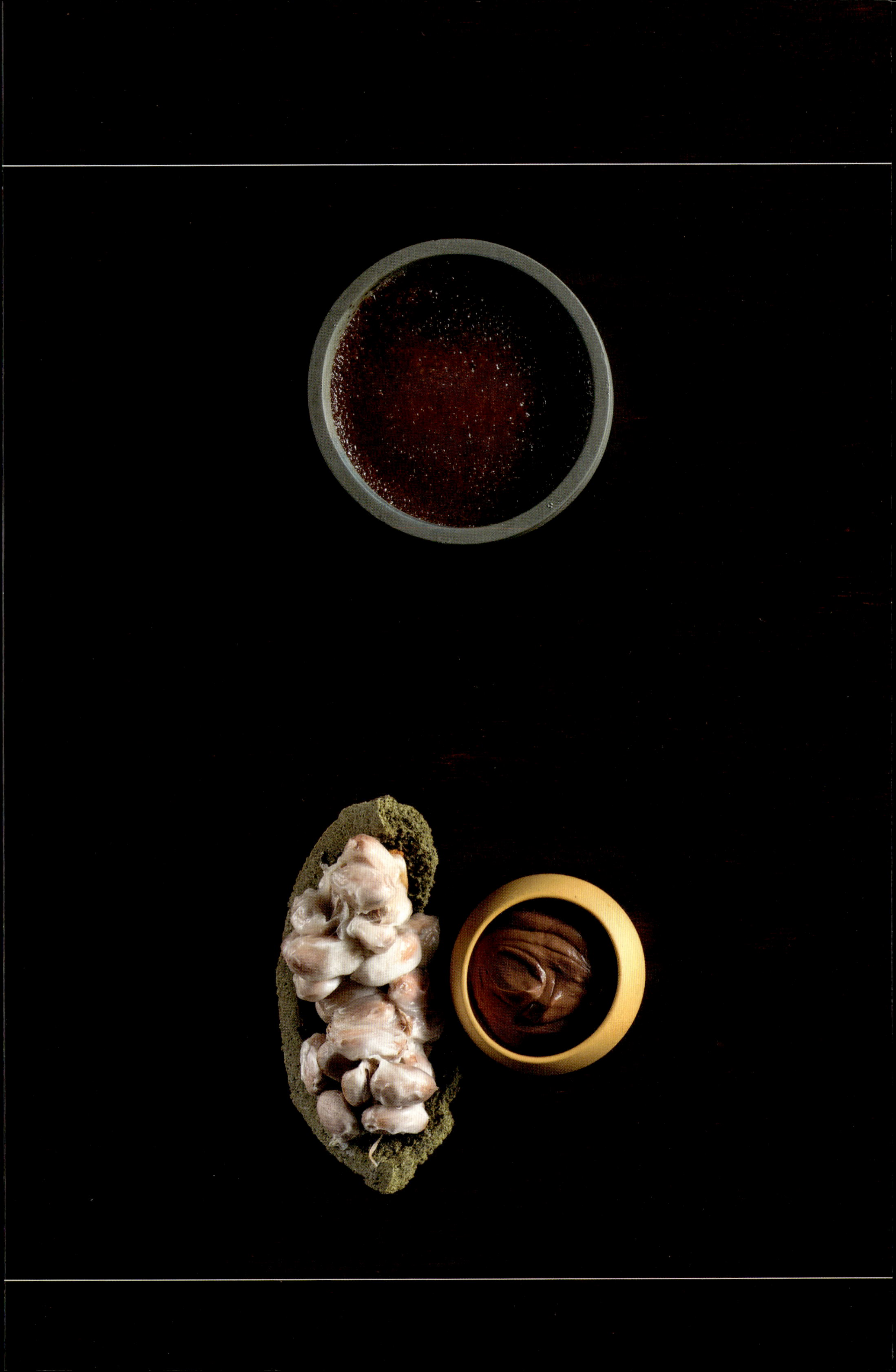

METHOD

CREAMY CHOCOLATE

MIL CHOCOLATE, 72 %
CREAM, 110 ml
MILK, 110 ml
EGG YOLK, 40 ml
RAW CANE SUGAR, 30 g

- Cut the Mil chocolate into small pieces.
- Warm the cream and milk in a saucepan.
- Whisk together the yolks and the raw cane sugar in a bowl. Slowly add and mix in the cream and milk to the yolk mixture then return the mixture to the saucepan over low heat until it reaches a creamy consistency. Pour the warm mixture through a strainer on to the chocolate and blend together for a creamy sauce. Set aside.

8.

HUATIA OF CACAO

Mashwa
Coca leaf
Cacao
Mucilage

PARA 4 PERSONAS

MUCILAGE GRANITA

CACAO MUCILAGE, 500 ml
CREAM, 100 ml

- Whip the cream until the peaks are firm.
- Mix together the mucilage and chantilly cream, transfer to containers and freeze before using.
- For serving, remove the granita from the freezer and use a fork to scrape it into very fine crystals. Keep in the freezer until it is time to serve.

YELLOW AND VIOLET MASHWA CANDIES

YELLOW MASHWA JUICE, 150 ml
RAW CANE SUGAR, 25 g
MAUKA STARCH, 25 g

- Measure out the ingredients and cook in a heavy-based saucepan until the mixture thickens.
- Briefly run the mixture through a food processor, roll out 3mm-thick sheets on silicone mats, dehydrate at 40°C (105°F) for 6 hours.
- Repeat this recipe but using violet mashwa juice.

FINISH AND PRESENTATION

- In a chilled deep dish, plate the creamy chocolate and cover with the mucilage granita. Add the two-colored mashwa candies.

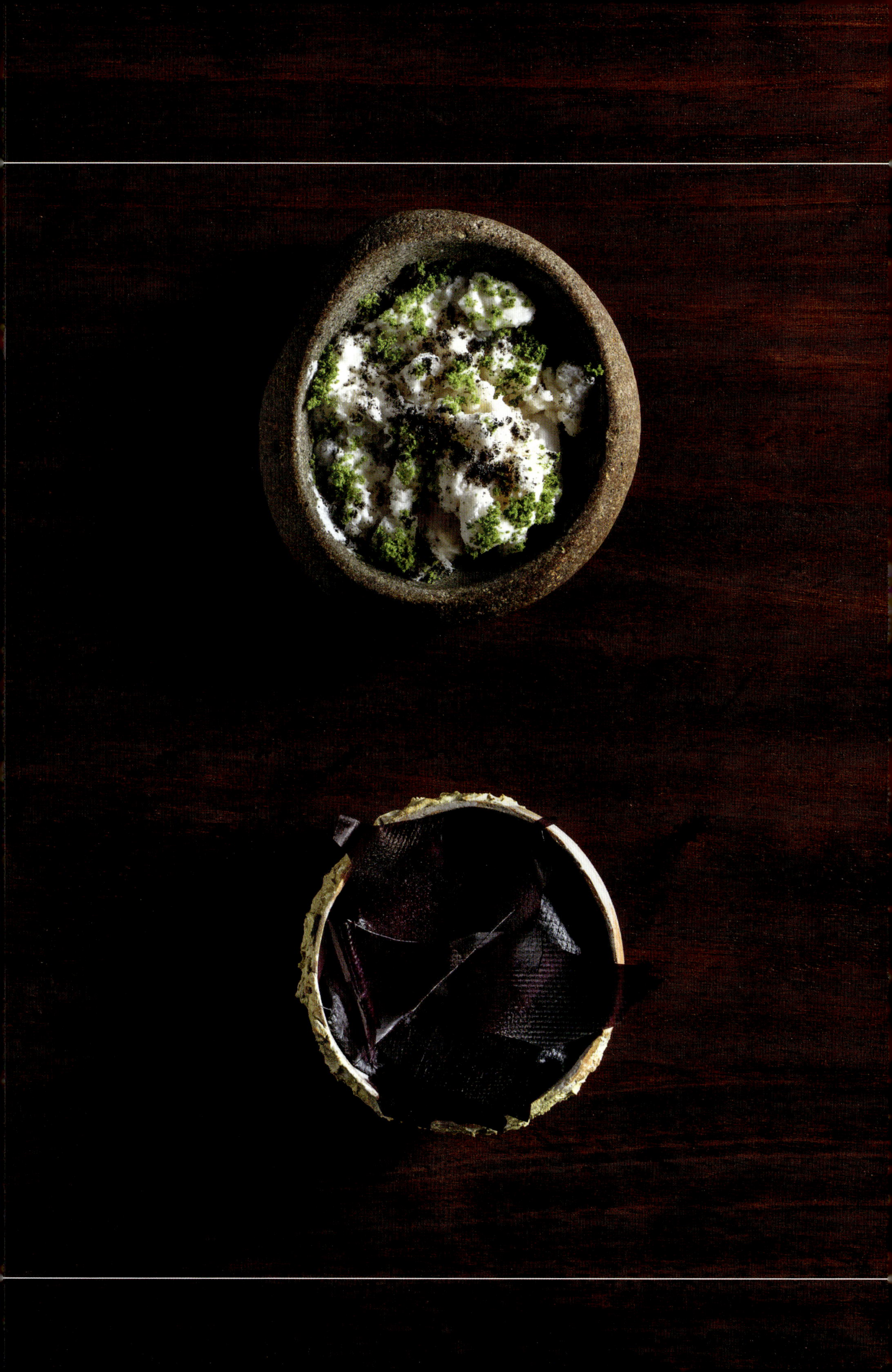

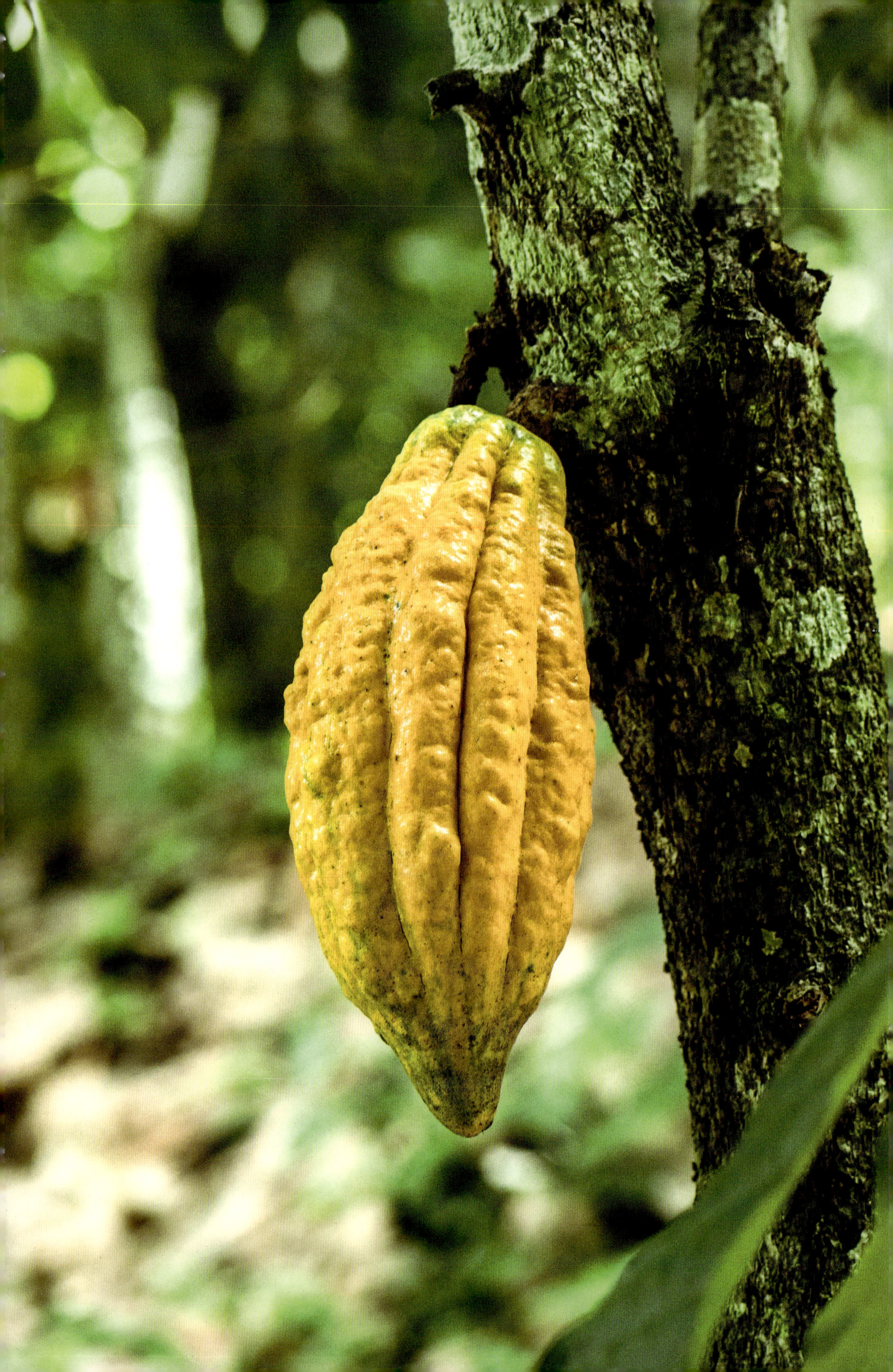

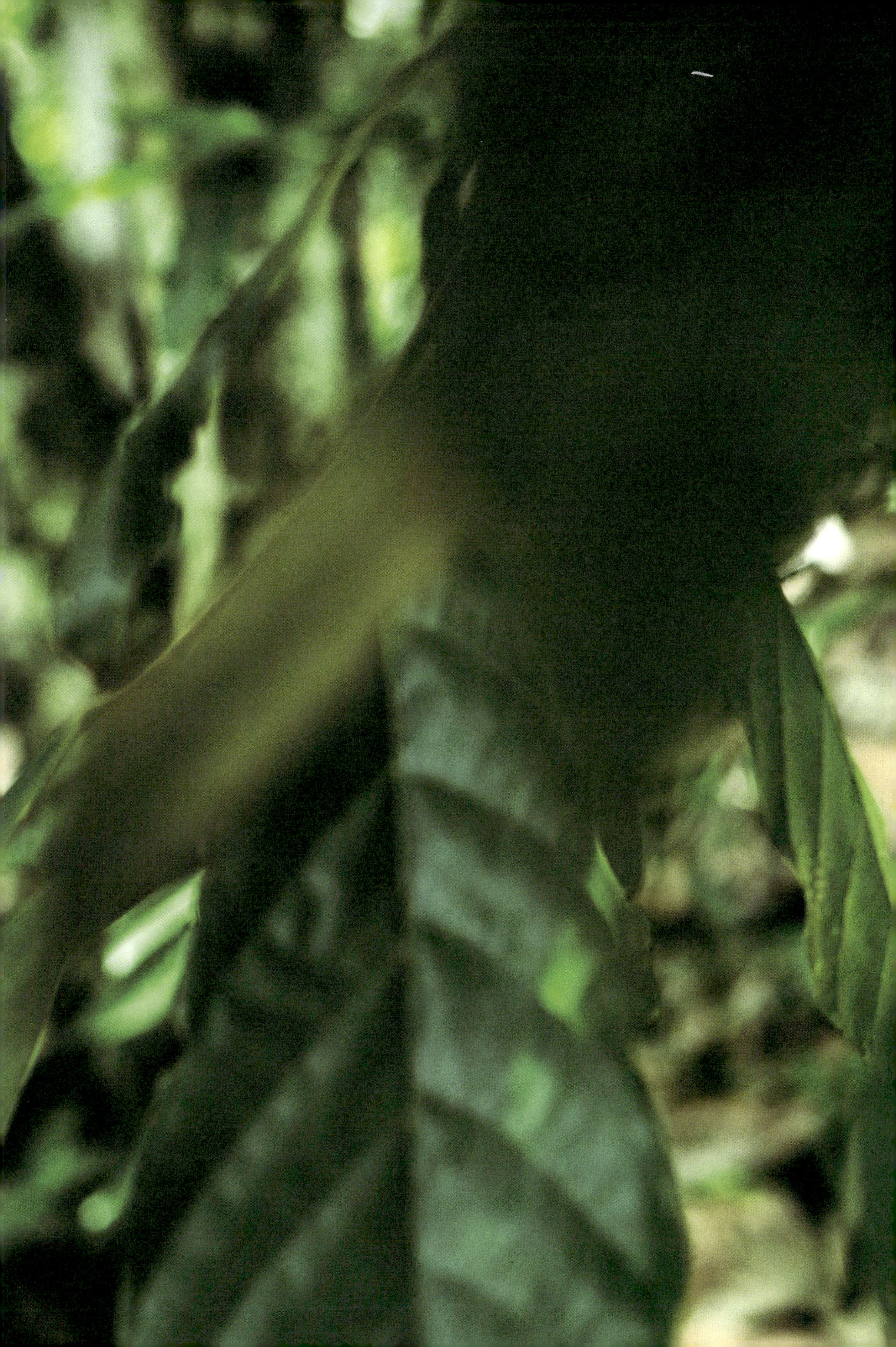

TRIBUTE TO HERITAGE

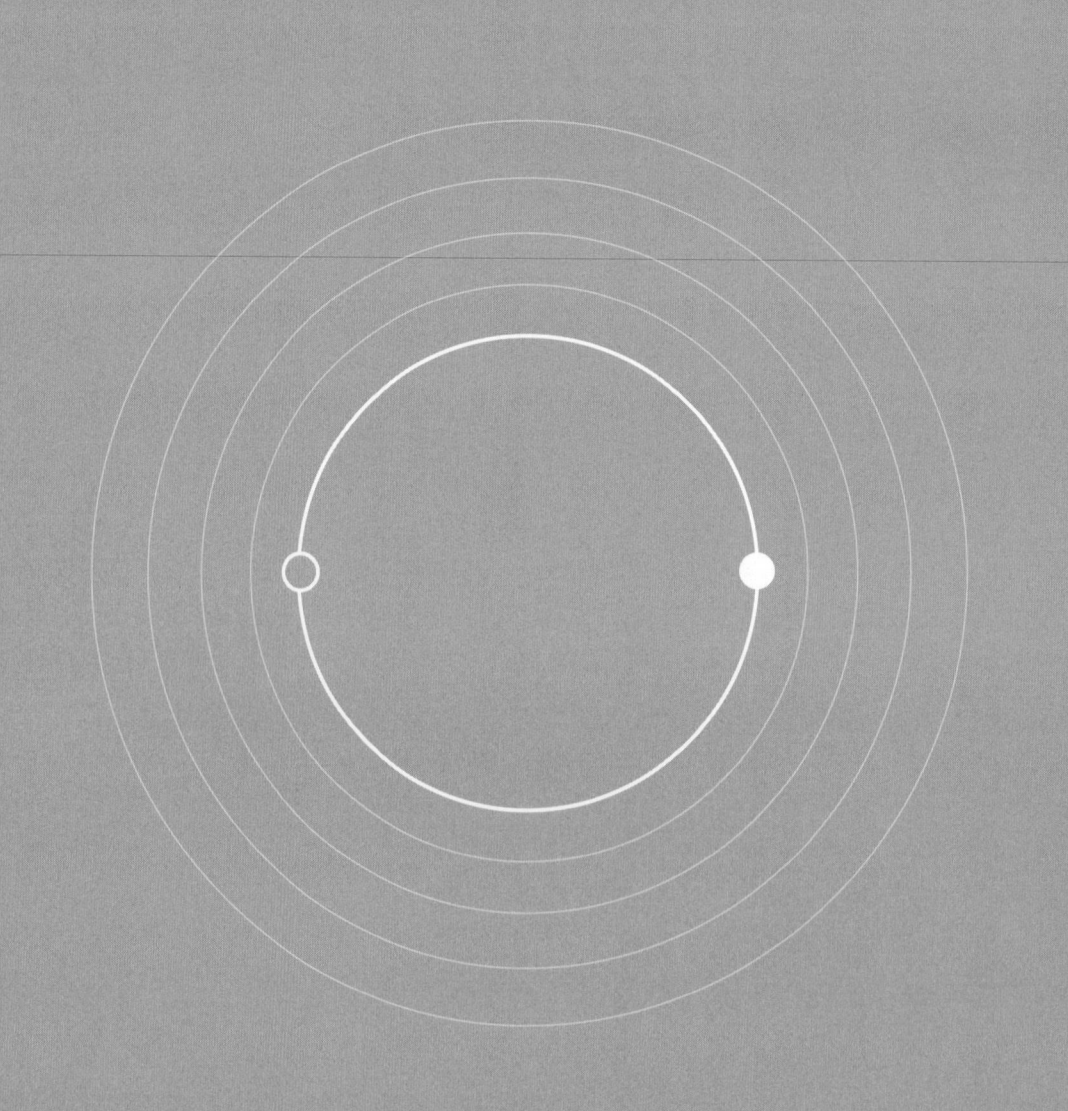

Stripping the adobe walls of their industrial makeover was also an important undertaking, one that would allow visitors to recognize the Andean landscape reflected in Mil's architecture. After removing a few centimeters of paint and cement, the freshly exposed interior walls were treated with a layer of *aguacolla* (Echinopsis pachanoi) cactus resin mixed with sand, local clay – which contribute gray, black, white, yellow or red tones – and tiny *ichu* fragments to create a natural plaster. The façade, meanwhile, features the adobe's burnt sienna tones, which are fading with time. But that's a positive, says architect Rafael Freyre. "Natural erosion isn't often well looked upon, but evidence of weathering by the elements – wind, rain and sun – imbue the building with nature, uniting it with both its environment as well as expressing seasonal transformations. When it was first laid, the roof was green-yellow but over time it's faded, which has helped the architecture to further integrate."

And, to fulfill the dual concept of both connecting and crossing over between Moray and Mil on entering the latter's threshold, the architect constructed a descending stairway and ramp using andesite, an extrusive igneous volcanic rock, crafted by a stonemason from Maras. Landscape architecture was also well considered, given that various non-native vegetation, such as large stands of eucalyptus monocultures, has been introduced into the local ecosystem. "We planted *queñual* (Polylepis), an indigenous tree that's nearing extinction, for example, back into the immediate surroundings and in the refurbished courtyard," he adds.

As for sustainability, Rafael, who also drew up the blueprints for Central and Kjolle in Lima, removed the courtyard's artificial pond, counteracting past extravagance by incorporating a wastewater treatment process. "H_2O is shared by local communities but as the source is scarce, it was paramount that Mil reclaims the water it uses; this first prototype irrigates the organic garden and the plan is for water to be returned to the bathrooms in the future."

By minimizing the impact on its surroundings and respectfully merging into Moray's natural, cultural and social settings as well as reviving and transforming local tradition, Mil ensures that its famous neighbor and the Andean landscape remain the protagonists in this evolving story.

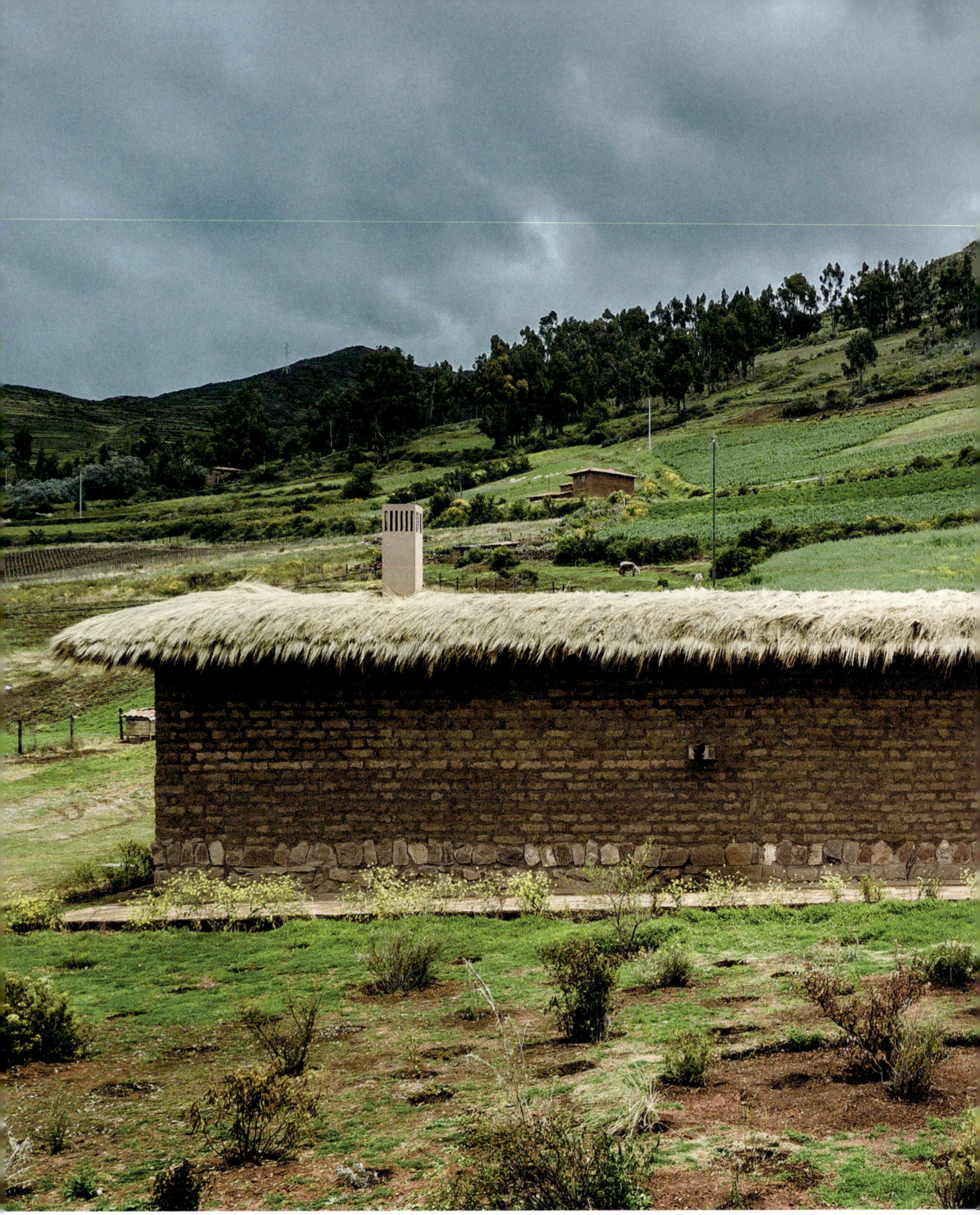

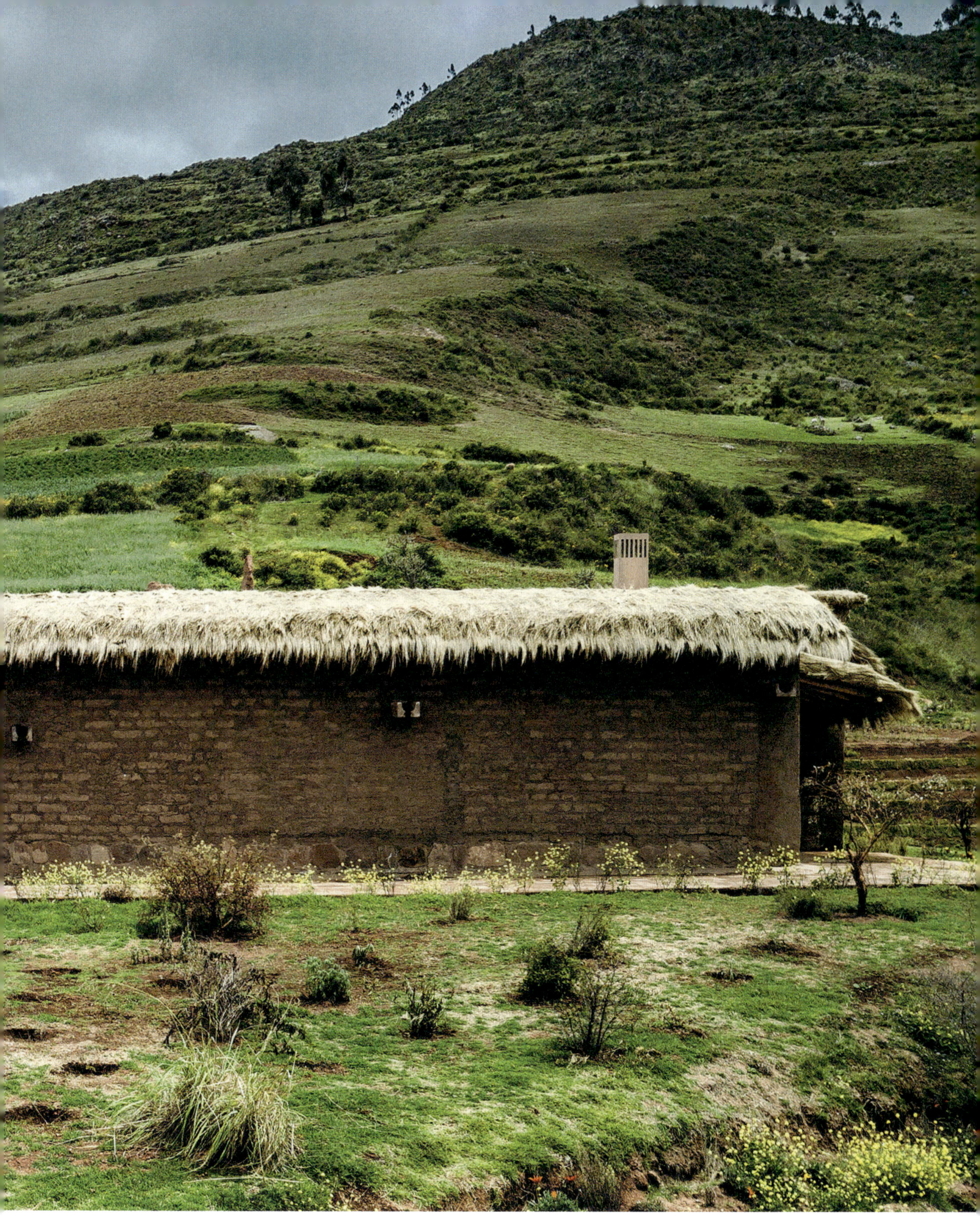

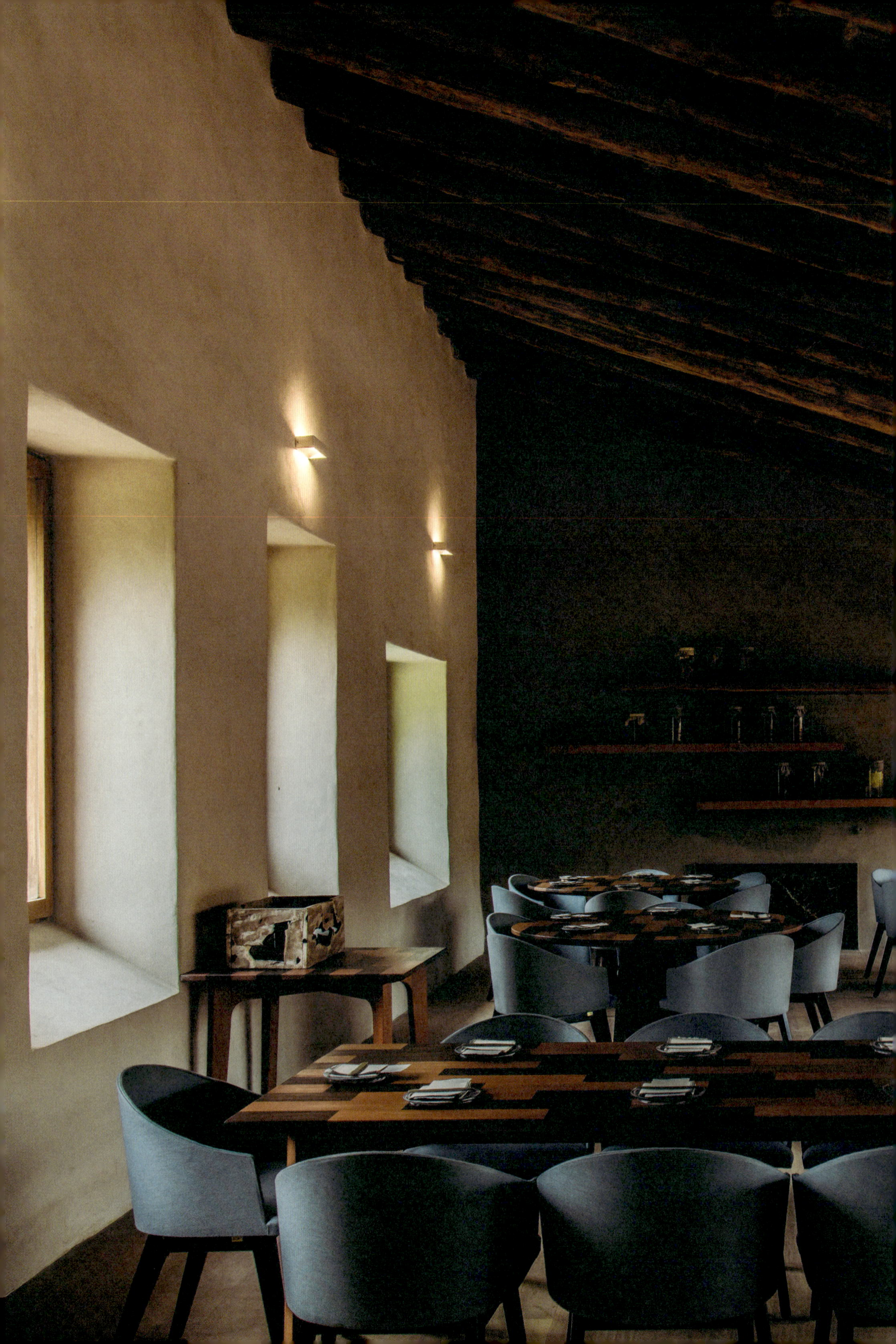

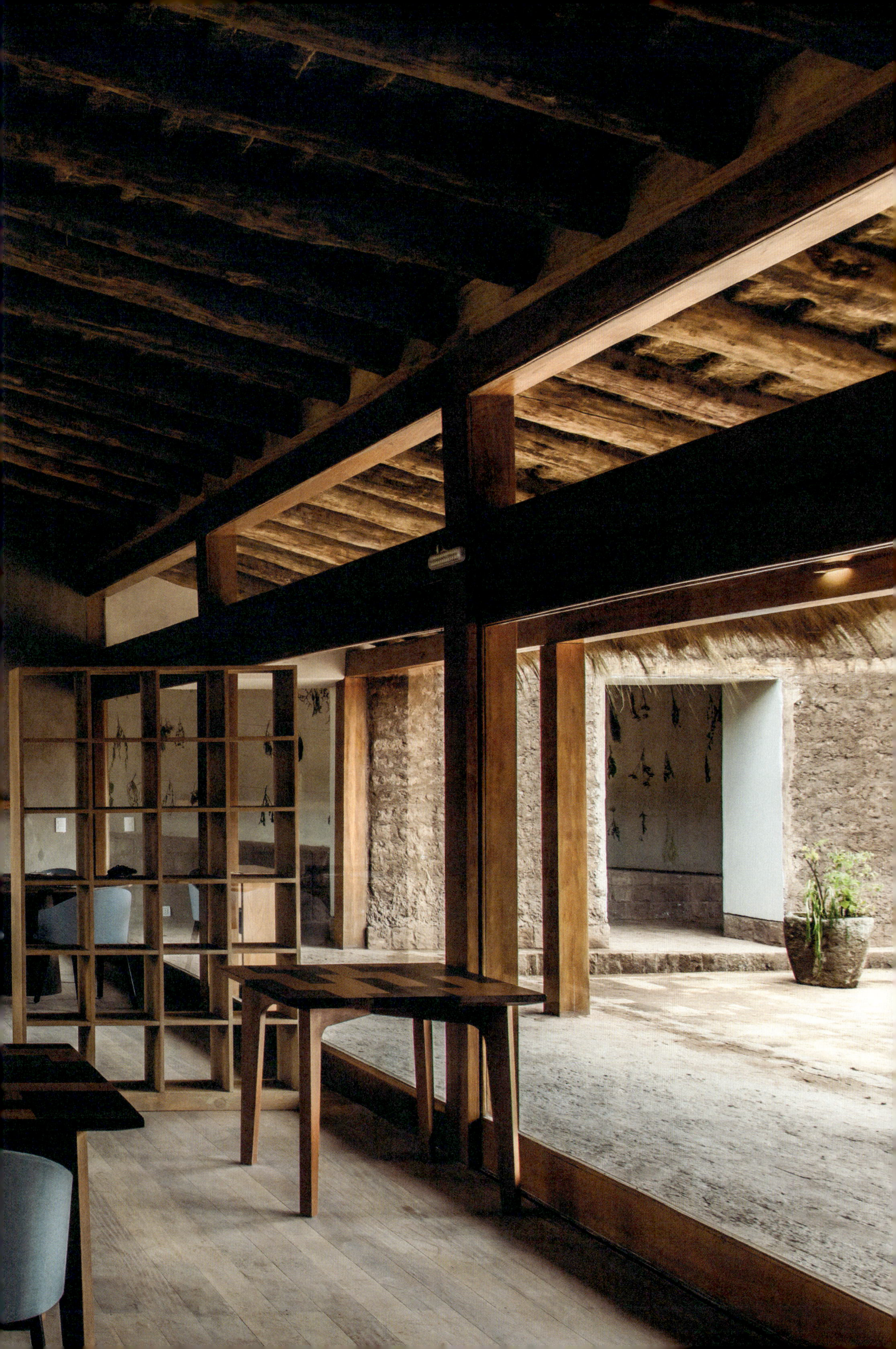

MIL
ECOSISTEMAS DE ALTURA
PRESERVACION
tunta, choclo
uchucuta, maca negra

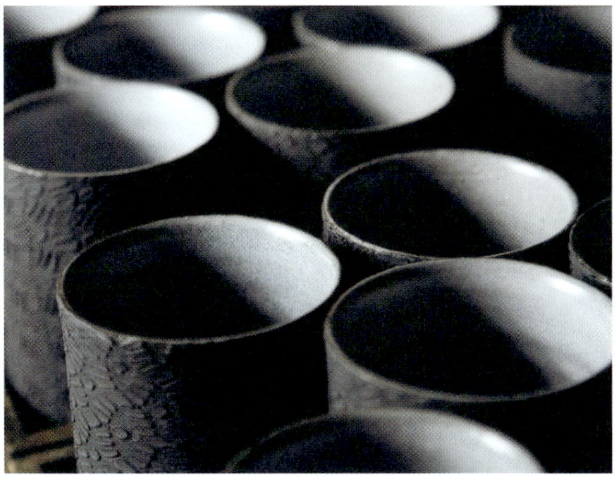

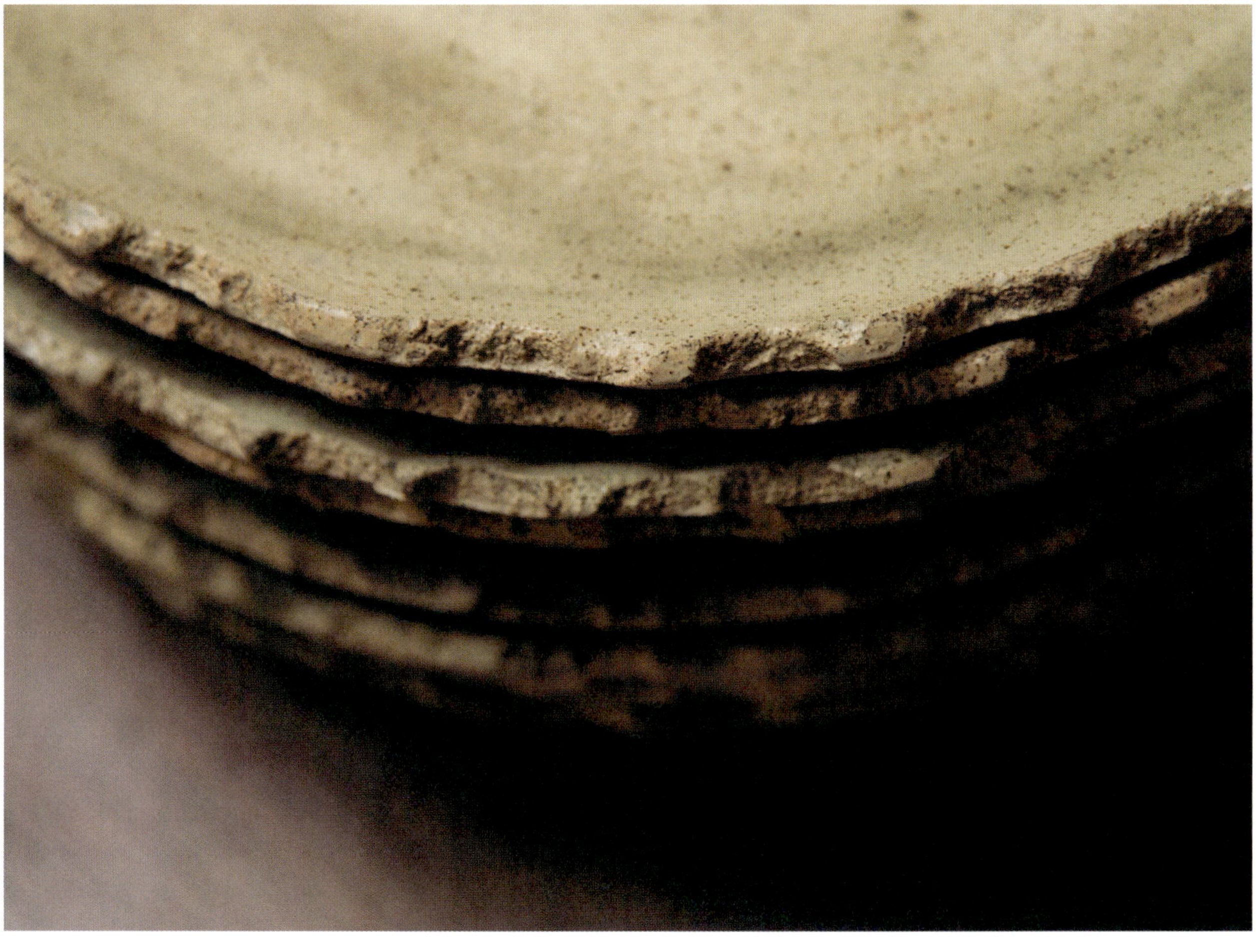

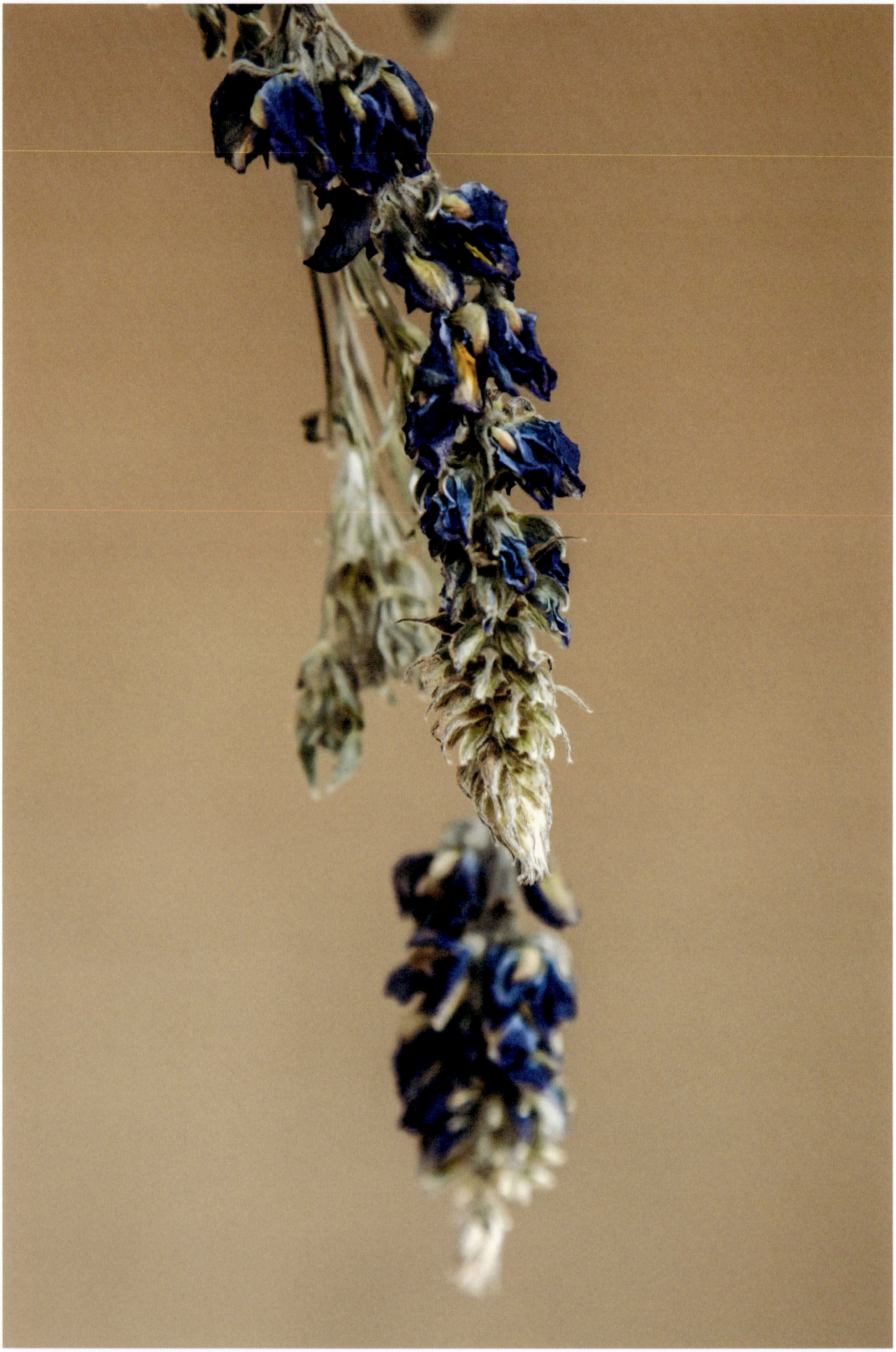

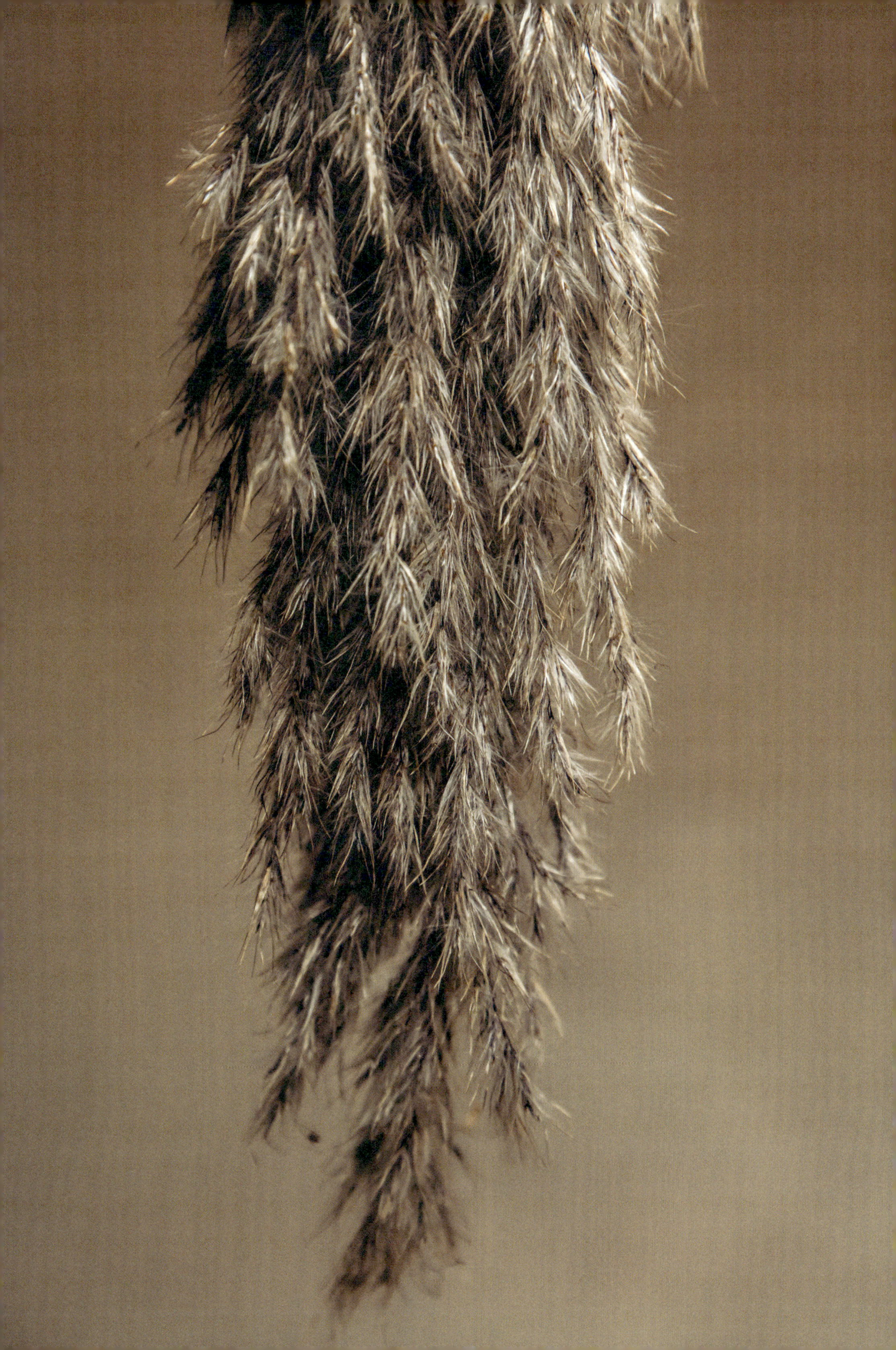

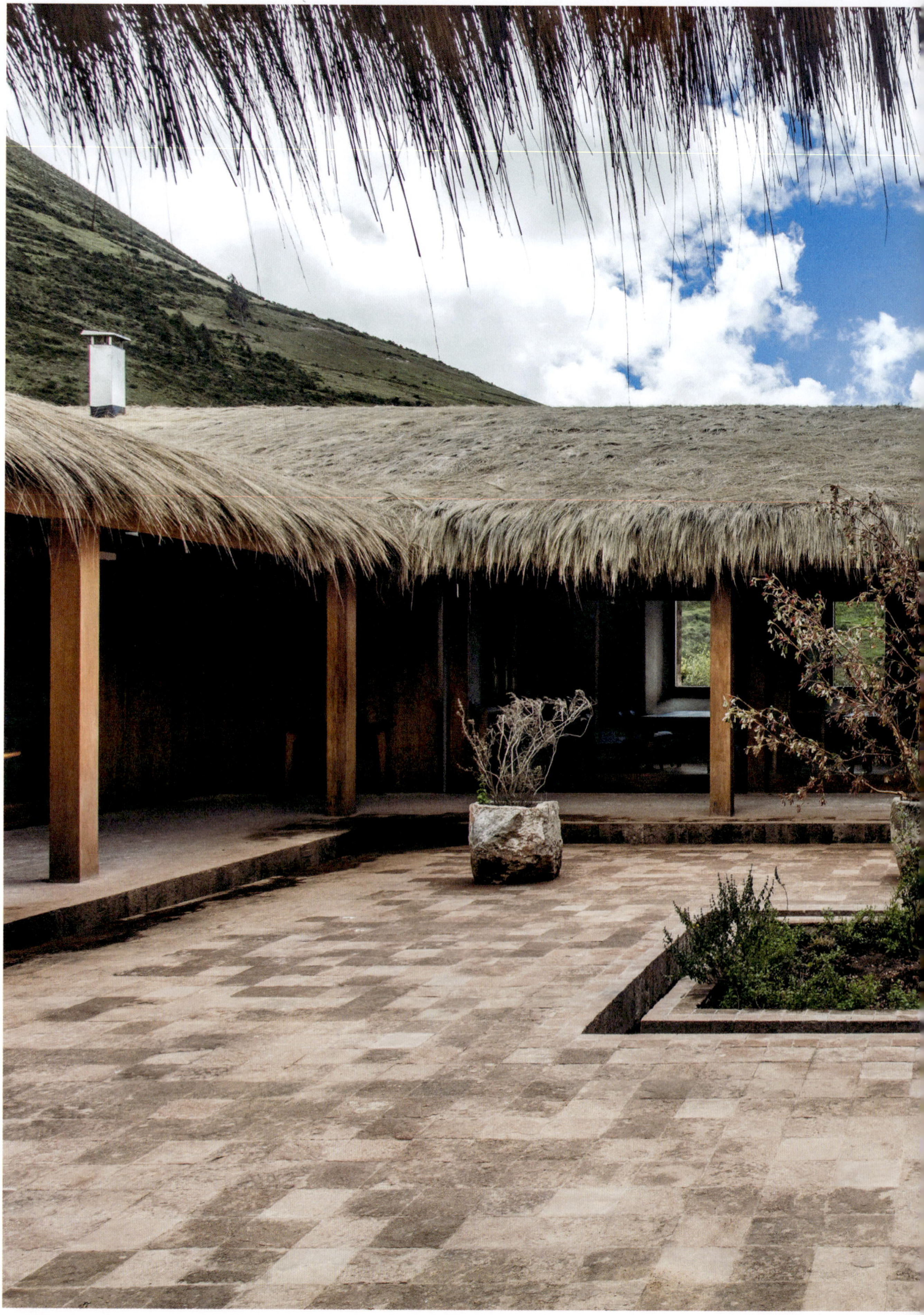

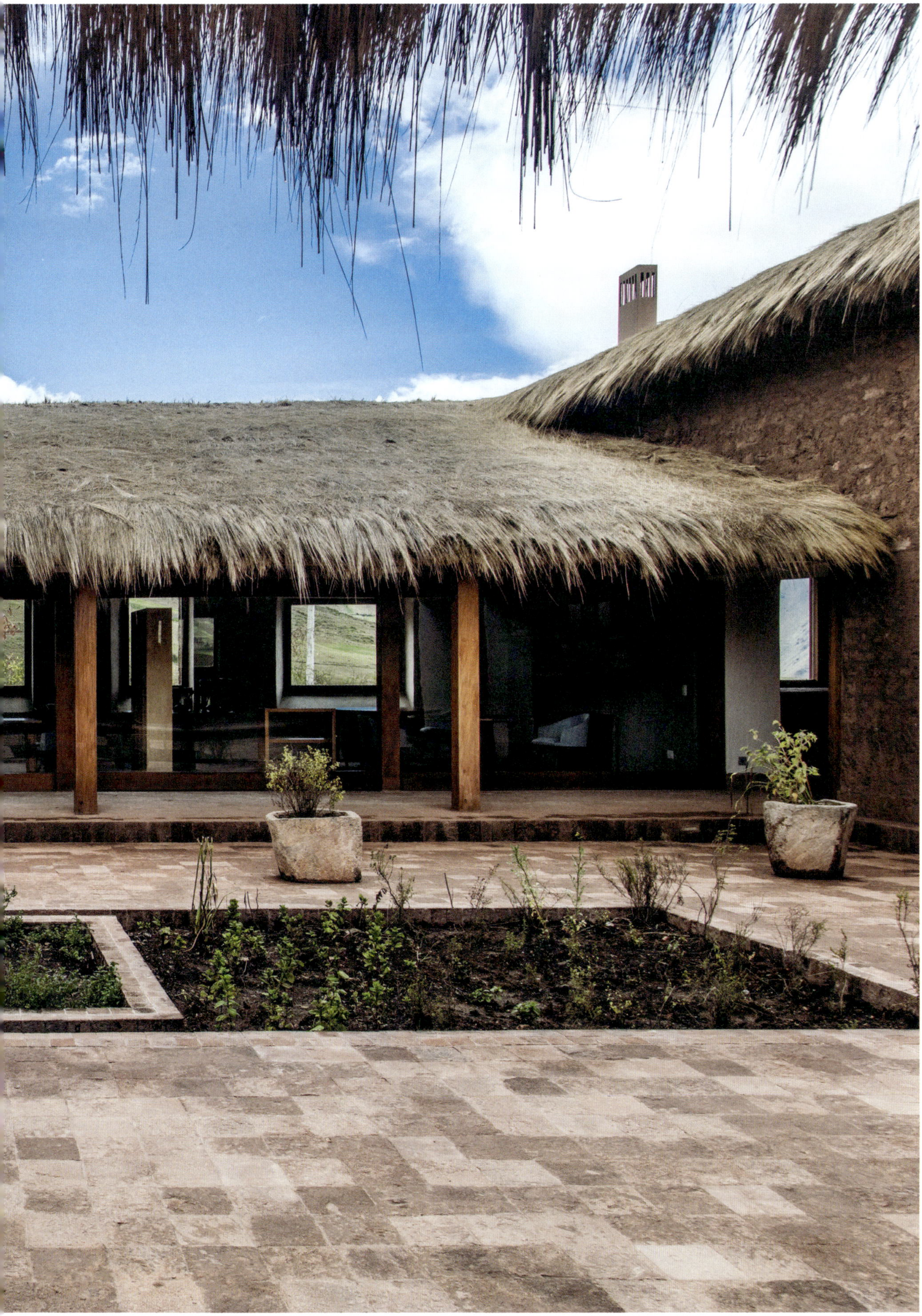

Every day we challenge ourselves to look closely at our territory

MALENA MARTÍNEZ
Codirector de Mater

> "Mil interprets the past in the present, and each interpretation has a short-lived nature. But it's also a vision of the future, always considering the possible effects on the communities."

Our first expedition to Cusco and the Sacred Valley as a very nascent Mater, with the vague notion of 'seeing what's in Peru', took me out of my professional comfort zone as a medical doctor. But I quickly realized that no matter where I was and with whom, we would always meet back in the middle by sitting down to eat together, exploring food – a richly diverse yet universal language – which made changing course a painless experience.

Raised in Lima, my three siblings and I spent many a spontaneous weekend in the countryside, swimming in the river and getting close to nature – it was our mom Blanca's way of returning to her roots. As a studious and organized child who took after her, that dogged discipline led me to medicine.

Growing up in the 1980s and 1990s, Peru was unstable and chaotic because of terrorism and armed conflict, so Blanca, an architect, and Raúl, our lawyer father, had always instilled the notion that we needed to study and live abroad, then return and apply ourselves. I had chosen my path from a young age and, after qualifying as a doctor in Lima, I undertook rural medical service in Iquitos in the Amazon for a year, an experience that further intensified my thirst for knowledge.

Like my brother Virgilio, I also moved abroad. I went to California in the USA for 18 months where I planned to specialize in pathology – an indication that my vocation wasn't directed at looking after patients – but instead I focused on nutrition.

Back in Lima to 'apply' myself, I was working at a laboratory in 2013 when Virgilio called me about his Mater blueprint. The idea of, as I said, 'seeing what's in Peru' made all the difference in that this project would heighten awareness of our country's diverse rainbow of products. Plus, the timing was impeccable given that gastronomy had recently become a source of national pride.

Woven together by ideas, passion and not even a wisp of funding, Mater really did seem like a project we could embark upon together. My brother had read me well: I was ready to leave the comfort zone I'd created for myself.

I had no idea how we would work together; while Virgilio is artistic and sporty, I'm more studious and academic. Although there's a small age gap and we were close growing up, we have very different personalities. Still, he generated enough confidence in the project that when we started traveling as Mater, it was easier to work side by side than any of us expected. I was still required to be analytical but the boundaries were different, less defined. There wasn't any sibling rivalry, we simply found a consensus and often held the same opinion – we complemented each other. And with her determination and adventurous character, Pía completed the nucleus.

As Peruvians, one of our shared past-times and pleasures that unites us as a nation is eating. Food is a universal language with many accents. Pick up a fruit and ask what it is – it invites conversation. On that first expedition to the Cusco region we met husbands and wives, parents and children, people from Andean communities who work their farmland every day of their lives, and learnt about the seeds they'd sown, nurtured then harvested. Our curiosity was piqued by shapes, origins, the difference in flavor intensity across elevations and purposes (Is it medicinal? What does it cure? Can we use it to dye other raw materials or even textiles?), opening up the playing field and appreciating that a single product can be interpreted in a dazzling array of ways. Then we'd all sit down to eat together – farmers, kids, the chefs and the doctor – connecting at meal times, with food at the center.

And the more we traveled, the wider Peru's arms opened to receive us…

Our laboratory is experimental, but removed from the constraints of a conventional research center. Mater has all the flexibility and dynamism of a *vitis vinifera* vine trained to bear bountiful bunches of grapes that, in time, will produce fabulous vintages.

Organically shaped by Peru's land, influenced by local people and global visitors as well as the confluence of cultures, Mater gives us freedom – one door opens up to others – and we've learned to improvise readily at Mil because while we strive for perfection, we're also tolerant and adapt quickly to the unexpected.

In its nascent period, Mater had a biological and gastronomical focus designed to serve and inspire Central's tasting menu. But its mandate grew quickly in ever widening circles to include multiple disciplines that nurture agricultural, anthropological, cultural and artistic projects through to fruition, projects led by both visiting and permanent staff from diverse global backgrounds. Today, it's an interdisciplinary multicultural research center that investigates Peruvian products, the engine that drives Mil, Kjolle, Mayo and Central.

When Virgilio comes up with an idea, my initial instinct is to analyze it and identify its possible implications. So when he suggested we open a restaurant in Moray, I aired some concerns: 'We'd need to send a team to work there. The administration would have to be managed from Moray. It's a 90-minute drive from Cusco, so where would we source products from?' Virgilio, meanwhile, had already visualized this unnamed restaurant in full fluid motion. That's how Mil originated and, once I stopped hyperventilating, I devised a real plan: anthropological input, architecture, logistics, staffing, products.

We started spending more time in this diverse region, which goes far beyond the lovely but stereotypical image of Machu Picchu. We think about elevations, mountains, the high-altitude plateau *puna*, *ichu* feather grass, snow and *apus* (mountain deities), but it's also jungle, Amazon, humid forests and high-altitude jungle, a whole colorful spectrum of ecosystems. As for Moray, it elicited a stream of questions (and back then, visitors could still walk across the lowest terrace): 'Who designed this? How did it happen? What was it used for?' Moray is truly unique.

We started building relationships so our neighbors, CC Kacllaraccay and CC Mullak'as-Misminay indigenous rural communities, would be willing to engage in dialogue, working alongside and sharing knowledge with us as we would with them. The interpersonal bridges constructed over the past three years have solid foundations and Mil's growth – from social, anthropological and agricultural points of view – has been so exponential, it's almost hard to contain. Through Mater and Mil, we're proving that a dining experience is more nourishing than simply eating a fabulous meal. And between us all – farmer, chef, doctor, anthropologist, agronomist, bartender, textile designer – we're showing that a single Peruvian object is, indeed, open to many interpretations and there's a whole world to discover.

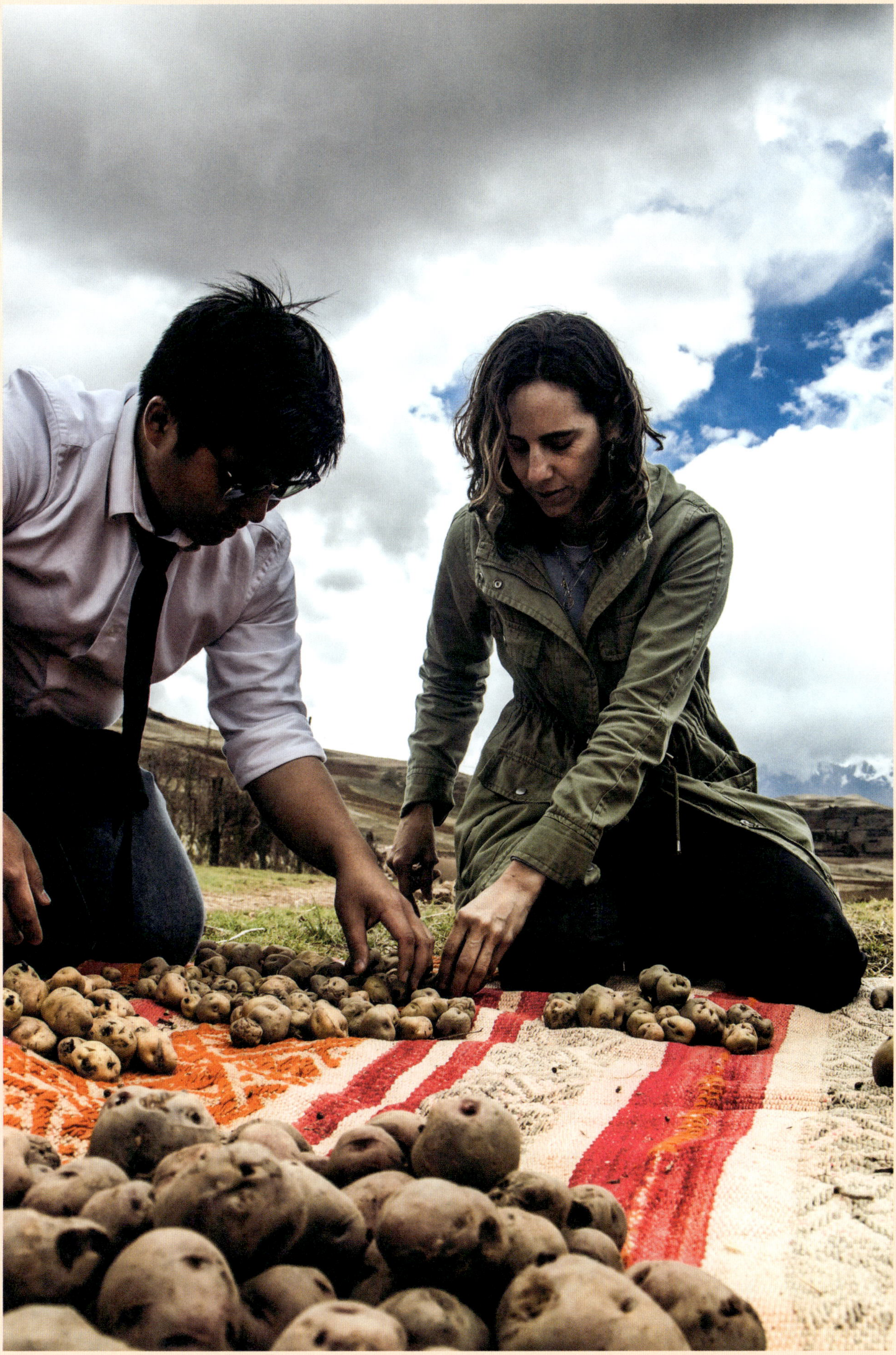

*TAULI!

1. Paras Nobias: Variedades
2. Cultivos: Quinuas: coti(es)
3. Kiwicha (amaranto)
4. Pastos Amazónicos) Natwias
5. Hugos: 2 tipos
6. Homa)
   Valor

COMUNICACION

Mater Iniciativa

= MATERMONEY
= MIL CENTRO
...

#MATERV

219

Land's history repeating itself

MANUEL ACURIO
Agricultural engineer and land manager of Mil

Although he was raised in Cusco, Manuel Acurio's connection to Moray is in his blood. As a child, he would visit his grandfather Washington, a farmer from Pauchi in Maras district, and Moray was Manuel's playground: weekends were spent running up, over and around the concentric formations on the high plateau with his cousins, playing *chapa chapa* (tag), and helping his family in the nearby fields. Three decades on and history has come full circle; the agronomist oversees Mil's agricultural research laboratory that's located on 3.2 acres of land next to the restaurant.

Having lived all around Peru, completing a master's degree in Lima and assessing land in Puerto Maldonado in the Amazon rainforest, Manuel has relished returning to the Cusco region. "Both my father and my grandfather worked on this land – now it's my turn. And, it turns out that I'm working with some of the same people as Washington; he's come up in conversations without their knowing my relationship to him. His legacy is one of the reasons I'm at Mil," he says.

Manuel's grandfather cultivated potatoes as well as barley, maize and quinua, standard crops for the area.

In an interview with Italian ecologist Bárbara D'Achille for *Ecología Volumén I* (1989), Washington recalls a maize rainbow was planted on Moray's terraces. (He also took Australian anthropologist John C. Earls to Moray, who later extensively researched the archeological site.) But, as chemicals became a normal agricultural practice and farmers rejected nutrient-rich potatoes for lucrative, high-yield, easy-care species, the production of native varieties such as *ccachun, huaccachi* – which is difficult to peel – and *queqorani* dwindled significantly in the Andes.

Manuel's mission at Mil's experimental biointensive farm – a contemporary version of the Quechua empire's own experimentation center next door at Moray – is to create an exchange program that recovers ancestral knowledge while recuperating biodiversity. A collaboration with members of CC Kacllaraccay and CC Mullak'as-Misminay, including Kacllaraccay's president Cleto Cusipaucar, this trailblazing project is managed on a daily basis by Mil co-worker and fellow agronomist Marcelo Gonzales Solis.

Besides discovering which native potatoes best adapt to today's land and weather conditions, Mil and Mater will share this newly created genetic bank with the communities, who, going forward, can sow seeds best suited to their ecosystems and harvest improved products.

Manuel says: "Rain is irregular and temperatures vary widely [as they did in Quechua times, according to *Ecologiá I*], so the 2019/2020 agricultural season has been planned specifically to identify the most productive way of working and which native potatoes best grow on Mil's limestone-rich land. Agronomist Ladislao Palomino from Peru's National Institute of Agricultural Innovation (INIA) donated 223 varieties of potatoes including 55 clones sourced from its germplasm collection, which we sowed in late 2019. Come harvest time, we can determine which varieties are most resistant to drought, frost and *rancha* (late blight) – the destructive water mold that caused the 1845 Irish potato famine – and share that genetic material."

Thirty-six native potato varieties and tubers cultivated by farmer Manuel Choqque were also sown in the same 2019 season to see how they, too, fare in Maras' rather water-deficient ecosystem.

While biodiversity and sustainability are destined to improve, farmers will continue using traditional tools such as *yunta* – a bull yoke – and *lampas* (hoes) to prepare the land, while modern *mochila fumigadoras* (spraying backpacks) are filled with specially prepared, microorganism-rich fertilizer rather than chemicals. Mil and the communities adhere to the *en compañía* method of working, a mutually beneficial scheme where the former provides the land and labor, the latter provides seeds, the *yunta* and organic material, and each entity benefits equally 50/50 from the harvest – without any money exchanging hands. "*En compañía* means '*Hoy por ti, mañana por mi*' or 'Today for you, tomorrow for me'. We want to help farmers become more efficient without changing the traditional way in which they work," adds Manuel.

A typical day starts early for farmers, attending to goats and herds of sheep at around 4:30 in the morning before breakfasting on boiled fava beans, *mote* corn or broth. At 11,480 feet above sea level, farming can be physically gruelling, sun beating down or icy rain pelting your face, and a series of three welcome breaks, accompanied by *chicha de jora*, a corn beer made from germinated maize, keeps up energy levels and morale.

Chicha de jora is a vital component for Andean farmers, says Manuel. "It's indispensable; not only is *chicha* refreshing and energy-giving, it allows people to come together, to relax and chat for a moment. Everyone drinks from the same cup and it's a fundamental part of rural life that complements the working day."

Extending *k'intu* (a bunch of three or four coca leaves) upwards towards Inti, the sun god, to ask for a good harvest, and offering known as a *pago a la tierra* or an offering is part of agriculture's ancestral convention in the Andes. Christianity also shows its hand: many farmers bless the land with a crucifix and a prayer, "just in case", says Manuel.

Come August, across Peru, indeed Latin America, they give thanks to Pachamama. Grateful to the goddess of earth and fertility for her generosity, farmers return her abundance, pouring *chicha de jora* into the ground and appreciatively burying their best potatoes, meat and coca leaves.

Working with Mater has given Manuel a wider perspective when it comes to agriculture. "At a workshop held in the Amazon, we were asked 'what value does this product hold for you?' I replied: 'How much I can sell it for.' The anthropologist said, 'the story behind this plant', while the biologist said, 'its biodiversity'. Mater has taught me that there are plenty of contexts behind a single product and that everything is connected."

But the most treasured aspect in agriculture is the circle of life, he says. "Being at one with the land and the sun, sowing a seed and watching it grow from the earth's bosom then gathering it is incredible – why wouldn't I celebrate every harvest?"

They call him Choco

NILVER MELGAREJO
Cacao technical researcher, chocolatier at Mil

For a self-confessed chocoholic, sourcing organic cacao pods from mountainous, jungle-based farms to temper single-origin beans into hand-crafted bars at our high-altitude Andean chocolate workshop is a dream assignment. After bagging exactly that position, chocolatier and cacao researcher Nilver Melgarejo rightly feels he's got the best job in the world.

Nilver's passion for converting cacao into finished bars [toasting cacao makes cocoa, which is used to make chocolate] was sparked during what he calls his "Willy Wonka days". Several years of mass producing at a large factory in Lima steered him through the technicalities of making chocolate, and despite never harvesting, fermenting, toasting or selecting beans first hand, he fell for cacao regardless.

From Lima, Nilver was only able to sate his hunger for chocolate-coated knowledge by watching bean selection videos and looking at photos of scarlet and yellow pods. So, he seized the opportunity to take his craft to a specialist, artisanal level and moved to Urubamba. At Mil's chocolate workshop, not only does he work in an idyllic setting atop a mountain, grinding nibs to create chocolate liquor, the sultry perfume wafting as he elegantly molds handcrafted bars made from 72 percent, 77 percent and 100 percent *cacao chuncho*, which are then sold via Mater Sostiene, he's finally got up close and personal with plantations and their carers.

High-altitude, subtropical rainforest in La Convención province set that first scene, home to the Andes' *cacao chuncho*, a native variety from the Forastero genetic group that holds unique characteristics such as mandarine and passion fruit aromas as well as floral and nutty flavours, and a high fat content.

Nilver says: "The first time I found out I was going to Quillabamba and the high-altitude jungle, I was the happiest man alive. I couldn't contain my excitement and kept asking the bus driver how long it was until we got there – time just wouldn't go fast enough."

Two years on as our chocolatier (his Mil co-workers have nicknamed him Choco), he's forged many friendships and regularly visits the 14 *cacao chuncho* producers in and around Quillabamba in La Convención, eager to learn as well as share his own knowledge with farmers such as Rómulo Cámara Moncada, with whom he undertook harvest in 2020. Nilver's philosophy is reciprocal: "If you don't have a connection with people, you'll never make great chocolate. Peru doesn't have a state entity that supports cacao producers, we have to create those networks and support them, so I visit Quillabamba regularly to continue strengthening our relationships.

"The older generations are very welcoming when it comes to inviting me to their farms. I love seeing the yellow cacao chuncho pods attached to the trees, then dried and hearing them crunch… *cacao chuncho* has so much potential and is worth its weight in gold. I'm in the best place in the world when I'm visiting a plantation – I tread slowly as I walk under the leafy canopies to spot as many colorful pods as possible."

The chocolate Nilver crafts is used in desserts at Mil as well as Central and Kjolle, and he also creates cocoa powder and bars, some made with nibs for additional crunch, which are sold by Mater Sostiene, products whose traceability, flavors and textures couldn't be further from his Willy Wonka days.

"When I slide open Mil's workshop door, I stop, and breathe in deeply. I love what I do every single day because there's a whole world to discover; it's also taught me to be patient. And recently I've started wondering, what would chocolate sourced from my own cacao plantation taste like?"

The greatest experience, however, is sharing finished bars with a producer. "I remember the first time Rómulo ate chocolate I'd made with his *cacao chuncho*; he'd never tried anything like it. That was the moment I realized I wanted to make chocolate for the rest of my life."

Plating first-person stories with regional products

LUIS VALDERRAMA
Head chef at Mil

Nothing about the daily routine at Mil is typical, starting with the commute up into the mountains, says head chef Luis Valderrama. He takes hairpin bends starting at 9,420 feet above sea level (asl) from the town of Urubamba up to Moray at 11,705 feet asl six days a week, a drive he considers an inspirational luxury.

"*Molle* (Schinus molle) and *kunuca* (Satureja boliviana) line the sides of the roads, plants we use in the restaurant, clouds hug the snow-capped mountains, and the Sacred Valley lies below. Morning 'rush hour' means goats trotting down the middle of the road: this landscape and its colors fill my mind with ideas," he says.

Born in Lima, Luis is one of three siblings including twin brother Carlos, one of Central's head chefs. When Luis realized an international relations degree wasn't his true calling, he followed Carlos into gastronomy then into Central's kitchen; he later became my assistant.

The day might start with Luis trekking up into the mountains to forage for products such as *marku* leaf (Artemisia vulgaris) or quinua and, depending on whether it's pre-rainy or dry season, sowing seeds or harvesting tuber crops with farmers from CC Mullak'as-Misminay and CC Kacllaraccay on Mil's farm situated next to the restaurant. The altitude, location and the fast-changing weather fronts ensure no mornings or afternoons are ever the same, but the biggest difference to working in the city is the close contact he and the team have developed with the land, and the exceptional relationships formed with our producers.

Our tenacious chef Luis loves caring for Mil's farm. Not only can he pluck organic, zero-kilometer ingredients such as *oca* (Oxalis tuberosa) and *mashwa* (Tropaeolum tuberosum) from the ground with his own hands and walk them back to Mil's kitchen just a few steps away, that experience undeniably brings a new dimension to his cooking and the menu. It means there's a first-person story behind every dish we plate.

Luis says: "The fields are our classroom, and the farmers my teachers. Learning about the whole agricultural cycle – sowing seeds or planting already-sprouting tubers, seeing them grow then cooking them is wonderful. Because, if we want to cook potatoes, well, we should have to pick them. The first harvest we shared with the communities left the greatest impact on me because it meant we're changing the narrative from third person to first person." Besides that relationship with the land, a personal connection with our producers is also vital in our story-telling process. "I know the person behind every ingredient at Mil; I see their faces, meet with them regularly, and know their stories. We work hard to establish respectful relationships, which, in many cases, blossom into friendship.

"In particular, I've connected with Santiago Amar from CC Mullak'as-Misminay and Santiago Pillco from CC Kacllaraccay. We joke around and have fun but there's also a level of trust that's developed over time – we often prepare a *huatia* together," he says.

Of course, there are challenges running a kitchen at this elevation and in this remote part of the Cusco region, and Luis cites distance as the greatest. "Some of the team might be tracking down ingredients that we urgently need, undertaking a physically exhausting trek up to 12,500 feet during which the weather can change in seconds, while others will be in service. But, as we aren't a typical restaurant that orders in products, it's one of many challenges we tackle in order to achieve our goals. Plus, it provides a fantastic education for cooks."

Besides sharing facetime with guests to explain some of the moments on our *High-Altitude Ecosystems* tasting menu, Luis was recently inspired to create a tuber seed bank.

"I wanted to show our diners how we store potato seeds for the following year's crop and how they develop." Located on the restaurant's patio in a bespoke glass-and-wood cabinet, it now forms part of Mater's Immersion tour circuit.

MIRRORING THE ANDEAN COLOR PALETTE

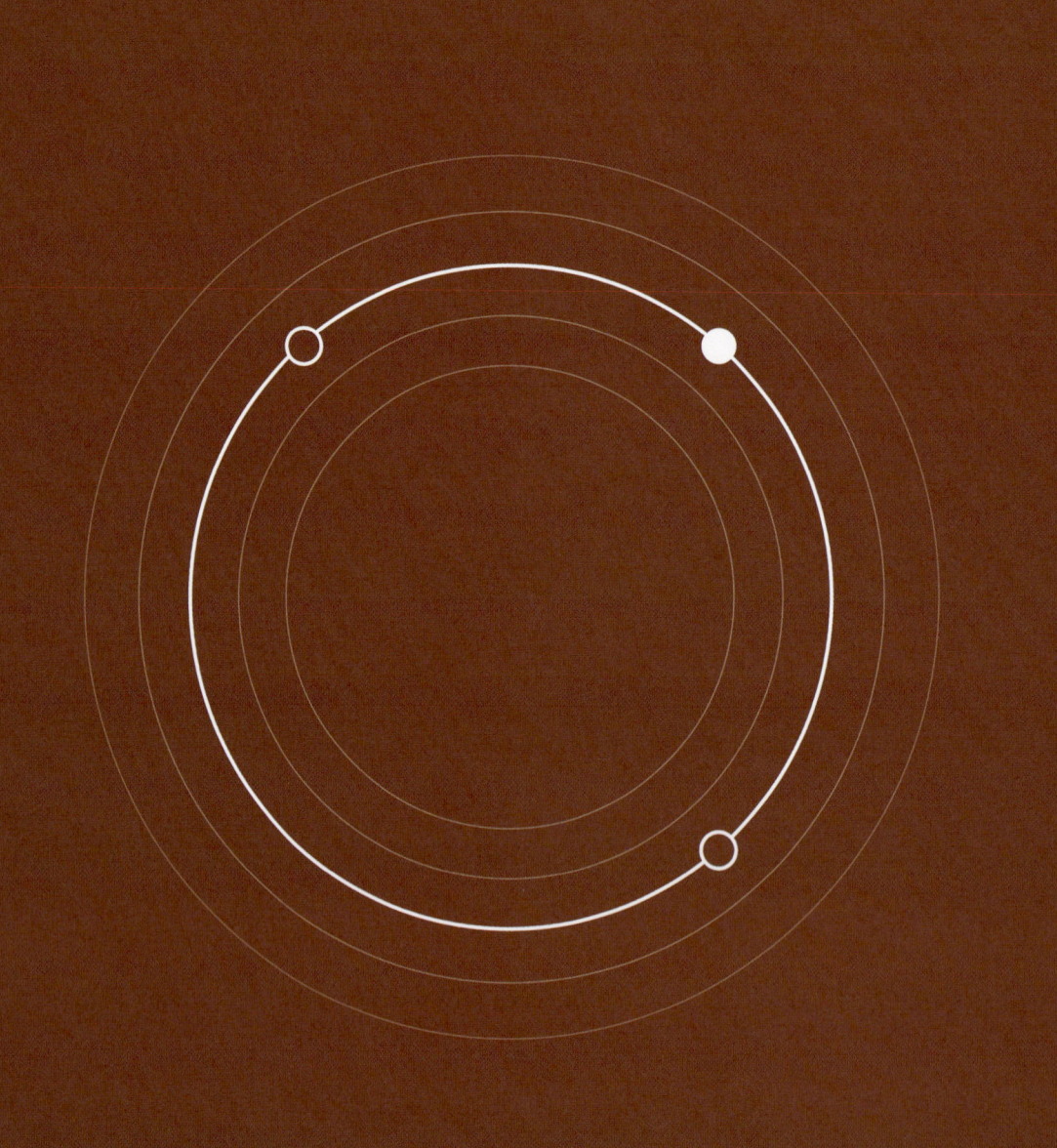

Vivid yellow *retama* (*Fabaceae*) broom bushes, their blooms blanketing the mountains during rainy season. The olive hues of *ch'ilca* (*Baccharis latifolia*) leaves paint a lush and green panorama. A field, recently ploughed by the *yunta*, resembles the sienna tone of *qaqasuncj'a* lichen.

These colors mirror the Andean landscape, and their hues intensify or soften depending on a specific moment of the dry and rainy seasons. Colors extracted from leaves, flowers and roots with love and patience to create a diverse palette.

Ceferina Pillco Gutiérrez captures that yellow-blanketed mountain and just-ploughed field in the guise of yarn so perfectly that she ad her Andean rainbow of hand-dyed alpaca *ovillos* (balls of yarn) were invited to exhibit at Ruraq Maki. And so she boarded a flight for the 2019 edition of Peru's prestigious traditional arts fair and flew to Lima (a double first for the artisan).

She and other women from CC Kacllaraccay have long used their foremothers' techniques to create textiles, dyeing sheep and alpaca wool with botanicals, spinning yarn and weaving with a *telar de cintura* (backstrap loom). Industry, however, has flexed its muscles, much to the detriment of those traditional skills, meaning authentic, artisanal wares are hard to come by in the Cusco region.

When Ceferina met Italian textile designer Giulia Pompilij, a Mater artist-in-residence, however, their mutual desire for knowledge bridged their respective ancestral and academic perspectives on dyeing techniques that would come to reveal the diverse plant ecosystems that surround Mil. Together they roamed fields and mountains, gathering leaves and flowers and unearthing roots, and conceived Warmi ('woman' in Quechua), an experimental workshop that uses botanical materials foraged from the Andean surroundings in line with the seasons.

"As the Warmi collective, we do everything together. We gather plants early in the morning, we dye together, stirring vats of boiling water filled with eucalyptus leaves or yellow *kjolle* (Buddleja coriacea) flowers, then add in wool or cotton totes, which 'cook' for around 15 minutes," says Ceferina.

Once the skeins have dried at the whims of the wind and sun, the *warmis* neatly order them, twisting their bodies to wrap the wool over their wrists, arms wide open at waist width: from skeins, they create perfectly spherical balls of yarn.

Ceferina shared her knowhow with the Italian textile designer, for example, that water from Maras is very salty so colors don't gain much intensity. "Her botanical knowledge is also extensive," Giulia says. "And, in turn, I showed Ceferina how to use mordants to see how many shades we could extract from plants. It was very experimental for us both in the beginning."

Their special, dynamic friendship meant the pair's enthusiasm fast encouraged other CC Kacllaraccay women to get involved, widening the creative web and fine tuning the workshop: today, the *warmis* connect with their environment, taking color inspiration from Apu Wañinmarcca mountain and its surroundings. Weekly meetings are held at Ceferina's barn, a couple of resting bulls and a few friendly mutts watching with vague interest as the 15 *mamis* – as the women refer to each other – not only undertake the task at hand but also enjoy lunch together. Each member of the collective brings a dish to share while they sit on the ground in a circle, a ritual of equal importance as the workshop itself.

The female-only collective's place within the community is crucial: not only does it lend renewed values to traditional artisanship and create sustainable products, it encourages members to interpret everyday objects with fresh eyes and tap into their environment. Meeting to share what's usually a solitary creative activity, they are empowered as they draw strength and inspiration from each other.

The women also labor in the fields along with their husbands, usually during sowing and harvest seasons, so in this regard, they contribute less economically. But every ball of alpaca yarn sold via Mater Sostiene (our Mater offshoot that reinvests in the interdisciplinary research organization's projects in order to continue preserving such traditional practices) notches up an additional source of income, with the menfolk supporting the project by helping to collect plants.

Warmi's hand-crafted approach also helps break the spell of textile sameness that flood fairs around the Cusco region, ceremoniously snapped up by tourists keen for a vacation bargain. Given that a machine-produced blanket takes a tenth of the time to make than a backstrap loom-woven *manta* (blanket) – then sells for a tenth of the price – it's hard for artisans to compete.

Ceferina was only too happy to stop selling somebody else's mass-produced wares at Moray's crafts fair, according to Giulia. "She hated carrying around a heavy bag filled with products she didn't believe in, and loathed talking about them even more," she says. "Creating yarn is much more her thing."

CC Kacllaraccay had double representation at Ruraq Maki; Elba Henrriquez Quispe exhibited homewares she makes at Mater's sister workshop Sacha (meaning plant or native in Quechua). A smaller, equally experimental project that brings together eight women artisans, the Sacha collective focuses on weaving with plant fibers, although its horizontal approach incorporates Warmi's wool in its creations.

Elba had largely stopped working with a traditional backstrap loom, choosing to crochet caps or buy, then sell on, mass-produced garments. And, while she's also a fountain of botanical information, she'd never considered using plant fibers in a weaving context. Together with Egyptian graphic designer Nada Atalla, another Mater artist-in-residence, Elba and Ceferina explored the Andes, gathering leaves and stems.

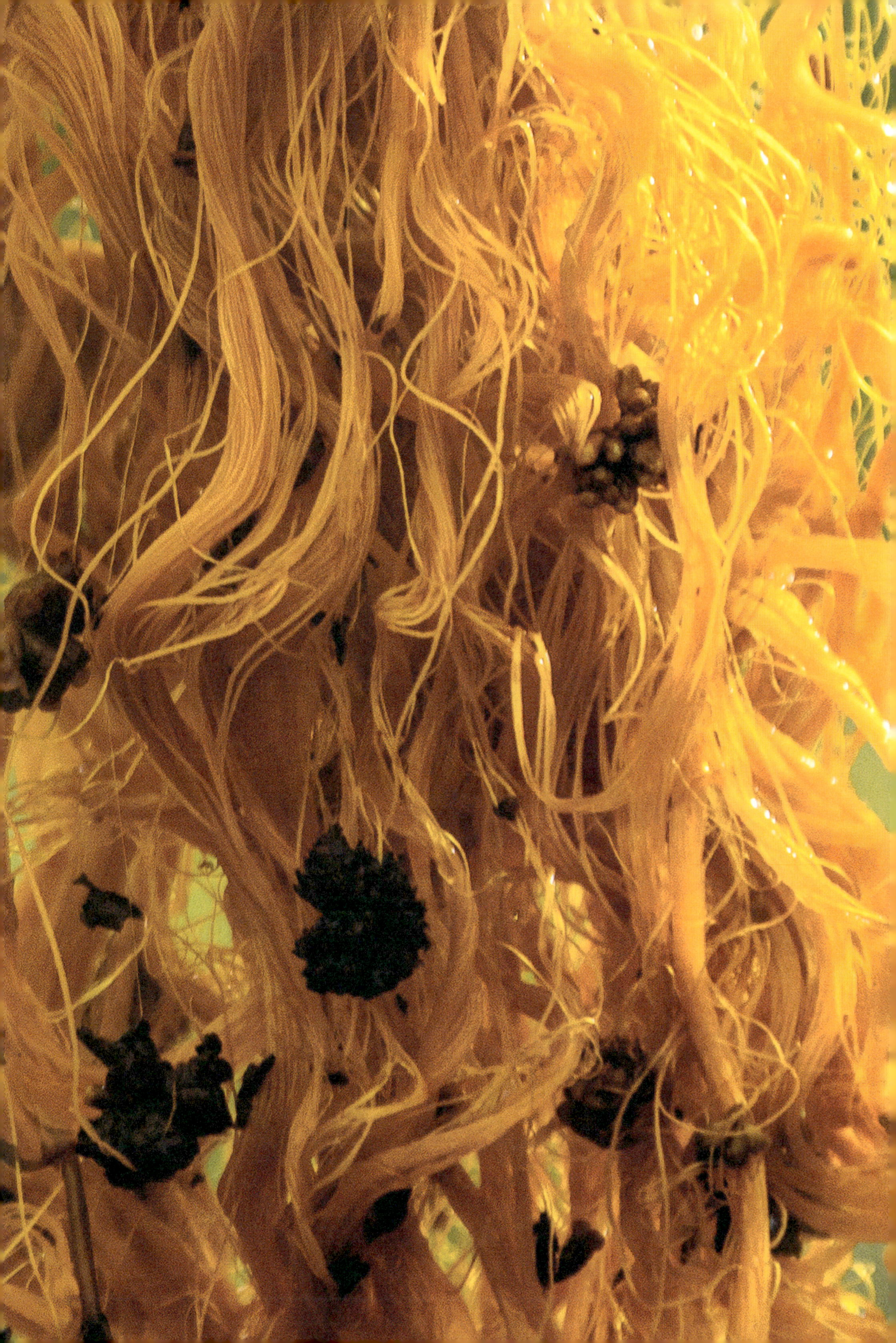

"None of us had weaved with botanical fibers before," says Nada, founder of a Cairo-based graphic design studio. "But Ceferina and Elba identify specific properties, for example, which plants bend easily or snap once dried." Together, they played around with *maguey* (Agave salmiana) fibers, sugar cane and quinua stems, and *panca de maíz* (corn husks) on the small frame loom that Nada had brought from Egypt. That inspired Elba to dust off her pinewood backstrap loom and start weaving again, this time incorporating botanical materials with more familiar animal wool fibers.

Panca de maíz, usually used to feed cattle, stood out for its easily pliable texture and the ease by which their light colored husks can be dyed. Nada adds: "Between violet, scarlet and yellow, the shades are outstanding, plus you can play around with patterns. It takes less time to weave with husks than it does with wool because patterns are less intricate." Woolen textiles tend to incorporate every-day iconography such as rivers, peaks and flowers, whereas Sacha's botanical weaves take a more linear approach.

Harvested around May, the dry season in motion, Elba keeps the husks damp so they retain flexibility. She pulls out a handful from her brightly colored *lliclla* shoulder cloth, six months after they were picked but as fresh as if they'd been plucked from the field earlier that morning.

Elba says: "If they retain moisture, I can work with them as and when I need to; I use purple, red and yellow corn husks to create patterns." She soon started creating table runners and now leads the Sacha workshop, passing on her newly honed knowledge with the community's young moms.

The future looks promising for both collectives. One ongoing Warmi project is producing yarn prototypes for a Peruvian women's wear brand, while plans are in the pipeline to develop a Kacllaraccay-specific iconography guide. And, together, Warmi and Sacha teamed up with Mater artists-in-residence Alejandra Ortiz de Zevallos and architect Constanza Gainza to create a 39-foot by 39-foot *khipu* (interactive knot-record), made with *ichu* and Warmi yarns. A tufty pale-yellow Andean grass traditionally used to thatch roofs, woven in a particular way *ichu* was used to record information in Andean communities. This 21st-century *khipu* – commissioned for an eponymous exhibition held at Lima's MALI art museum in 2020 – was inspired by the Q'eswachaka Bridge in the Cusco region's Canas province (a structure that is rebuilt annually).

Thanks to the knowledge, creativity and dedication of CC Kacllaraccay's *warmis*, the living matter surrounding the Apu Wañinmarcca mountain deity is just starting to leave its mark on the world of art and design.

231

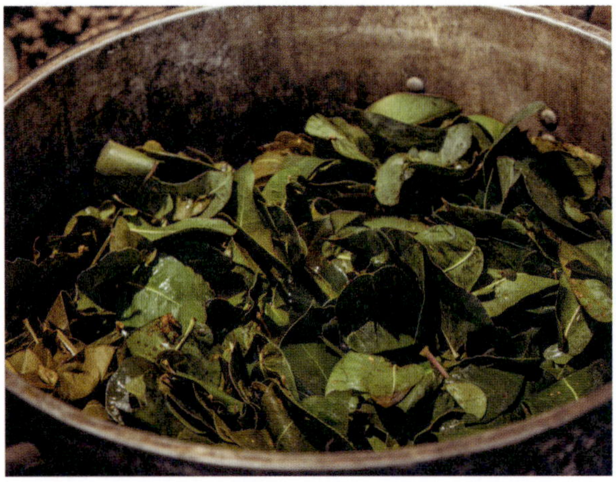

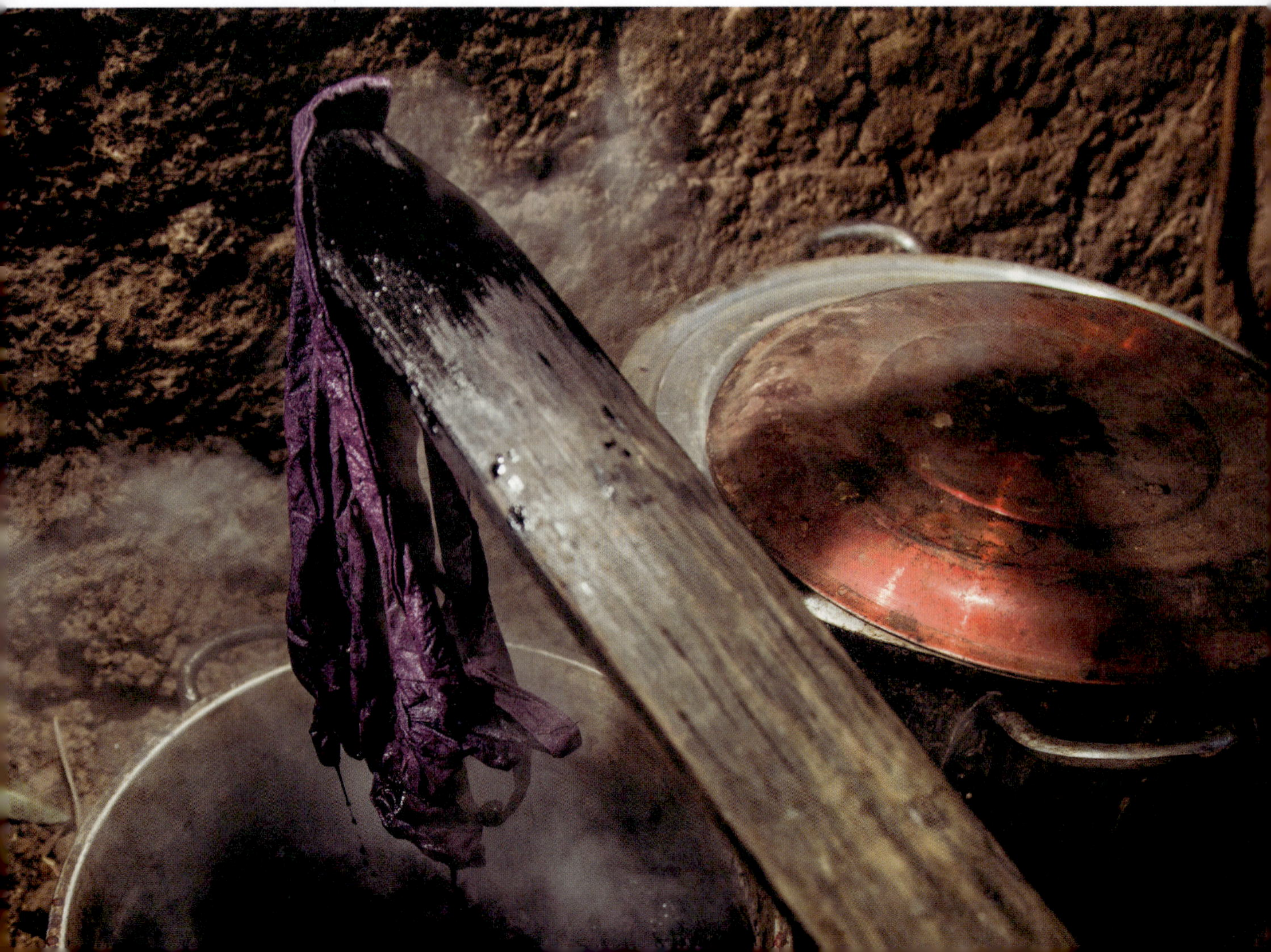

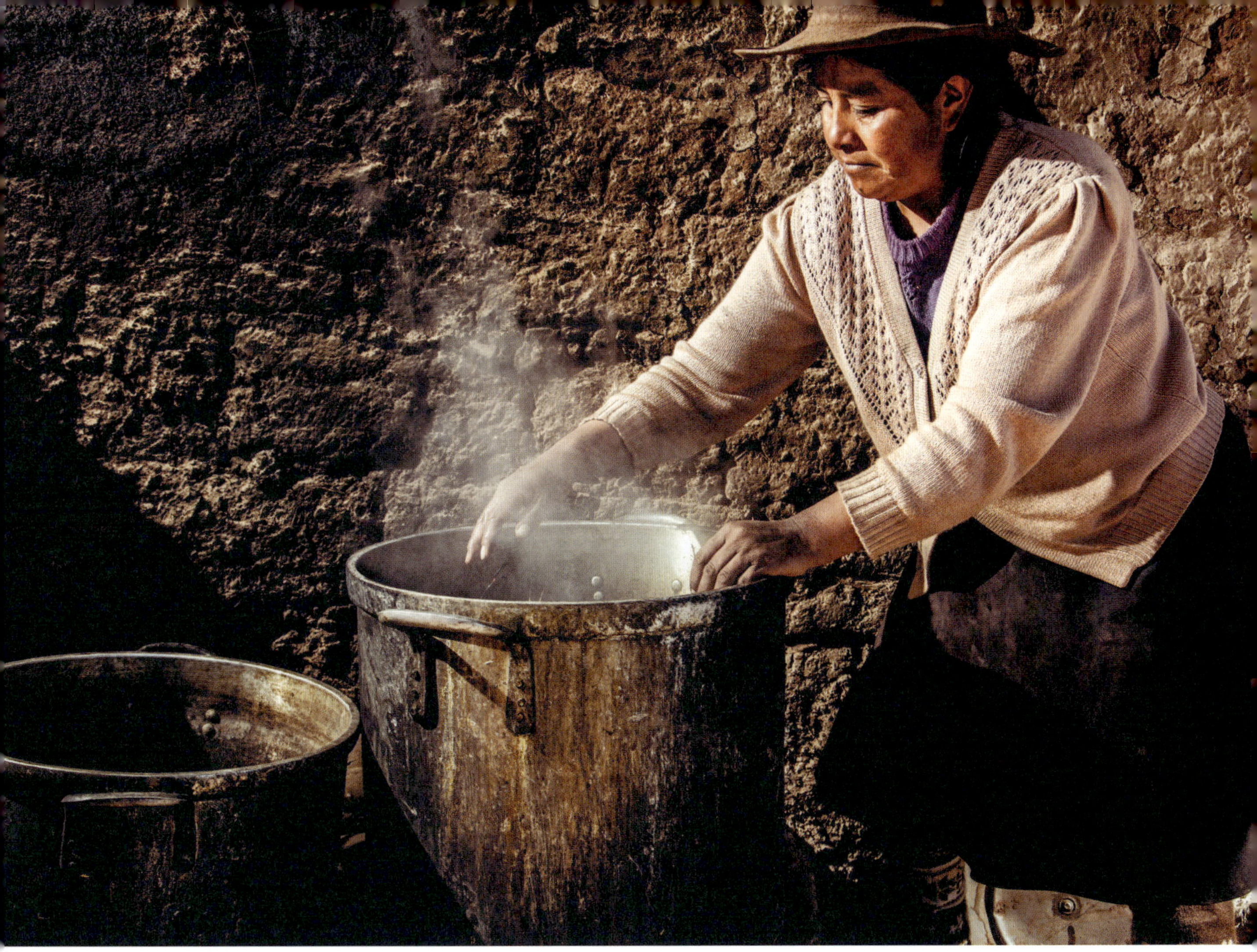

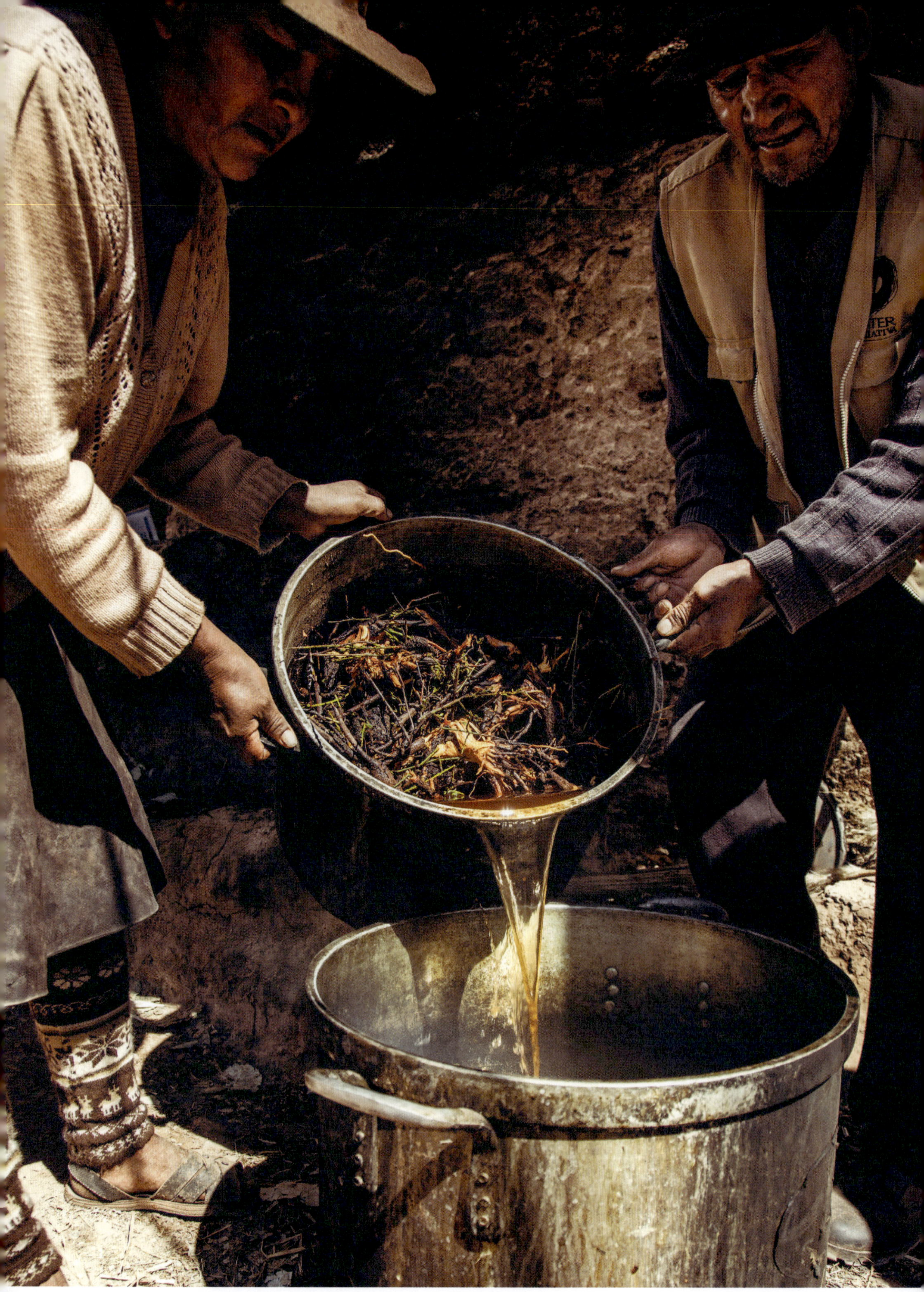

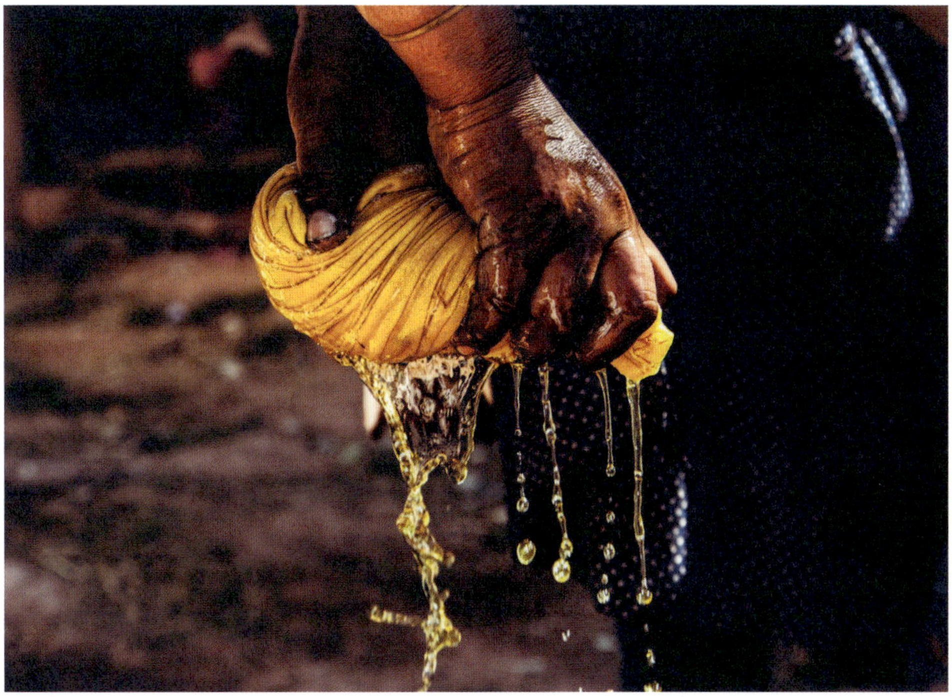

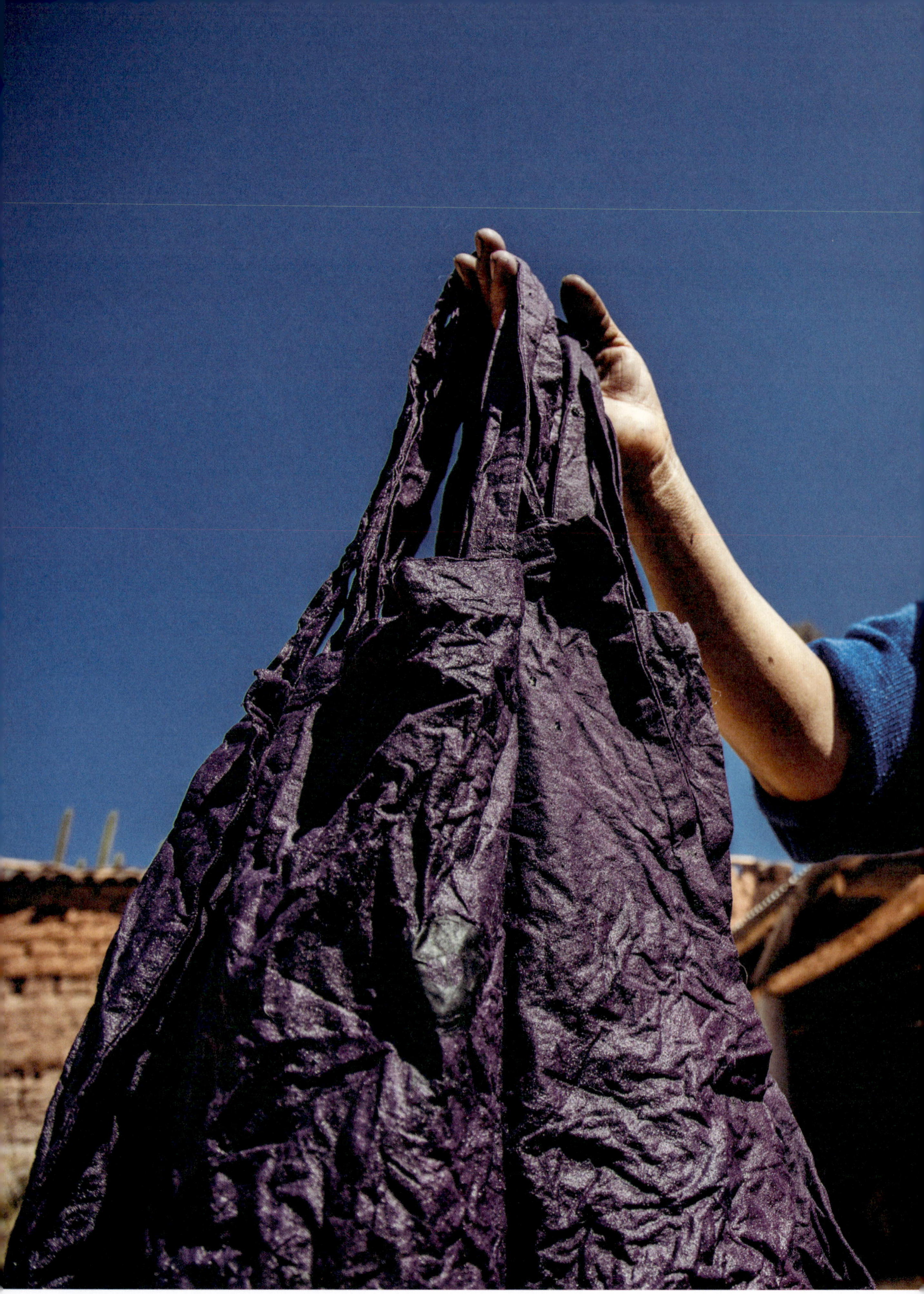

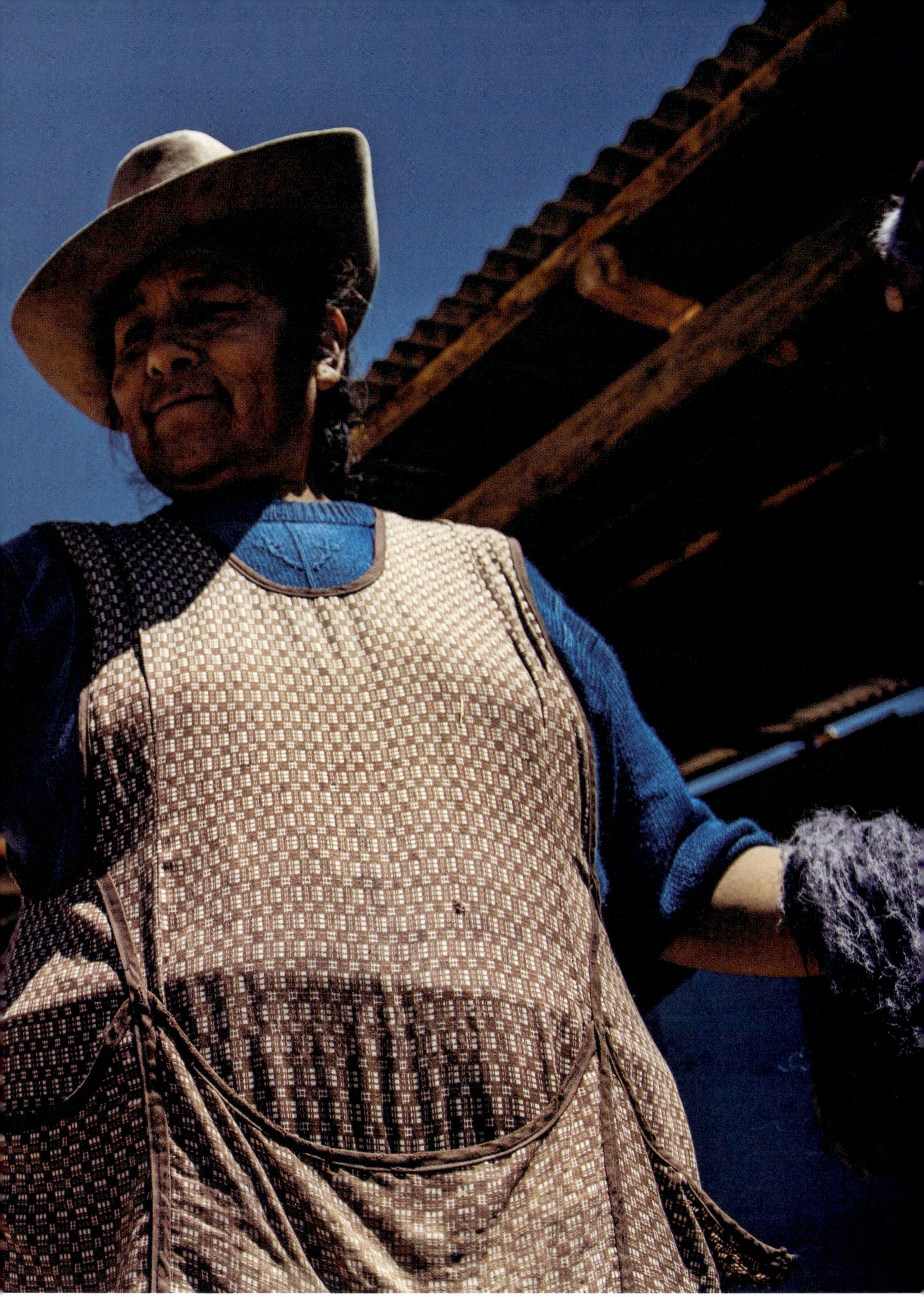

238

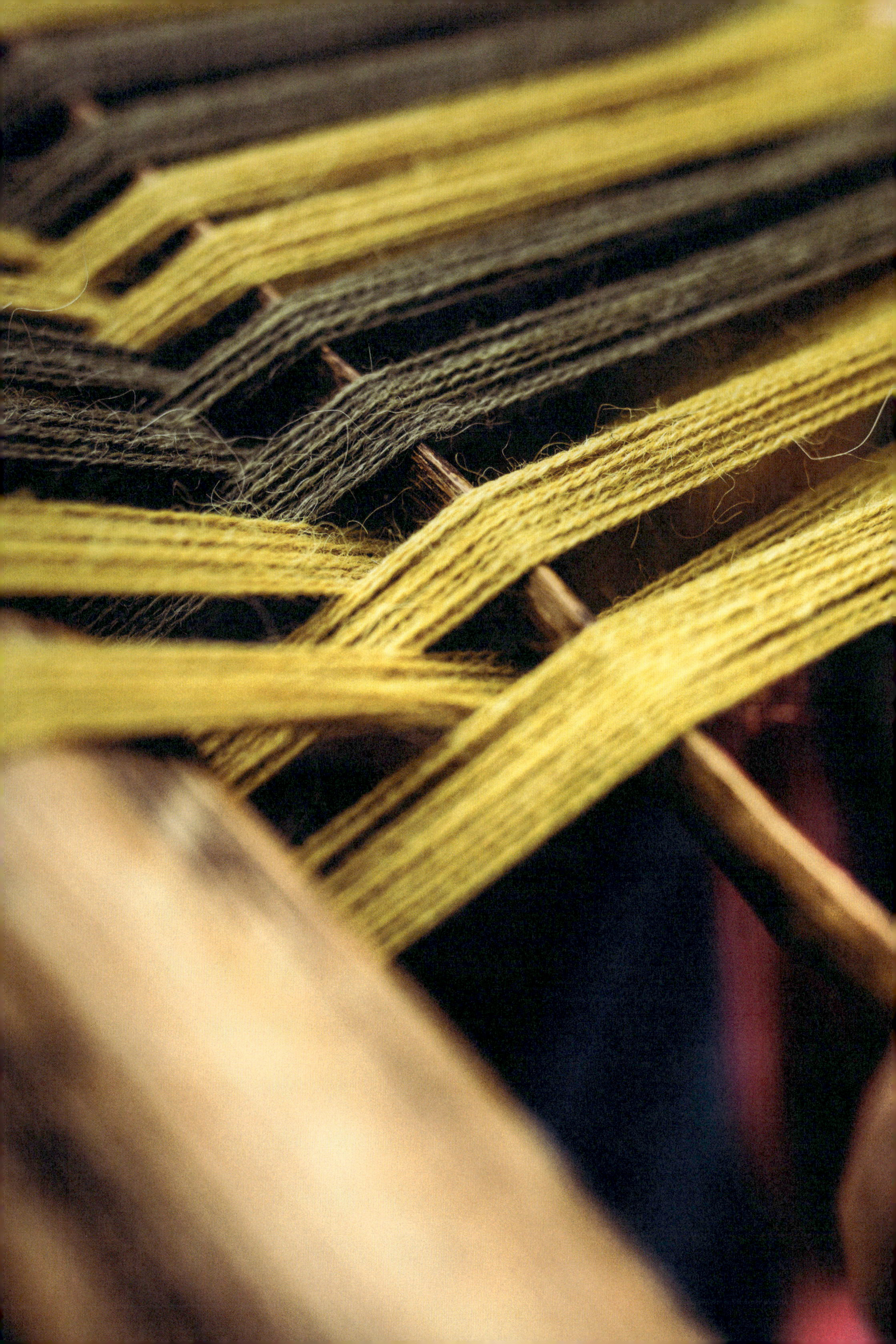

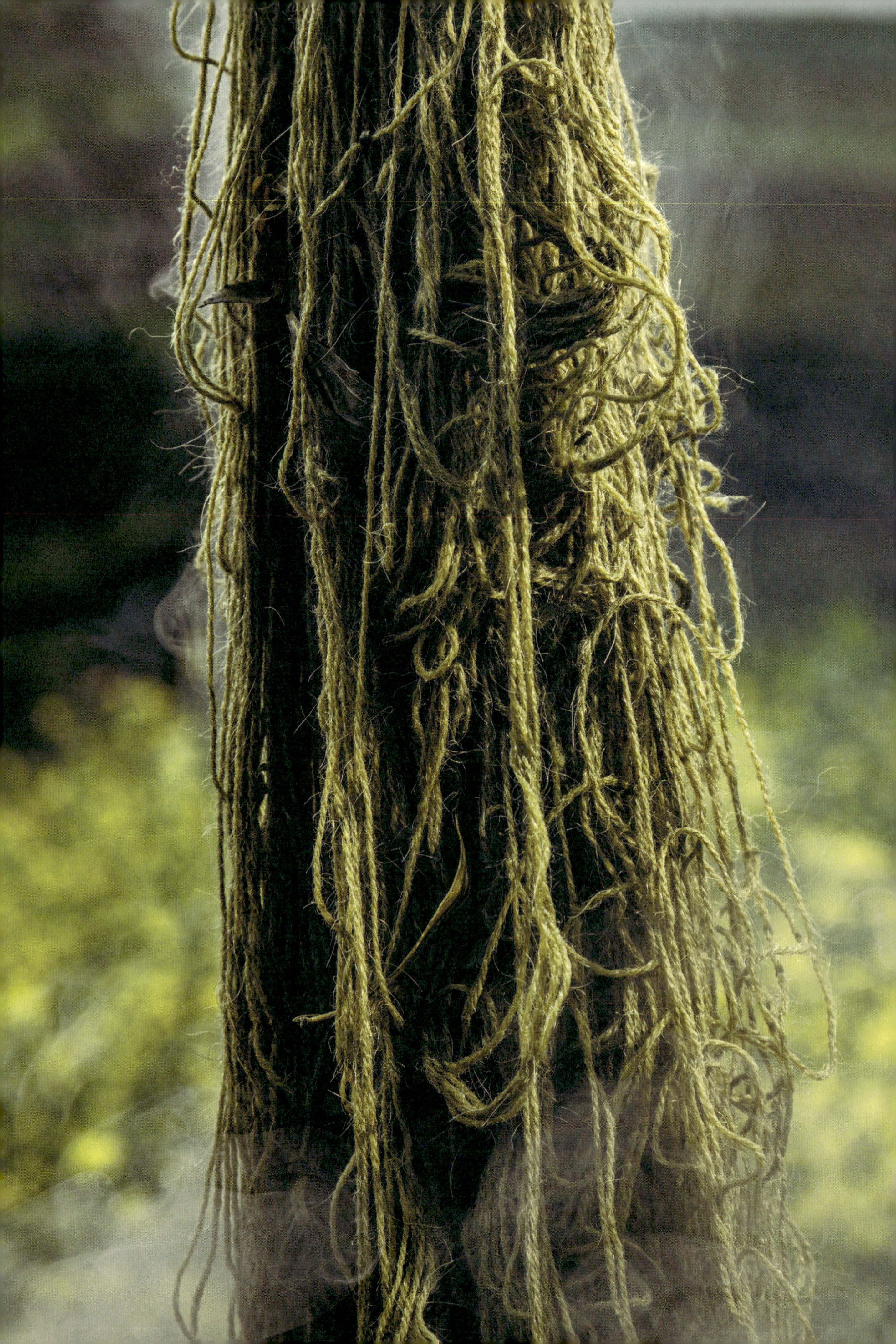

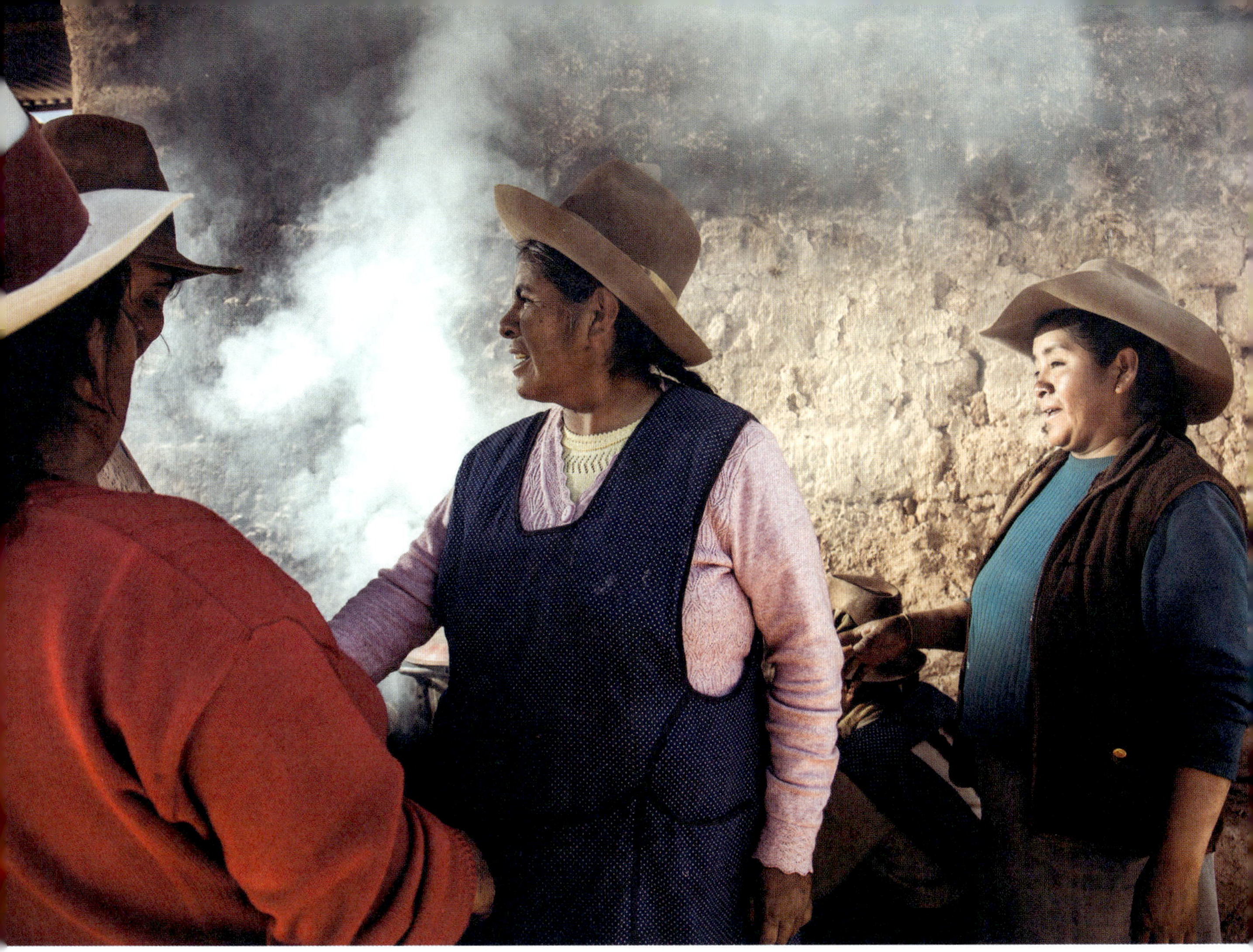

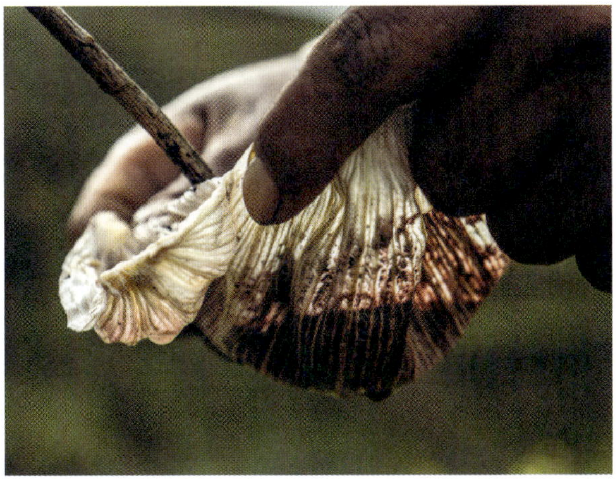

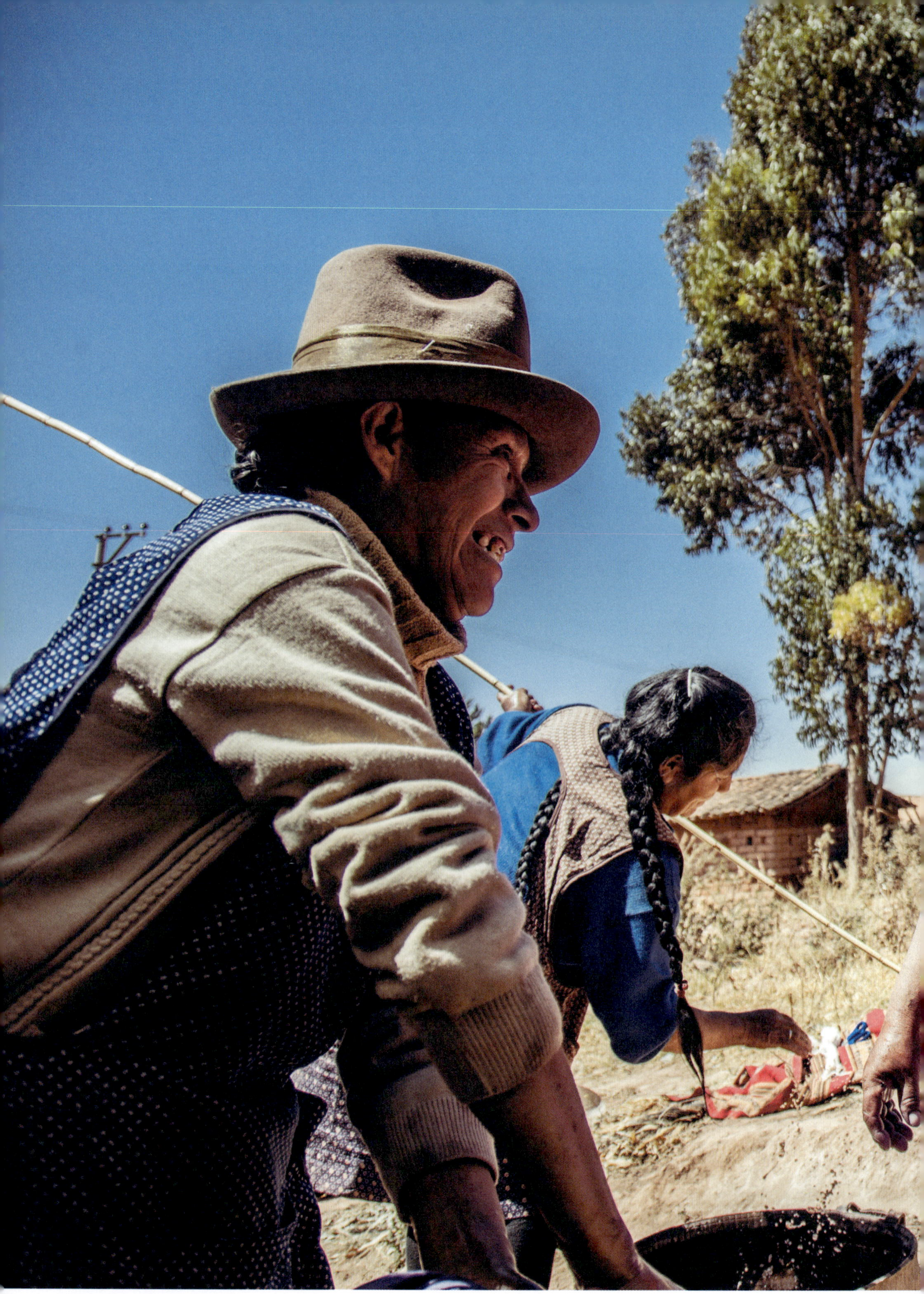

243

DOWN-TO-EARTH CREATIONS

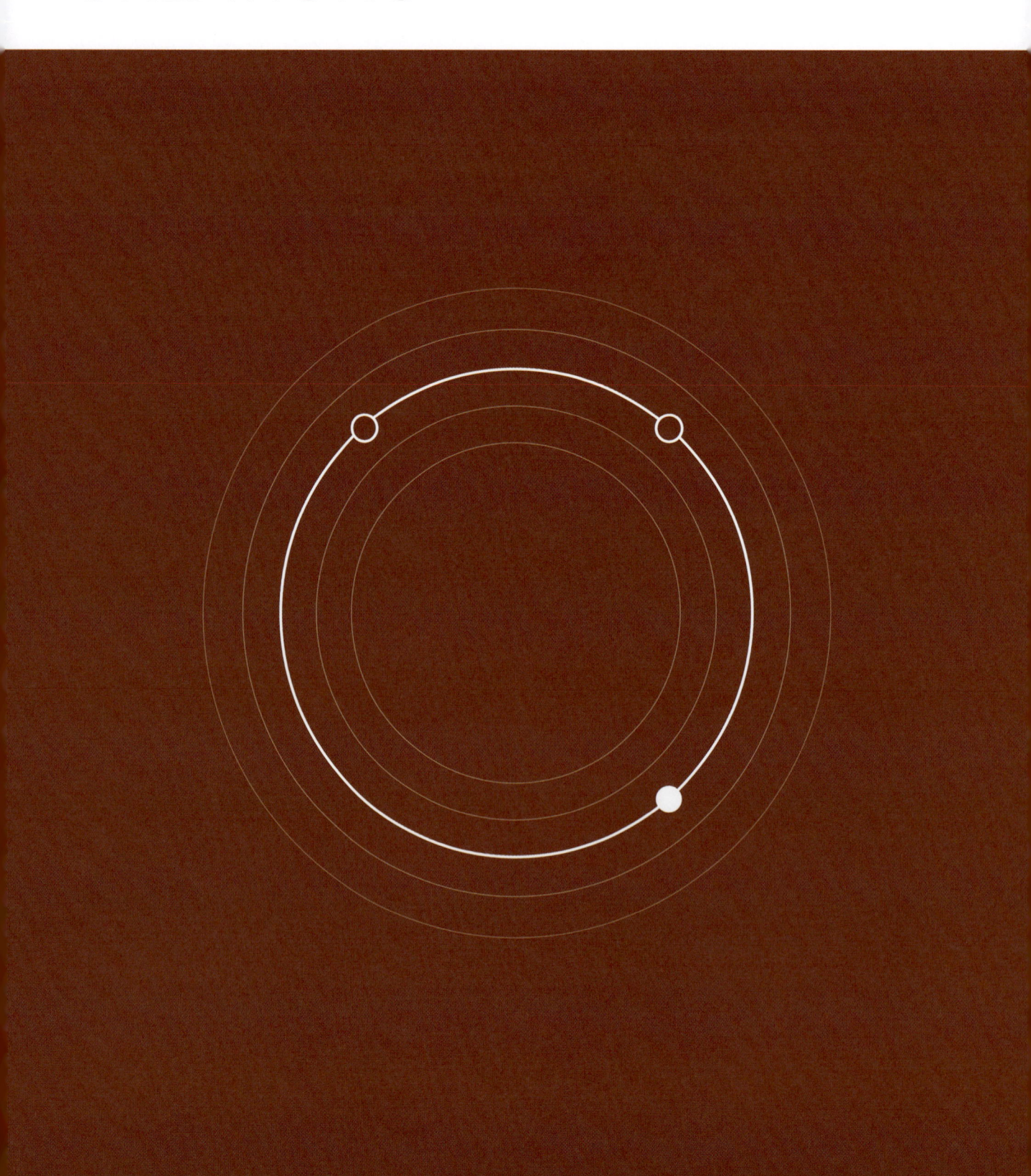

For Mater's T'uru Maki pottery workshop, we take inspiration from our surroundings, scooping up the earth to creatively transform its texture and shape. Earth, whose porosity and plasticity means dwellings in the Cusco region have long been constructed from hand-molded adobe bricks shaped from this red-brown mud, water and *ichu* feather grass – including our own Mil, a former vicuña breeding center. In the rainy season, thick mud clings to sandaled feet that have traversed the elevated fields, or artfully splatters over windscreens like a Pollock. In the dry season, brisk breezes whip the ground up into vigorous dust devils. Mud, glorious mud, is everywhere – brimming with potential.

Besides using wet earth for building materials, during the Quechua civilization the Cusco region's inhabitants adhered to a strong tradition of creating pottery for practical, everyday use as well as ceremonial ones, and for trading at Tiobamba [the *raqui* pot used for fermenting *chicha de jora* served both purposes, given the corn beer's sacred status]. But, similarly, albeit to a greater extent than textiles, this craft has faded away, failing to be passed on down the generations. Only Raqch'i, based in Cusco's San Pedro district in the province of Canchis, is noted for – and today continues – its excellence in pottery.

In CC Mullak'as-Misminay and CC Kacllaraccay, families build their homes from scratch with local resources. Women and men team up to collect clay – pits are especially notable in the former community – then make adobe bricks. Combining water and *ichu* grass, they then tread on the clay, leaving it overnight to dry; small houses are built in four or five days. What these communities are constructed upon, and their surroundings, are put to practical, rather than artistic, use.

So when Berlin-based product designer Cindy Valdez approached Mater to research clays in Mil's vicinity, it provided the impetus to create an artistic project that would weave social, sustainable, gastronomical and environmental elements into a new venture, while resurrecting lost traditional skills, ticking all the boxes for Mater's director of art and cultural projects, Verónica Tabja. "This kind of collaboration can help sustain, share and revitalize a legacy of identity that's nearly been forgotten," says Verónica.

Cindy was the first person to dig up, then identify, some of the distinctive clays that form part of the Andes' ecosystems: she then evaluated their properties with the aim of showing the importance of biodiversity and human intervention of earth, simply, what is behind a dish in *Migration of Matter*, her thesis project. "The red, white, and yellow clays we sourced from a hill in CC Kacllaraccay have high mineral content, which influences biodiversity, and in turn, defines a potato's attributes," she says.

Cindy's clay-catalog baton was then picked up by Lima-based sculptor Valeria Figueroa, who specializes in pottery, to collaborate with Mater and Verónica, and together they established T'uru Maki (Quechua for 'clay hands'), a ceramics workshop for women who live in CC Mullak'as-Misminay that resurrects and inspires a 21st-century interest in the art with the end goal of crafting dishware sold by Mater Sostiene, which reinvests back into the workshop.

"By using locally sourced raw materials, Mater re-opened the doors of this ancestral technique to one of our neighboring communities – a skill dating from the Quechua empire and developed in the Sacred Valley – with the aim of generating a commercial channel for those participating in the workshop. It has also allowed us to discover a whole new universe," adds Verónica.

The timing was inspired for Valeria, who was reassessing the value of her own work and looking for a new base outside of Peru's capital. She says: "In Lima, we potters buy already-prepared clay and have no idea where it comes from or its composition. You simply buy a 26-lb bag, then get to work with it. I wanted the opportunity to collect my own clay and start the whole process from scratch, possibly even building my own kiln.

"The idea of putting together a ceramics workshop outside of the city was formidable. Working directly with the community, learning from their intuition with clay, sourcing materials directly from the earth, learning the differences between the various earths and creating pieces from elements that surround their territory, seemed like one of the most honest and enriching experiences I could expose myself to."

Just one woman – Dominga Cusihuaman Acostupa – out of an initial group of 10 recruited by Mater's anthropologist Francesco D'Angelo for the first live laboratory, had dabbled in pottery; memories of her grandmothers shaping bowls or plates were hazy, however. "It piqued my interest that this tradition was actively pursued during the Quechua empire but no longer exists today," says Valeria.

With the sky for a roof, that first gathering of many over six weeks took place outdoors in Anccoto, a sub-district in CC Mullak'as-Misminay. An experimental exercise, it started by gathering clay from the surroundings, one of various motives behind the project including female empowerment, independence and forming a creative outlet inspired by the immediate vicinity. "We used finished plates as molds to jump in more quickly," she adds, "although those first pieces were coarse."

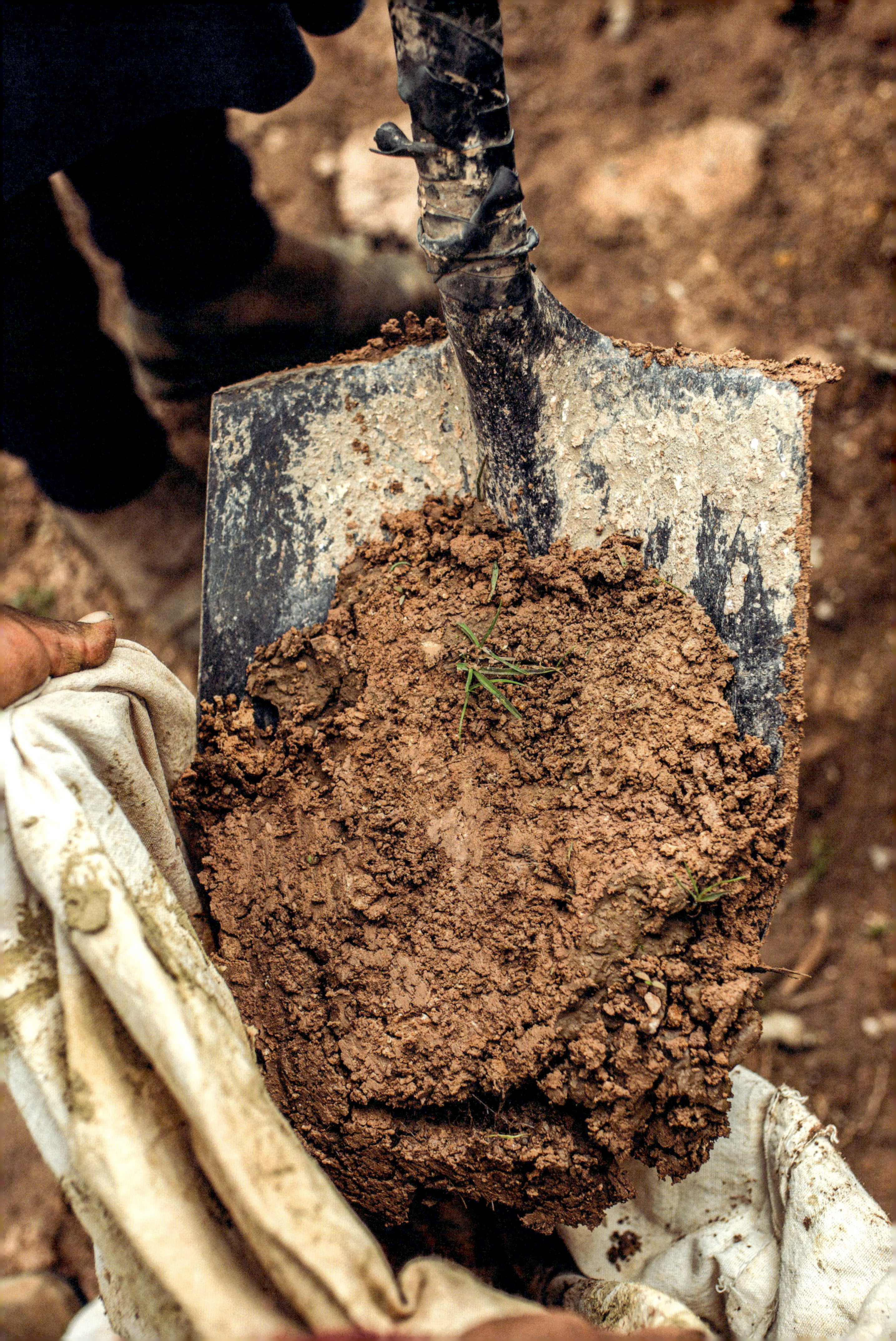

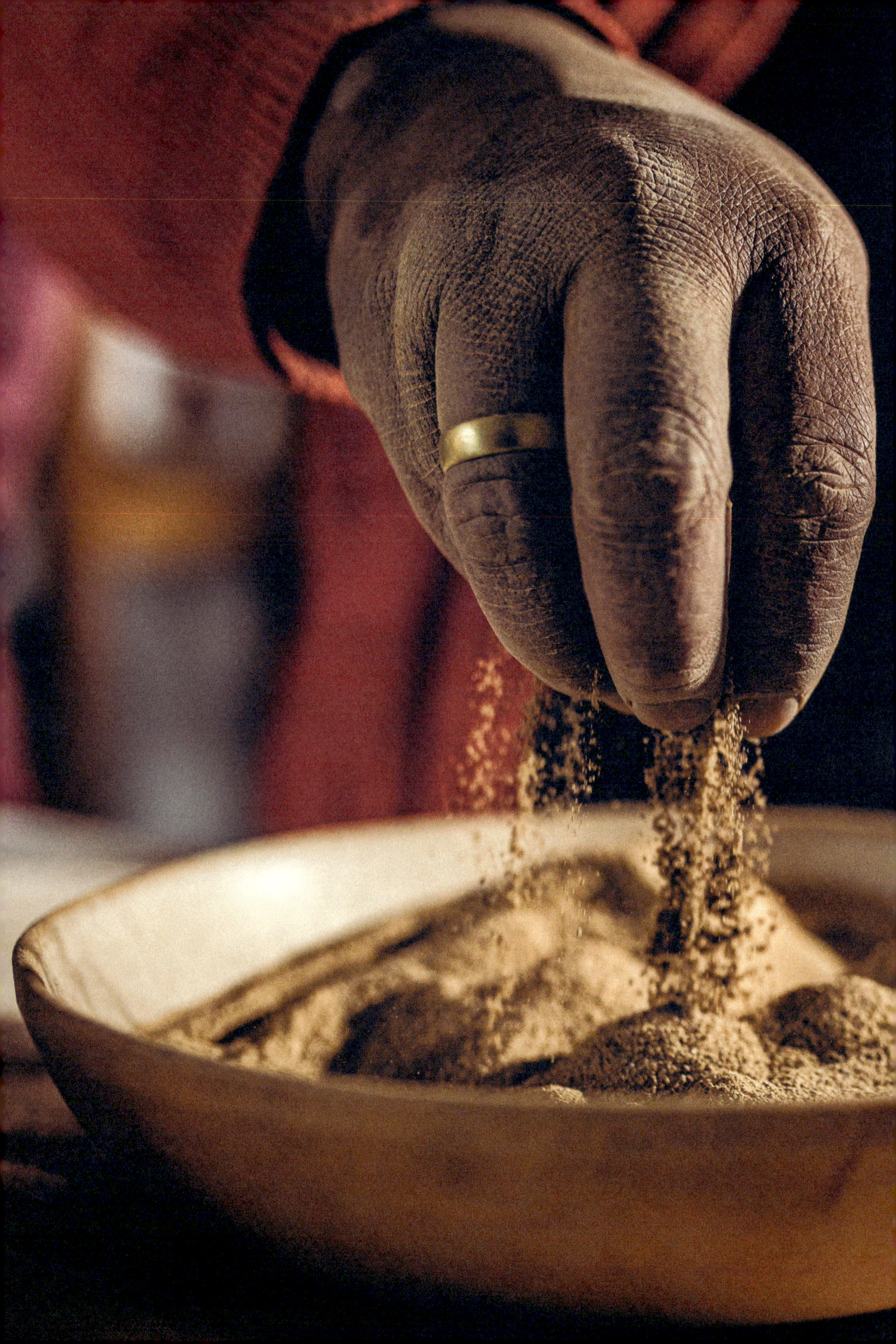

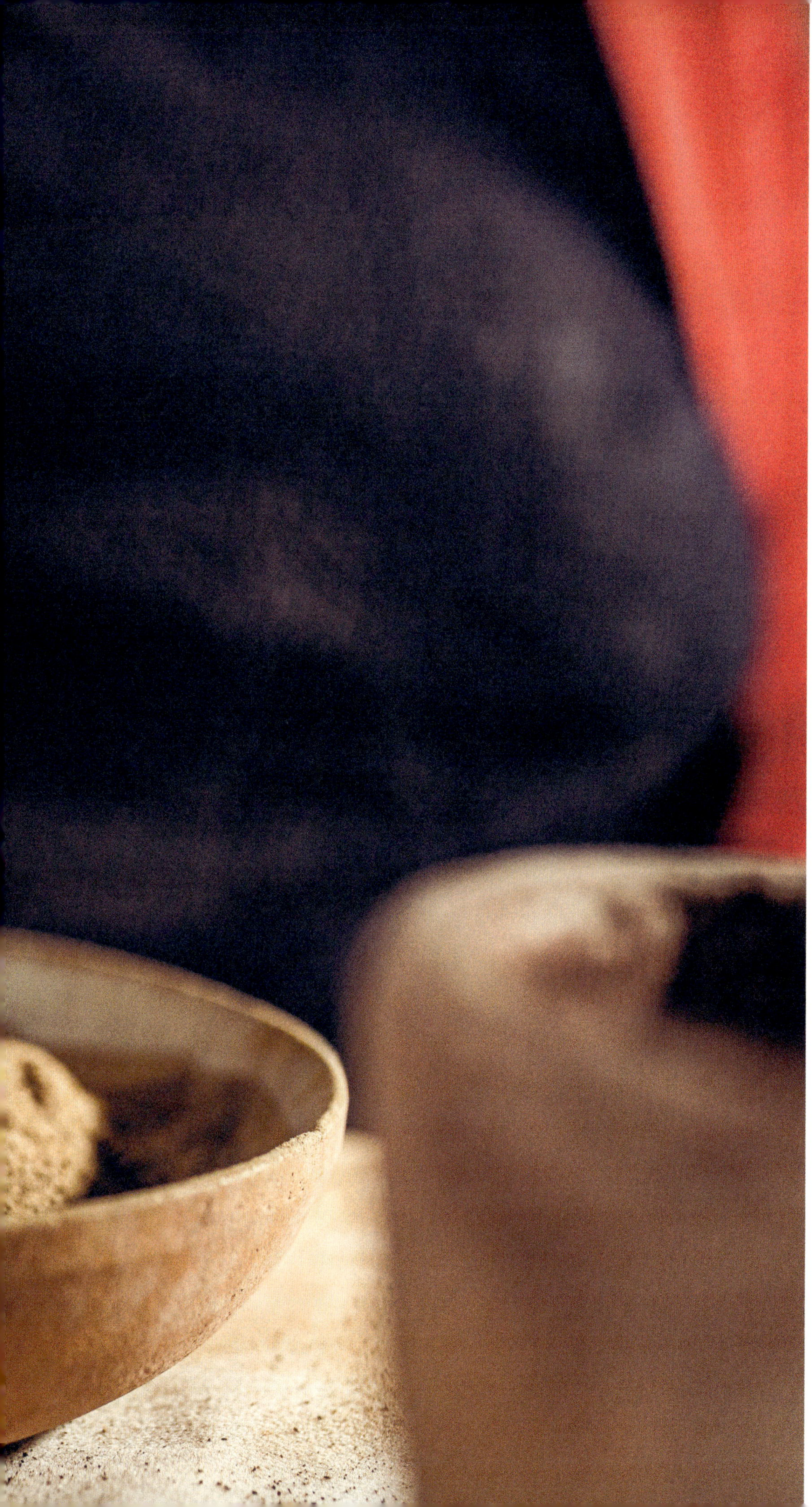

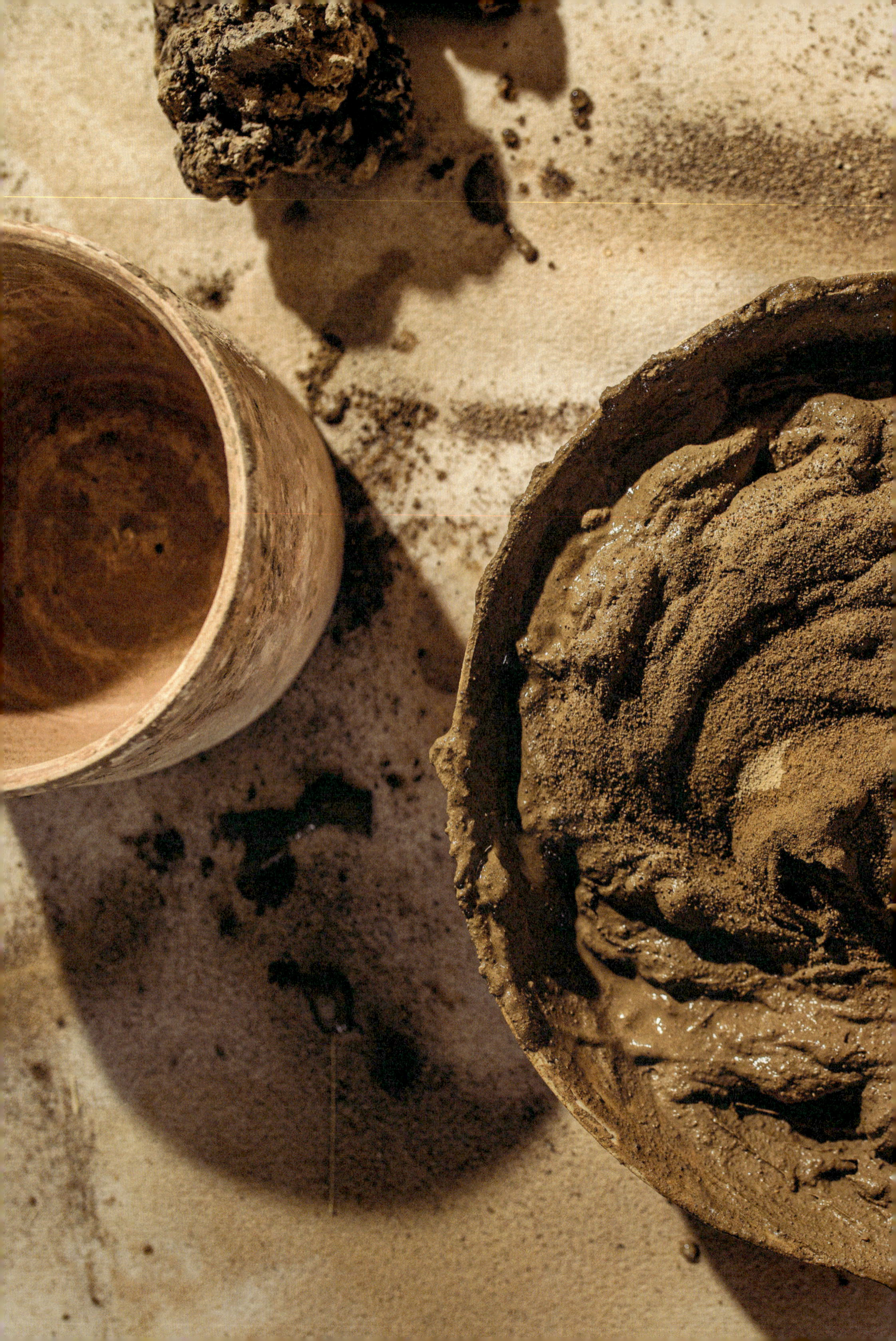

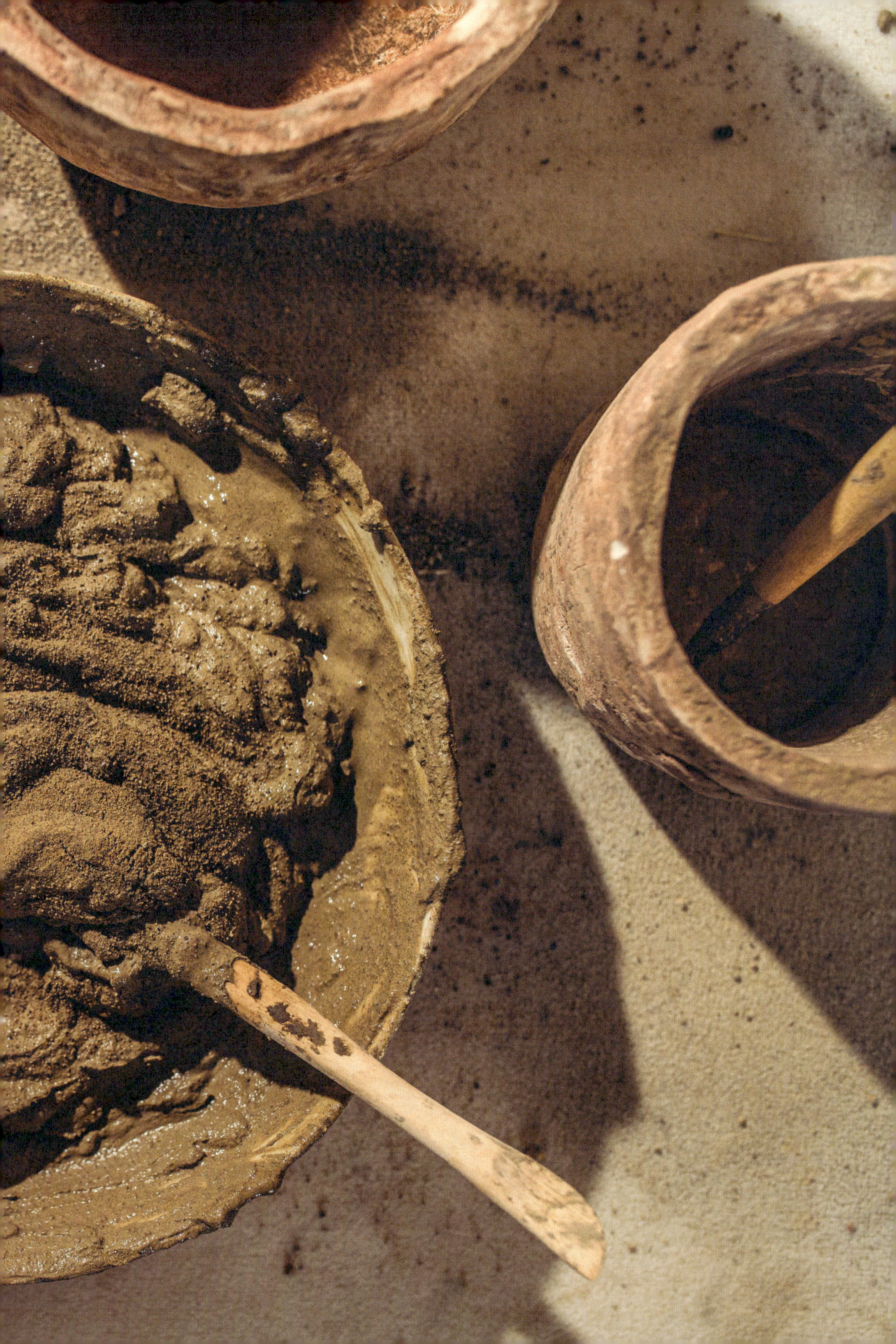

An ancestral technique dating from the Quechua empire, the art of pottery making in the Cusco region has dwindled in recent times. Our live laboratory digs up raw material – red, white and yellow hues with surprisingly distinctive textures – straight out of the Andean ground to experiment with and revive this enriching yet lapsed skill by forming the T'uru Maki collective (Quechua for clay 'hands') with women from CC Mullak'as-Misminay.

Together, the collective dug up three types of earth that had different textures and colors. This meant a trip up into the mountains with a mule to haul the load back, but on discovering that the green-gray clay from Pillahuara was best to work with, that several hour-long journey instantly became worth it. Adding in eucalyptus ashes taken directly from each woman's clay oven at home gave additional texture to finished pieces before they were fired. They built *huatias* but they never reached high enough temperatures (from 1,800°F/980°C upwards) and so used a kiln rather impractically located in Urubamba for those first 16 pieces; they are now in use at Central in Lima.

T'uru Maki remains an experimental work in progress, given that the collective is sourcing a wood-fired kiln to fire bowls and cups in Anccoto, rather than taking them to Urubamba. But, they've made headway. Dominga and co now work out of a small workshop in Anccoto, and every time they scoop up earth, mixing it to obtain the right composition before forming it into a plate or bowl is another step closer to empowerment, artistically appreciating their surroundings and retrieving the identity of this traditional skill.

"The materials that come from these surroundings are so simple and incredibly beautiful. They aren't just minimal and contemporary but also share the story of day-to-day living in a community and working with local resources. This skill was lost – we're simply trying not to forget it existed," says Valeria.

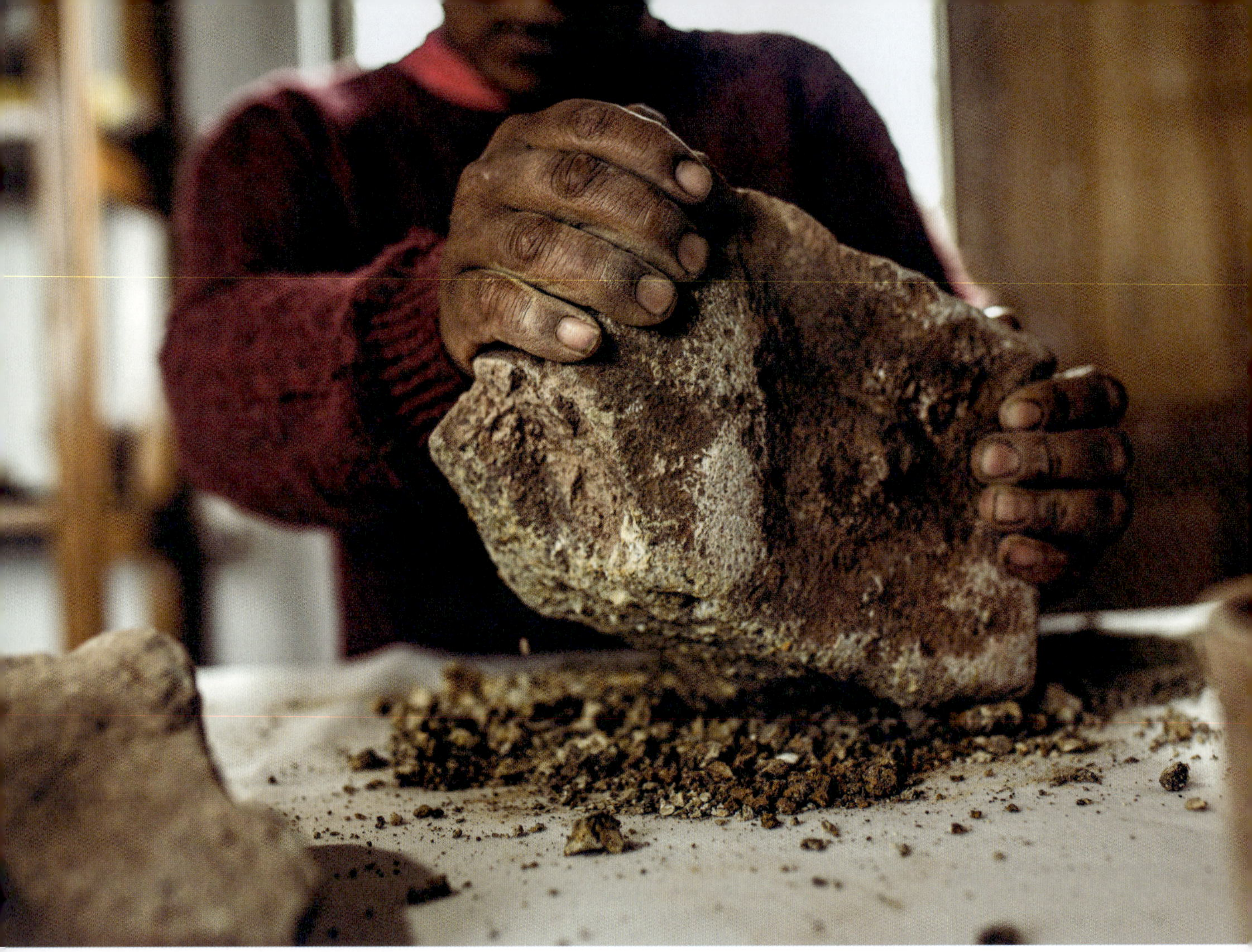

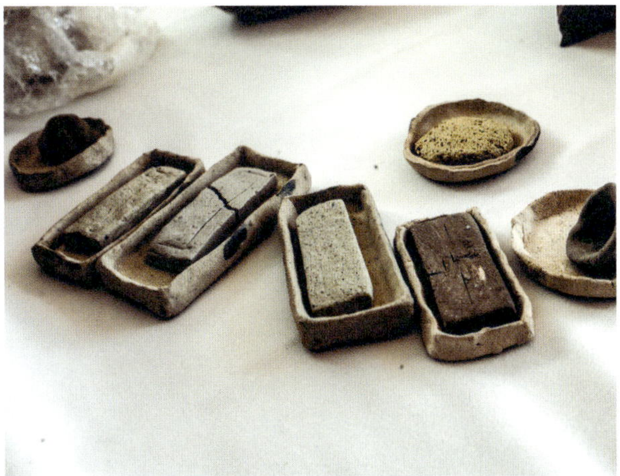

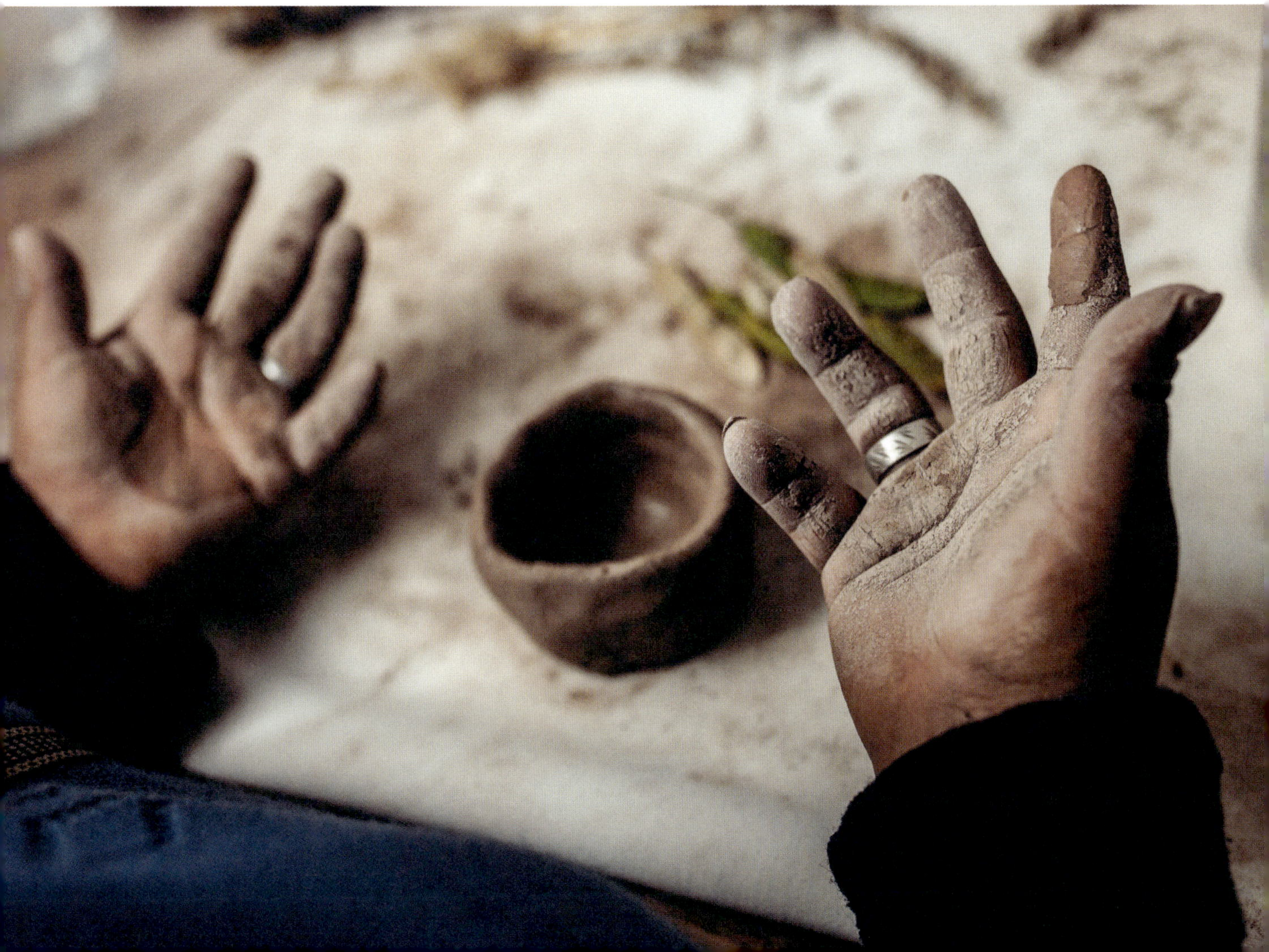

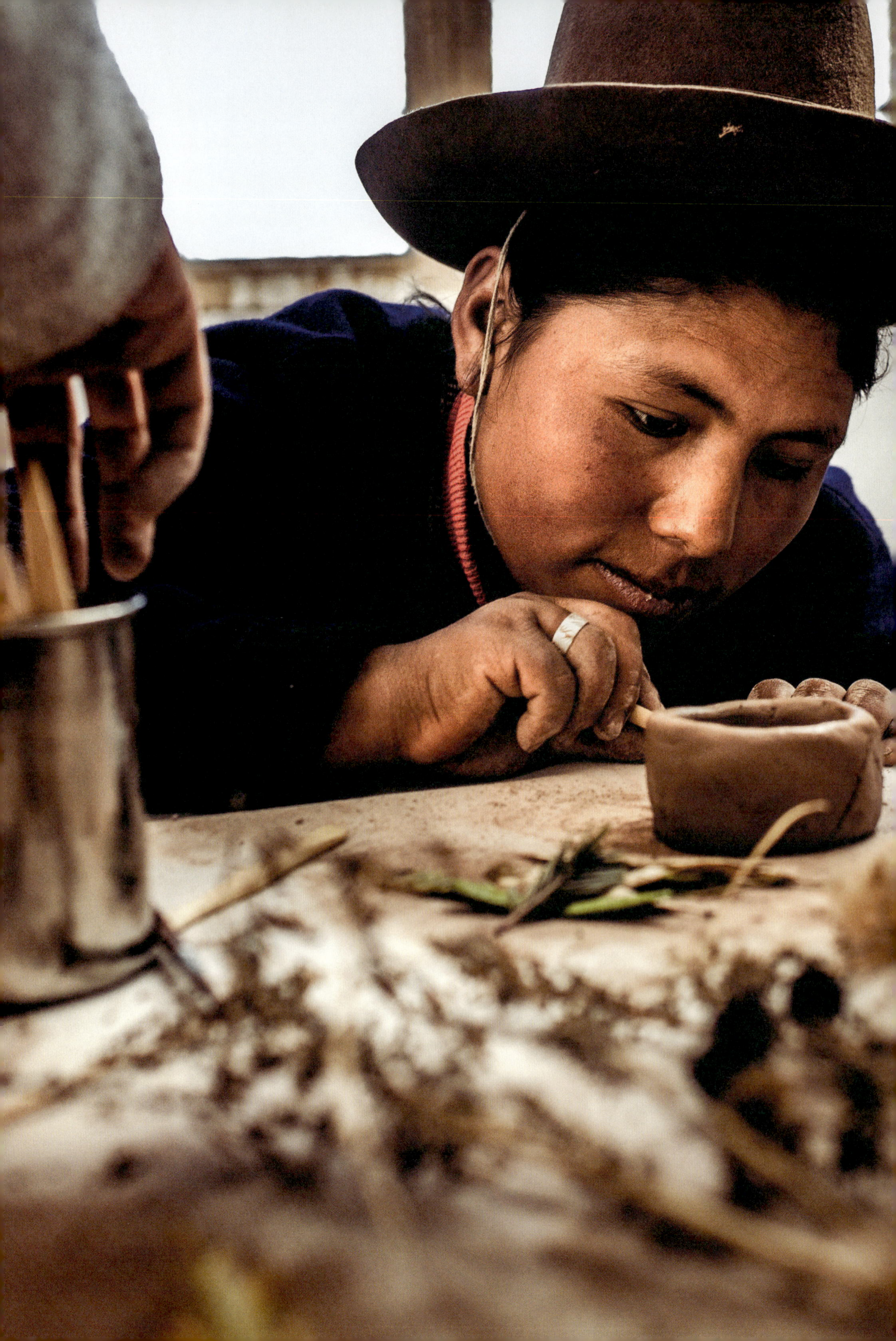

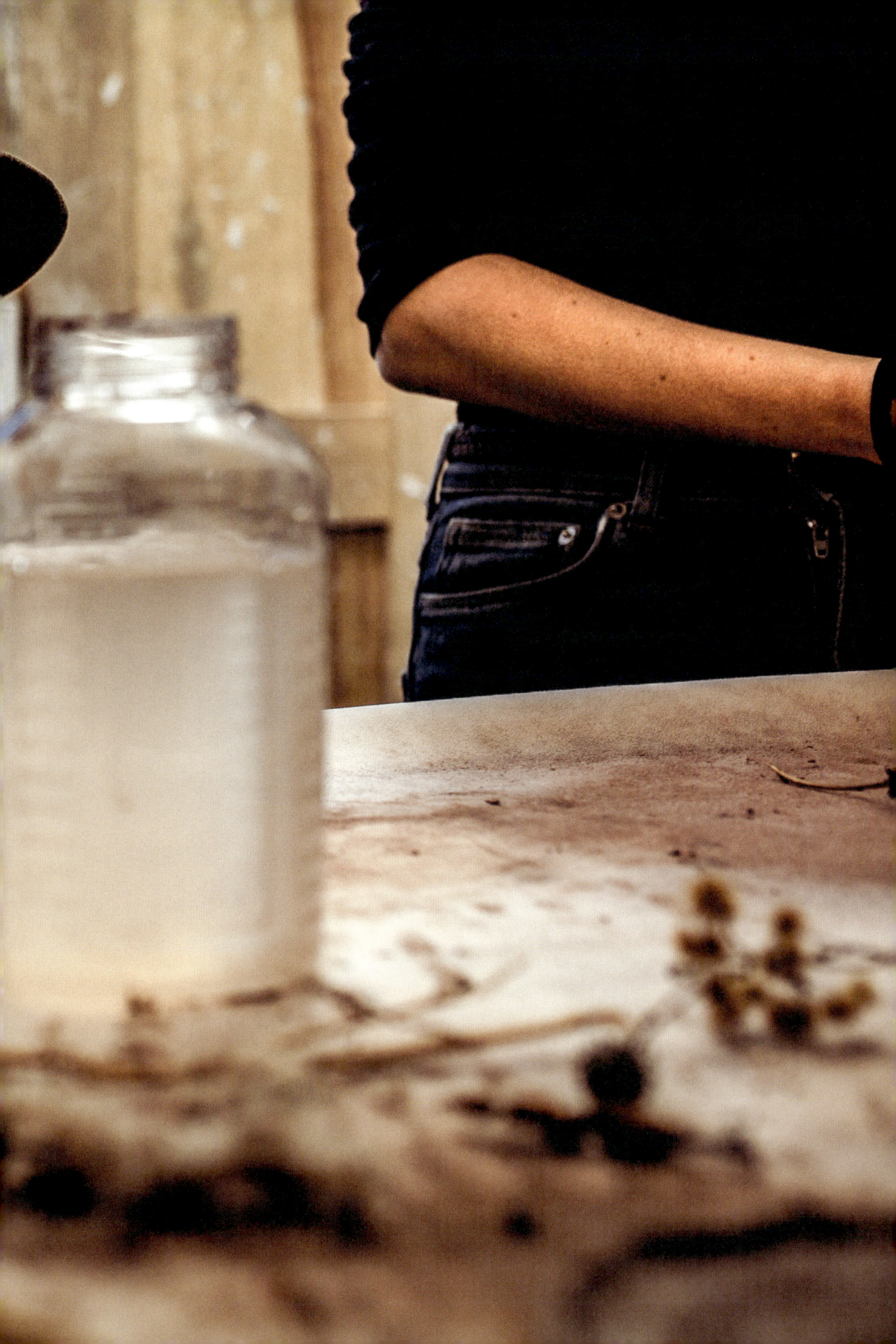

ORGÁNICA LAMAY

HORTICULTURIST

The life cycle of land

While Cusco was the administrative heart as capital of the Quechua empire, its location at the 'the navel of the world' was near perfect, agriculturally speaking, embraced by the bosom of Sacred Valley. Hundreds of years after feeding its citizens and armies, these elevated fertile lands, whose crops were cultivated on vast terraces that are still seen today in Pisaq and Ollantaytambo, while its arteries, the Rivers Vilcanota and Huarocondo, vigorously wind through the valley, bursting out over their banks in rainy season to quench thirsty corn and fava bean crops and feed people. Communities have long thrived here, working the land and understanding the two seasons to use them to their advantage; indeed Cusco has been continuously inhabited for 3,000 years, the oldest such city in the Americas, thanks to the region's bountiful pantry.

Traveling between small towns such as Pisaq, Calca and Ollantaytambo, farmland drapes many steep, impossible-to-plough slopes; every usable inch is devoted to agriculture. Rows of corn sway in the mountain breeze, while blooming tubers in the rainy season weave pretty carpets of yellow, pink and violet flowers.

In the foothills above Lamay found at 9,645 feet above sea level, an hour's drive from Mil, there's a farm using that every-last-inch philosophy to create a sustainable and organic farm on less than a hectare of the Andes. "Everything flourishes here," says Alex Rocca, daily operations manager at Orgánica Lamay, "thanks to the fertile, volcanic soil and varied weather." (Continue climbing up into the mountain for another 3,280 feet and you'll reach CC Huama-Chuquibamba, where the foraging Quispe sisters and botanical expertis live.)

A need for fresh, varied produce gave light to Orgánica Lamay a decade ago. After opening his first establishment in Cusco, restaurateur Rafael Casabonne quickly realized the ingredients he sourced from Lima rarely reached the kitchen intact. He discovered a fertile area of Lamay next to the Carmén stream – a corner filled with buzzing bees and merry parakeets calling joyfully as they fly between eucalyptus trees – at 9,810 feet above sea level and founded a farm that would meet his own needs.

Applying a natural approach from day one – ensuring product diversity by rotating soils, using natural herbicides

LOCATION
Lamay,
Calca, Cusco

ELEVATION - ECOREGION
9,500 feet
Dry valleys of the Selva Alta high jungle

PRODUCTION CHAIN
Orgánica Lamay plants, cultivates, harvests and washes its produce for distribution. Should they be short of produce to fulfill a Mil order, they'll source what is needed from neighboring communities.

SEASONALITY

PLANTING
Year round (depending on variety)

HARVEST
Year round (depending on variety)

Organic agriculture (methods):
compost, biol, bokashi, lime-sulfur solution, diatomaceous earth, pollination, crop rotation

CLIENTS
Cusco area restaurants

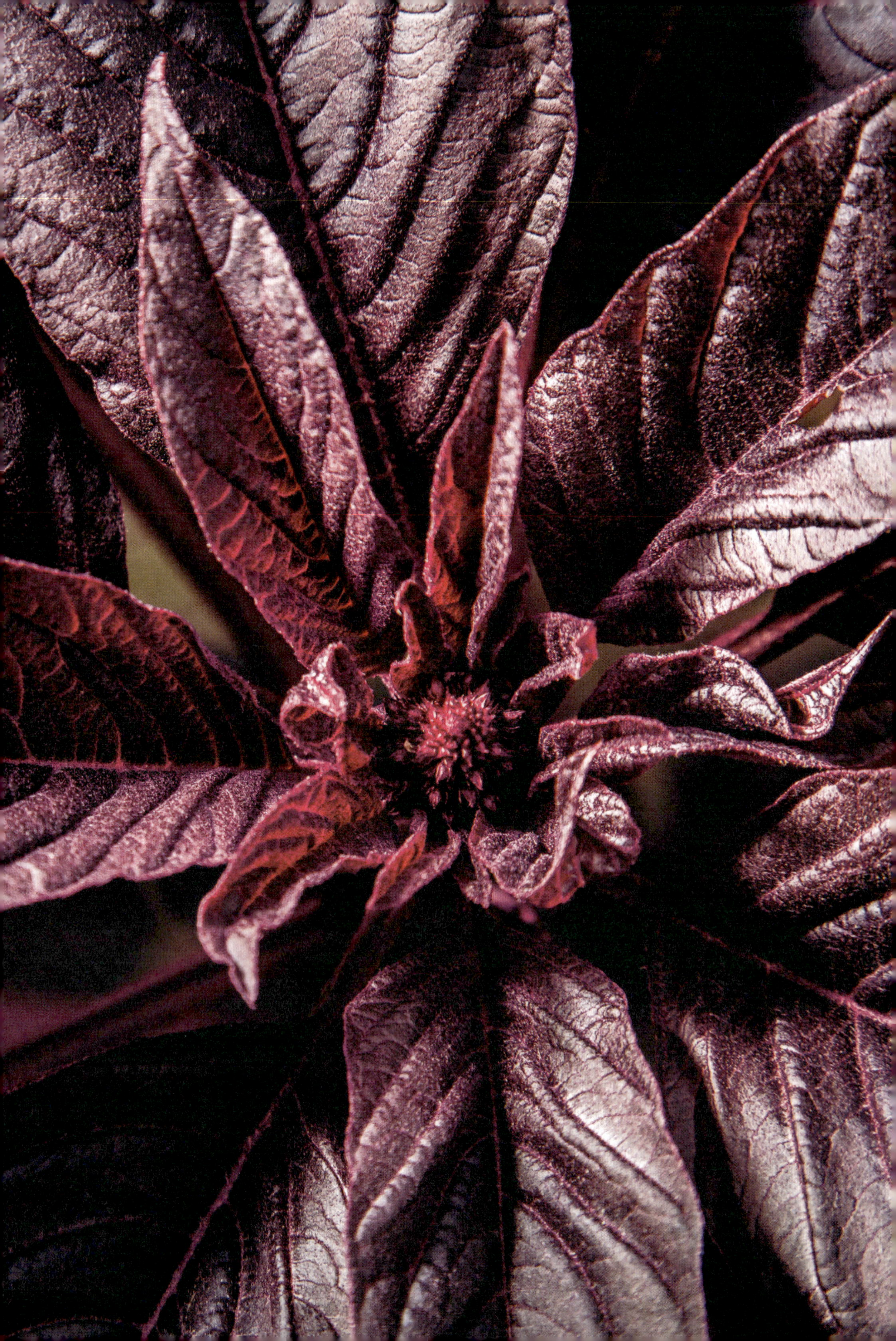

such as chili pepper sprays, producing their own seeds and optimizing space – today, Orgánica Lamay cultivates 97 species of herbs, edible flowers, grains and leafy vegetables year-round, including kale, pot marigold, elderflowers, red and green sorrel, and oracle leaf, all of which are used in the *Andean Forest* moment of Mil's tasting menu.

Orgánica Lamay's product diversity has broadened over time, and of the 97 varieties, around half are autochthonous to the Andes, such as *muña* (Minthostachys mollis), *kiwicha* (Amaranthus caudatus) and quinua. The nine-strong horticultural team, all born and raised in Lamay, uses traditional agricultural techniques, such as the *yunta* (bull yoke) to turn over soil on these small plots – it's more efficient than a tractor, which simply flattens the earth, according to Alex – paired with bio-forward farming methods such as self-prepared, microorganism-rich compost.

"We use everything – leaves, flowers and stalks – and make it more fertile by adding in sheep, cow, goat and guinea pig poop before vermicomposting with California earthworms. It then returns to the land two months later as biofertilizer: we optimize everything to ensure zero waste," he says.

The orchard also relies on nature's own remedies rather than chemicals to keep crops in good health. "In order to avoid blights, we mix up plant species, always sowing a barrier of natural repellents such as garlic or basil to deter bad bugs from attacking, say, tomatoes. As we don't use any chemicals, I can pull a carrot straight out of the ground and eat it – that's the best part of working here," he adds. The sustainable philosophy, much like giving thanks to Pachamama, means everything returns back into the ground to complete, then re-start, a new cycle.

Orgánica Lamay's team also calls on Mother Earth for an extra vote of confidence. "Besides pouring the first glass of *chicha de jora* corn beer into the ground, our security guard makes a *pago a la tierra* (offering) to Pachamama every day," says Alex. "He offers *k'intu* (a bunch of coca leaves) to the sun god Inti before burying them in a secret sacred spot that none of us knows about, then asks for a good day on the farm."

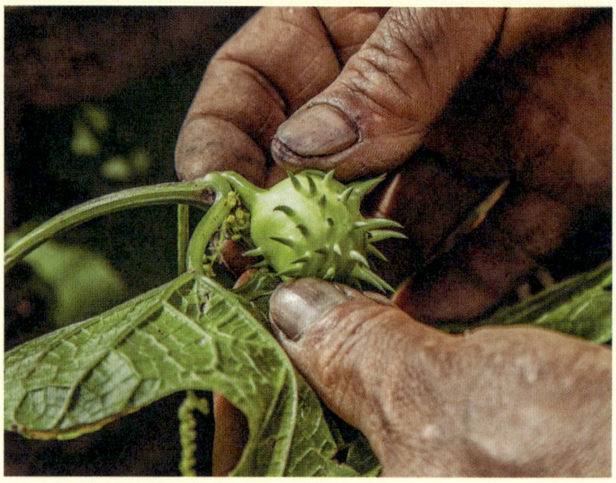

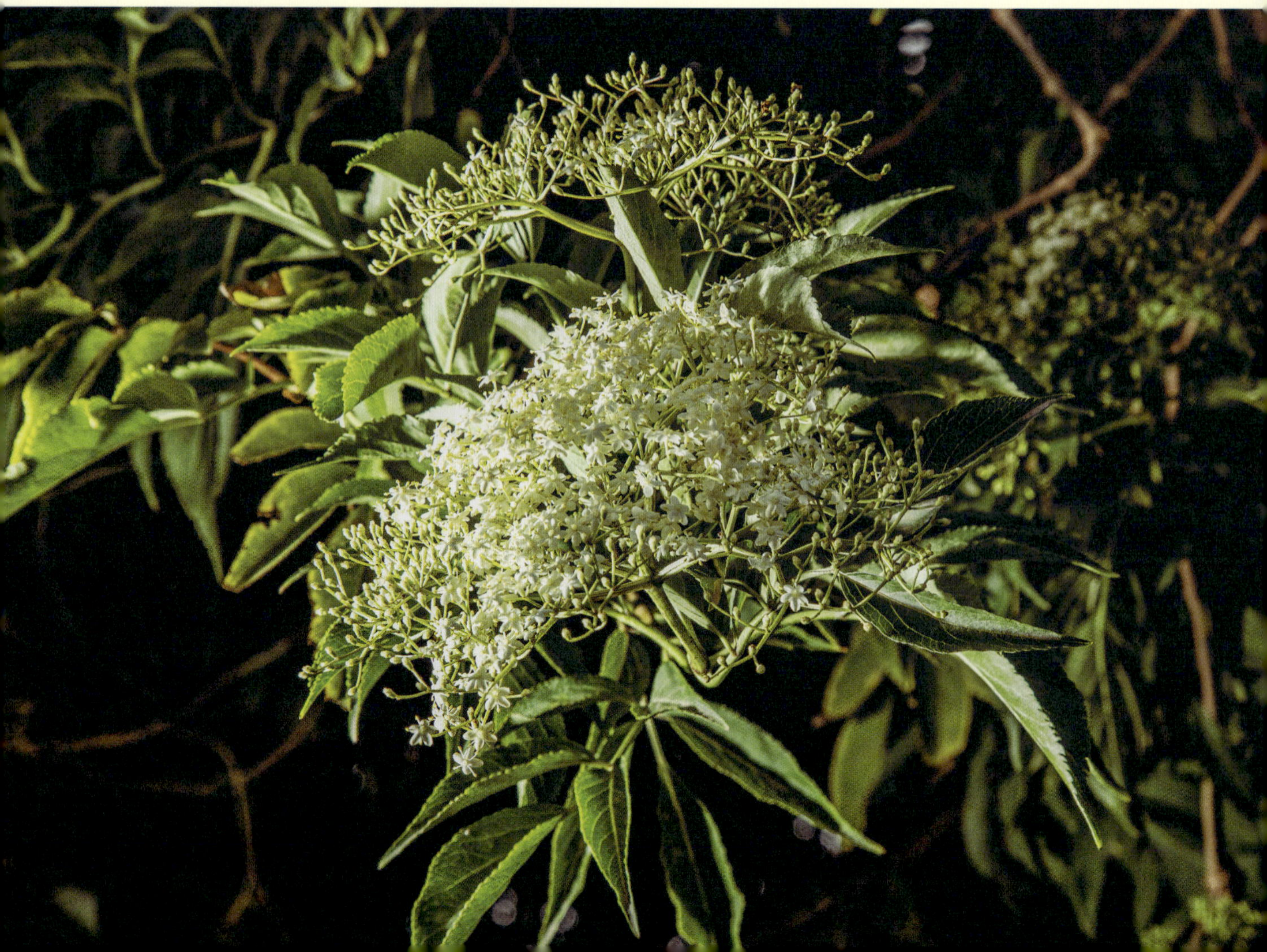

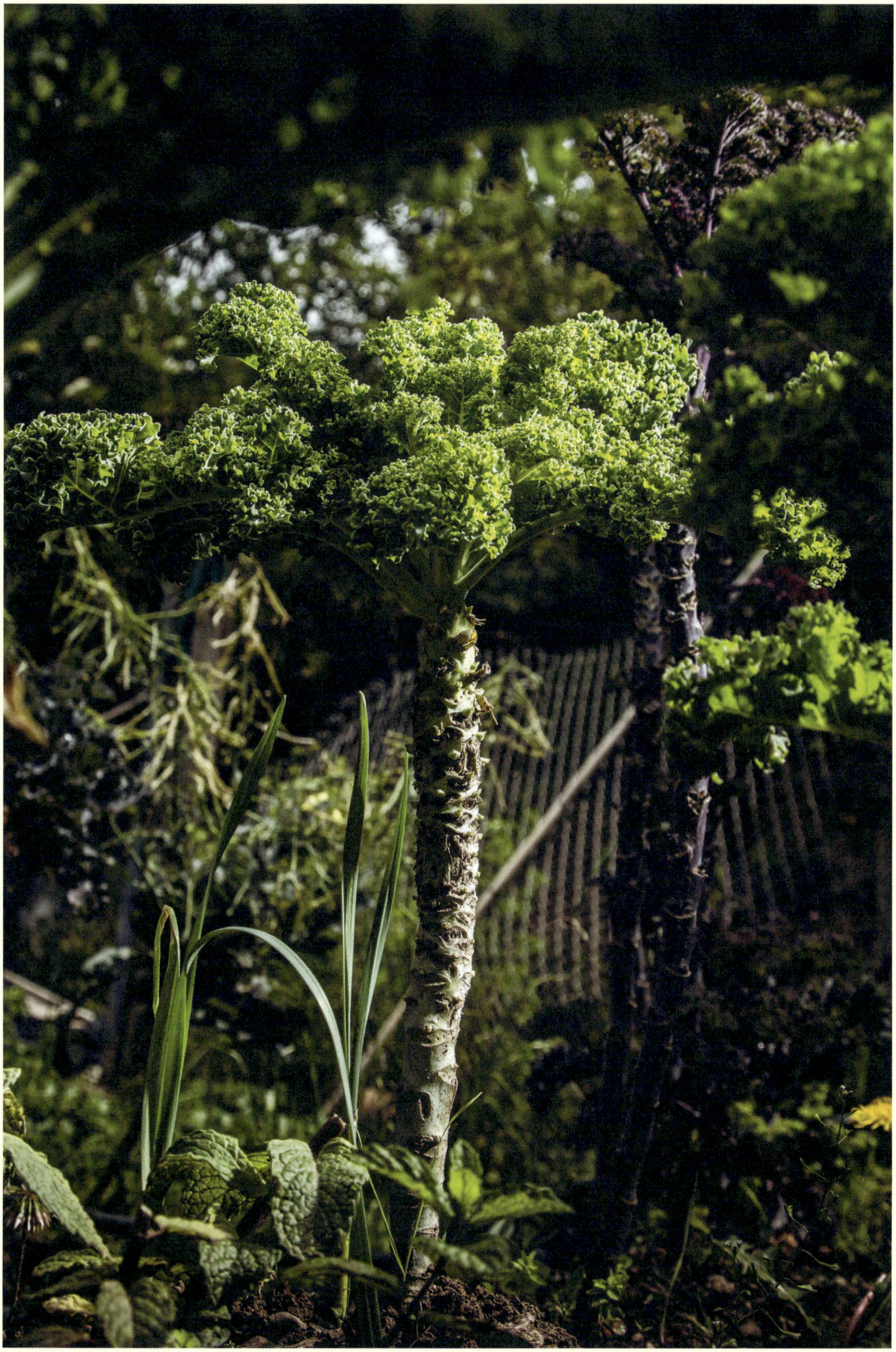

CERVECERÍA DEL VALLE SAGRADO

ANDEAN BEER

A veritable Andean Brew

Donde hay montañas, el agua inexorablemente percolará su
Where there are mountains, water will eventually percolate its way through the layers of rock. Add hops, malt and yeast, and you've conquered the basic recipe for a beer that Ninkasi, the ancient Sumerian goddess of brewing, would likely have savored.

But what if those rocks were Andean? And rainwater and snowmelt have filtered slowly but surely down through South America's rocky backbone, from 14,435 feet above sea level (asl) down to the community of Rayan at 9,185 feet asl? And instead of contemporary stainless steel tanks, this brew is cooked up in a traditional *chomba* clay pot usually used for fermenting *chicha de jora* corn beer?

Huatia, an ancestral and single-use clay oven used across the Andes, is the inspiration behind one of Mater's ongoing collaborations, and this particular beverage project is a work in progress with Cervecería del Valle Sagrado.

Based in the village of Pachar in the Sacred Valley, an hour's drive from Mil, Cervecería del Valle Sagrado's brewmaster Carlos Barroso, a former personal banker, already plays around with unusual flavors, sourcing cacao nibs and paste from our chocolatier Nilver Malgrejo to make an Imperial Stout called Dalí and the Chocolate Factory as well as a Roja (red beer) made with *airampo* (Opuntia soehrensii). But by cooking up samples of a *huatia* brew, the micro brewery's beer buff aims to capture the Andes themselves in a glass with an ale that's cooked with rocks and earth, an idea inspired by the landscape by Mater's anthropologist Daan Overgaag.

The *huatia* is built with dried clods of adobe clay found around the fields and mountains to create a small standalone oven, and a fire is lit inside. Once it's hot enough, potatoes and herbs such as *huacatay* (Tagetes minuta) are placed inside, then the *huatia's* roof is broken down on top of them, the bricks' heat penetrating the whole tuber. Carlos is brewing up that cooking method. "The idea behind the *huatia* ale is to obtain those clay and stone flavors that come straight from the ground, while bringing the mineral, herbal and smoky aromas that emanate from the *huatia* to liquid life," he says.

LOCATION
Ollantaytambo
Puente Pachar, just above the town of Pachar

ELEVATION - ECOREGION
9,200 feet

PRODUCTION CHAIN
Cervecería del Valle Sagrado's beer is brewed from malted grains, yeast, hops and natural spring water, occasionally using other ingredients such as local fruits and herbs. After cooling and fermentation, the beer is transferred to pressure chambers to create a final product that's rich in aroma, flavor and body.

SEASONALITY
Year round

CLIENTS
Restaurants
Local and visiting consumers

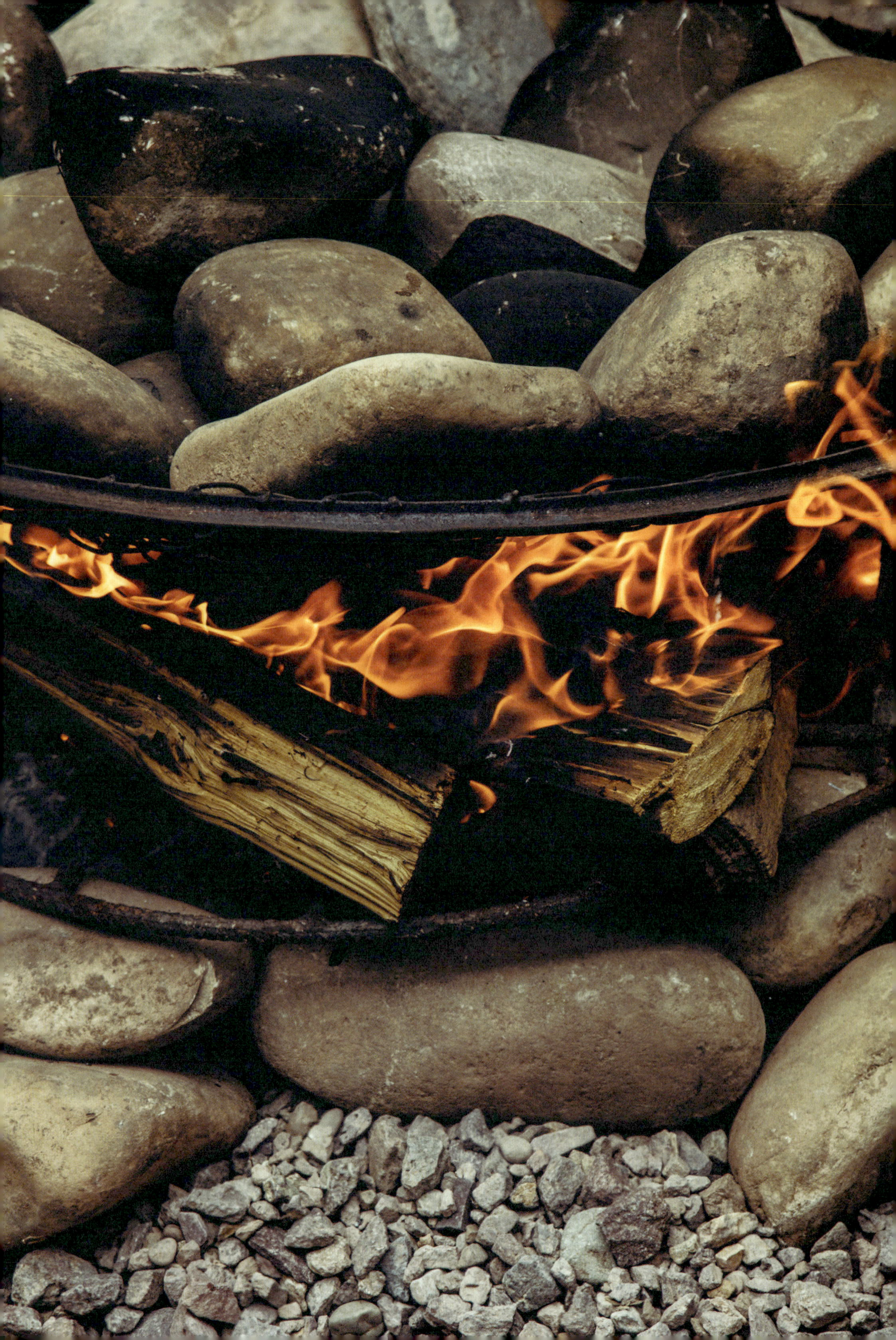

Acquiring the correct geological elements is of particular importance, else they could break down in the boiling process. "This granite is unique and comes from a specific source in the valley from a former river basin. Rocks need to stay whole for as long as possible and if you don't use the right type, they could crack. I've tried using other clay-based stones but they went soft in the first boil; plus, the beer came out dirty. As it retains heat for sufficient time, this granite is perfect," he adds.

By cooking up the ale's base ingredients along with this river granite in a *chomba* (three-feet-high ceramic pot) at a scorching 450°F (230°C) temperature for between 60 and 80 minutes, this boiling liquid absorbs all these earthy and mineral flavors from the pot as well as the stones themselves. Add *huacatay* and rocoto chili pepper into the bubbling mix, and he's brewed the uniquely earthy flavors of the Andes, ready to be poured into a glass at Mil.

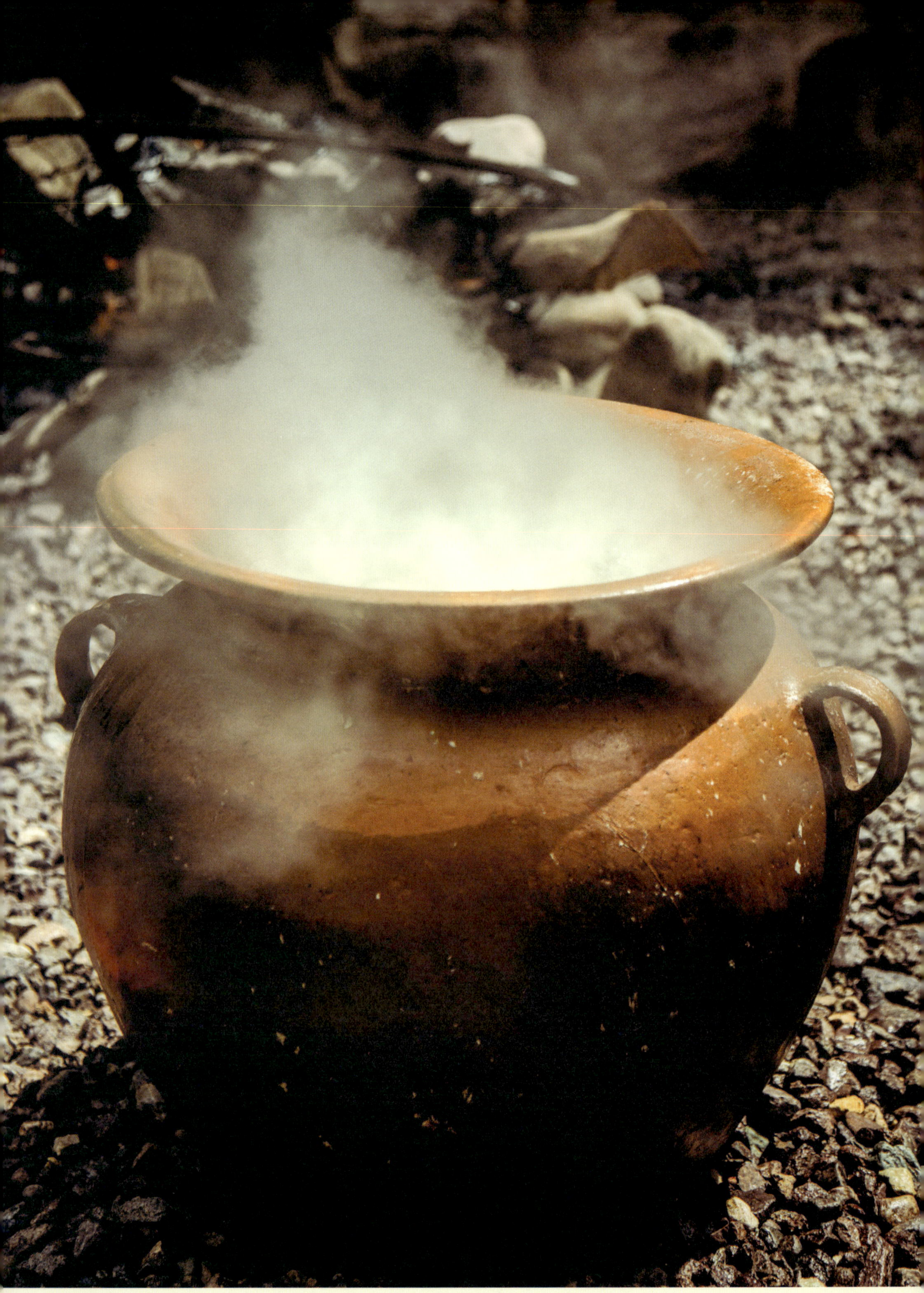

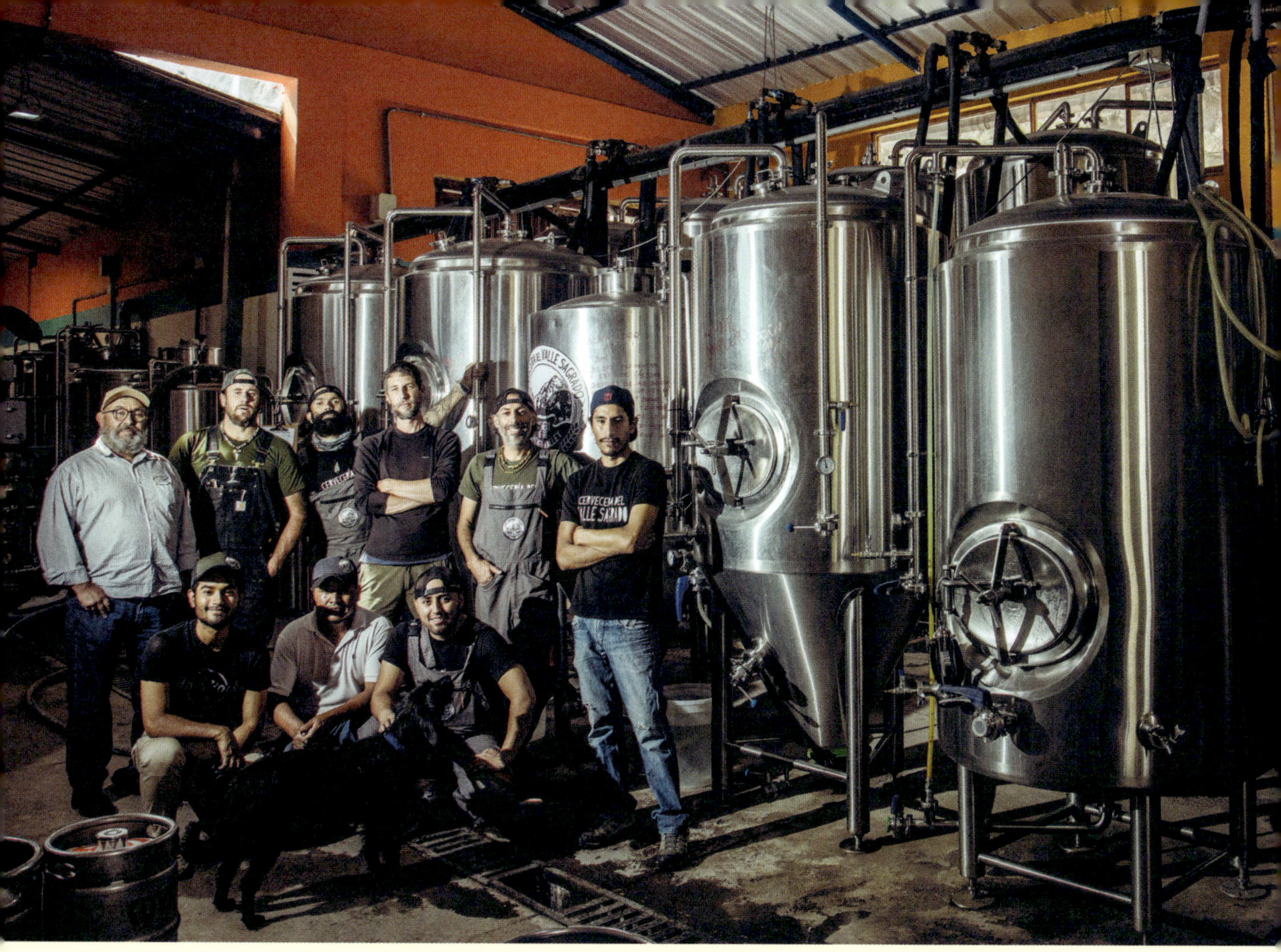
VALLE SAGRADO

MERCEDES CHAMPI AND FAMILY

LACTOCANEÑITA DAIRY PRODUCER

White-gold liquid

The plains of Jilayhua in Yanaoca district, Canas province, stand out for two reasons: their status as unusually high-altitude flatlands located at 12,795 feet above sea level (asl), and for the variety of natural crops grown that nourishes dairy cattle, resulting in high-quality milk that is crafted into honest, curdled wares. And there's another reason: the cheese produced here improves quality of life.

Besides growing maize, barley, potatoes, *mashwa* (Tropaeolum tuberosum) and fava beans for her family in this elevated valley, smallholder-turned-entrepreneur Mercedes Champi Ccalloquispe has long raised a tiny herd to provide fresh milk. And, she's always fed her children homemade Andean cheese. Over the years, others started benefitting from her agricultural expertise, given that she's worked with Sierra Productiva, a rural-based non-profit agricultural network that works inclusively with the Cusco region's small-scale farmers such as Francisco Quico Mamani and Trinidad Mamani Cascamayta in Unión Chahuay for social change, for more than two decades.

Since undertaking Sierra Productiva-run courses in dairy farming and cheese-making, Mercedes has become one of the NGO's – and Yanaoca's – agricultural success stories as the head of LactoCaneñita, a small, family-run dairy purveyor she founded in 2016 that takes pride in its organic, artisanal Paria and Quesillo cheeses. Paria is her star product, delivered every Tuesday to Mil's kitchen by youngest daughter Karen Taype Champi to be plated on our *Diversity of Corn* moment.

"Our mom has always been committed to agriculture and it's nice we can work together as a family," says hotel administration student Karen. "Although I live in Cusco, I visit Jilayhua every weekend to spend time in the countryside, to breathe in the fresh air, just like when I was younger – and to make cheese."

A fresh, semi-hard pale yellow cheese, molded in a rectangular block like butter, Paria is traditionally made in the high flatlands at between 9,840 and 13,120 feet. What makes this particular Paria stand out is the care and consideration that goes into every made-to-order batch, Mercedes choosing quality over quantity – and that starts with the cattle.

LOCATION
Yanaoca,
Canas, Cusco

ELEVATION - ECOREGION
13,800 feet
La Puna and High Andes

PRODUCTION CHAIN
Mercedes Champi milks the cows, which is then pasteurized at 149°F (65°C), cooled to 95°F (35°C) and rennet and salt added. After 45 minutes, the curds are gathered and molded.

SEASONALITY
Year round

PRODUCTION
Year round

CLIENTS
Local and regional markets
Restaurants

This project is supported by Sierra Productiva.

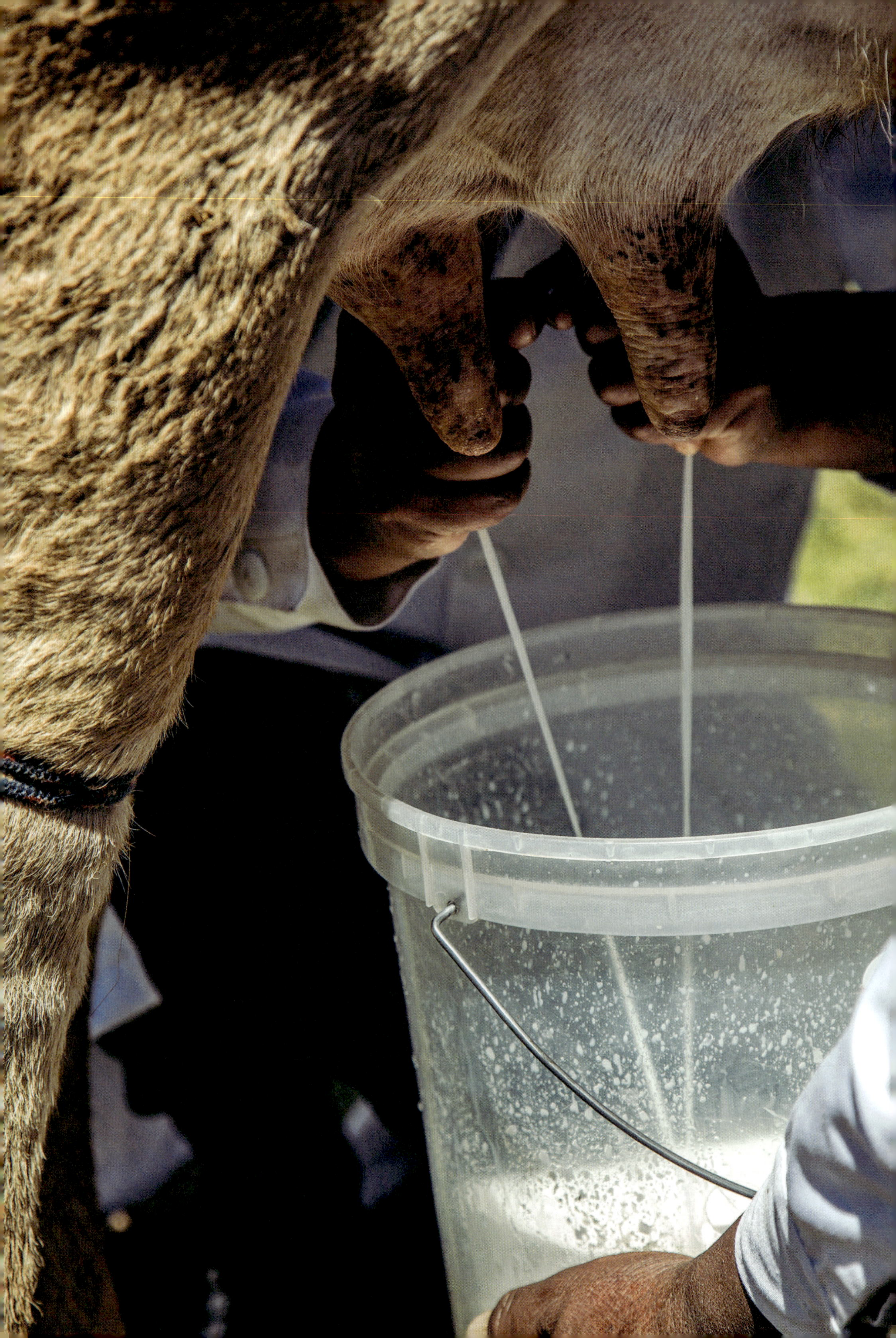

Mercedes used to raise Criollo, the oldest livestock breed in the Americas, but in order to improve milk quality, she switched them up for tan-colored Brown Swiss. She and husband Carlos Taype tend to the meadow, farming crops for their milk producers named Cata and Zorrita. Only pure and simple fare such as oats, alfalfa, straw, clover and green, green pasture, nurtured by the rain and the sun, reach Cata and Zorrita's slow-chewing mouths. Come late afternoon, they are herded home into a spacious barn to protect them from nocturnal mountain chills.

Family-run LactoCaneñita means each person has a particular role: Carlos gathers feed for the even-toed ungulates, daughter Yeni Lisbet Taype Champi and Mercedes milk the cattle, while Karen undertakes administration and logistics. But, there's always room for development. While she taught her daughters to make a version of the fresh Quesillo when they were little, after honing her skills on Sierra Productiva courses, Mercedes has now passed down more precise cheese-making skills to them. Having branched out to produce natural Greek-style yoghurt, she has also become a figure of inspiration for other rural female farmers and entrepreneurs in the Canas province. And, milk has also helped to bring about transformations at home.

"It's changed our lives," says Lisbet. "From the way we obtain milk, to the food we eat and even financing Karen's college education, producing cheese means it's not just our parents who are maintaining our family but all of us, making Paria and Quesillo, and working together as a team."

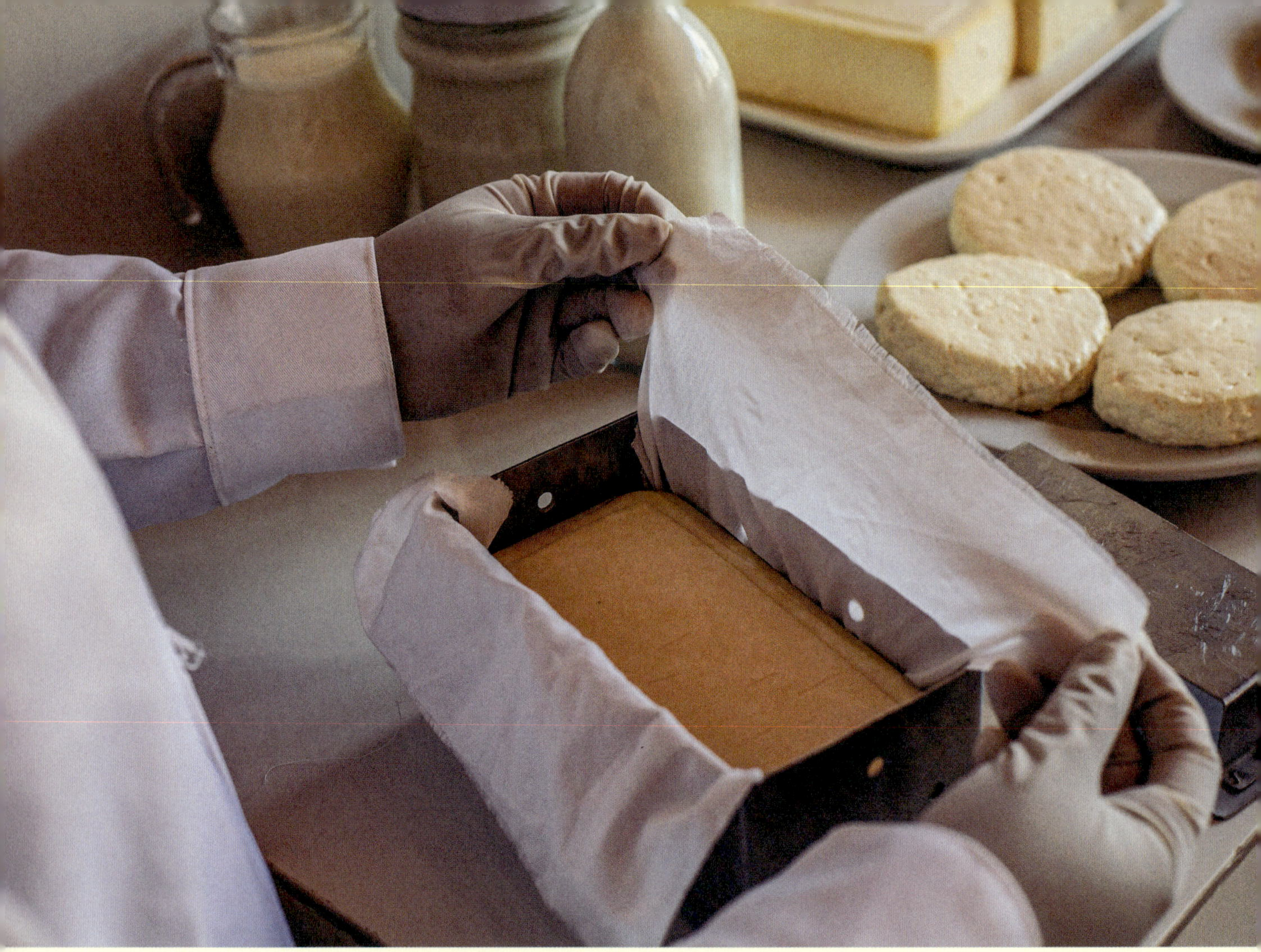

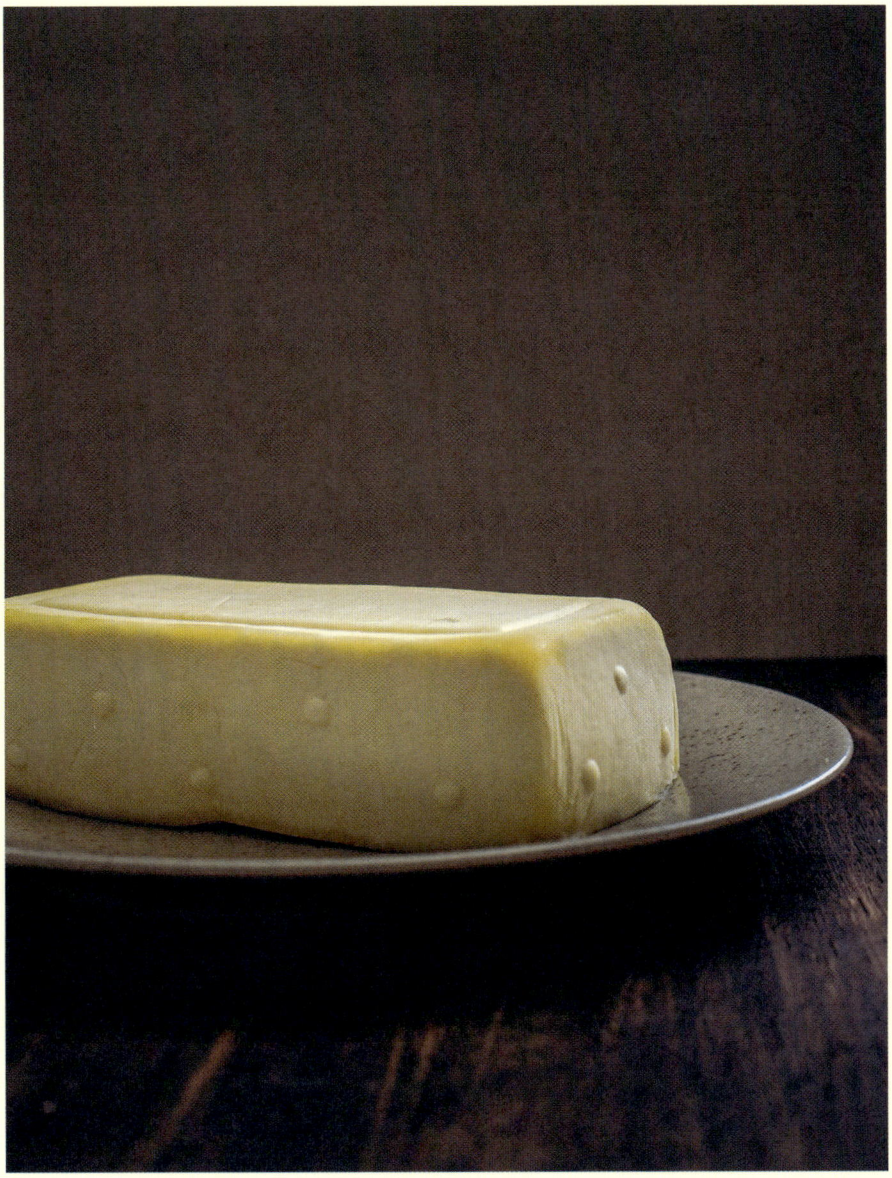

RÓMULO CÁMARA MONCADA

APA VALLECITO, CACAO FARMER

Chuncho, the golden cacao

Two worlds merge at Rómulo Cámara Moncada's cacao plantation – the Andes and the subtropical cloud forest. From Mil, cross the Abra Malaga pass at 14,175 feet above sea level (asl) and zigzag down the vertiginous road to Chahuares. The rather stark mountainscape shifts almost incongruously to take on a tropical topography at first dominated by banana and mango trees, and the rising temperature means we are suddenly shedding layers of unwelcome insulation like an onion.

The village of Chahuares, near Quillabamba in La Convención province, is found at 3,315 feet asl, a rather lowly altitude in terms of the Sacred Valley's usual elevations. Here, coffee, passion fruit, pacay (Inga feuilleei), yuca and cacao thrive alongside each other like one big happy family, the nearby peaks frequently enshrouded by low clouds.

Rómulo was born and raised in Chahuares. He completed the third year of high school, inheriting his parents' land and devoting himself to what became his future. "Who else was going to manage what my family had started?" he says.

It's a poignant question, one that many might not be willing to answer with a commitment, given how physically demanding cacao cultivation is, especially in the subtropical Andes. Weeding between trees locked onto muddy inclines is an ongoing process, while the dogged persistence of leaf-cutter ants can cause substantial mayhem in this particular ecosystem. At harvest, pickers scale trees that can top out at 40 feet to hook, then skillfully twist off – without damaging – the fruit, or pods, that hang individually from branches. Pods are easy to spot: the golden-orange *cacao chuncho* variety shines through the dense jungle like Mercury in the night sky – though less elusive – while the *híbrido* variety's scarlet capsule resembles a static flame.

Rómulo, wife Celia Cruz Sánchez and their four nephews work on their species-rich plantation, but *Theobroma cacao* wasn't always the in-demand product it is today. "Coca leaf and coffee used to bring in much better incomes," he says, referring to crops he used to cultivate. But, following a government initiative to eradicate the controversial leaf a decade ago, coca was

LOCATON
Chahuares,
Echarate, Cusco

ELEVATION - ECOREGION
3,120 feet
High jungle forest;
Mountain rain forest

PRODUCTION CHAIN
Romulo monitors the growth of the cacao trees – which bear fruit after three years – on his land. The cacao beans are harvested along with their pulp and fermented for five to six days. After drying, the beans are hand-selected by size and stored.

SEASONALITY

PLANTING
Wild growth

HARVEST
December–May

Organic agriculture (methods):
cacao rind compost

CLIENTS
Distributors
Chocolate manufacturers
Mil restaurant

This project is supported by Concytec and ProCompite.

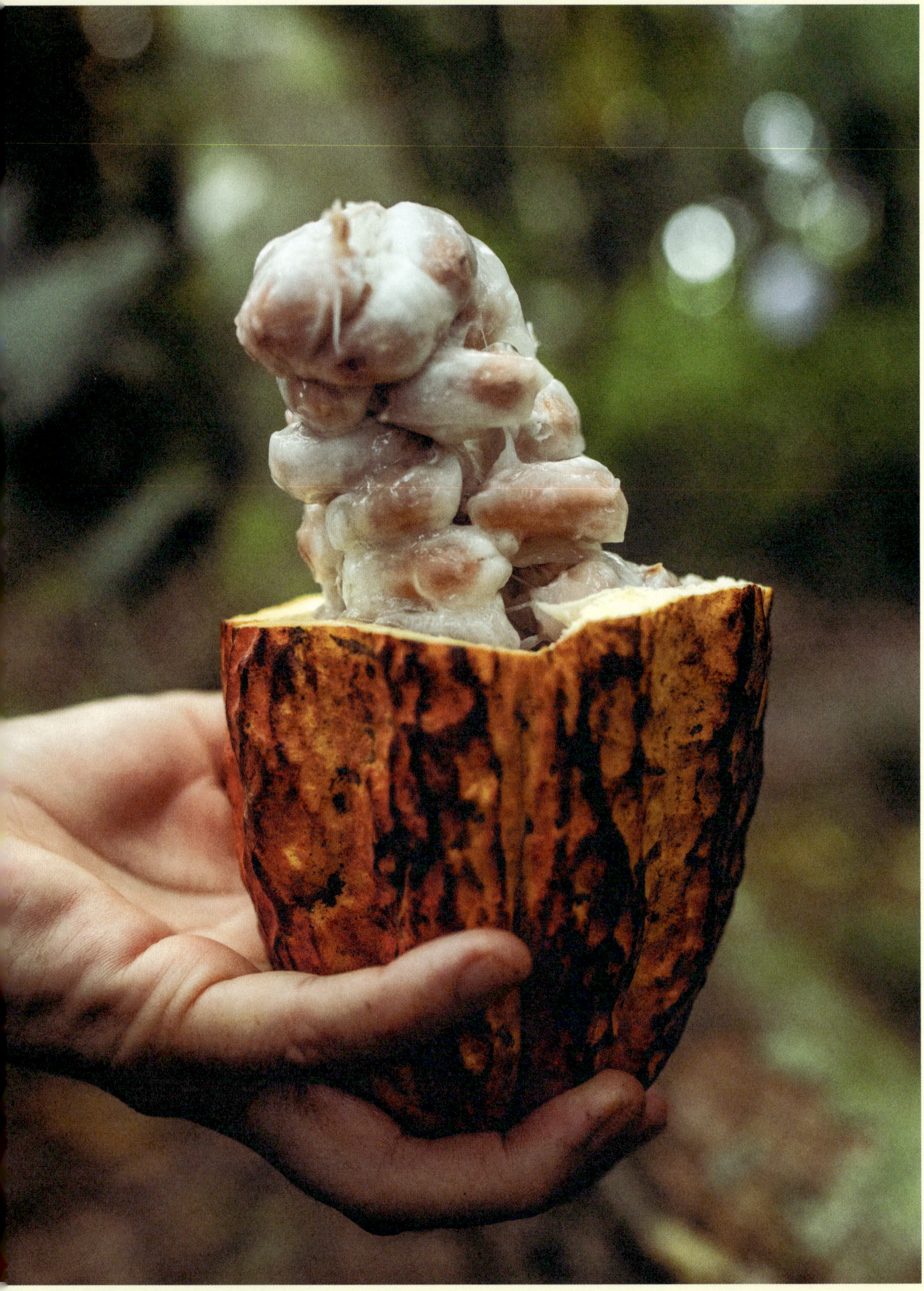

replaced with cacao – first, by the high-yielding CN51 *híbrido* clone and later the native *cacao chuncho*. It's this latter variety that's been gaining a name for itself in a chocolate-obsessed world that increasingly demands single-origin beans with high quality aromas and flavors, and it's the variety we use at Mil.

For many years, Rómulo flew solo, fermenting and drying beans in basic facilities at home next to his small guinea-pig farm. It wasn't particularly comfortable for anyone. Then, in 2018, he and some fellow cacao farmers from La Convención received a small government grant to further their knowledge, learn post-harvest techniques and build a small facility, allowing them to ferment beans. APA Vallecito, a 14-strong association specializing in cacao, was born.

Ensuring cacao provides a living for families such as Rómulo's meant it was essential to join forces, says Celia. "One person can't do all this work and harvest on their own, so we neighbors had to band together." They adhere to *ayni*, the reciprocal way of taking turns to work on each other's plantations, laboring throughout the day drinking rata rata, a beverage made from burnt cacao skin, tree bark and water that's sipped while *chacchando* (sucking) coca leaves to keep energy levels up.

Cacao chuncho is the association's star product, a native variety from the Forastero cacao family that was discovered in the 1800s. Given that its organoleptic profile was classified just two years ago (there are six such crops), it's only recently started to capture cacao lovers' attention. Its green pods sprout from a cream-colored flower before maturing to a vibrant golden-orange; they're easy to spot, given that other varieties such as *híbrido* mature to scarlet. As a finished product, *cacao chuncho's* intoxicating – and unusual for chocolate – aromas include mandarine and passion fruit as well as floral and nutty flavors.

Since setting up APA Vallecito, Rómulo and his fellow growers have attended several workshops, learning, then applying new skills to improve on-the-ground operations. Pod selection now forms part of the harvesting process, capsules carefully cut open by hand and checked for diseases as soon as they reach the ground, an important step in quality control that ultimately leads to better prices. They have also branched out with 'new' products: following suggestions from anthropologist Daan Overgaag who heads up Mater's traceability program, the association now saves mucilage, the delicious white pulp that covers beans inside the pod and is usually discarded, to sell to Mil. And, in the quest to supply superior beans, APA Vallecito now ferments all their beans at the purpose-built plant. "Cacao has given us greater quality of life, in terms of health and education. I know that if I continue to produce beans of excellent quality, our lives will continue to improve – and I'm prepared to do that," says Rómulo.

The outstanding aromas and flavors of *cacao chuncho* ensure its place on Mil's menu: in-house chocolatier Nilver Melgarejo creates bars and blocks from APA Vallecito's nibs, while *Huatia of Cacao*, the final moment, is made with 72 percent *chuncho*, *mucilage*, *mashwa* (Tropaeolum tuberosum) and coca leaf, best taken with a delicious 75 percent hot chocolate sprinkled with *chuncho* nibs prepared by bartender Manuel Contreras.

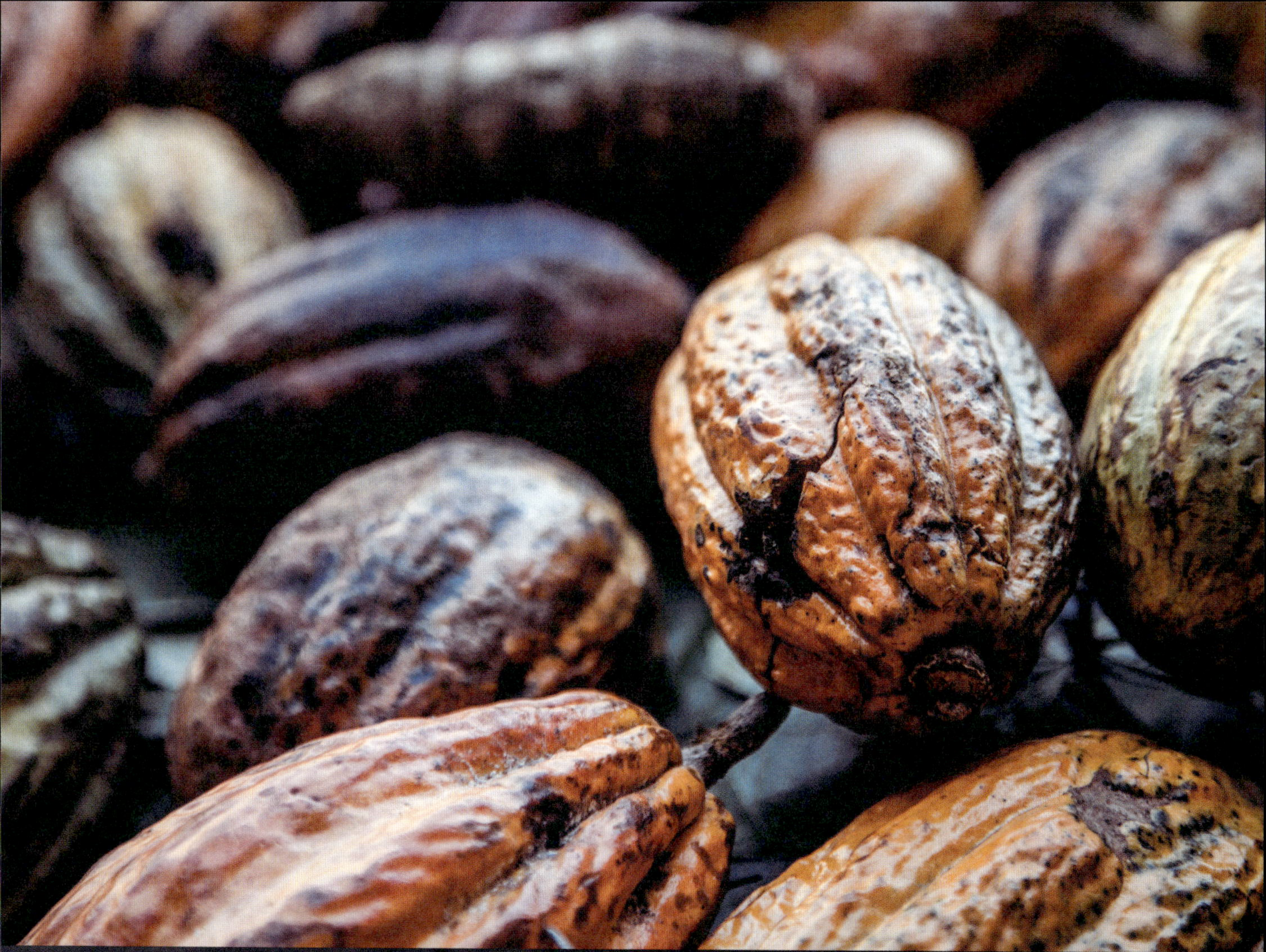
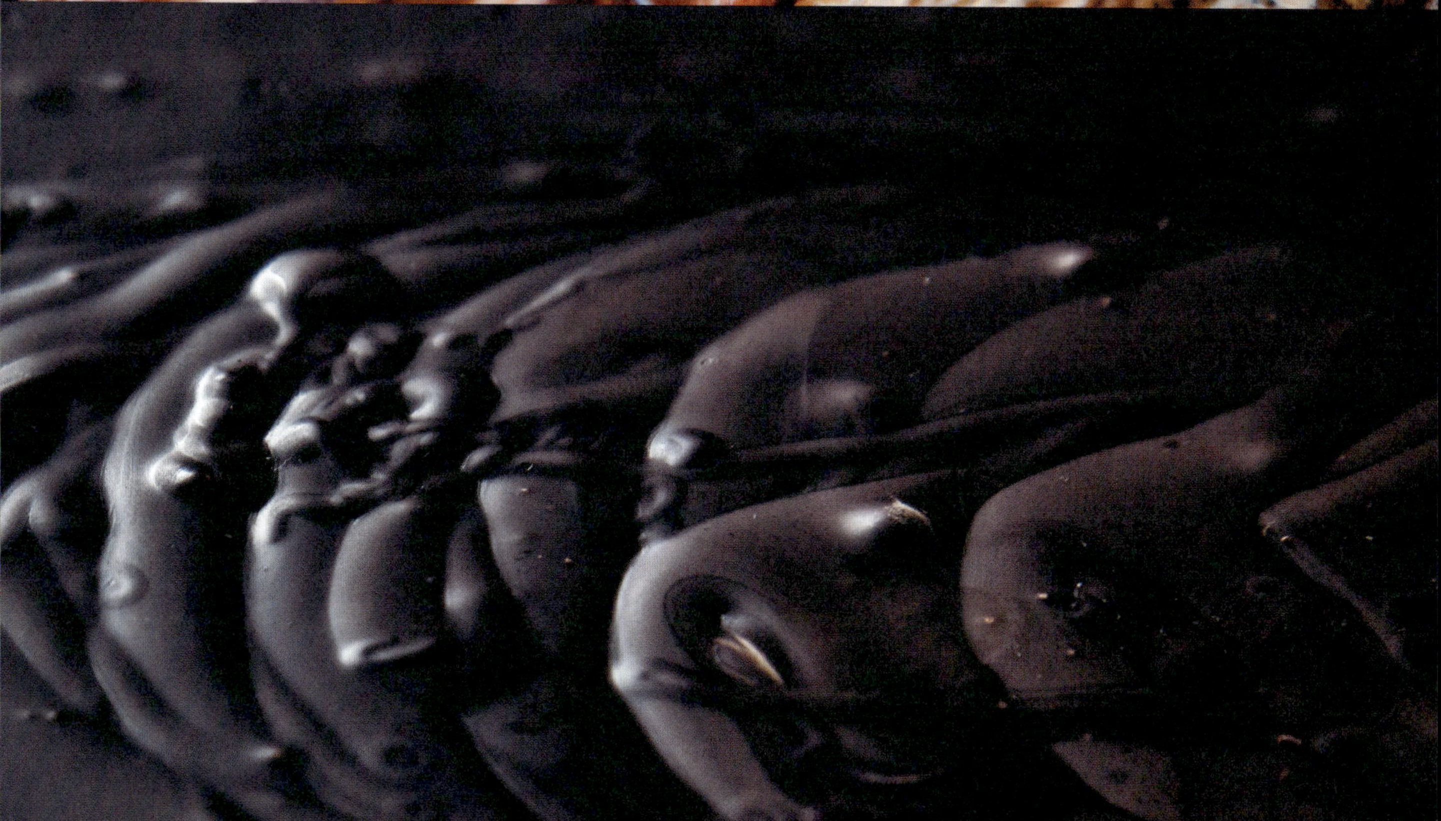

ROSA FERRO GIRALDO
SALINERAS DE MARAS SALT PRODUCER

Salt of the earth

During the Andes' dogged rainy months of November through April, the elevated terraced salt ponds of the Salineras de Maras become a patchwork of brick, rouge and cappuccino hues, their muddy beds depicting the palette. Come May, however, when the dry season kicks off and mountain spring water is irrigated across the 3,800 unevenly fashioned shallow pools, it's as if a polar front had hit overnight, solar evaporation leaving halite deposits as dazzling as freshly fallen snow.

The ponds Rosa Ferro Giraldo owns at Salineras de Maras, a 15-minute drive from Maras' main square Plaza de Armas, represent a family enterprise that includes her father and two brothers. Each holds the deeds to a minimum of four salt pans, their birthright as members of this small Andean community, as it is for their neighbors in Pichingoto. And while the Ferro Giraldo family is relatively new to the sodium chloride game, given that they acquired their pools when MaraSal started formal commercial operations in 1999, this picturesque tapestry of ponds slotted into the Andes has been producing salt since before the Quechua ruled the land, 11,105 feet above sea level (asl) and 557 miles from the nearest ocean as the condor flies. Despite the complex topography, whose terraced composition resembles that of Moray, Salineras de Maras is tucked into a gorge with views over Pichingoto and the Río Vilcanota river on a complex formation of sedimentary rocks formed during the Cretaceous period between 145.5 million and 65.5 million years ago, according to Spanish archeologist Marc Cárdenas. Saturated with calcium carbonate, calcium sulphate and magnesium, the mineral-rich water gushes out from a mountain spring and is channeled through the labyrinthine mosaic of open-air terraced ponds that incline 20 degrees down the mountain to feed the 3,800 pans in use today: taste the water, it's like swallowing a mouthful of ocean.

Long a valuable resource, more recently within the past two millennia, salt has held various roles. In the 'Old World', the Roman empire paid its soldiers a *salarium* or salary so they could buy commodity-of-the-moment salt, while in the Andes, the Quechua used *ch'arki* (Quechua for jerky), salt-curing and preserving fish, vegetables and alpaca meat so food

LOCATION
Maras – Urubamba
Cusco

ELEVATION - ECOREGION
10,100 feet
Salineras de Maras

PRODUCTION CHAIN
Rosa Ferro Giraldo begins by first shoring up the perimeters of her salt ponds and then irrigating them with sodium chloride-rich mountain spring water every three days for a month. The top layer, the *flor de sal*, is harvested, then the pink second layer, then the red final layer for industrial and medicinal use. The salts are dried for five days and transferred to a central storehouse for registration and the addition of iodine, after which it's packaged and labeled.

SEASONALITY

HARVEST
April-October (monthly)

CLIENTS
Own consumption
Local businesses
Travelers and tourists

could travel long distances to feed their armies, a conservation technique still used today where refrigeration is unavailable or impractical. The mineral also played its part in ceremonial rituals as a vital element in the mummification process of the *incas* (Quechua kings) and was also exchanged in trueque for other goods at the Sacred Valley's Tiobamba fair.

Carved into a gorge that ranges between 10,100 and 10,500 feet asl within the Maras Formation that encompasses Qaqahuiñay, Cruz Mocco, Llully Mocco and Chupayoq hills, there's often a more captivating and romantic account to explain events and phenomena in the Andes. In the case of Maras' salt-crusted history, folklore has it that nearby Weqey Willka, also known as Mount Verónica (18,640 feet), at the start of the Quechua empire, is where the Ayar brothers abandoned their strongest sibling. Ayar Kachi wept so much at his fate that his tears turned into crystals. From his destitution, Maras salt's pale pink hue and notable trace mineral content has made it an emblem for Peru on the world gastronomy stage. It should be noted that the Salineras are not another example of remarkable Quechua architecture; the site dates back to the Early Horizon period 900BC-200BC, according to Unesco.

Following tradition, Rosa and her family gather their crystals by hand, a laborious process that involves scraping, cleaning then carrying 110 lb bags under blazing sun up the mountain to the curing chamber. The collection season is short, one day a month for six months, as the mountain source gently floods pans every three days, which are left to the elements to evaporate and crystallize. "It looks like it just snowed May through mid-October," says Rosa. Less rainfall in the dry season means fresh water is less likely to interfere with quality and trace mineral content such as calcium, magnesium, iron and zinc, she adds, ensuring superior crystals that we bag and sell via Mater Sostiene.

A hodge-podge of sizes varying between six to 16 feet in length that spans 255 acres of mountain, pans can produce between one and eight quintals – 220 to 1,760 pounds – of salt. The process is methodical, says Rosa. "We start in the middle, gently scraping up *fleur de sel*, then we tread on the pan, which is still a little humid and an inch thick with salt, to ensure it's pristine white. Then we gather it with a hoe or between slabs of wood, rinse it in the basket with the same water from the channels, then take it to dry for a week."

Harvesting salt makes a difference, financially speaking, to Rosa's life: working on the *chacra* (farm) is her only other livelihood, and that feeds her family. As the owner of four ponds, the parent company part-pays her in salt, one 110 lb bag of salt a year, with which naturally Rosa cooks, as we do in Mil's kitchen. "My favorite dish is *Soltero de habas*, a fava bean soup with carrots, onions, tomatoes, dried potato, *cochayuyo* alga (Chondracanthus chamissoi), fresh cow's cheese and a pinch of pink Maras salt. I also prepare lamb *ch'arki*, which we eat on special occasions."

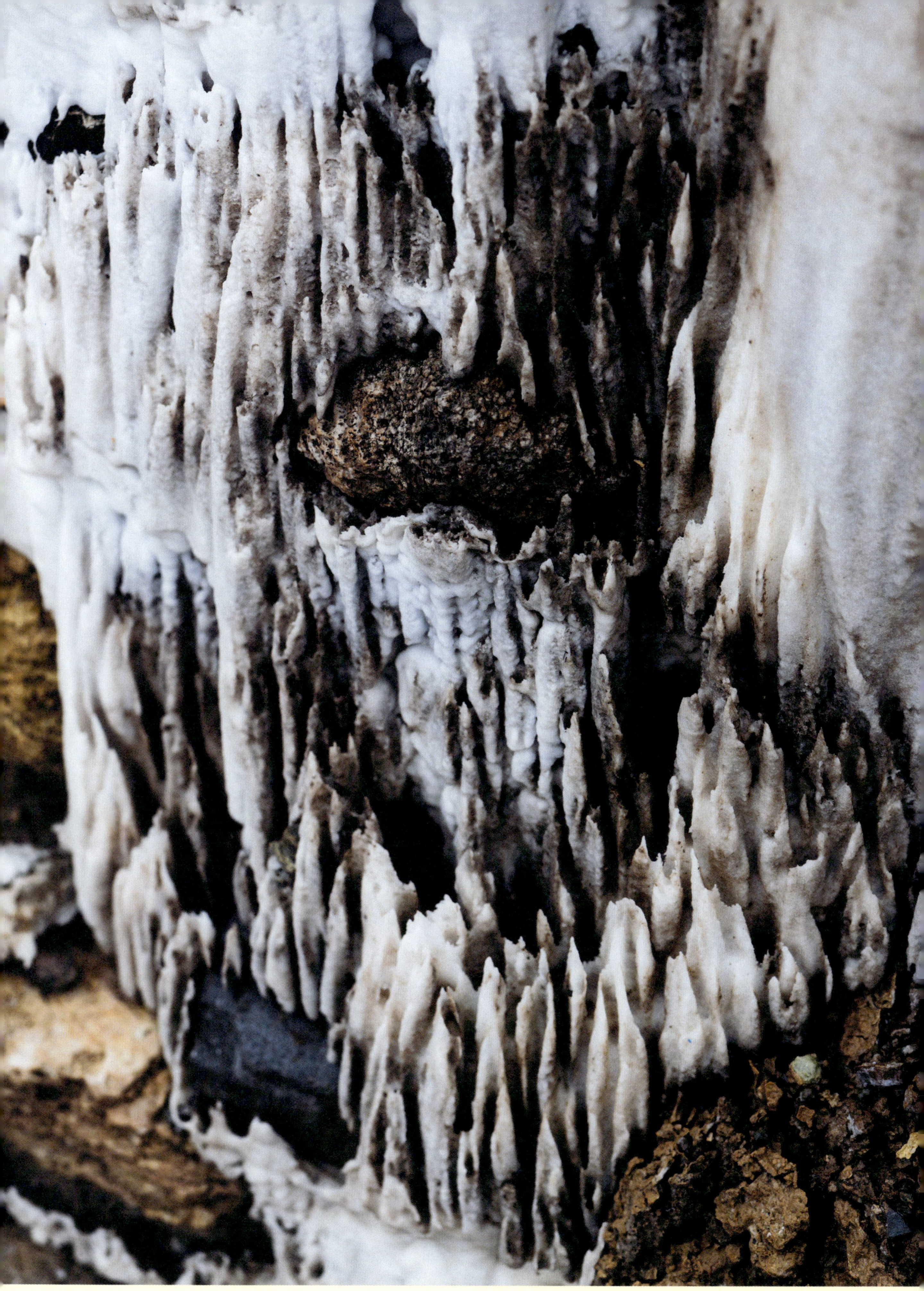

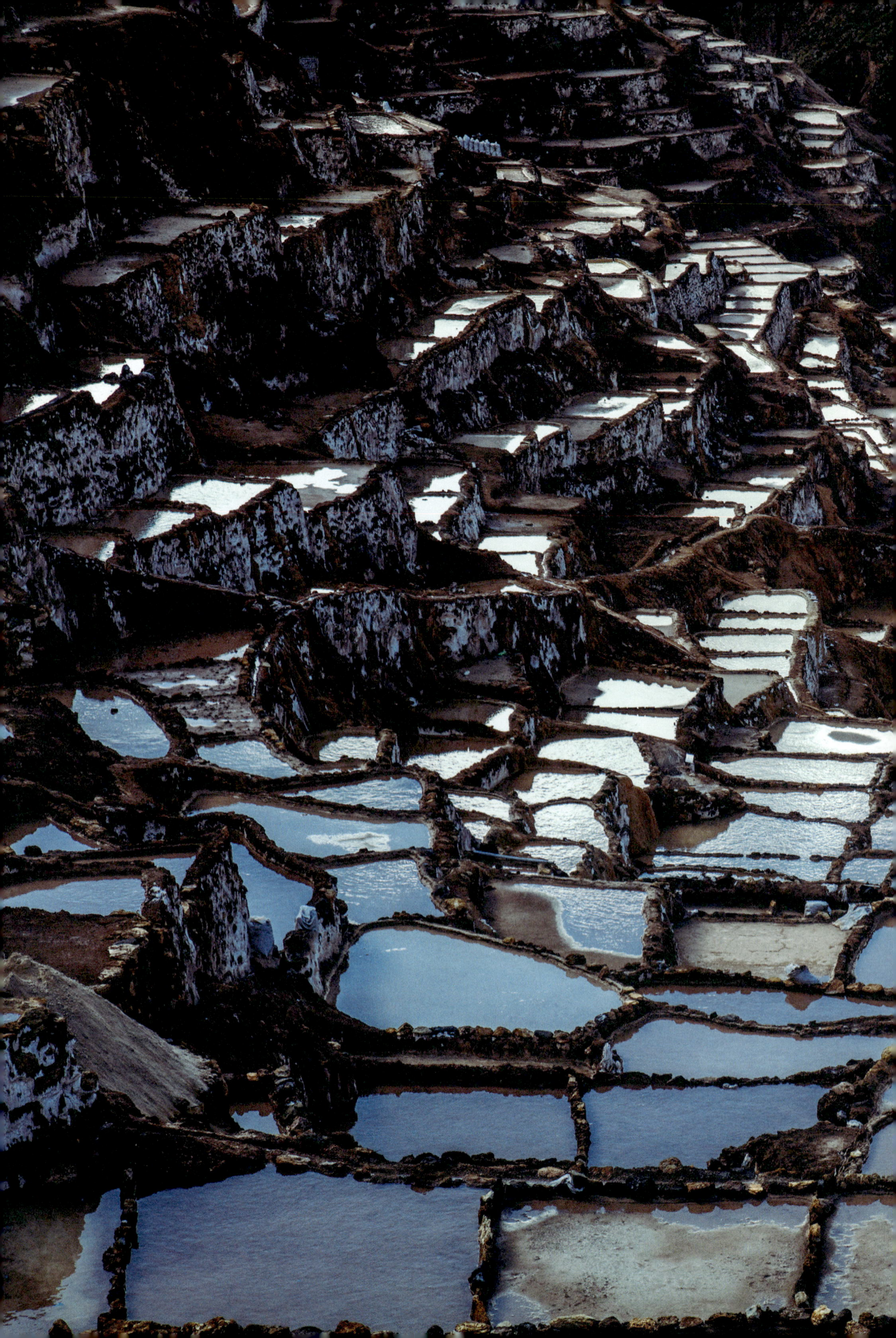

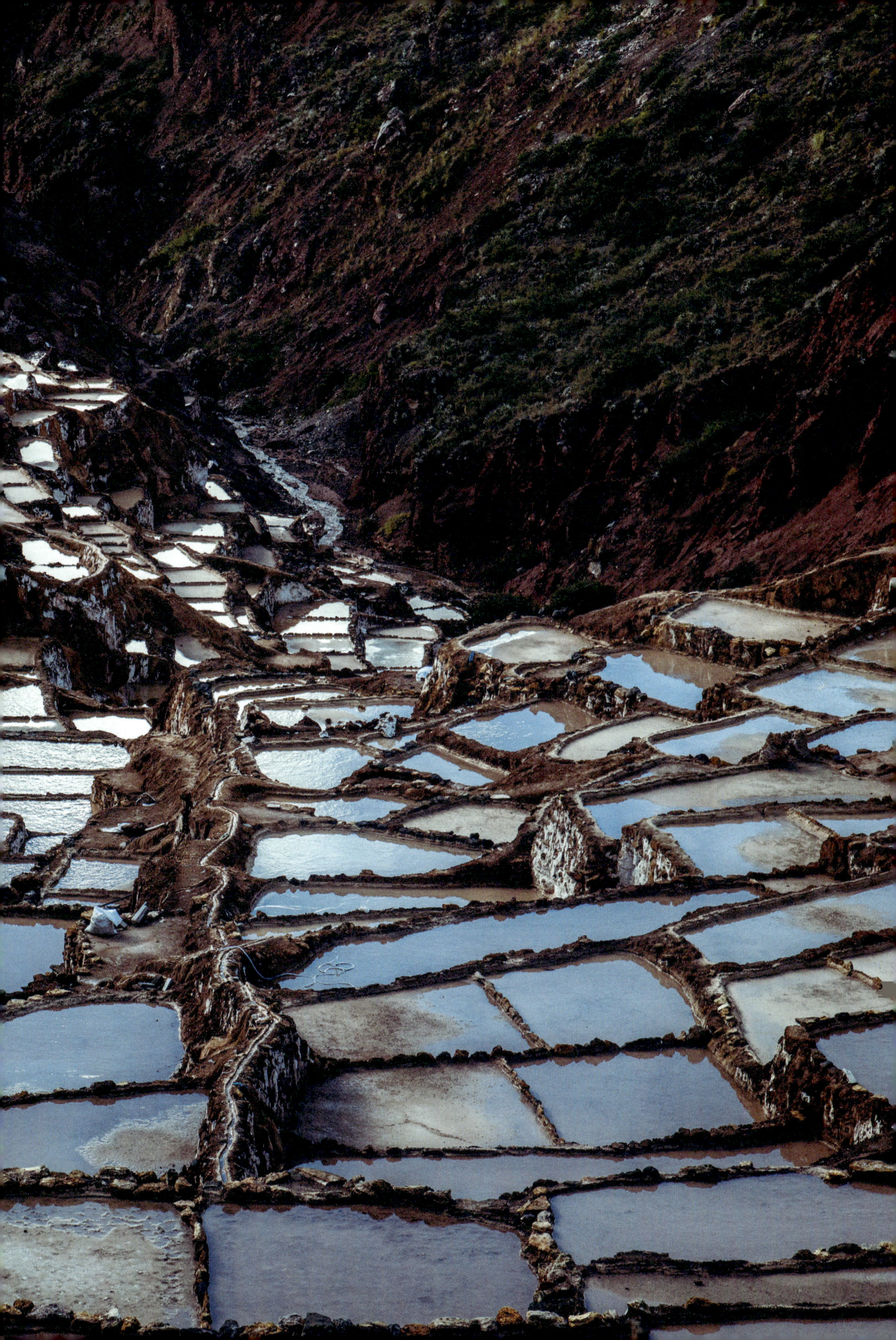

THE SACRED VALLEY

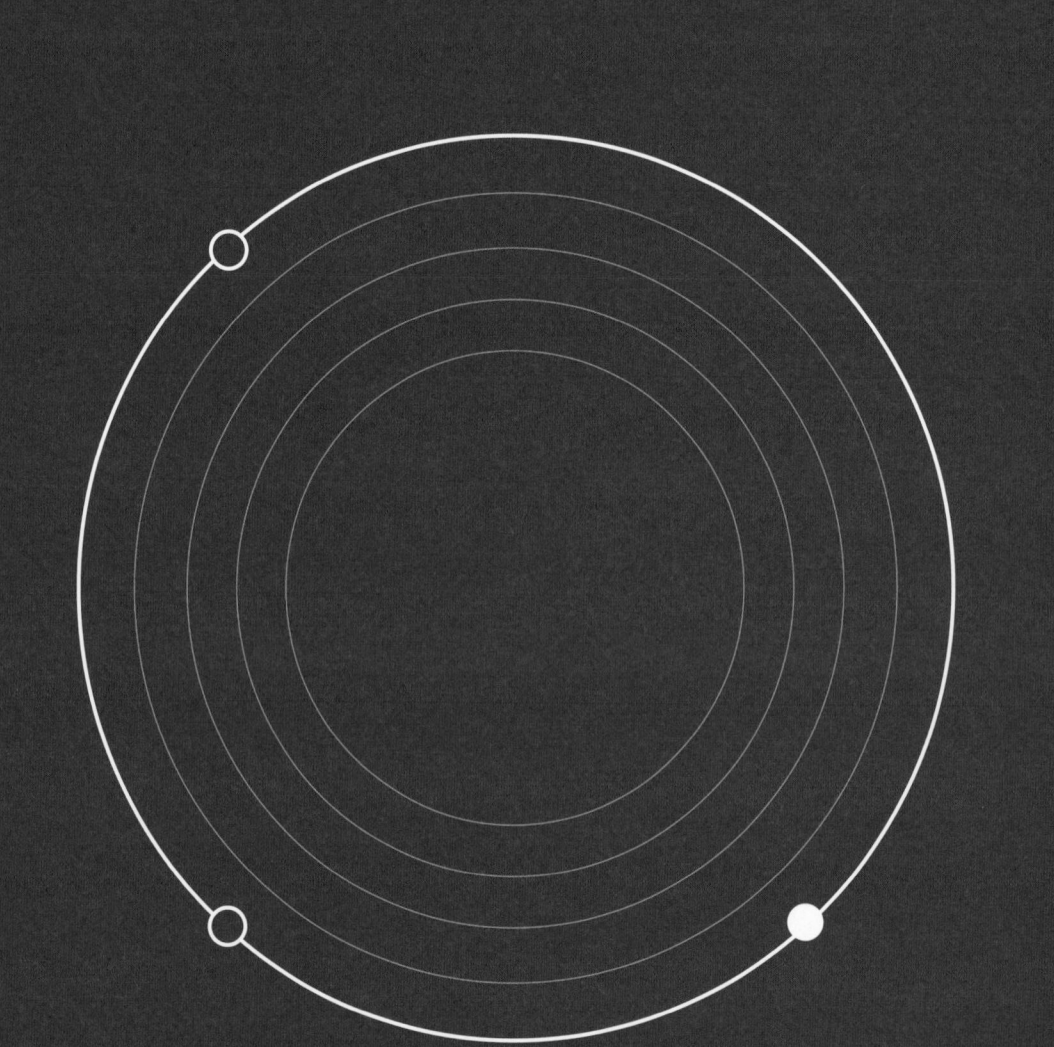

Tawantinsuyu, as the Quechua empire was called in its eponymous language, was the largest pre-Columbian civilization in the Americas and the largest civilization in the world throughout its existence. But, as destiny would have it, after succeeding a number of Andean cultures that spanned three millennia, it was to be the last.

Founded at the start of the 13th century by a tribe that originated in the Andean highlands, its dynasty of 13 *sapa inca* or kings ruled over the empire from 1438 for a relatively brief period, less than a century. It is for these rulers that the civilization is commonly but erroneously referred to as the Inca empire. The tenure of the last *sapa inca* Atahualpa was cut short after a year when Spanish conquistadors invaded from the north in 1533 and he was assassinated later that year in Cajamarca. Despite its brevity, the Quechua empire was a mighty and far-reaching territory, its well-trained armies extending it to parts of modern-day Colombia and Ecuador in the north, and Chile and Argentina to the south. Always dominating elevated Andean sectors, its population is, rather widely, estimated to have numbered between 4.5 and 14 million people, forming a well-structured society that adhered to a strict hierarchy that started with the *sapa inca*, passing down to royalty then nobility and ending with *allyus* (peasants) on the bottom rung.

Cusco (also written as Cuzco, Qusqu and Qosqo), a thriving, urban center known as the navel of the world, established at 11,155 feet above sea level (asl), was the empire's administrative, military and political hub, one of its most revered sites. Laid out in the form of a puma, one of three sacred animals in Quechua cosmology representing *kay pacha* or the world of the living as well as strength and wisdom, its most important temples were built within the confines of the puma 'head'. The longest continually populated urban center in the Americas, Cusco is tucked into an elevated valley, surrounded by towering peaks and the confluence of three rivers; all relevant reasons why the Quechua chose this for their key base.

Today, centuries later, it remains a lively city but also a living artifact, the confluence of the vastly different worlds of both the Quechua and Hispanic cultures, the former guided by the Andean cosmovision and *yanantin-masintin* or complementary dualism and the opposites of existence, the latter by institutional religion.

While some Quechua structures such as the Sacsayhuaman citadel survived the conquest's ruthless razing, today, colonial architecture including the Plaza de Armas square and the Basílica de la Virgen de la Asunción cathedral dominates the contemporary urban landscape. Qoricancha sun temple is one example that includes components from both cultures, as the Spaniards made use of the Quechua ground-floor stone foundation to build the Santo Domingo convent, its later upper level known for its wooden façades. A popular destination with visitors who stop off on their way to or from legendary citadel Machu Picchu, the city of Cusco was named a World Heritage Site by Unesco in 1983, one of countless recognitions that corroborates its relevance at anthropological, historical, architectural, industrial and cultural levels, not just in Peru but in the world.

While Cusco was the administrative heart of the far-reaching and powerful Quechua empire, the Urubamba Valley was its lifeblood, a thriving, regional hub dedicated to agriculture. Civilizations such as the Wari and Killke who predated the Quechua had already made this fertile land their home during the previous 3,000 years. The Río Vilcanota river (also known as the Río Urubamba) forges its path as it winds through these elevated plains, full of vigor after flooding in the rainy season, energy that nourishes crops such as maize and grains that have provided sustenance for thousands of years. It was the Quechua, however, who knew how to develop and best exploit the 70-mile valley's geography, ecosystems and microclimates to their advantage.

Located some 32 miles northwest of Cusco, today, the Urubamba Valley's most lucrative and renowned commodity with regard to tourism is Santuario Histórico de Machu Picchu, the mystical, elevated citadel that contributes to the valley's popular 'sacred' moniker, the iconic, lost city tucked into a sub-tropical corner of the valley to which local farmers led Hiram Bingham III in 1911; the North American explorer has been lauded for 'discovering' it ever since.

A multi-purpose complex constructed in circa 1450 at 7,980 feet asl for the ninth *sapa inca* Pachakutiq Inka Yupanki (responsible for transforming the Kingdom of Cusco into the Quechua empire), not only is Machu Picchu a masterful feat of engineering given its remote mountain location, it was designed to fulfill religious, ceremonial, astronomical and agricultural roles. As the Vilcanota flows, it also marks start and end points between the Quechua capital and this royal estate, which is strategically tucked away in a difficult-to-access northwest corner of the valley.

Machu Picchu provides remarkable insight into life at the top of the Quechua civilization's social order, and one's very first encounter with it, gazing across the dry-stone-constructed temples [mortar is not used] with the lofty and slender sister mountain Huayna Picchu in the background, low clouds clinging to its silhouette, imagining daily activities on its grounds such as farming on the agricultural terraces from a time more than 600 years ago, confirms this site's magical image. But, like any good legend, the citadel remains shrouded in mystery: was its main purpose as a fortress or did the ruling *sapa inca* use it as a decadent seasonal retreat? And how did the Spaniards fail to catch on to its existence? Archeologists remain undecided.

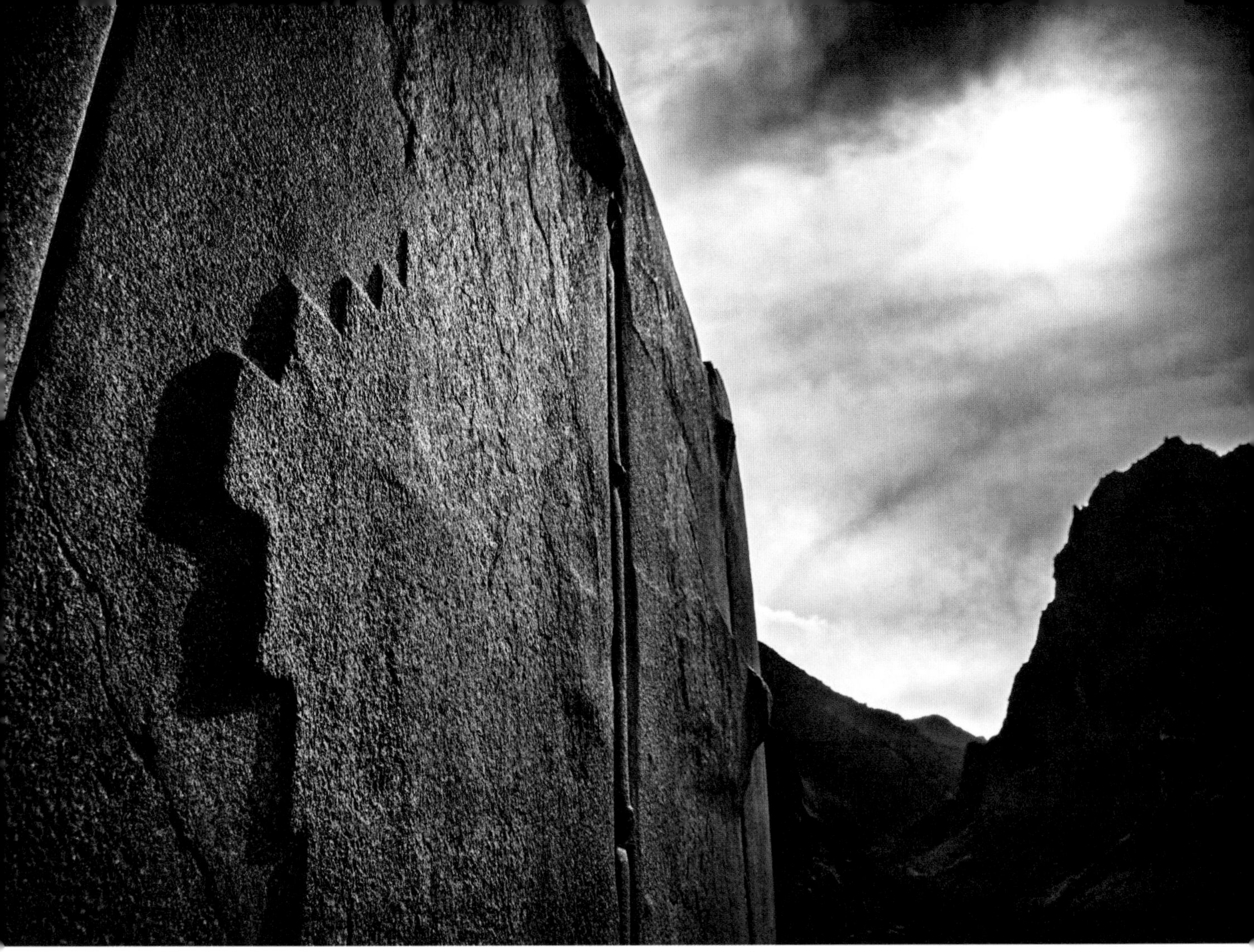

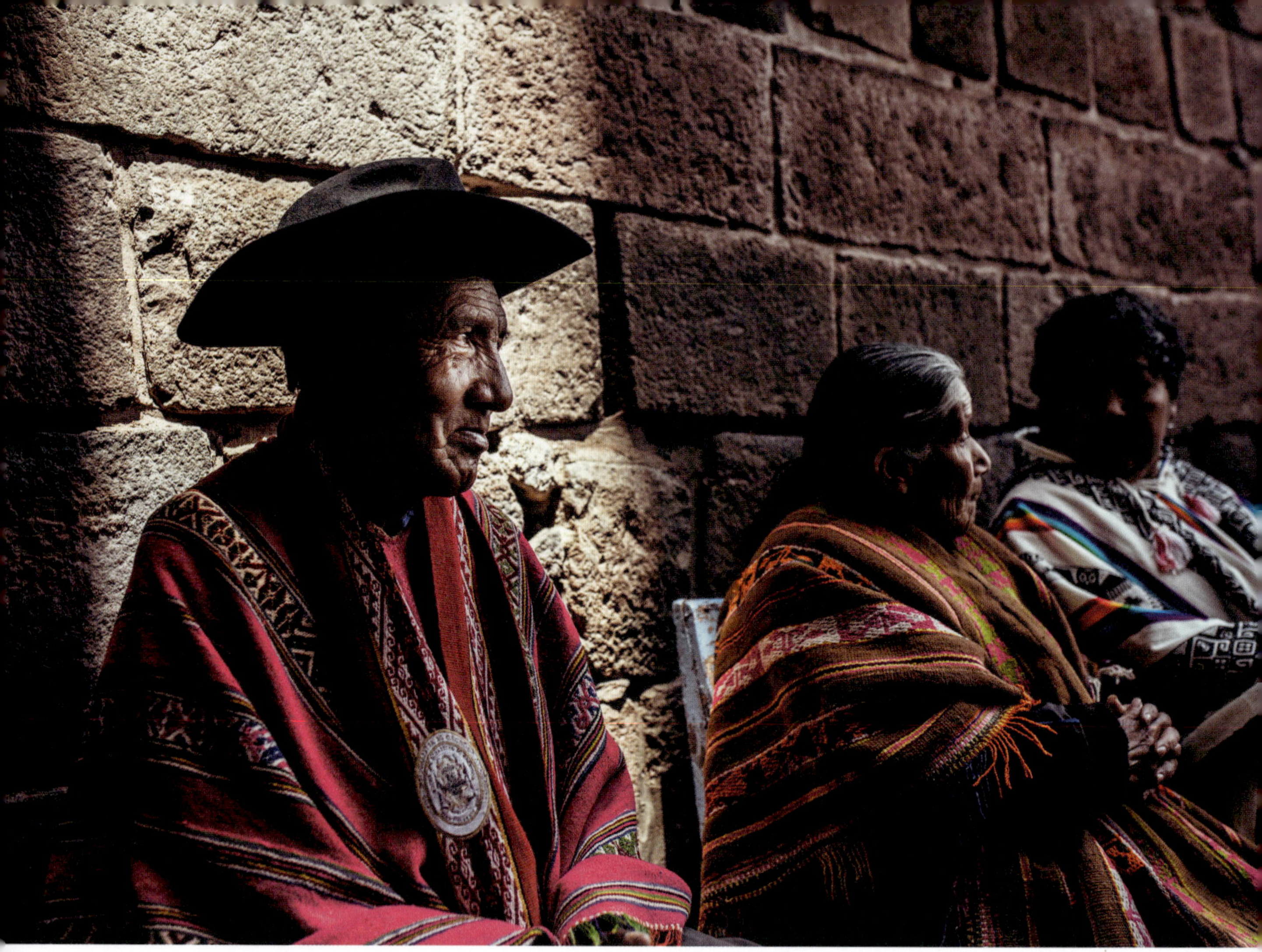

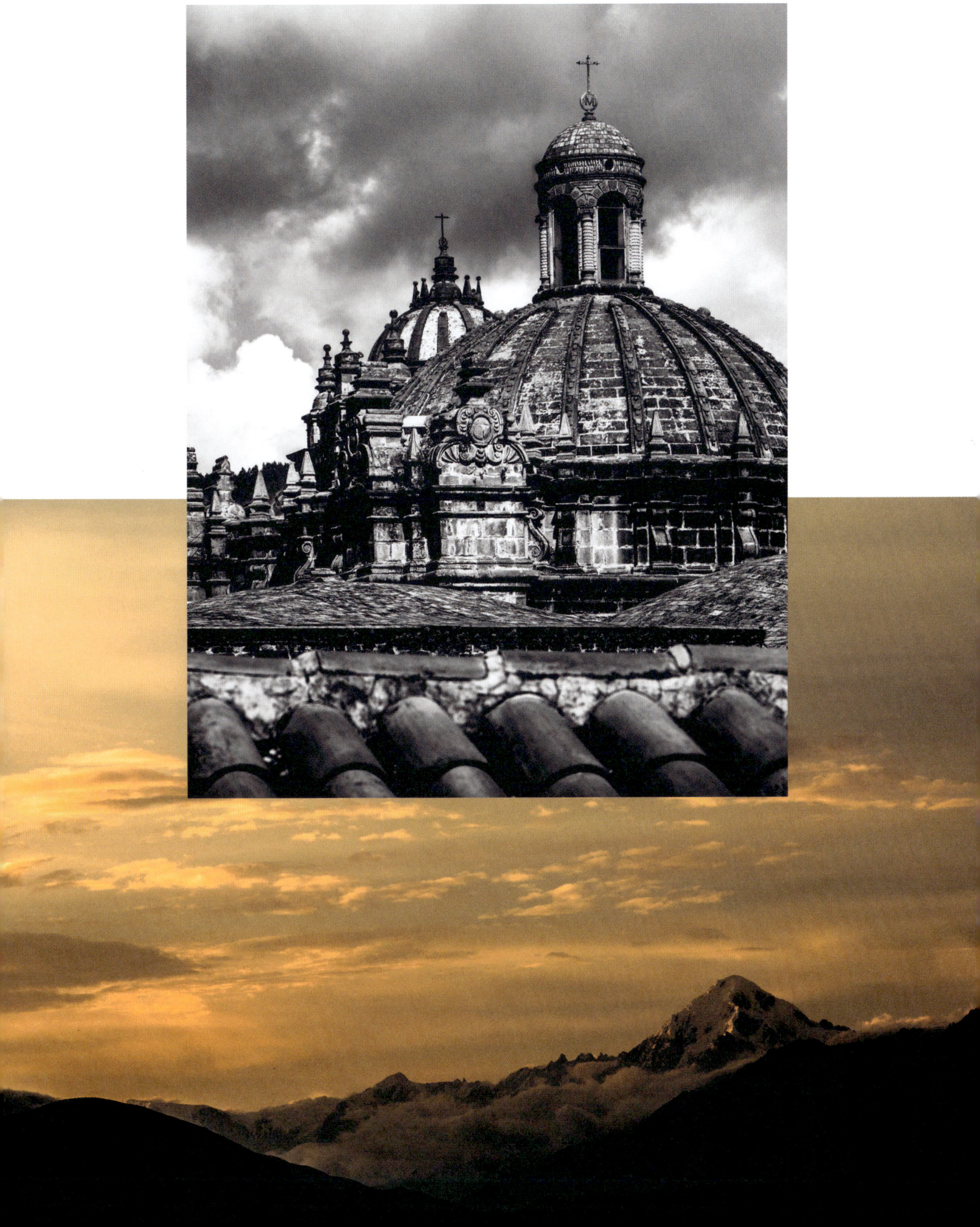

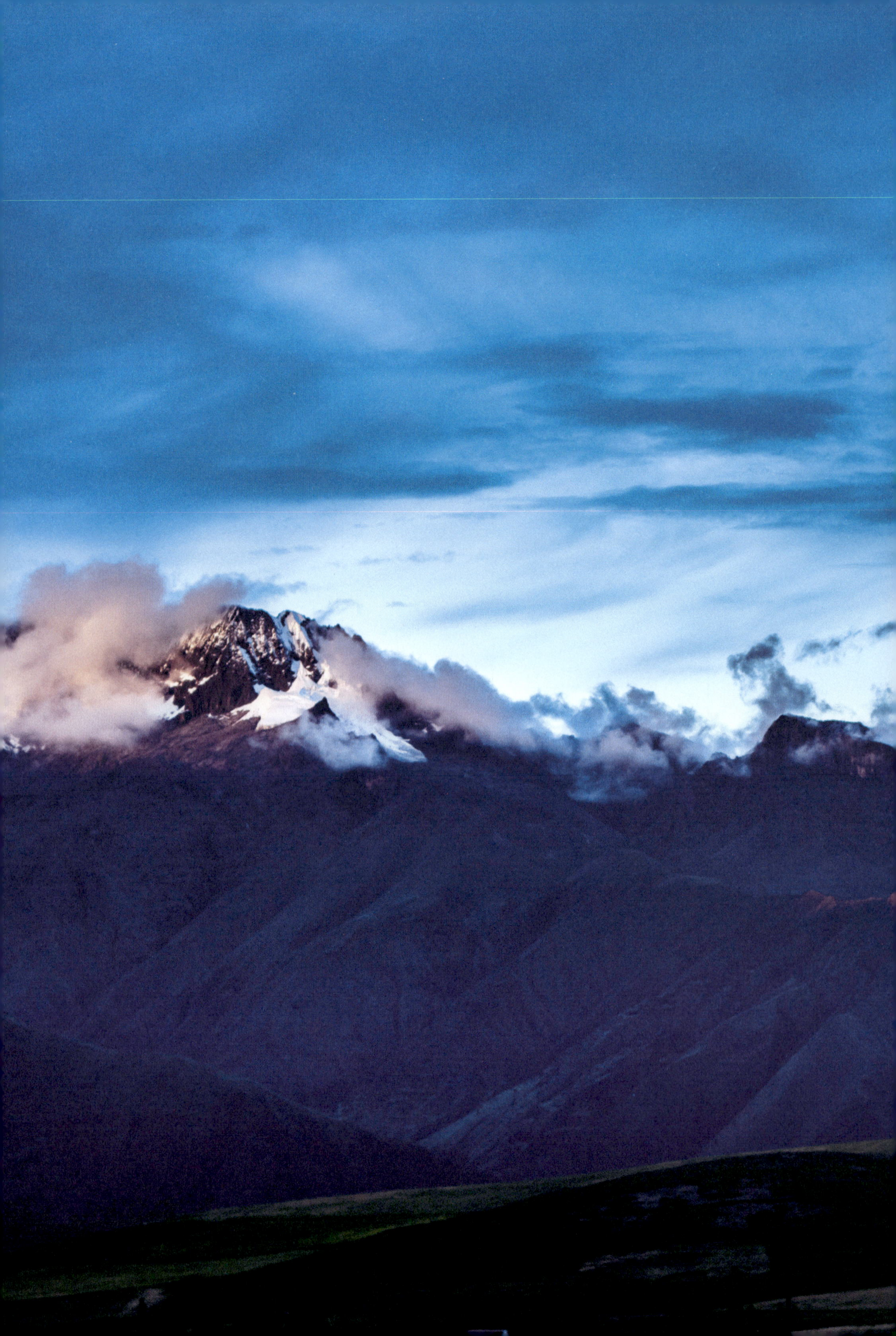

As the condor flies, the distance between Cusco and the Sacred Valley is relatively short, but driving the zigzagging, at times notorious, roads, the first visible brushstrokes of an endless, rolling landscape are applied to the Andean canvas. First, the elevation rises to 12,470 feet asl passing through the small town of Chinchero, known for its artisan textiles, then the winding descent of more than 3,280 feet into the valley begins.

Depending on the season – here, the options are dry or rainy, rather than the four classic equinoxes – the hues create an intense tapestry of vibrant emerald, chartreuse and forest green, the shades changing according to the crop sown and how close it is to harvest time. Once the rainy season initiates toward the end of November, and sprouting seeds burst through the sienna earth, swaths of gold and violet denoting blooming *oca* (Oxalis tuberosa) or *tarwi* (Lupinus mutabilis) splash bright pigments upon the often cloud-obscured vista a few weeks later. The fields are well and truly alive, showered alternately by beams of brilliant sunlight and pelting rain. Once harvest is underway, with products from tubers, grains, herbs and fruits plucked from both above and below the ground, the palette becomes more muted, taking on tan and cappuccino tones, and the land begins its regeneration for the forthcoming sowing season. And so the circle of life continues.

Spread across lower elevations than the city of Cusco, the Sacred Valley runs between 6,500 and 9,900 feet asl and it's a magnet for visitors today, the gateway for those determined to complete a modern-day pilgrimage by foot through the high Amazon basin along the 20-mile 'Inca Trail' to reach and wonder at this captivating treasure (or by taking a bus up the winding road to the ticket entrance).

Architecturally less grand but equally notable in historical and cultural value is the cluster of towns such as Ollantaytambo and Pisaq dotting the valley, close to the banks of the river. The combination of diverse geography, fertile ecosystems and ideal microclimates meant the Quechua needed little convincing that they should set up key agricultural centers in this area.

The Sacred Valley was so valuable with regards to its religious, ceremonial, astronomical and agricultural roles, it wasn't considered part of the empire but, in fact, a possession of the ruling *sapa inca*.

A strategic and powerful regional capital, Cusco and its Sacred Valley remain as multicultural today, given the influx of international travelers, as they were during the Quechua civilization, which relocated people from conquered ethnic groups, known as *mitimaes*, from around the empire to populate the area. Each settlement fulfilled several functions, although one operation might outweigh others, such as housing soldiers at the fortress found in regional administrative center Ollantaytambo, undertaking research at the purpose-built agricultural experimental station at Moray and adhering to the Quechua cosmovision at Pisaq's astronomical observatory.

It's an early start in the Sacred Valley, communities rising at dawn to tend to their flocks, refueling with breakfast at home then returning to the elements to spend the daylight hours tending land. Come nightfall, rest is welcomed, the constellations and the moon gently illuminating the apus, ever watchful, always protecting the communities.

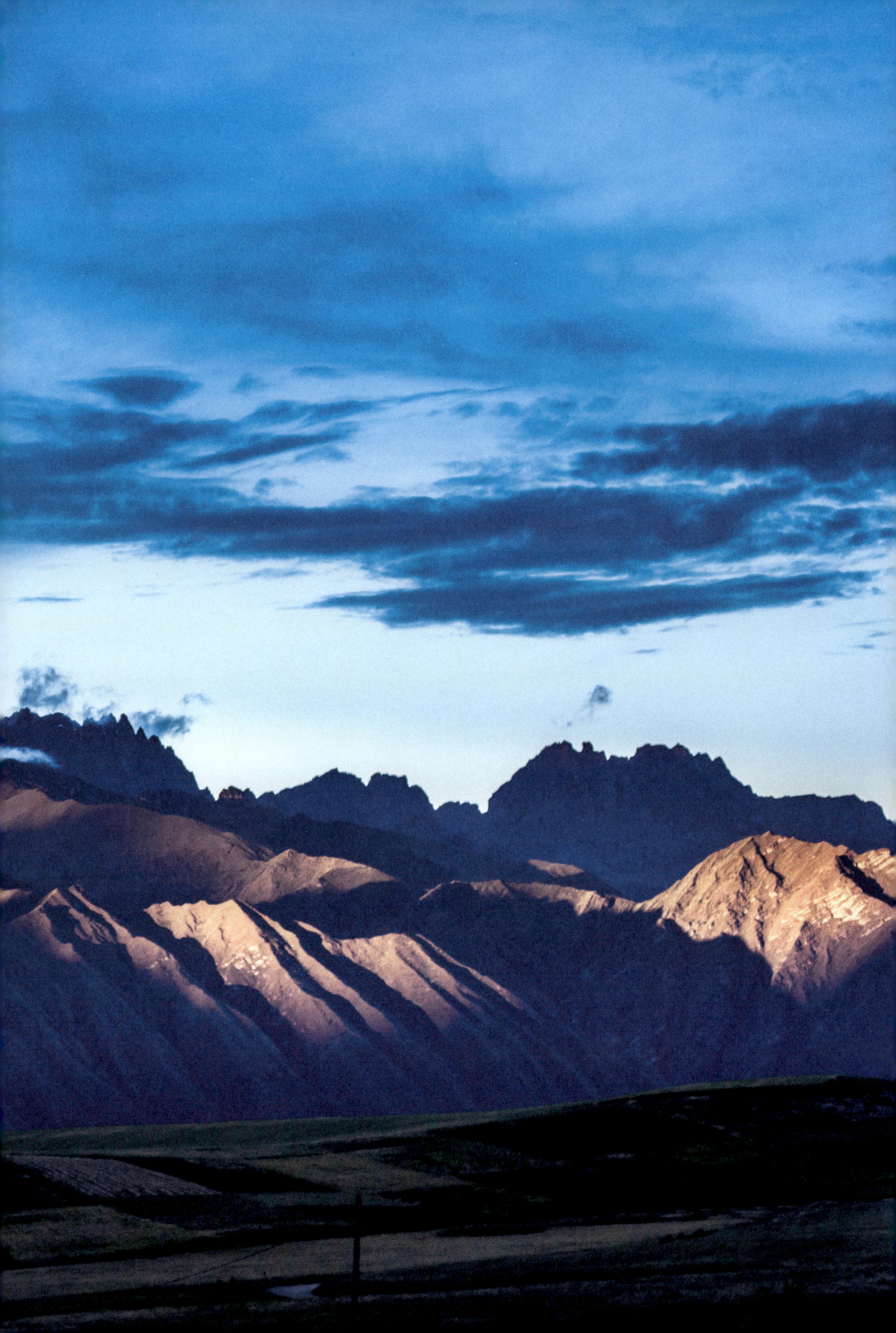

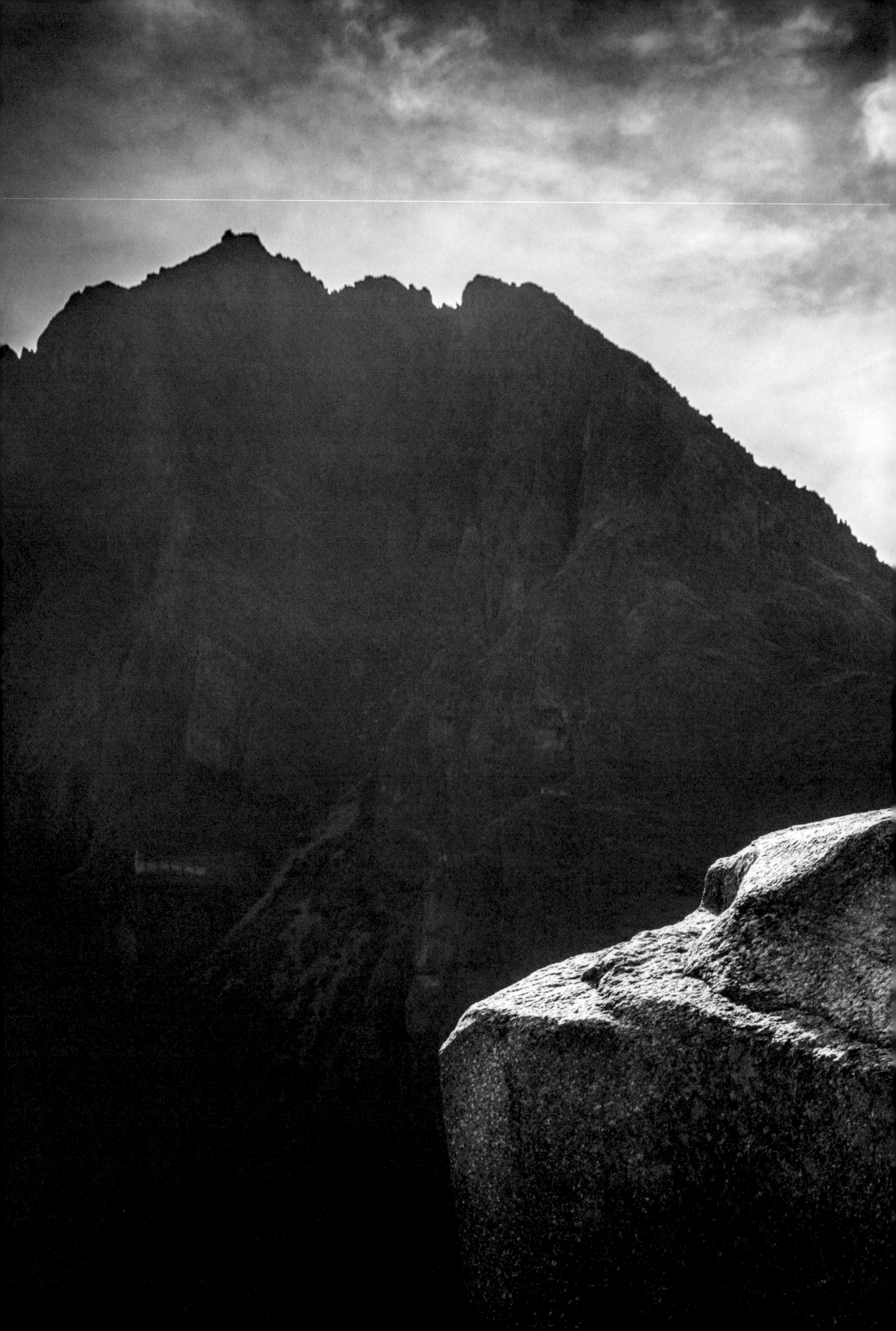

In the past, many of these settlements and villages, much like Machu Picchu, quickly displayed their value, they too became treasured royal estates. Even today, as they were several hundred years ago, Maras' salt pans are harvested, the pink-tinged grains used then and now for bartering, payment and food preservation. Now, just like then, the Sacred Valley's lands are of inconmensurable value.

Located at 9,750 feet asl, Pisaq was one of the more sophisticated, multi-purpose Quechua administrative centers that also fulfilled religious functions, verified by the proximity of a burial site populated by Quechua mummies that was discovered higher up in the mountains. Also of interest is Pisaq's impressive set of agricultural terraces carved into the hillside.

Nourishing a widely dispersed population was one of the Quechuas' strengths when it came to successfully extending the empire, and the Sacred Valley was key to that process. Besides the luxury of excellent climate conditions, sufficient sun and rain, enough wind to deter destructive insects, river flood irrigation for low-lying crops and fertile soil, the Quechua also identified potential in these formidable landscapes that would usually be impossible to develop for agriculture. Given that they had so much manpower and engineering acumen, teams could cut an enormous series of platforms into the side of a mountain, a way of preventing landslides [a common peril in rainy season] that could potentially destroy an entire crop plantation, and also incorporate irrigation systems to channel water from the mountains.

The platforms were then covered in topsoil carried in from more fertile lowlands. Crops such as maize, the valley's principal commodity, fava beans, potatoes and quinua would have been cultivated here for human consumption, while other crops served as feed for herds of easily domesticated llama and alpaca.

While Ollantaytambo, located at 9,160 feet asl, is one of the modern-day gateways to Machu Picchu, its railway station filling twice daily with excited passengers early in the morning and late afternoon, this settlement was another key regional administration center; it was also the site of a battle fought between the Quechua and the Spaniards in 1537, one of the few wartime success stories against the conquistadors (resistance continued for a further 35 years).

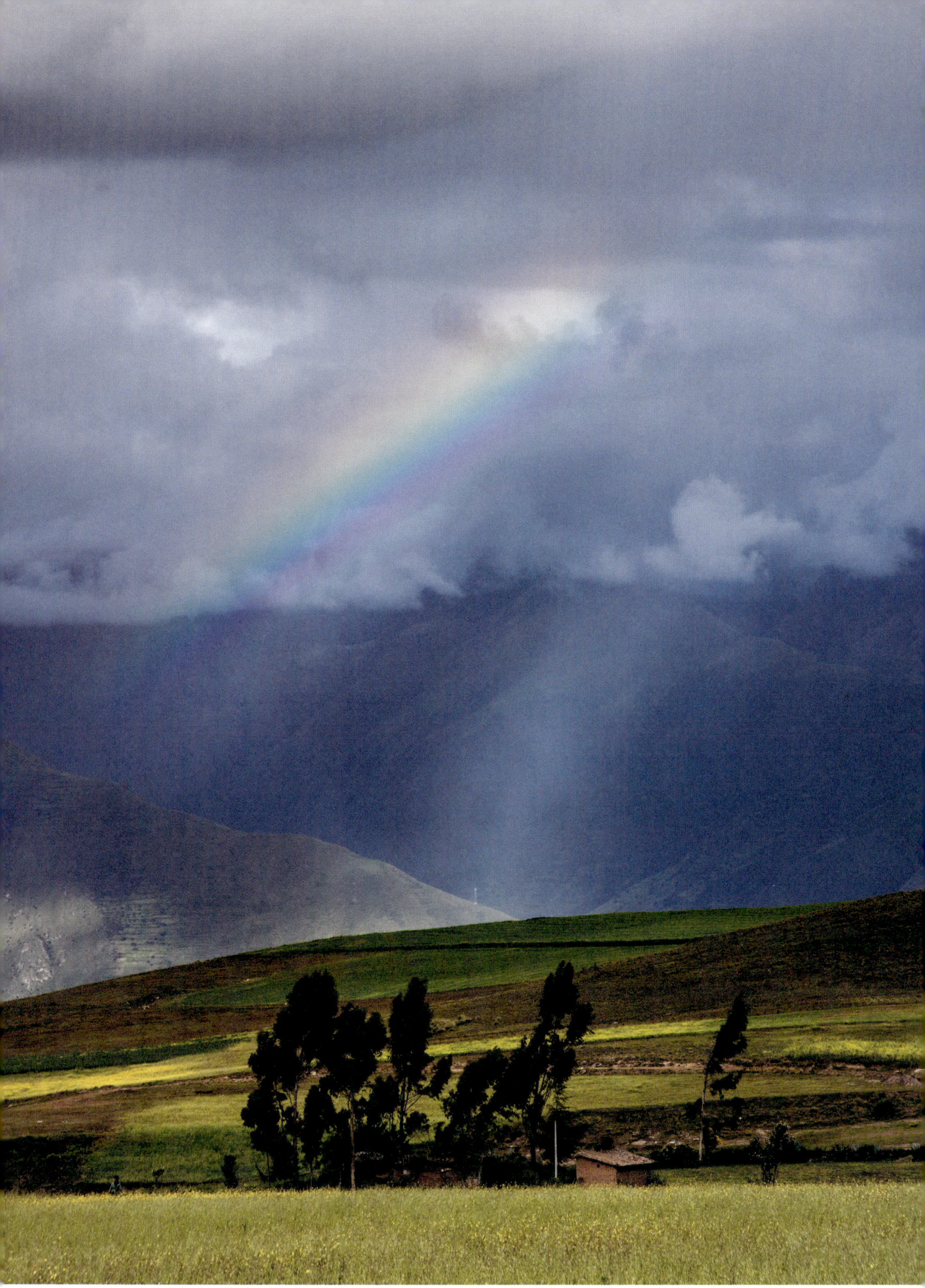

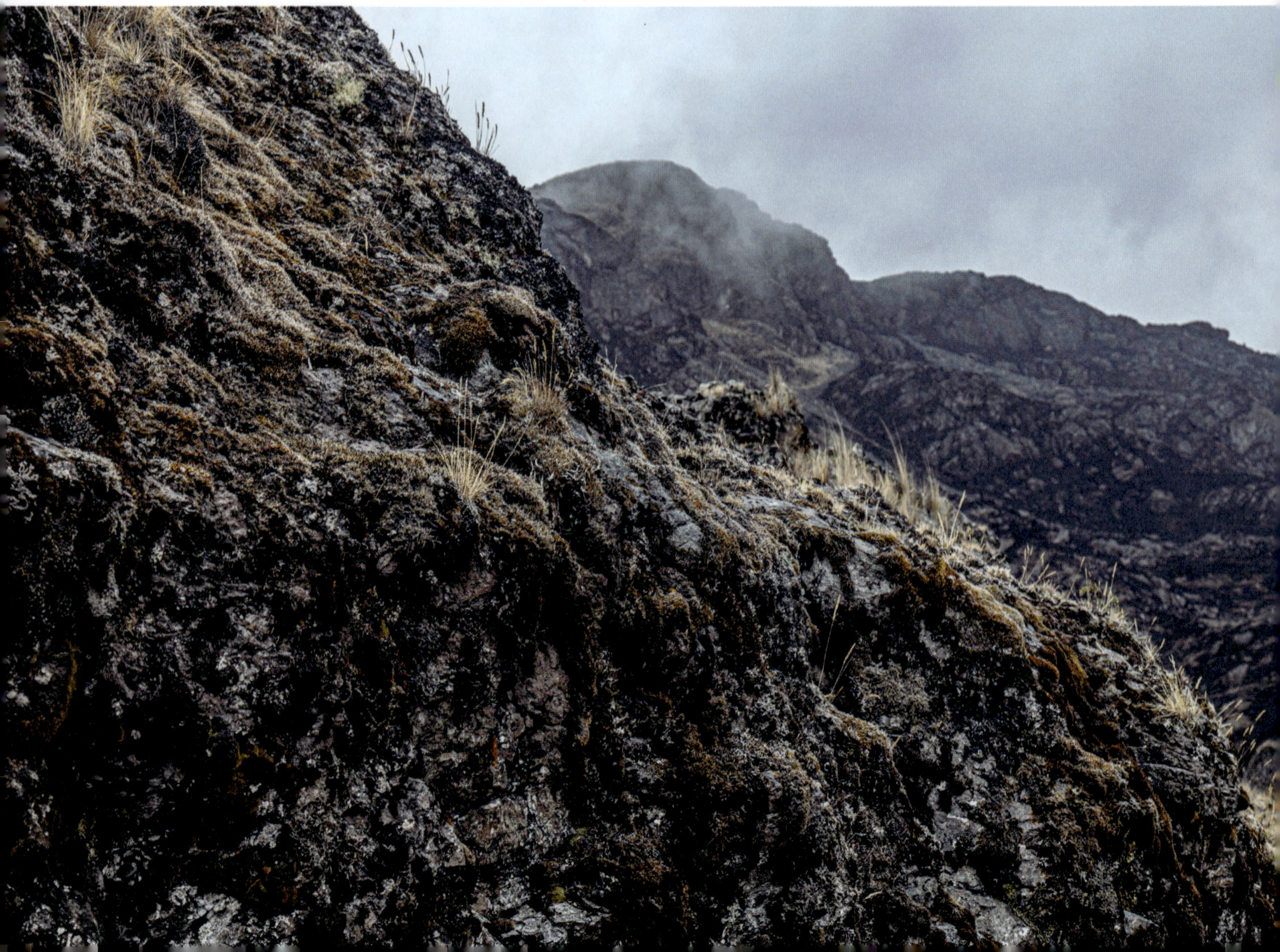

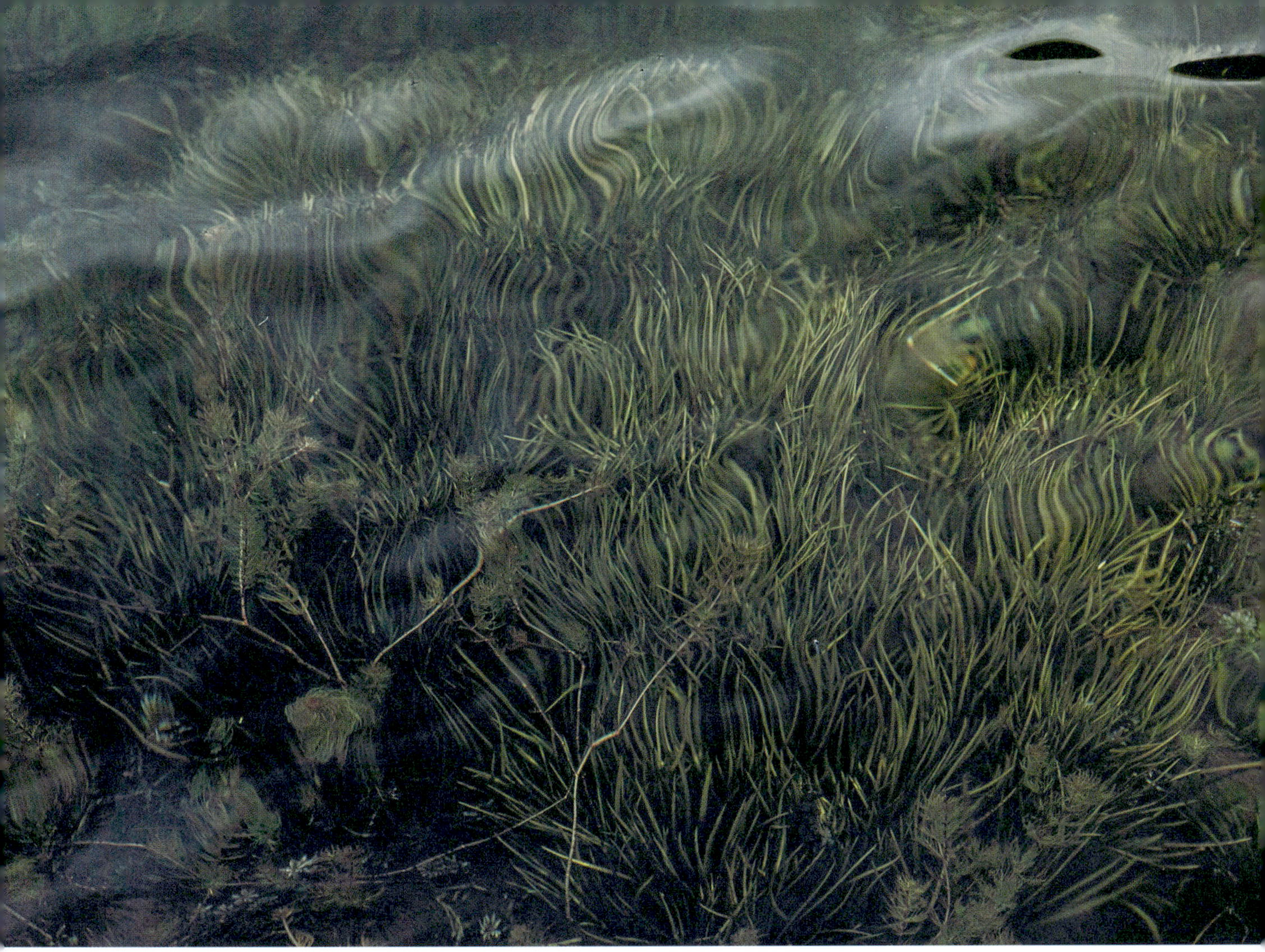

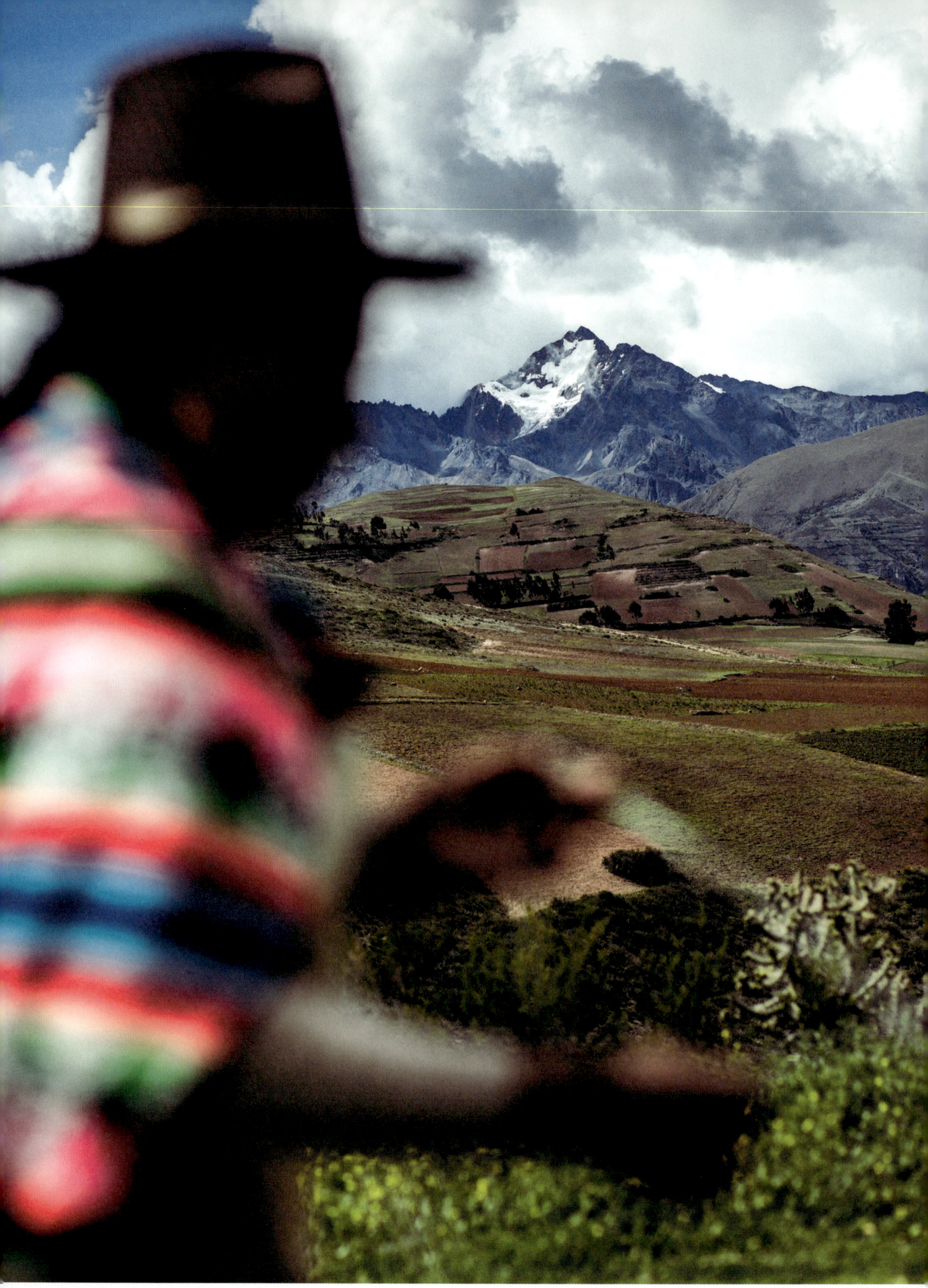

Ollantaytambo was first razed by, then rebuilt by and for the *sapa inca* Pachakutiq Inka Yupanki, and, like Pisaq and Machu Picchu, it's the site of rectangular, man-made agricultural terraces. The small town is home to numerous sophisticated architectural and engineering feats, including multi-room palaces while those agricultural platforms stand out for their fine workmanship and fitted cut-stone masonry. Besides making the most of these terraces' microclimates to grow an array of crops that might not otherwise successfully produce on this rocky land without some form of intervention, the Quechua took food production to another level and constructed *qullqas*, storehouses designed in a way to protect and ventilate the deposited grains.

And then there is Moray, the Quechuas' most elaborate agricultural research center, a monumental construction formed by a group of *muyus*, concentric terraces with an otherworldly appearance designed to replicate some of Peru's elevations and ecosystems in this single, hard-to-reach corner of the high plateau found at 11,515 feet asl.

While crops were already cultivated on platforms by civilizations prior to the Quechua, their exceptional civil engineering skills took this farming technique several steps further, using the geography and climate to their advantage. Here, they created a 59°F (15°C) temperature differential and a selection of high-altitude ecosystems between the highest and lowest terraces, allowing products that are poles apart when it comes to farming zones to be cultivated in this rather inhospitable part of the Andes. In any other place, it would be unthinkable to imagine that cacao and tubers could ever grow just vertical feet apart. But Quechua efforts proved successful. And today, their descendents continue to plow, sow and reap, living and working from their land, rising with the sun, resting when it sets, always in harmony with *yanantin-masintin* in mind. This is the place that inspired – and continues to inspire – Mil.

Elevated, bountiful, beautiful and unique, the fascinating Sacred Valley and everything it has witnessed since before the arrival of humankind, everything that it represents today, inspired us to set up a restaurant high in the mountains, above the Andean lowlands and the revered plains. Generous and plentiful, there's diversity in every corner and every field, and we pay tribute to the valley and to Pachamama by interpreting the complex landscape in ways that go beyond plating it. Drawing exclusively from the Sacred Valley's ecosystems ensures the authentic nature of our Andean restaurant and interpretation center, and, just like Moray's complex series of terraces, we too will create ever-increasing circles in our efforts to express and share the array of nuances of this magnificent region.

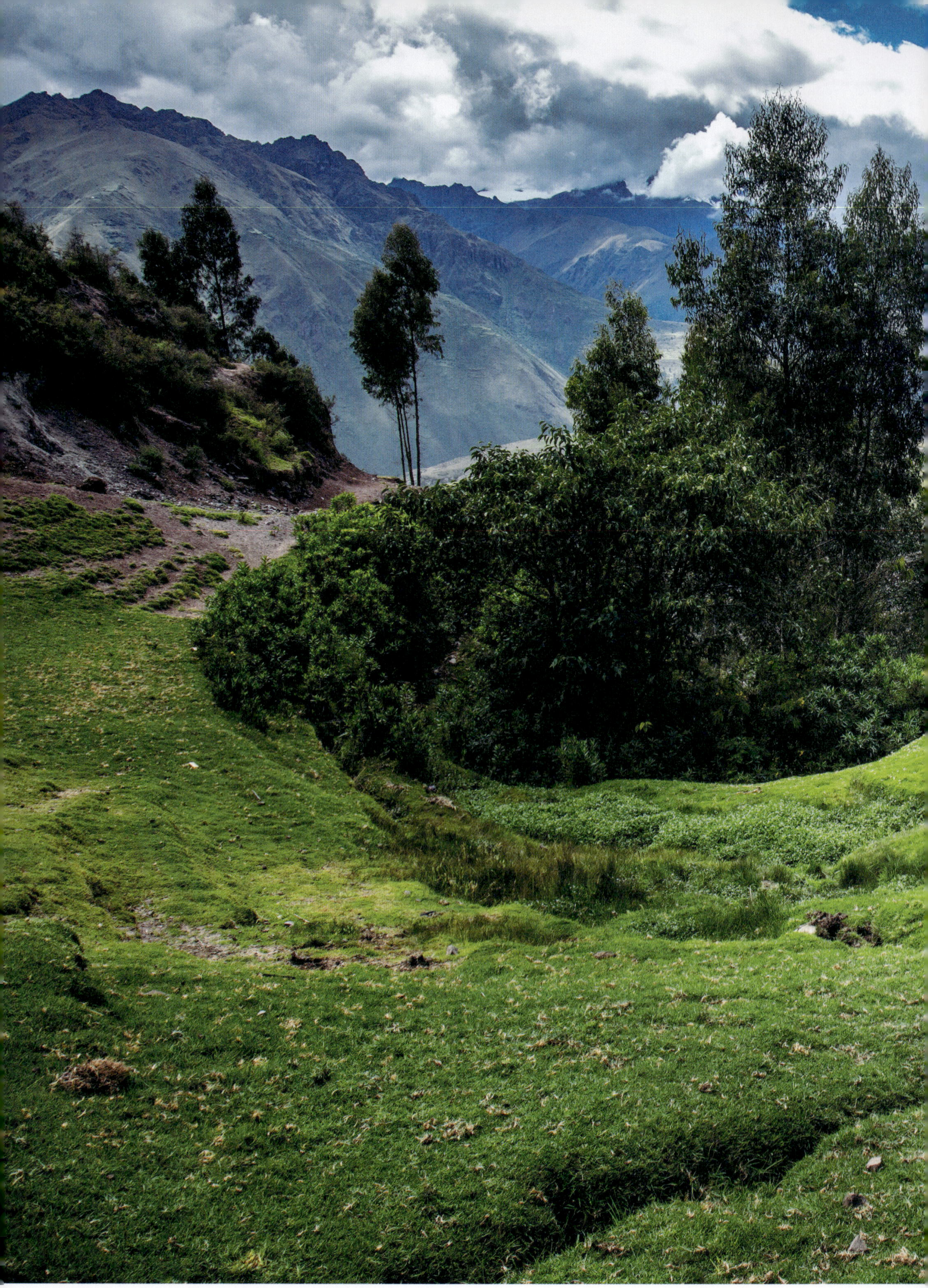

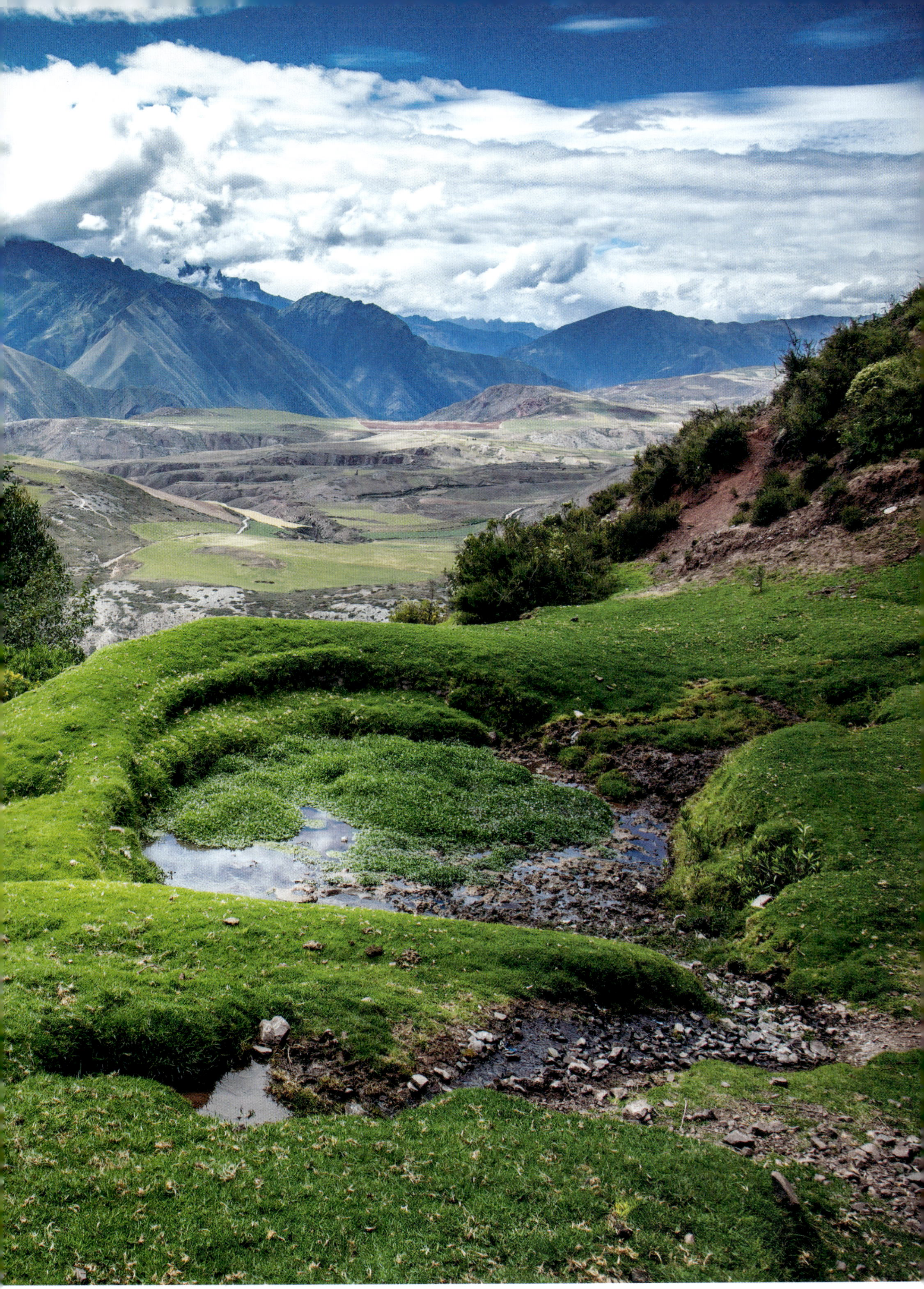

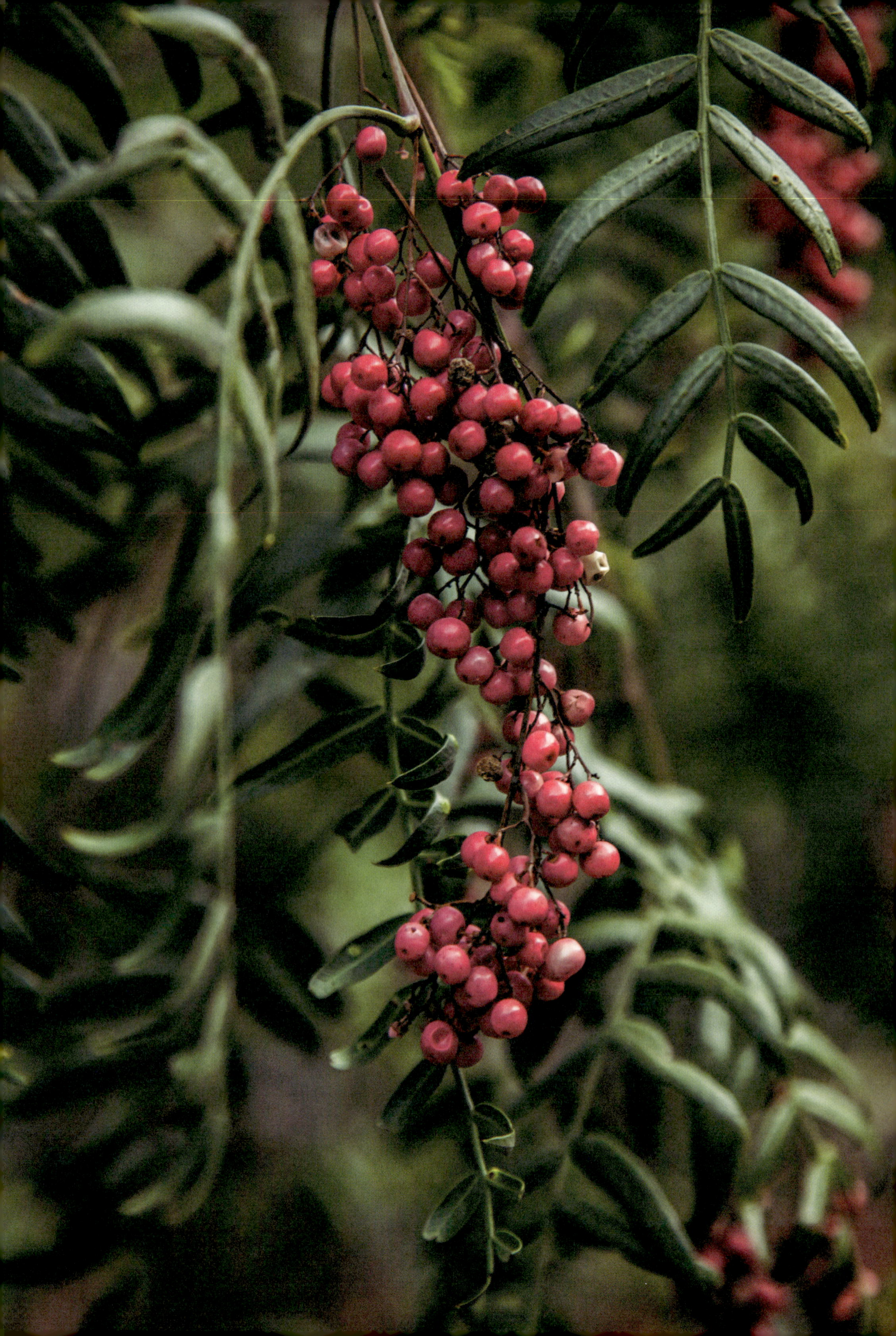

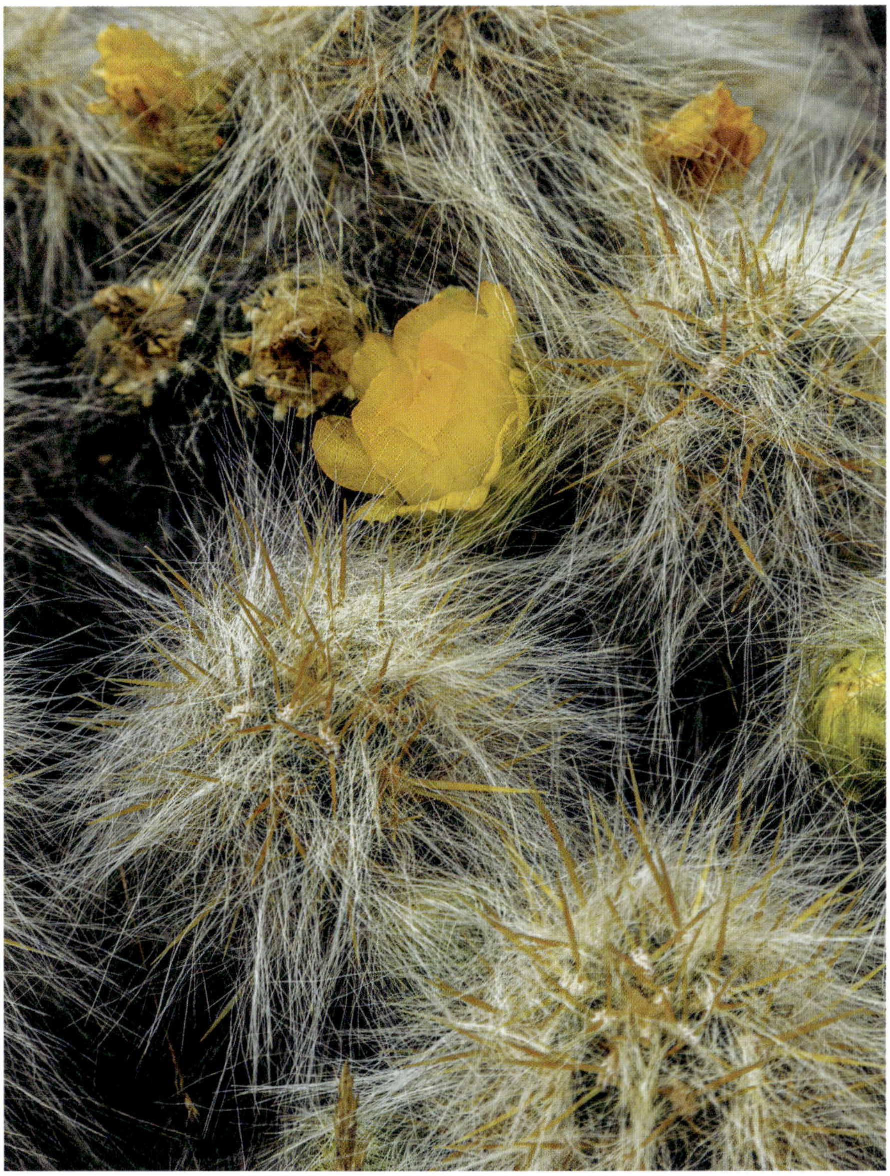

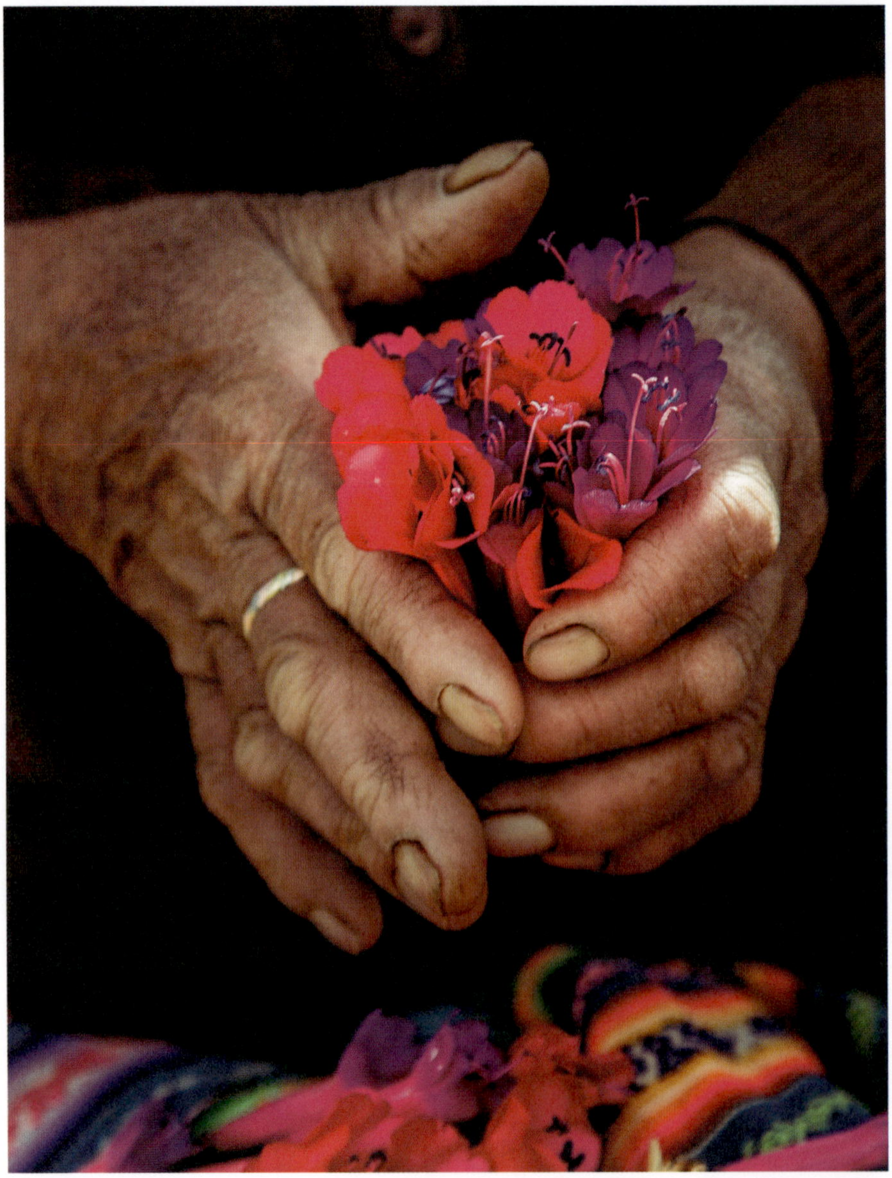

311

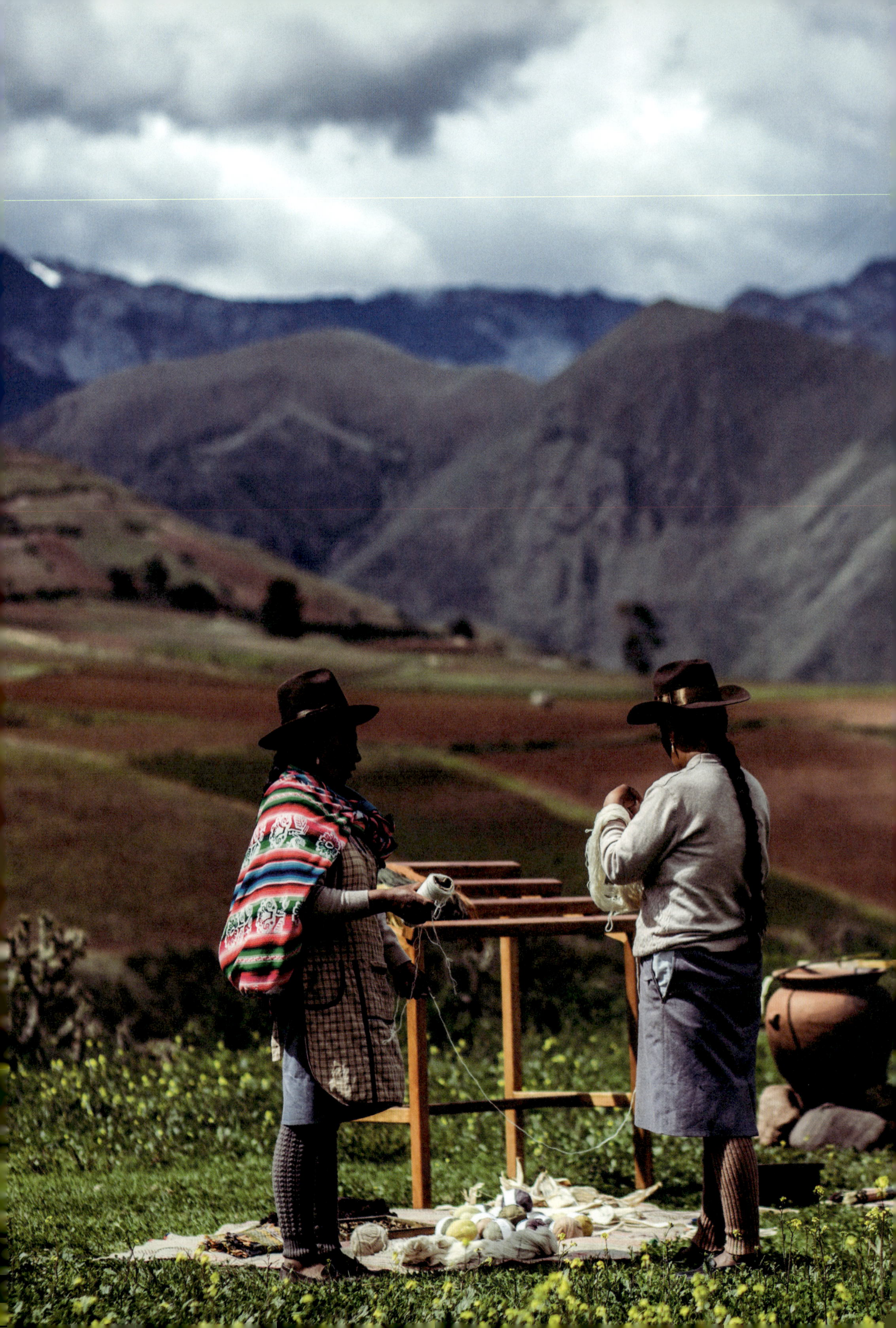

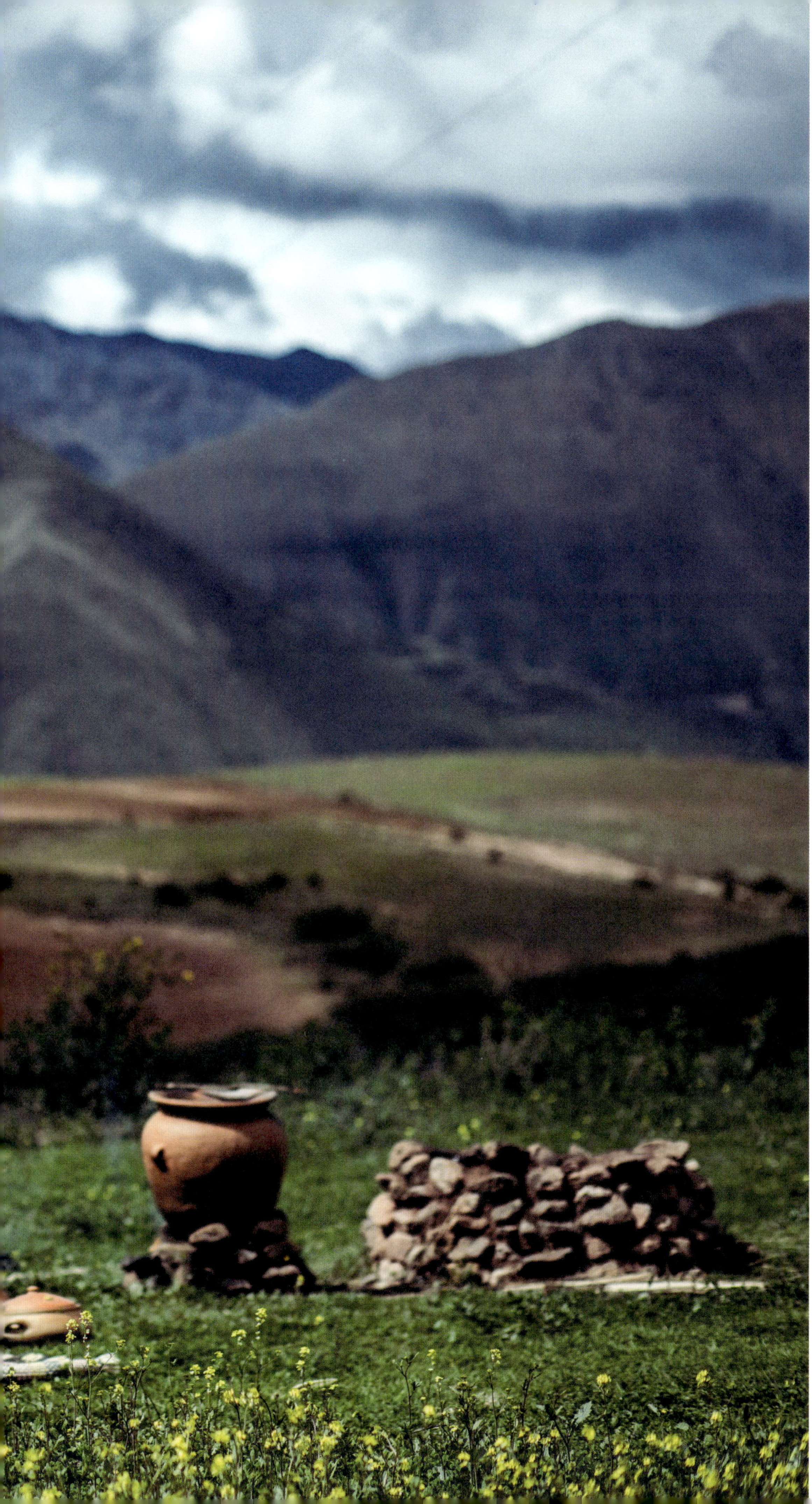

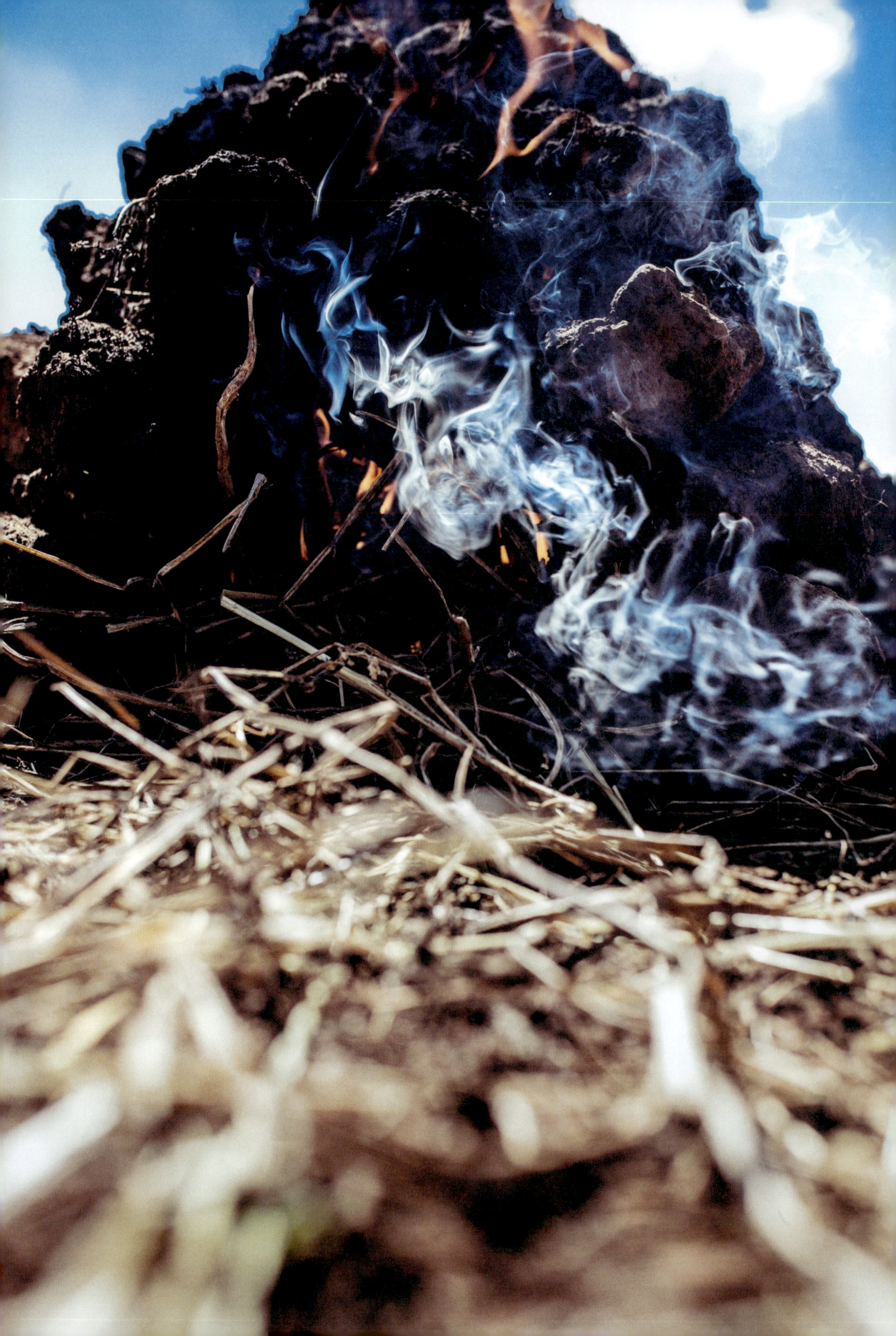

Fire stokes the cold nights in the mountains, illuminating hands digging into a pile of *chuña* before dipping them into freshly made spicy uchucuta salsa, just as their forebears did. And, when the harvest has been completed, communities show their gratitude to Pachamama by preparing a *huatia*, an ancestral cooking method created out of the ground with clumps of earth.

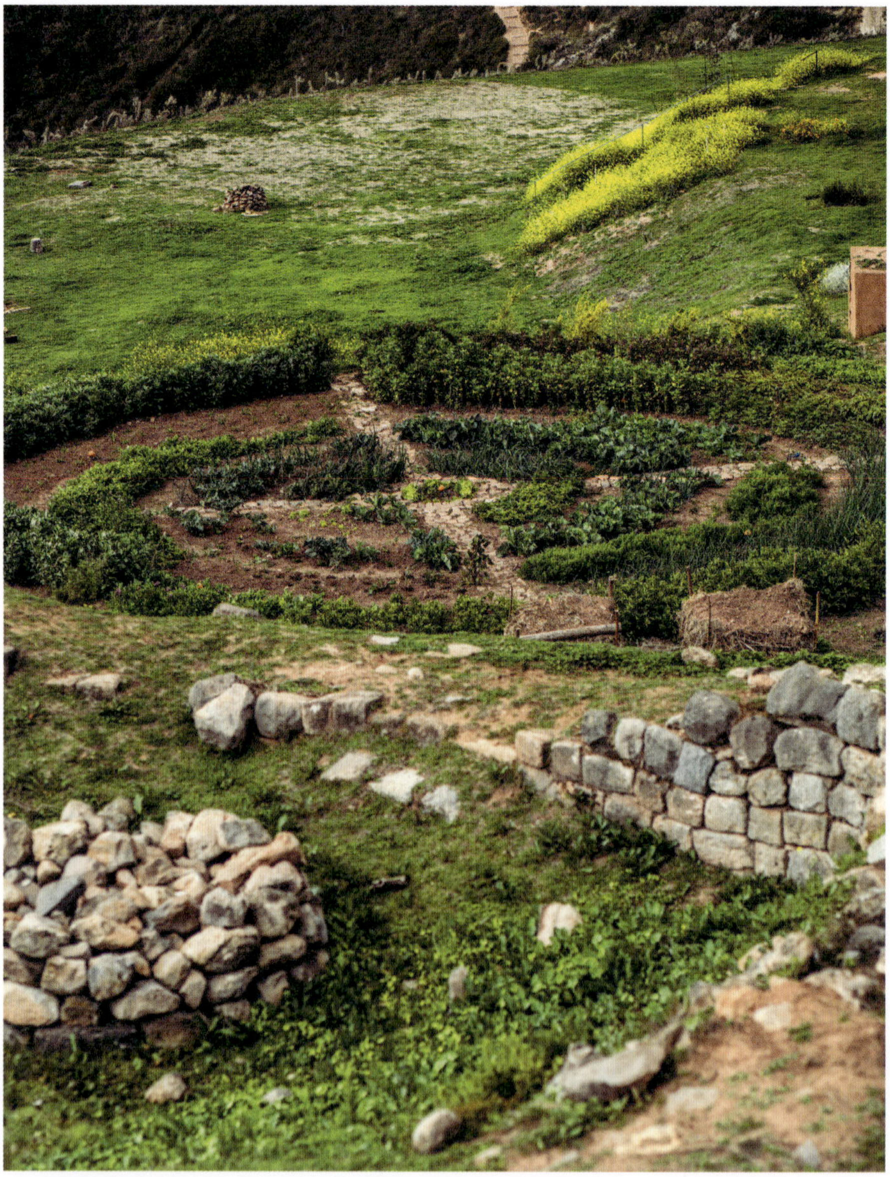

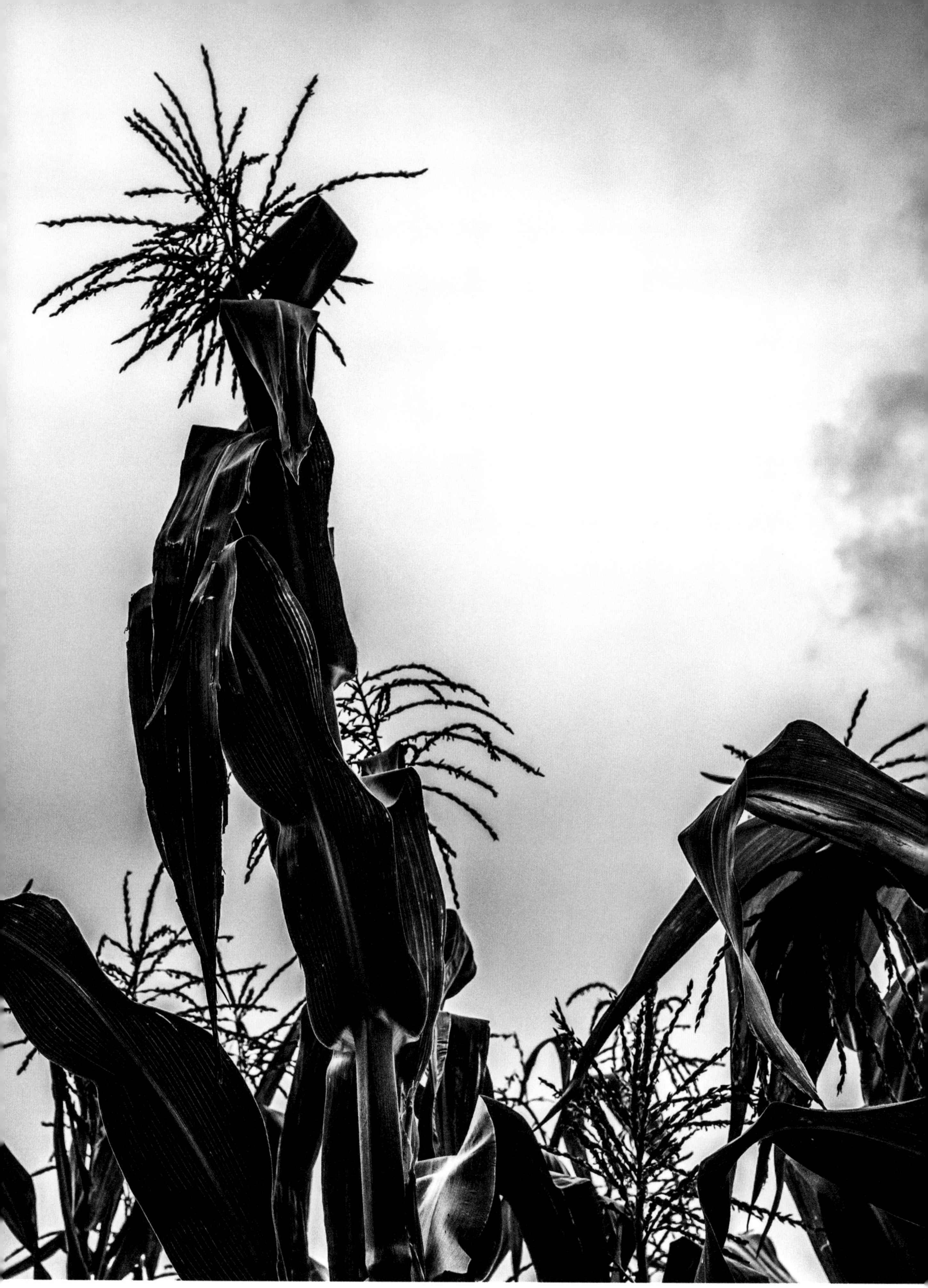

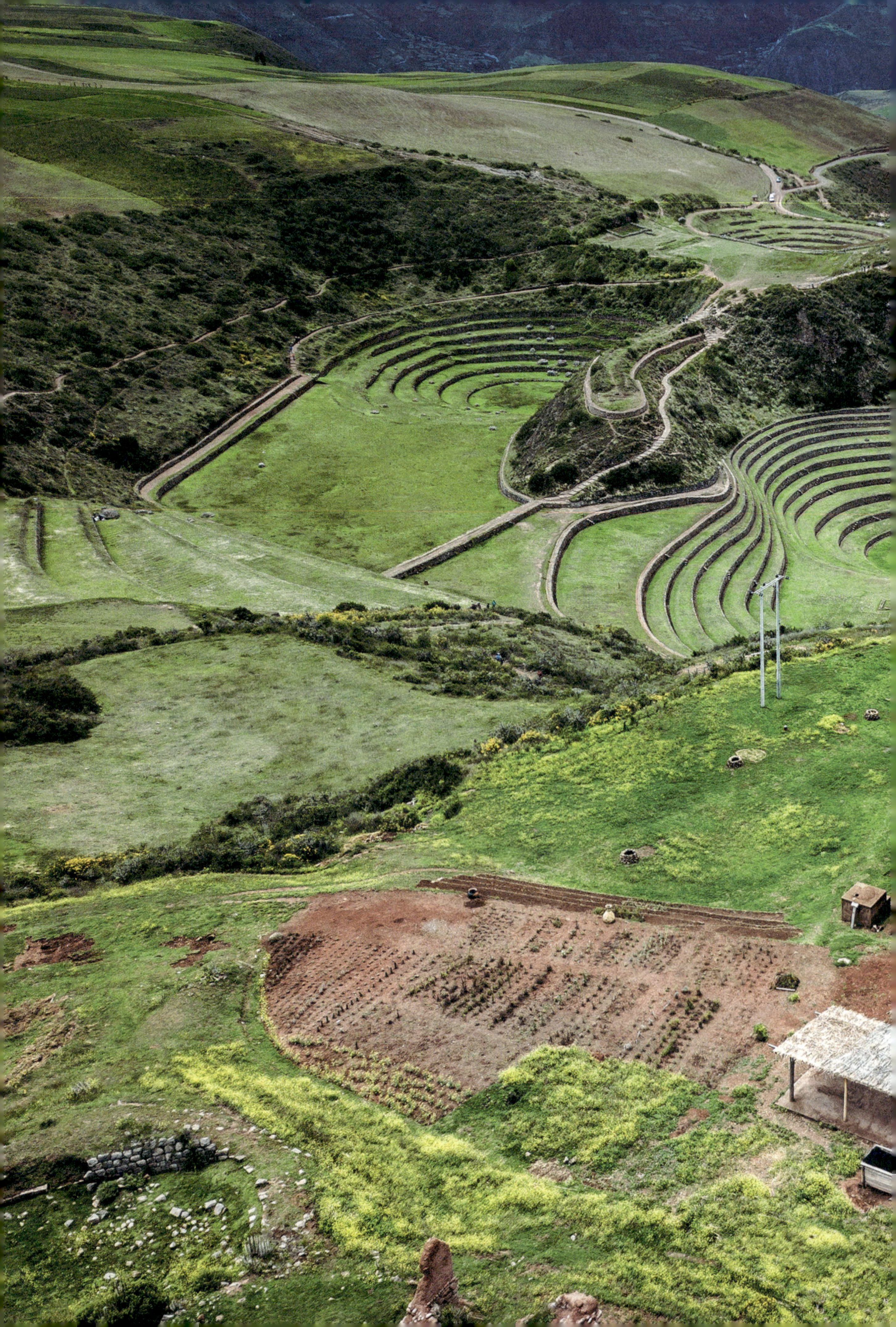

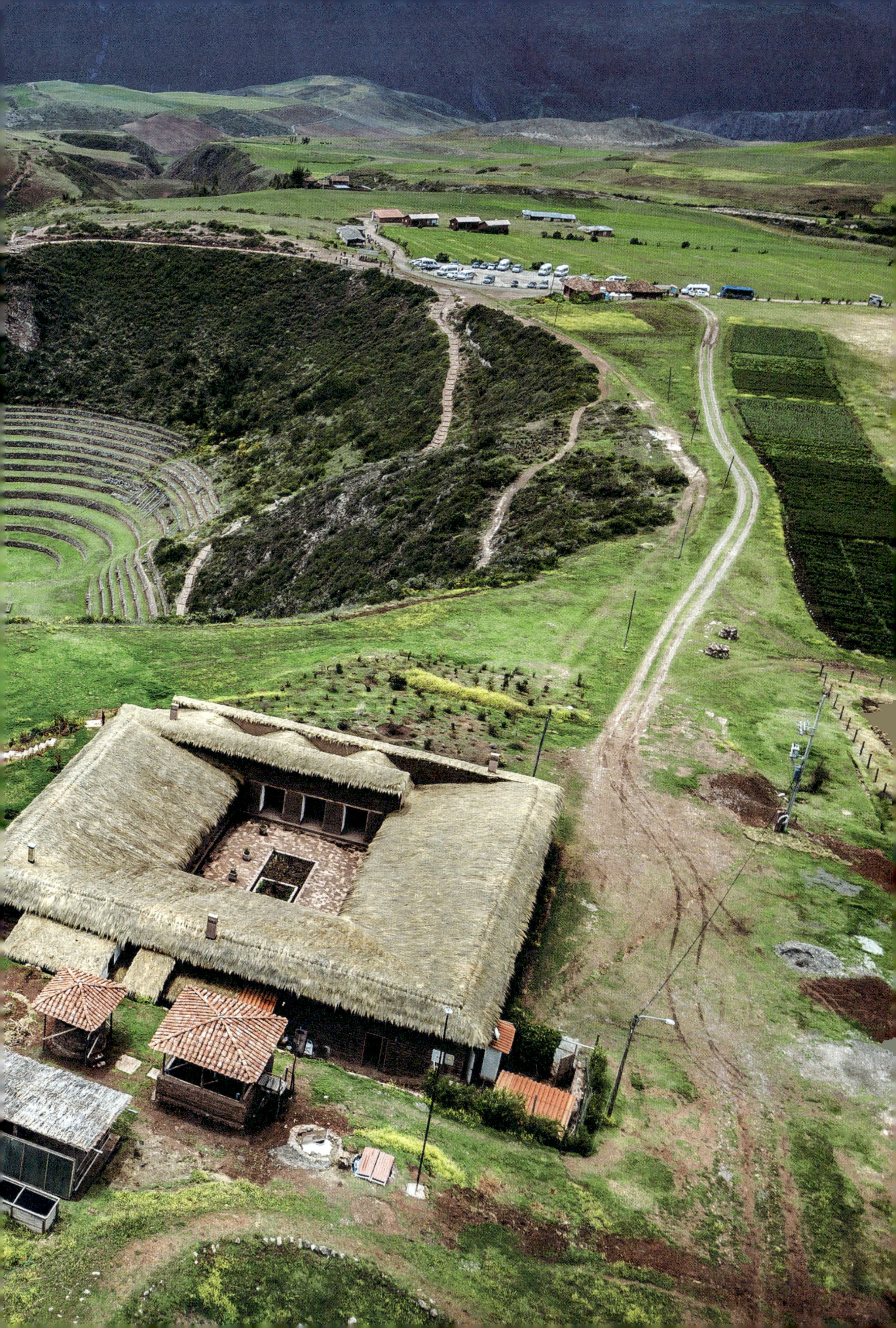

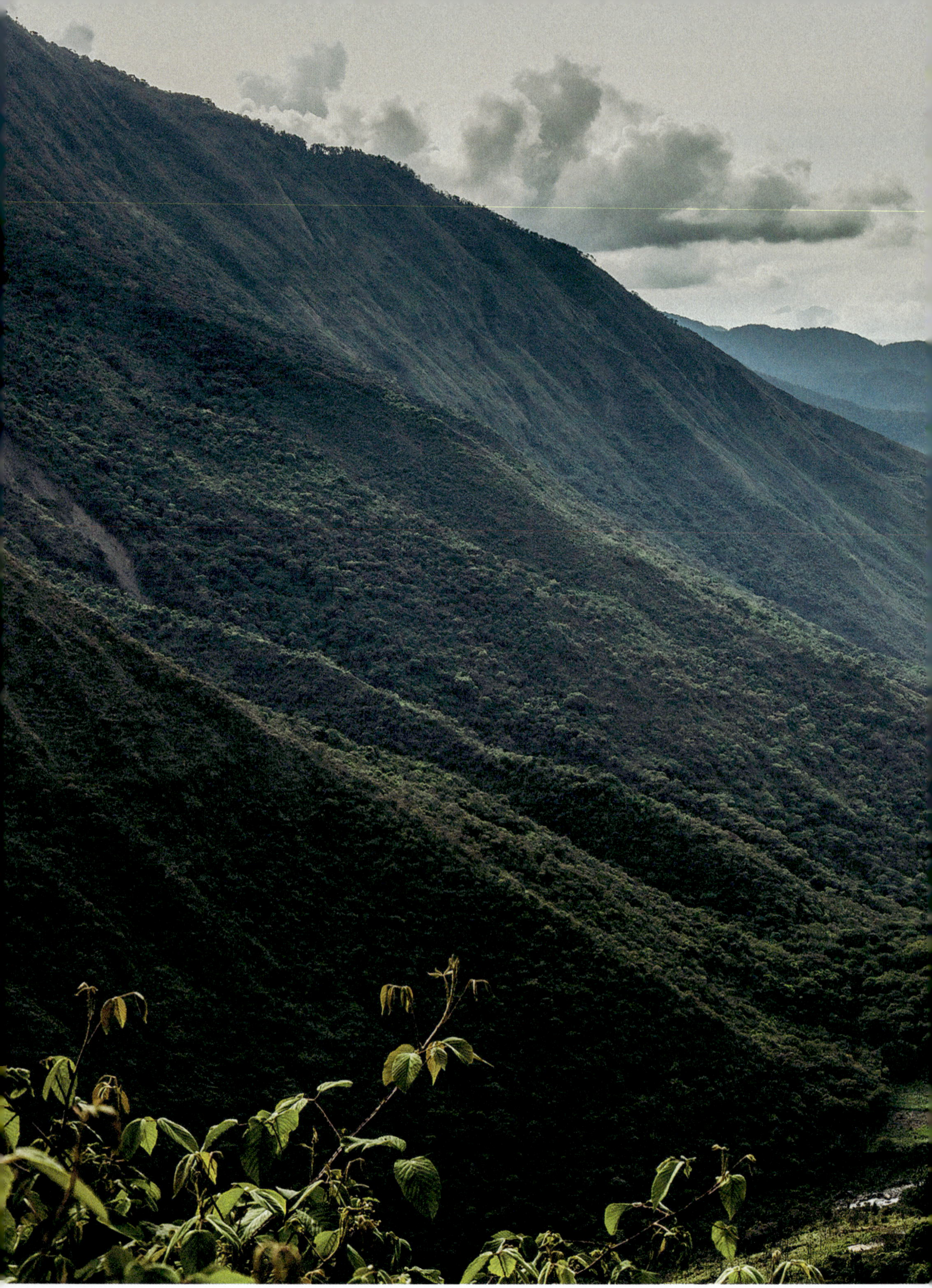

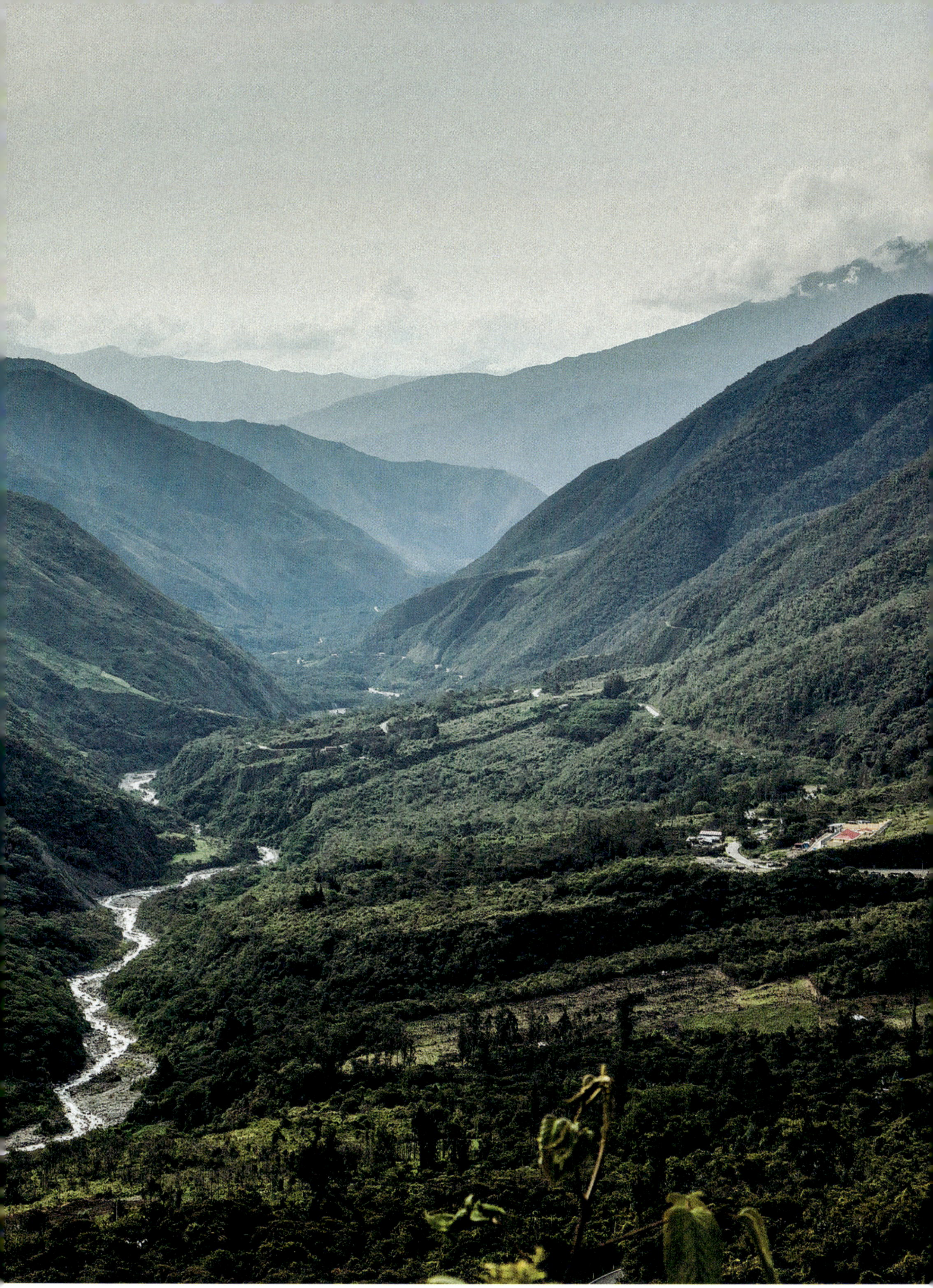

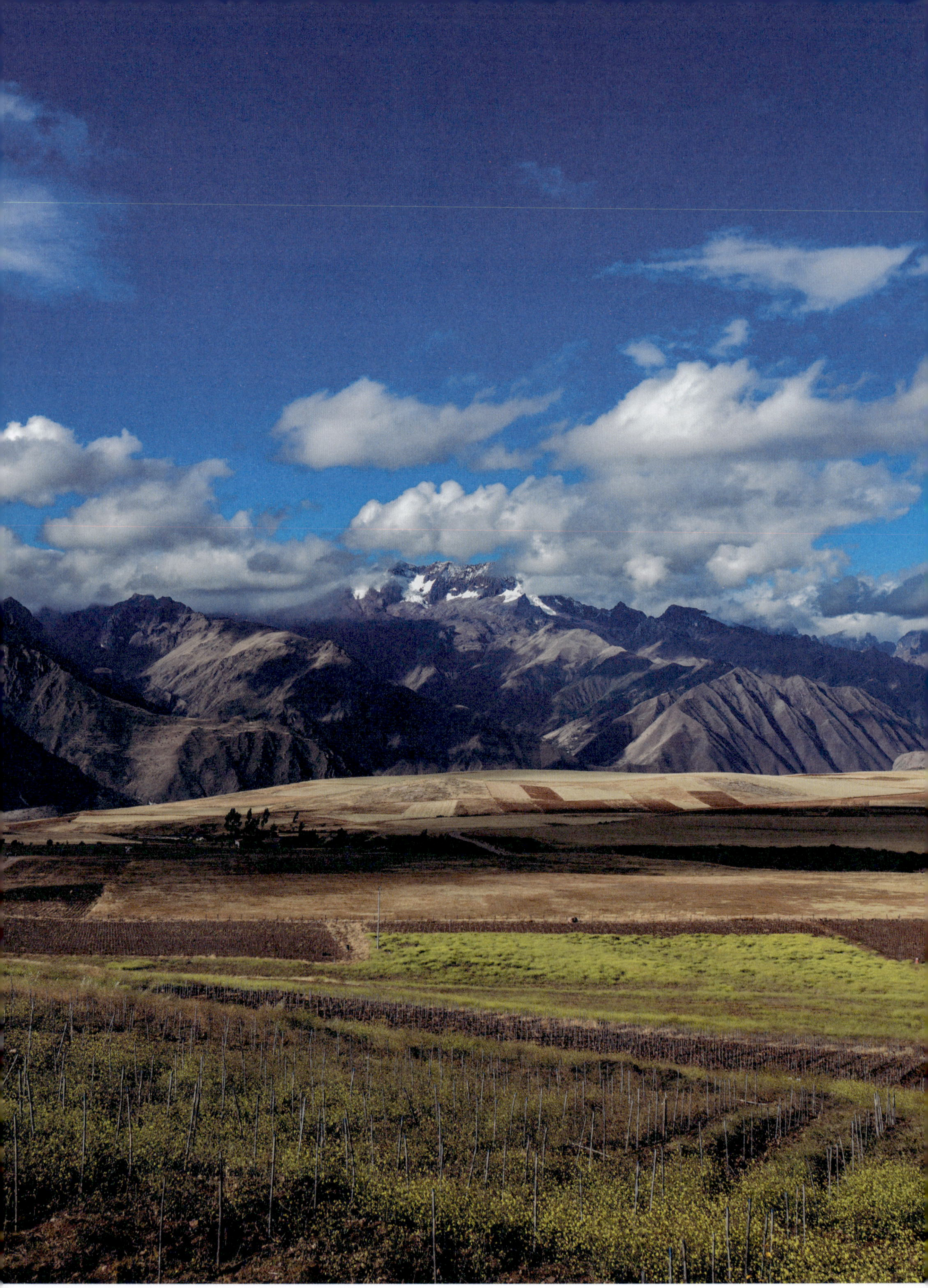

The truth is, it's impossible for us to pull together a complete list of the names of all the people who in one way or another have been part of the concept, construction, and the start-up and/or expansion processes of everything that Mil involves. Our Mil transformed into a universe, and each personage a part of the cosmos, an expansive network that continues to discover ways to interconnect, and that gives us great satisfaction, and paths we've learned and others from which to learn.

We are grateful to life, to the Sumaq Tarpuy association that granted us a magical space five years ago, trusting that we would hand-mold an entirely new concept with deep roots and branches reaching to touch the sky. And we're grateful for this beautiful land and to all those in Cusco who opened their homes, their farms and their hearts to us, regardless of whether what we left in exchange was monetary, a handwritten recipe, a photograph or a sincere handshake. What we value most in all cases has been, is and will continue to be that we forge relationships so that they last forever, that we can call each other *compañeros*, comrades, not of work but of life.

Thanks to each visitor, everyone who has crossed the threshold – even if just to take a peek inside – to each person who surrendered themself to a new experience, for hours, days or, in the case of the craftspeople, months. They all left their mark.

May all those who joined us feel that they are mentioned here, that their names are imprinted on Mil's very soul and upon every space between the massive and sturdy adobe blocks that form it.

Gracias.

Virgilio, Malena, Pía

MIL
VIRGILIO MARTÍNEZ | PÍA LEÓN | MALENA MARTÍNEZ

1st edition.

Catapulta
Av. Donado 4694 - C1430DTP
Buenos Aires, Argentina.
www. catapulta.net
info@catapulta.net

GENERAL EDITING
Victoria Blanco

COORDINATOR
Agostina Martínez Márquez

DESIGN AND ART DIRECTION
Santiago Goria and Tomas Ruíz
www.thisistender.com

TEXTS AND RECIPE REVISION
Sorrel Moseley-Williams

PHOTOGRAPHY AND RETOUCHING
Gustavo Vivanco

PHOTOGRAPHY ASSISTANT
Manuel Vivanco León

PICTURE on page 170 was taken at:
Hacienda Sarapampa, Valle Sagrado, Cuzco.

DRONE OPERATOR
Enrique Nordt

GRAPHIC PRODUCTION
Verónica Álvarez Pesce and Mariana Voglino

EDITING
Martina Serrot

ENGLISH EDITING AND RECIPE TRANSLATION
Allan Kelin

SPANISH TRANSLATION
Marco Vermaasen

Printed in China in July 2021
ISBN 978-987-637-942-7

Martínez, Virgilio
 Mil / Virgilio Martínez ; Malena Martínez. - First ed. - Autonomous City of Buenos Aires:
Catapulta , 2021.
 360 p. ; 29×21 cm.

ISBN 978-987-637-942-7

 1. Gastronomy. 2. Tourism. I. Martínez, Malena. II. Title.
 CDD 641.591

C 2021, Virgilio Martínez, Pía León, Malena Martínez
C 2021, Catapulta Children Entertaiment S.A.

Made the deposit required by law N° 11,723.

Book edited in Argentina.
The partial or total reproduction, storage, rental, transmission or transformation of the present book in any form or by any means whatsoever, whether electronical or mechanical, photocopied or digitalized is not allowed, or by any other means is forbidden without the prior written permission of the publisher. Any violation will be punished by laws N° 11,723 and N° 25,446.